THE LEGACY OF HICKS

THE LEGACY OF HICKS

His contributions to economic analysis

*Edited by Harald Hagemann
and O. F. Hamouda*

London and New York

First published 1994
by Routledge
11 New Fetter Lane, London EC4P 4EE

Simultaneously published in the USA and Canada
by Routledge
a division of Routledge, Chapman and Hall, Inc.
29 West 35th Street, New York, NY 10001

Typeset in Times by Solidus (Bristol) Limited

Printed and bound in Great Britain by
T.J. Press (Padstow) Ltd, Padstow, Cornwall

British Library Cataloguing in Publication Data
A catalogue record for this book is available from the British Library.

Library of Congress Cataloging in Publication Data
The Legacy of Hicks : his contribution to economic analysis / edited
by Harald Hagemann and O. F. Hamouda.
p.   cm.
Essays written by an international group of economists in tribute
to Sir John Richard Hicks.
Includes bibliographical references.
ISBN 0–415–06874–6
1. Hicks, John Richard, Sir, 1904– . 2. Economists–Great Britain.
3. Economics–Great Britain–History–20th century.
I. Hicks, John, Sir, 1904– . II. Hagemann, Harald. III. Hamouda, O. F.
HB103.H47L44
330'.092–dc20   94–13602
CIP

CONTENTS

CONTENTS

vi

CONTRIBUTORS

Christopher Bliss is Professor of Economics at Nuffield College, University of Oxford, UK.

John S. Chipman is Regents' Professor of Economics at the University of Minnesota in Minneapolis, USA.

Nicholas Georgescu-Roegen is Distinguished Professor Emeritus of Economics at Vanderbilt University in Nashville, Tennessee, USA.

Richard M. Goodwin is Professor Emeritus of Economics, University of Cambridge, UK, and University of Siena, Italy.

Harald Hagemann is Professor of Economic Theory at the University of Hohenheim in Stuttgart, Germany.

Frank H. Hahn is Professor Emeritus of Economics at the University of Cambridge, UK, and Professor of Economics at the University of Siena, Italy.

Omar F. Hamouda is Associate Professor of Economics at Glendon College, York University in Toronto, Canada.

John D. Hey is Professor of Economics and Statistics at the University of York, UK.

Charles Kennedy is Honorary Professor of Economic Theory at the University of Kent at Canterbury, UK.

David E. W. Laidler is Professor of Economics at the University of Western Ontario in London, Canada.

Axel Leijonhufvud is Professor of Economics at the University of California in Los Angeles, USA.

Robin C. O. Matthews is Professor Emeritus of Political Economy at the University of Cambridge and former Master of Clare College, Cambridge, UK.

Michio Morishima is Professor Emeritus of Economics at the University of London and the former Sir John Hicks Professor of Economics at the London School of Economics and Political Science, UK.

Kurt W. Rothschild is Professor Emeritus of Economics at the University of Linz, Austria.

Robin Rowley is Professor of Economics at McGill University in Montreal, Canada.

Roberto Scazzieri is Professor of Economics at the University of Bologna, Italy, and Life Member of Clare Hall, Cambridge, UK.

INTRODUCTION

Harald Hagemann and O.F. Hamouda

The idea of gathering into a volume essays in honour of Sir John Hicks occurred to us a few years ago. His sudden death in May 1989 has strengthened our desire to go ahead with producing *The Legacy of Hicks*. This volume is thus a collection of essays written in his memory.

Sir John Hicks made a significant impact on almost every aspect of modern economic theory. He wrote more than fifteen books and over 200 articles that have all left a mark on the discipline. The articles in this volume not only stress his contribution to economics in general but also consider Hicks's impact on the specific foundations of economic theory as perceived by the contributors, a special group of scholars.

The objective of *The Legacy of Hicks* was to put together in one volume a dozen essays written by authors (Hicks's friends, colleagues or former students) who each not only are familiar with Hicks's contributions in a particular field, but also have made a contribution in the same area. For many, Hicks and economics have become almost synonymous, and from this perspective the volume will be viewed as an assessment of the evolution of the discipline of economics in the last five decades. In a look backward in each essay, Hicks's work is related to that of authors who influenced him. As a whole, however, *The Legacy of Hicks* looks forward and suggests which of the many contributions of Hicks will be remembered by future generations and where he left unfinished work for future economists to pursue. The volume thus encapsulates the achievement of the prolific self-critical economist, Sir John Hicks, and also assesses the influence his work has had and will continue to have.

There are numerous scholars whose interest or personal relationship to Hicks, as admirers, antagonists or observers, qualifies them to write and discuss Hicks's work both in retrospect and prospect. For our project we invited many of these scholars to contribute. The positive response was more than overwhelming. Some, Hicks's especially close contemporaries, although they wanted to participate, were unable to do so in the tight time limit we had set for submissions. It is without doubt that those scholars who did accept to contribute have all, each with a very personal touch, shed interesting light on issues which not only concerned Hicks but which are still of pertinence in the economic discipline. These essays that mesh well in their complementarity will certainly help historians of thought and those interested in the development of economic ideas to grasp the significance of Hicks's own contributions and those of Hicksian economics.

Hicks died in his home in May 1989. The following October a service was held in his memory at the University Church of St Mary the Virgin in Oxford. Robin C.O. Matthews, whose first encounter with Hicks was when Hicks served as his tutor in economic theory in 1946–7 at Nuffield College, was honoured to be asked to deliver the memorial address. We thought it appropriate that his address be reproduced in this volume as an introductory contribution (Chapter 1). In the few moving words reprinted here as 'In memoriam', Matthews captured the character of the Sir John Hicks he knew, but also the Sir John Hicks recognizable to almost all who knew him.

'John Hicks the theorist', by Frank H. Hahn (Chapter 2), was originally written for the *Economic Journal* just after Hicks died. For Hahn, as for many others, Hicks served as a strong intellectual mentor. Like Hicks, Hahn is a product of the London School of Economics, representing its next succeeding generation. Although Hahn's love for the technical or mathematical approach to economics far and away supersedes Hicks's, to a large extent Hahn shares Hicks's disdain for the abusive use of mathematics when words will do and his intolerance of the pretentious use of complex mathematics when more elementary methods are sufficient. Among technical economic theorists Hahn is perhaps the most qualified to assess both the technicalities and the subtleties of Hicks's theoretical contribution. It is no surprise that Hahn esteems almost exclusively Hicks's *Value and Capital*, while appraising to a lesser extent his monetary theory and Keynesian economics.

With one other exception (Chapter 10) all the remaining essays were written specifically for this volume, beginning with Michio Morishima's 'Capital and growth' (Chapter 3). As Matthews remarks in 'In memoriam', it is known that Hicks, as a theorist, was a loner. Despite a few joint papers, he did not seek out sustained collaboration. Morishima's was an exception. Morishima was very close to Hicks from the early 1960s until his death in 1989. Hicks frequently sought his opinion, for he found Morishima's original approach to economics and his mathematical expertise to be challenging and up to date. It can be said that Morishima was truly part of the making of Hicks's *Capital and Growth*.

Morishima's contribution here on capital and growth has the same breadth as Hahn's. It explains the interaction between Hicks and himself in the making of *Capital and Growth*, especially that part of the book that deals with the von Neumann model and the turnpike theorem. In an interesting way Morishima discusses Hicks's distinction between fixprice and flexprice both as theoretical concepts and as methodological and sociological–historical constructs. The reader might find of particular interest the later sections of the

2

essay in which Morishima follows Hicks's ideas through *Capital and Growth* to *Capital and Time* to set Hicks's method within the context of von Neumann's growth model.

Shortly after the publication of *Capital and Growth*, Hicks acknowledged his indebtedness to Charles Kennedy, author of 'Capital theory' (Chapter 4). One harsh criticism directed toward *The Theory of Wages*, published in 1932, that Hicks was to remember well and for a long time was Shoves's remarks about Hicksian capital theory. As a later influence, Charles Kennedy played a similar but more constructive role in redirecting Hicks's capital theory from its treatment in *Capital and Growth* to that in *Capital and Time*. In his essay Kennedy has combined his knowledge of Austrian theory, capital theory and Hicks's theory of capital. Some of his special concerns about the treatment of capital in economics, as pertains to situations of the steady state and the traverse, and technical progress and statistical problems of measurement are spelled out in his contribution.

In 'The theory of wages revisited' (Chapter 5) Kurt W. Rothschild focuses on what has happened to Hicks's first and major book. The Vienna tradition in economics had many facets. On one side it had, for example, much to say about production and capital theory, in the line of Böhm-Bawerk and the outsider Wicksell, and Hicks was very attentive to that variant. On yet another, the Austrian economists following Menger and Hayek might have found the underlying spirit of *The Theory of Wages* as being perhaps the work, among all of Hicks's contributions, which is most compatible with their variant of Austrian market economics. Kurt W. Rothschild, who knows quite a lot about the latter tradition and who, like Hicks, also wrote his own *The Theory of Wages* (1954), reassesses the theory that ironically made Hicks both famous and embarrassed during his formative years. As Rothschild rightly emphasizes, Hicks spent a great deal of subsequent time demolishing parts of his own work. These revisions, Rothschild notes, make his assessment task a bit awkward. Rothschild discusses in particular the merits of Hicks's concepts of the elasticity of substitution as well as his bargaining process in which he introduced an 'employer's concession curve' and a 'union's resistance curve'.

In his 'A reformulation and extension of Hicksian dynamics' (Chapter 6), Richard Goodwin shifts the attention to 'economic dynamics' and the trade cycle. When Richard Goodwin left Harvard in the early 1950s to go to England, Hicks, who recognized his pioneering talents in mathematical economics and economic dynamics, wanted him at Oxford. None the less he ended up, for reasons we do not need to elaborate here, in Cambridge. At the time, Hicks was more preoccupied with Harrod's dynamics than with Goodwin's non-linear system, but their work had much in common. Hicks himself had recognized it by 1950 (1950a: xii) and Goodwin likes to repeat jokingly that Hicks's *A Contribution to the Theory of the Trade Cycle* spoiled his own share of the then lucrative market for business cycle theories.

Goodwin recognizes that Hicks's crude model, although it uses linear analysis in which the cycle is dissociated from its trend, had in fact embedded in its theory a more complex non-linear dynamic system. Goodwin thus suggests an alternative formulation in terms of growth of both the labour supply and the labour cost relationship in which a feedback mechanism both relates wage, productivity, profit and growth and explains the dynamics of the interaction between output and employment. This manner of setting the dynamics, he says, is a variant of von Neumann's model. Goodwin demonstrates that when Hicks's crude and simple model is extended to a more complicated form, the traditional notion of equilibrium and regularity takes a different meaning, and under certain conditions the dynamics of the system can become chaotic.

Among his many achievements in economic theory Hicks will perhaps be remembered most for his contribution to general equilibrium and Christopher Bliss chose in 'Hicks on general equilibrium and stability' (Chapter 7) to reassess and concentrate on the issue of stability in Hicks's work on general equilibrium. Christopher Bliss joined Hicks's college, Nuffield in Oxford, after Hicks had retired and moved to All Souls. He knew Hicks as a colleague and had many discussions with him. Some of them helped him directly to write an enlightening and comprehensive entry of Hicks's contributions for the *New Palgrave Dictionary*.

Much has been said about Hicks's notion of stability and the rudimentary mathematical tools Hicks used in his pioneering work *Value and Capital*. More than five decades after its publication Bliss, in his reconsideration of this issue, argues that now that mathematics consists of more powerful tools, it is topology and non-linear differential equation theory that are needed to analyse both the existence problems and the stability problems of general equilibrium. Ironically, however, he also remarks that with the use of more advanced mathematics, theorists are reaching a rather disturbing conclusion: technical refinement does not necessarily lead to the neat outcomes in terms of existence and stability that most economists had sought earlier, but rather to a potentially chaotic result. It seems, according to Bliss, that Hicks's own analysis, though very simple, provided all that was needed for the issue of stability of an economic system, without entering high water full of surprises.

Hicks was one of the fathers of modern welfare economics. In fact, he received the Nobel Prize together with Kenneth Arrow in 1972 for his 'pioneering contributions to general economic equilibrium theory and welfare theory', the latter referring to a bunch of papers published between 1939 and 1946 (collected in Part II of Hicks 1981). According to Hicks the major tasks of welfare economics are the study of conditions of Pareto optimality and of deviations from this optimum, and it is here that Marshall's concept of consumers' surplus has a major role to play. John S. Chipman, a specialist in international and welfare economics, noted for his command of the history of economic thought, reviews in 'Hicksian welfare economics' (Chapter 8)

Hicks's contributions to welfare economics under four main headings which correspond to Hicks's main contributions to 'new welfare economics' or 'Kaldor–Hicks welfare economics'. He shows that John Stuart Mill came very close to but fell short of developing a quantitative underpinning to his compensation argument like in the Kaldor–Hicks approach, and advocates the abandonment of statics in favour of an intertemporal framework in which uncertainty plays a crucial role. Chipman is critical of Hicks's strategic retreat to the cost approach and concludes that without consulting preferences there is no basis for deciding which products to include in the 'social income' and which to exclude and likewise for the measurement of either welfare or productivity. In his re-evaluation of Hicks's rehabilitation of the Marshallian concept of consumers' surplus, Chipman shows that this concept can be treacherous and misleading, which is illustrated by taking up the Hicksian example of the effect of an excise tax imposed on a particular commodity. Finally, Chipman comes out as a champion of Hicks's equivalent variation (as opposed to compensating) as a universal measure of value.

Modern macroeconomic theory has been shaped to an extraordinary degree by Keynes and by Hicks. Hicks's interpretation of Keynes's *General Theory* through the IS–LM diagram, developed in his famous 'Mr. Keynes and the "classics"' (Hicks 1937a), set the course of Keynesianism and the ensuing development of modern macroeconomic theory, although Hicks ceased to use it in his later reconstructions of Keynesian theory (see, for example, Hicks 1974b, 1980a). From his first impressions of Keynes, Hicks felt that while he himself had begun as a Walrasian, Keynes's *opus magnum* was more part of a Marshallian tradition, that it was *not* a general theory. Axel Leijonhufvud in his 'Hicks, Keynes and Marshall' (Chapter 9) discusses the issues surrounding the IS–LM model and its influence on the development of modern macroeconomic theory. In particular Leijonhufvud focuses on the question whether Hicks's 'suggested interpretation' neutralized Keynes's revolution or diverted it off the 'right' track.

Leijonhufvud, who was a close friend of Hicks for many years, himself became well known with his classic *On Keynesian Economics and the Economics of Keynes* (1968) in which he disposed of the income–expenditure model as the 'economics of Keynes' because the comparative static nature of that model cannot deal with the genuine dynamic question of self-adjustment. In a later attempt to find out 'What was the matter with IS–LM?', Leijonhufvud (1983) came to the conclusion that IS–LM ignores the sequence of events *within* the period and fails to capture essential elements of Keynes's theory. The IS–LM apparatus is a hybrid consisting of a Walrasian element of a simultaneous equilibrium on interdependent markets and built on Marshallian microfoundations. The problem was that theory in the Marshallian tradition was 'in time', whereas theory in the Walrasian tradition was not, as Hicks later came to recognize.

Another area in which Hicks's achievement will be remembered is that of the theory of money. We asked Robert Clower, who was Hicks's student in Oxford in the 1950s, and who has himself made a number of contributions to monetary theory in particular, to give an account of Hicks's contribution to monetary theory. Unfortunately, his recent poor health has slowed up his work considerably and he suggested that David Laidler be asked instead to carry out the task. Despite the short notice Laidler accepted. Laidler's own work in the area of monetary theory and the history of monetary theory and his knowledge of Hicksian monetary theory is well known and does not need to be emphasized here.

Given the tight time limit set and also the fact that Laidler has in numerous instances commented on and published many review articles on Hicks's work on money, the editors reconsidered asking him to contribute a whole new paper. Laidler was asked instead if he could combine ideas from his already published work. The outcome is an analysis of 'Hicks's later monetary thought' (Chapter 10), derived from a fortunate amalgamation of the contents of two separate review articles on *Money, Interest, and Wages* (1982a) and *A Market Theory of Money* (1989a). Readers interested in monetary thought should also be aware of another interesting and more extensive paper by Laidler, 'What was new about Liquidity Preference Theory?' (1990), in which the author discusses Hicks's notion of liquidity in relation to both the pre-Keynesian and Keynesian revolutions.

The next two essays – 'In time with Hicks: probability' by Omar Hamouda and Robin Rowley (Chapter 11) and 'Risk and uncertainty' by John Hey (Chapter 12) – are about Hicks's theory of uncertainty and probability. Choice under conditions of uncertainty is another area in which Hicks did some pioneering work. As pointed out by J.L. Ford, Hicks was the originator of the use of moments in economics, which he used in his portfolio theory. Although Hicks's contribution to the portfolio approach received recognition in monetary theory, his suggestions as to how to handle risk and uncertainty have gone less noticed. There are three independent and complementary papers written at more or less the same time assessing Hicks's contribution to the theory of risk and uncertainty. Those of Hey and Hamouda and Rowley are printed here, while the reader interested in the issue could also consult Ford (1991).

Neglect of Hicks's contribution to the area of risk and uncertainty may be due to two reasons. One is that the theory of risk and uncertainty has become an extremely technical area, and many may doubt whether Hicks had the expertise to carry what is often seen, perhaps wrongly, as crude mathematical techniques to a sophisticated level. The other has to do with the purpose of studying choice under uncertainty. There are clearly many circumstances in which risk and uncertainty are present. Hey subdivides them into cases involving (a) a form of insurance, (b) a Knightian 'true' uncertainty, (c) a purchase of lottery tickets and (d) the ordinary running of business. The neglect of Hicks's theory may come from the fact, which Hey correctly observes, that most economists are fascinated (perhaps under the influence of statisticians) by case (c), while Hicks was rather mostly concerned by cases (b) and (d) that have more to do with economics.

'In time with Hicks: probability' (Chapter 11) was read at the 1989 conference, *'Fifty Years of Value and Capital'*, in Bologna in Hicks's honour. In the essay Hamouda and Rowley explore Hicks's early contribution to the theory of profit and uncertainty and Hicks's knowledge of probability at a critical time when the theory of probability itself was undergoing a tremendous evolution. Hicks often criticized his own *Value and Capital* in which he said he neglected uncertainty. Hamouda and Rowley undertook the exercise of probing what would have happened to that classic book if in it Hicks had seriously considered uncertainty rather than certainty equivalence by applying his knowledge of probability. Hamouda discusses in much greater length Hicks's use of uncertainty in his book *John R. Hicks: The Economist's Economist* (1993), and probability in general with Rowley in a book forthcoming from Routledge.

John Hey is among a small group of scholars whose expertise in the theory of choice under uncertainty, the theory of risk and uncertainty and the theory of expected utility is undeniable. His numerous contributions and valuable surveys in the field of risk and uncertainty serve as reference to students. Hey's present article 'Risk and uncertainty' (Chapter 12) is another addition and is of great help both for translating Hicks's language and techniques into today's standard terminology and, most of all, for explaining Hicks's concept of 'the disaster point in risk theory' and for clarifying some of Hicks's debate with the state of the theory.

Finally, the last three chapters are about topics that especially occupied Hicks's mind in the later part of his life when he grappled with the analysis of major economic changes or 'impulses', like the impact of an innovation on the development of an economy over time. Here we reach the territory of 'deep Hicks' (Collard 1993) who was concerned with economics becoming a historical social science. Clearly, the author of *A Theory of Economic History* (Hicks 1969a), who investigated the evolution of the market economy culminating in the Industrial Revolution, wants us to think about this book jointly with the subsequent *Capital and Time* (Hicks 1973d), where key assumptions are substantially the same as those effects of the English Industrial Revolution which are at the very centre of Hicks's historical explanations.

This holds in particular for Hicks's analysis of the Ricardo machinery effect which is taken up by Harald Hagemann in his essay 'Employment and machinery' (Chapter 13). The analysis of economic growth and technological change is one of the oldest subjects in economics. Technical progress is not only a major growth stimulus which increases the level of productivity and real wages in the long run, but is also a source of many adjustment problems in the short and medium run. The diverging expectations on the employment consequences of new technologies mirror the ambiguous character of technological change which both creates jobs and eliminates them. Hicks always had emphasized the relevance of the time dimension in studying the compensation process. To analyse the adjustment problems caused by a change in technology, he switched over to a neo-Austrian model in which productive processes are completely integrated vertically. Deep Hicks used the Austrian insights of the importance of the temporal structures of productive processes to achieve his primary target, the construction of a theory of a growing economy which is not on a steady-state path but on a traverse from one path to another. But Hicks's theory is as much inspired by Ricardo as by the Austrians. Hagemann's contribution links the breakthrough Hicks has achieved, despite all shortcomings, with the analysis of the traverse to the starting point of the Ricardo machinery problem and reflects on the potential of Hicks's contribution for future research work.

Hicks's interest in history, economic history and the history of economic thought is evident in many of his writings. He made ample use of economic history and the history of economic thought as necessary instruments in the process of advancing economic theory. In his contribution, 'Economic theory and economic history' (Chapter 14), Roberto Scazzieri attempts to bring together Hicks's constant concern with theoretical rigour and his awareness of the historical dimension of economic theories. Scazzieri focuses in particular on time-related phenomena as the distinction between stocks and flows, on fixprice and flexprice models, on the association between the time structure of productive processes and money, decisions and sequential causality as well as on specific institutional arrangements to explain Hicks's method of building blocks for a theory of economic history.

The last essay, but by no means the least contribution, is by Hicks's closest contemporary Nicholas Georgescu-Roegen on the theme 'Time in economics' (Chapter 15), with which Hicks eventually came to struggle. Hicks was aware of the difficulty it presented in his treatments of dynamics, capital, uncertainty and expectations as he grappled with general equilibrium, IS–LM, marginal productivity, monetary theory and the production function. This is nowhere more explicit than in his paper 'Some questions of time in economics', which he wrote for a Festschrift in honour of Georgescu-Roegen (1976f). Georgescu-Roegen, like Hicks, has been a loner theorist, but, unlike Hicks, who remained in his native country surrounded by admirers, Georgescu-Roegen has found himself in a foreign land where, while he was respected by the economic establishment for what he had to say, his advice was not always listened to. He must have been very pleased when Hicks finally echoed the concerns he had been hammering out since the early 1930s, that time is of critical importance in economics and that its consideration gives an entirely different meaning to production and utility functions and all derived concepts used by economists.

After an opening treatment of the obvious need for a consideration of a concept of time in the economics of expectations and change, Georgescu-

Roegen subtly shifts his attention to the significance of time in the use of the standard economic variables of the production and utility functions. With refreshing creativity and stylistic flourish, the author explores the idea of economic change as evolution.

This set of essays is revealing not only of the work and character of Sir John Hicks but also of the nature of the economic discipline. Economists in increasing numbers believe that their discipline is a science and somehow must, *de facto*, be mathematical. The very few at the forefront aware of the nature of economic problems think that economics has not been mathematized enough and that the kind of mathematics required for economics is yet to be developed. There are, however, also a number of perceptive economists who believe that mathematical economics at the stage in which it is now has lost touch with the societal problems that economics is supposed to analyse.

Hicks always resorted to simple examples and used accessible mathematics. This rather middle-of-the-road approach earned him lots of praise but also criticism from both extremes. For example, very early on Shackle and especially Joan Robinson blamed Hicks for being responsible for leading economics into general equilibrium, for making it mathematical and for promoting 'useless neo-classical economics'. Attacks from other outsiders, such as Morgenstern, were equally virulent:

> The so-called 'mathematical' economists in the narrower sense – Walras, Pareto, Fisher, Cassel, and hosts of other later ones – especially, have completely failed even to see the task that was before them. Professor Hicks has to be added to this list, which is regrettable because he wrote several years after decisive work had been done – in principle – by J. von Neumann and A. Wald.
>
> (1941: 369)

Morgenstern was frustrated by the slowness of the profession to embark upon using the types of mathematical techniques developed by von Neumann. Bliss, in Chapter 7, records some of these attacks.

Whether he was a poor mathematician or simply restrained himself from sophisticated techniques, whether he over-simplified his models or overplayed the equilibrium theory, Hicks was conscious of both the implications of his theories and the limits of his approaches. He was very attentive to his critics while attempting to hold firm to the middle ground.

Confusion seems to stem from the inability of many to distinguish between tools and methods of analysis for the fundamental premises and propositions underlying a mode of reasoning, whether it be deductive, inductive or a mixture of the two. To this distinction also is grafted another peculiarity, that of the inescapable balance between the positive and the normative natures in economics. Each presents its own difficulty and challenge.

John Hicks was aware of all these aspects. He was ingenious enough to have pushed the abstractions of his arguments to make them rigorous by using whatever appropriate tools were available, but he chose to keep his theories simple enough to be able to make sense of them and to be able to switch gears and retract from formal models when explanations of the real world were needed. He often relied on intuition and common sense to complete his economics and to make it adaptable to situations that deal especially with human nature.

Recently, on the occasion of the 'centenary year' of the *Economic Journal*, its editor John Hey published a special volume in which many economics scholars were asked to speculate on economics a hundred years from now. Many very cautiously refrained from speculation. Here the question can be rephrased, what will economists think of Hicks in a hundred years' time? A hundred years from now Hicks's tools will no doubt be seen as crude and primitive, but his models, like those of Smith, Ricardo and Marshall, will probably have remained classic examples for students in economics for that long time to come.

All the essays in this volume have been published as submitted, except for minor editorial changes to bring about internal consistency. One of the major changes is that all the references to Hicks's work have been removed from the individual essays' bibliographies and gathered into a single complete bibliography of his works at the end of the volume.

We want to express our gratitude to all those institutions and persons who contributed to the realization of this volume. Thanks are first due to Glendon College, York University, and the University of Hohenheim for providing research facilities and financial support. Thanks are also due to the University of Cambridge, and in particular to Clare Hall, for providing an intellectual environment that has stimulated our work in an important way. A particular thanks to Professor B.B. Price who read the entire manuscript and made valuable suggestions. We are also indebted to Kerstin Gehringer and Sophie for secretarial assistance. Finally, we would like to thank the *Economic Journal* for permission to reprint Frank Hahn's paper and the *Journal of Money, Credit and Banking* and the *Journal of Monetary Economics* for permitting us to use extracts from David Laidler's review articles.

BIBLIOGRAPHY

Baumol, W. J. (1990) 'Sir John versus the Hicksians, or theorist malgré lui?', *Journal of Economic Literature* 28: 1708–15.

Bliss, C. (1987) 'Hicks, John Richard', in J. Eatwell, M. Milgate and P. Newman (eds) *The New Palgrave. A Dictionary of Economics*, vol. 2, London: Macmillan, pp. 641–46.

Collard, D. A. (1993) 'High Hicks, deep Hicks, and equilibrium', *History of Political Economy* 25: 331–50.

Ford, J. L. (1991) 'Uncertainty, liquidity preference and portfolio choice: aspects of the Hicksian approach', *Review of Political Economy* 3: 320–48.

Hamouda, O. F. (1993) *John R. Hicks: The Economist's Economist*, Oxford: Blackwell.

Laidler, D. (1990) 'What was new about Liquidity Preference Theory?' *Greek Economic Review* 12, Supplement: 9–37.

Leijonhufvud, A. (1968) *On Keynesian Economics and the Economics of Keynes*, New York and Oxford: Oxford University Press.

—— (1983) 'What was the matter with IS–LM?', in J.-P. Fitoussi (ed.) *Modern Macroeconomic Theory: An Overview*, Oxford: Basil Blackwell, pp. 64–90.

Morgenstern, O. (1941) 'Professor Hicks on value and capital', *Journal of Political Economy* 49: 361–93.

Rothschild, K. W. (1954) *The Theory of Wages*, Oxford: Basil Blackwell.

1

IN MEMORIAM

Robin C. O. Matthews

It is not in doubt that Hicks was the most distinguished British economist of his generation, many would say the most distinguished in the world. Yet it is more difficult to convey in a few words the nature of his greatness and his contribution than it would be for others of comparable stature. His fame did not come from some strong policy recommendations, like those derived from Keynes; nor from some strong empirical finding. And subtle though much of his writing is, he is not remembered mainly for sharp and startling deductive theorems, achieved through complex chains of reasoning.

His chief contribution, rather, was as a conceptualizer. He was one who showed new methods of analysing economic problems, methods that might sometimes be used for one purpose, sometimes for another. This is not the place to enumerate these concepts. They were wide ranging, but related. They run from income and substitution effects in his early days, to others which he was continuing to develop even in his extreme old age. Hicks gave to economics a conceptual apparatus which is now taken for granted as part of the grammar of the discipline.

John Hicks was born in 1904. His father was a journalist–editor and part-proprietor of the *Warwick and Leamington Spa Courier*. There were intellectual traditions on both sides of his family, which had a connexion with Graham Wallas. A strong intellectual impulse was given to Hicks also by the Headmaster of his Prep school, to whom he felt he owed more than he did to Clifton or (alas!) to Balliol, where he was not well taught, at least on the economics side of the new PPE school. His undergraduate contemporaries, like Denis Brogan, recognized him as something out of the ordinary; but they knew too, even before the results were announced, that something had gone seriously wrong with his performance in the schools. His failure to get a First was a severe setback, and after doing a B.Litt. he actually tried for some months following his father's profession as a journalist, on the *Manchester Guardian*. Balliol, through the person of its Master, Lindsay, then made restitution by helping him in 1926 towards the job in the London School of Economics (LSE) that turned out to be so decisive for his career.

Those nine years at the LSE were tremendously productive. They included contributions to value theory, to welfare economics, to the portfolio theory of money and to general equilibrium theory. Any one of these contributions the average economist would be proud to have as his chief life's achievement. Hicks signalized the debt he felt to the LSE by giving for their new library the proceeds of his Nobel Prize – the first Nobel Prize in economics to be given to a British economist.

It was at the LSE, too, of course, that he met Ursula Webb, who became his wife. For the rest of his life, until her death a few years ago, they were seldom parted even for a few days. Their marriage was a marriage of opposites. He was shy, she was outgoing; she was direct, he was subtle. She protected him and organized their lives. Their loyalty to each other was unswerving.

The LSE years were the only important phase in his career when Hicks worked in close association with others of his own age and standing in his own field. Even then he was something of a loner, working things out on his own in his own way. Later, he talked a good deal to some selected younger economists; and throughout his life he saw much of his near contemporary who came to be a neighbour in Blockley, the economic historian T. S. Ashton, a pre-eminent scholar in a field which Hicks did not regard as his own, but in which he was deeply interested. The close intellectual contacts of the LSE days with his peers in his own field were not repeated. On the other hand, he gave encouragement and discerning help to an army of graduate students now spread over the globe. Many of them came from Ursula's college, Linacre, where he was an Honorary Fellow and a frequent visitor.

Chance plays a part in the development of even the greatest thinkers. I suspect that the near *tabula rasa* that Hicks brought to the LSE as a result of his lack of economic education in Oxford had a permanent effect on his approach to the subject. He felt he had to work out his own way of thinking, in part almost from first principles, and this habit persisted throughout his life. He had to chew things through and make them part of his own system of thought.

Had chance taken him as an undergraduate to Cambridge instead of Balliol, his intellectual starting point would have been quite different: he would have become deeply imbued in a single tradition, ready-made, the tradition of Marshall; and his initial task would have been to add or else to escape, rather than, as it was, to construct afresh. This desire to construct an edifice is witnessed by the remarkable breadth of his work. It shows also in his practice, almost unique among modern economic theorists, of making most of his main contributions not in journal articles but in books (or at least developed into books) – over a dozen of them.

This is not to say that in his process of construction he was uninfluenced by other thinkers. Indeed, the evolution of economic thought became a central preoccupation of his. He returned again and again to the great classical authors. As an undergraduate, I had the good fortune to be sent to him for tutorials in economic theory in 1946–7, soon after he came to be a Fellow of Nuffield after his sojourns in Cambridge and in Manchester. I was struck instantly by the complete difference between his approach and the approach of the other economics tutors I had had – and by the difference too from what I had expected (hard work on *Value and Capital*). With my other tutors, I had studied *topics*, using textbooks and other convenient but usually undistinguished sources. With Hicks I studied, not the instability of the price level, but Wicksell on the cumulative process; not discriminating monopoly, but Pigou's theory of it and his chapter on railway rates.

Chance played a part too, in determining which earlier thinkers initially influenced him the most. Hugh Dalton, of all people, still on the LSE staff when Hicks went there, said to him, 'You can read Italian, you should read Pareto'. So he did. And from Pareto it was natural that he should proceed to Walras and to general equilibrium theory. Hence, and also from Hayek's presence in the LSE, came the paradox that Hicks, English of the English in his personal character, was of the great British economists of our times the least English in his intellectual antecedents.

Hicks was conscious of his own place in the development of economic thought, and took a justified pride in it. There was one aspect of his influence that aroused mixed feelings in him. At school and in his first year at Oxford, he had become a proficient mathematician, without, I think, ever falling in love with mathematics. His own most influential book, *Value and Capital*, published in 1939, contained more mathematics than was usual in those days (as it had to, given its concern with the interaction of multiple markets). Together with the much further elaboration by American economists after the war of the lines of thought he had opened up, it had some responsibility for the present-day mathematization of economic theory. That process went much further than in Hicks's view was appropriate to the nature of the real-life problems that economics should address. That to him was the decisive criterion for economic theory. He was deeply academic in his outlook, but never scholastic.

There was also a matter of temperament in this. 'My home lies in the humanities', he said, with increasing emphasis as he grew older. That was one of the reasons why All Souls was so congenial to him. Here was a community of distinguished scholars, spanning the humanities – a community of which he could be proud to be a member, but a community in which privacy was respected. The honour that the College conferred on him by having his portrait painted was something that he appreciated with an intensity that surprised economists who knew of his renown in their own world. He was a Fellow of the College for 35 years. The rather parliamentary style of its governing body meetings suited him. He was a man for the single well-considered contribution, not a man for the cut and thrust of debate, whether in a College meeting or in an academic seminar. He did not relish the role of academic entrepreneur – hence his move at the age of 61 from the Drummond chair to a Research Fellowship. Still less was he attracted by the corridors of political power. He did have views on current economic policy issues; and sometimes they were strongly held. But his style was to state the argument, with his characteristic clarity, very likely also showing the issue in some larger context, and leave persuasion to others.

The breadth of Hicks's intellectual interests was apparent to all who knew him. It was given more rein in his later writings than earlier. It embraced architecture and music, as well as literature and above all history, which linked with his lifelong preoccupation with the treatment of time in economic theory. This wide range of interests in the humanities was one of the reasons why he so enjoyed being a Delegate of the University Press. Less widely known, perhaps because of his reticence, was the range of his emotional sympathies. He was interested in children; in his old age he took much pleasure from the company of his great-nieces. Poetry was important to him. He held no strict religious faith and he was unsympathetic to organized religion or to religion tainted with sentimentalism. But Dante, that most Christian of poets, was the poet most loved. And these lines by a poet of very different temper, from *Kim*, moved him to tears when he recited them:

> My brother kneels (so saith Kabir)
> To stone and brass in heathenwise,
> But in my brother's voice I hear
> My own unanswered agonies.
> His God is as his Fates assign –
> His prayer is all the world's – and mine.

2

JOHN HICKS THE THEORIST

Frank H. Hahn

Hicks's contribution to economic theory deserves and surely will receive serious and extended scholarly assessment. The present essay written so soon after his death, which, characteristically, came to him while completing a new book, does not provide this. It is written to evoke for the many for whom Hicks was a decisive influence the Hicksian spirit and approach. It will of course discuss some, but by no means all, of his contributions but these discussions will, in the nature of the case, not be exhaustive. The main aim is to remind us of what we owe to his work.

I

We live in an age of American economics. (Hicks (1963b) regarded 1946 as the 'eve of a great moment in American economics' and the start of its pre-eminence.) When he began his career as a theorist (he started economics in a very practical vein (Hicks 1963b: 305–6)) it was still very much a British subject with a recognizable British tradition. The latter is hard to pin down precisely but it had certain distinctive characteristics: (1) The study of economics is not to be regarded as an end in itself. It lacks the beauty of mathematics or art or the possibilities for precision and prediction of physics. The main motive for its study must be the improvement of the condition of mankind. 'The complicated analysis which economists endeavour to carry through are not mere gymnastic. They are instruments for bettering human life' (Pigou 1928: vii). (2) While certain aspects of the subject require precision and rigour it does not lend itself to the formulation of a general 'system'. A good economist is a pragmatic economist. (3) Economic phenomena are only one part of the phenomena of importance to the study of society. While *ceteris paribus* concerning all the non-economic variables may often be legitimate, explanation and understanding is often impossible without a knowledge of the history, mores and social norms of the society concerned. It is the duty of the theorist who has arrived at a formal result to consider whether it is robust when applied to different societies and particularly when it is applied to his own society. (4) It is pretentious to use mathematics when words will do and it is equally pretentious to use 'highbrow' mathematics when more elementary methods will do almost as

16

well. (5) As far as possible (given (1)) the economist should attempt to communicate with the educated non-expert.

It seems to me that, except in one important particular, Hicks belongs to this tradition and that he was conscious of it. The exception is point (1). He no doubt was interested in the amelioration of the 'human condition' but he seems to have felt strongly that the condition must be understood. Indeed it is this departure from the tradition which appeals to many of us now. Reading Hicks always renews one's faith in the importance of economic theory as a means of understanding (and not necessarily of prediction). No one can doubt that he took this enterprise seriously. He returned to the same problems over and over again over many years because he brooded on them and became dissatisfied with his earlier answers.

On the other hand it must be admitted that other aspects of the tradition exacted a certain cost (as well as conferring benefits). Amongst the costs I would put Hicks's relatively small box of mathematical tools. He plainly had considerable mathematical ability but he seemed disinclined to learn 'new tricks'. To some extent this cut him off from some new developments to which he could otherwise have contributed. Again he wrote *A Revision of Demand Theory* (1956a) of which he says: 'Those who rely on mathematical methods will not get much from the present approach which they could not get from the mathematical appendix to *Value and Capital* (p. v.).' It is thus an example of point (5) of the tradition. However, it must be doubted that the non-mathematical reader would get very far with the 'translation' which is offered. The tradition also made him reluctant to read widely in the new technocratic literature. He read the 'greats' like Samuelson, but judging by his references missed much that was relevant to him from the pen of the 'smaller fry'. These are genuine costs but they are happily vastly outweighed by the benefits of his work.

II

Although it was not his first book it seems clear that reflections on Hicks's work should start with *Value and Capital* (1939a). There can be few books which have had as much influence on the course of economic theory not only in the years which immediately followed its publication but to this day.

Although there were distinguished predecessors (e.g. Slutsky) and no doubt Hicks gained much from Roy Allen's early co-operation (Allen and Hicks 1934), the exposition of consumer's choice in the first part of *Value and Capital* is a *tour de force*. Of course much work has followed and many refinements are now available, but in its essentials it stands like a rock. The argument is always clear and decisive. Hicks's forte of coining new terms plays an important expository role as one moves from income and substitution effects to the compensating and equivalent variations. Later this yielded new insights into consumer's surplus and the economic theory of index numbers

(Hicks 1956a). Even when he falters, as he does in his discussion of the convexity of indifference curves, the reader is learning. Of course there is nothing yet on duality and revealed preference. But one guesses that there are many economists who are not specialists in the theory of household choice for whom the *Value and Capital* account is all they know and all that they need to know.

But the real delight is the appendix. We no longer need bordered Hessians but to come across the analysis here presented in the 1940s was an exhilarating eye-opener. Most importantly is this the case for those sections of the appendix where Hicks used the theory of the individual agent to discuss certain problems of the interaction of these agents. We learned for the first time the rôle of income effects and substitution effects in the analysis of the economy as a whole. It is true that Hicks's notion of stability was both stilted and, in the end, unsatisfactory. But it was not as flawed as Samuelson (1941/2) supposed (see McFadden 1968; Hahn 1991). It remains true that now it was possible to see how the Walrasian enterprise could be started from the 'bottom up', i.e. from a well-articulated micro-theory.

But of course *Value and Capital* contained much more than this. Perhaps the most lasting and important part is that on sequence analysis and the accompanying discussion of expectations. Even if we somehow convince ourselves that an economy is typically approximately in steady state with correct or rational expectations, it is hard to see that we can rest content before explaining why that should be so. Indeed it has been a central question since Adam Smith how rational greedy agents could lead an economy to a coherent disposition of resources. On this matter we have not been served well by many American economists who often seem to take the evident need to simplify as an injunction not to ask awkward questions. They thus leave out of consideration a large part of the subject matter of economics. In any event Hicks knew what he was about here and indeed, over the years, repeatedly returned to the subject (see Hicks 1965a, 1973d, 1974b, 1985a). He had well-known Swedish predecessors (in particular Lindahl) and he has had distinguished successors who adopt a period approach (e.g. Radner 1972; Grandmont 1982). His period analysis in *Value and Capital* was the beginning of Hicksian dynamics but it was only in later writings that it emerged as a recognizable theory of a process. In *Value and Capital* the story stops at short period equilibrium. 'The Temporary Equilibrium Model of *Value and Capital* is "quasistatic"' (1965a: 65). None the less that sufficed to signal to the reader that both equilibrium and the future would depend on expectations or, more accurately, on the manner in which expected values were derived from past experience. Reading this part of the book now one can see how it contained the seeds of what was to come later. Of course for a proper dynamics we want to pass from 'week' to 'week' and we need to decide on the way in which it is best to regard this time interval. One way is to suppose that prices decided on Monday cannot be altered until the following Monday – the 'fixprice method' (1965a). Here one is led to consider rationing and/or inventory changes during the week. Another is to suppose that trading in the week takes place at 'Grandmont short period equilibrium prices' – the method of 'short period equilibrium' (1965a). Here the expectations held on Monday need not be those of the previous Monday. This sort of analysis lends itself to an economics of mistakes and of their correction. It thus allows us to explain a situation in which agents make no systematic mistakes by the learning induced by past mistakes. It is good economics.

The reason why it is only now that attention is being given to this way of doing dynamics is that we have no axiomatic theory of learning. This invites the use of *ad hoc* learning rules and that is 'bad'. There is some evidence that Hicks was not immune to this foolishness. In *Capital and Growth* (1965a) on page 183 he is pleased to 'emerge' from 'Growth Equilibrium' which has been 'fertile in the generation of classroom exercises'. By page 201 he excuses himself from studying investment behaviour and error adjustment on the ground that 'they would be no more than exercises'. It is hard to avoid the conclusion that in spite of his wisdom he here fell into the commonplace trap of regarding deductions from axioms as more 'real' than observation. What is bad about this is that it is logically indefensible in economics where, for instance, as he rightly notes, growth equilibrium is just as much of an exercise as, say, adaptive expectation models. Economics is not physics and where our evidence is so poor and one is hard put to find *any* theory which we all agree that the evidence has refuted, we must use everything that is available – intuition, diverse observations, knowledge of the world together with a rigorous theory and good statistical inference. The idea that we have avoided *ad hoc* by the postulate of rational or correct expectations is absurd.

It is good to see that all of this confusion is coming to an end. Excellent work is appearing from the pens of Marcet and Sargent (1988), Grandmont (1988), Woodford (1988) and Evans (1989). As it proceeds it will be seen as a natural outgrowth of Hicks's sequence analysis. He knew all about the need for such work and indeed posed the right questions.

His own treatment of expectations was determined by what he felt he could handle. He noted that one might deal with the problem by considering the path 'that would be determined by correct expectations' (1973d: 56). He rejects this because he now wants to pass beyond steady-state equilibrium. The theory which emerges with correct expectations 'is not a sequential theory of the kind we are here endeavouring to construct, past and future are all at one level' (1932b: 56). He then opts for static expectations although, as usual, there are many warnings on the way. But that is a pretty poor piece of *ad hockery*. It meant that the analysis of the 'traverse' was never very convincing. My guess is that had Hicks disposed of more varied mathematical equipment he would have proceeded quite differently since it is plain, not only in this book (1973d) but elsewhere, that he understood fully what needed doing but did not feel himself able to do it. This can be seen from the fact that he was most at home with the postulate of single-valued expectations although he shows full awareness that this is unsatisfactory and can be misleading (see, for instance, 1965a: 71). He does discuss the propagation of random shocks in *The Trade Cycle* and later felt unhappy with the popularity of the 'elasticity of expectations'. But again and again he needed to invoke static expectations to get his models to work.

That there are many other important and influential parts of *Value and Capital* goes without saying. I reserve the 'Keynesian' parts and those dealing with money to the next section. But before I turn to that I must take explicit cognisance of Hicks's contribution in this book to the definition of income and the latter's relation to interest rates. The distinction between the receipts of any one date and an agent's income is central to an understanding of the agent's intertemporal disposition of resources and hence also to the agent's savings and portfolio decisions. Friedman (1957) magnificently combined the correct income view with a properly based savings theory and produced much empirical evidence. But Hicks was a close predecessor.

On one matter, however, Hicks had comparatively little to say: imperfect competition. In *Value and Capital* he takes the 'Lucasian' view that it is too hard and untidy for incorporation in a model of an economy. Later he returns to it in *Capital and Growth* but only very formally. However, he notes there that imperfect competition would entail the need for more than price expectations – there would also be demand expectations. An article on excess capacity (1954a) is all that a quick search reveals of further work on this problem. In retrospect he was probably right – the time for considering these questions is only now approaching with the flowering of game-theoretic economics and much greater technical know-how.

In my view, although Hicks wrote many more books after *Value and Capital* and in doing so made numerous important contributions, *Value and Capital* remained his masterpiece. It is not clear that he would have agreed with this judgement (see page v of 1973d). He came to feel perhaps that the book was too Walrasian (or, if you like, neo-classical) and that he had not come sufficiently to grips with either monetary theory or process analysis. It will have been noticed that I indeed went to and fro between the later Hicks and the Hicks of *Value and Capital* when 'dynamics' was discussed. But that is because I hold the view that that book signalled, and not only to Hicks but to others, where the next advance was to be. It was clear to me and I am sure to many others when we had fully absorbed it that *Value and Capital* pointed in the direction of research and thought on sequence analysis and, in particular, on expectations. We saw some of the flaws but rightly regarded them as minor and inevitable at that stage. By its grand structure, by its many novelties and by its wonderful style it had and has the marks of a true classic.

III

Hicks was an early Keynesian and, as we know, his first understanding of what that entailed became the understanding of most of us ('Mr Keynes and the "classics"', 1937a). The famous diagram is of a distilled general equilibrium model but with fixed prices and no explicit future. He wrote (concerning this paper), 'I have never regarded it as complete in itself. In fact only two years later in *Value and Capital*, I myself put forward what is surely a very different formulation' (*The Crisis in Keynesian Economics*, 1974b: 6–7). And so he did but by then it was too late. The IS–LM construction was too seductively simple to be abandoned by the many who encountered it either directly or in textbooks. It is not clear that that was an altogether bad thing. As Solow (1984) notes, most economists to this day when considering some macro-problem take Hicks's construction as a first step into the inevitable complexities. It helps to provide a rudimentary framework for thought and is not dangerous to the economist with a proper grasp of economic theory not least of *Value and Capital*. But it does have its dangers, not least to the critics of Keynes. Just as so many critics of neo-classical theory took the textbook production function in labour and capital as the paradigm of that theory, so many modern anti-Keynesians consider that Keynes's thought is fully encapsulated in Hicks's famous paper. One supposes that it is not possible to be protected from the intellectually lazy.

In *Value and Capital* as well as in *The Crisis in Keynesian Economics* Hicks shows that Keynes is to be taken as concerned with short period equilibrium and short period processes. It was in perhaps his least successful book (*A Contribution to the Theory of the Trade Cycle*) where he introduced the 'supermultiplier' that he extended Keynesian analysis to the long run. But here the process of stock adjustment and its potentially cyclical consequences is given prominence – the steady state was there in the analysis mainly to demonstrate that the economy would not easily get to it. However, except for wages, Hicks did not succeed in combining quantity and price adjustments into a complete theory (but then, so far, no one has done so).

The famous 'Mr Keynes and the "classics"' must be understood in this context. The diagram represents a short period equilibrium and not a long-run one. There is no formal articulation of expectational and price assumptions. But it is obvious that we are to think of inelastic expectations and of a regime where average prime costs are almost constant – the 'economics of depression'. Money wages are taken as given as they ought to be in short period analysis. But one can relax all of these assumptions and still have some use for the diagram. For it can be considered as a projection from an eight-dimensional to a two-dimensional space. The eight dimensions are current and expected values of interest, income, price and wage. Indeed it is helpful to think of it in that way before adding further dimensions for the capital stock and perhaps inventories. Proceeding in this way we illustrate by the point we choose to project, how we interpret Keynesian short period equilibrium.

But one thing we should not do is to choose that representation which gives a steady-state equilibrium. Keynes is not about that and Hicks knew it. That is why much recent criticism of Keynes is so baffling. In essence it consists of showing that Keynes does not apply in steady-state equilibrium. This is like attacking a cobbler for not being a tailor on the unexplained hypothesis that no one needs shoes. But we do need to know how and if steady state comes about.

Hicks in 1932 (*Theory of Wages*) started more or less where the 'new' macroeconomics is now, although in that book he was concerned with stationary states and correct foresight rather than with steady-state growth and rational expectations. He wrote the book, he says, under the influence of the powerful London School of Economics (LSE) economists of the time, especially Robbins and Hayek. But 'Within months of publication of my *Wages* book I was writing papers which diverged from the regular LSE line; and by the end of 1934 when my ideas were more formed, I was publishing things which were recognised by Keynes (in correspondence) as being more on his side than on the other' (1974b: 5). The 1963 edition of this book gives an extensive discussion of his change of view and takes his earlier self to task. Here are some examples: 'It was nonsense to maintain that the unemployment of 1932 was in any sense *caused* by excessively high wages ... the movement in real wages during the Great Depression ought clearly to have been treated ... as an effect and not as a cause' (p. 313). He proceeds, however, to note that in the post-war era rising real wages may have been an independent influence on the working of the economy. Later he remarks that while much of what he said in 1932 concerning stationary states remained valid for growth equilibrium, 'I do not much care for the approach myself' (p. 314). The labour market he regards as 'very special kind of market, a market which is likely to develop "social" as well as economic aspects' (p. 317). A reason for this is that the relation of employer to employee 'will be a continuing relation' (p. 317). And so on. By 1963 Hicks, one might say, had fully absorbed the lessons of *Value and Capital*! The neo-classical steady state may provide a jumping-off ground for the analysis of certain important features of an economy, but it cannot help much with the old and central question of economics of how decentralized economies may or may not deliver what Adam Smith claimed for them. Hicks struggled with this problem throughout his life and he deserves to be honoured on that account alone.

He also continued to struggle with *The General Theory*, which he recognized to be theoretically incomplete. Reading Myrdal's *Monetary Equilibrium* and talking to Lindahl had already in 1935 led him to some anticipations of Keynes's book and of *Value and Capital* ('Wages and interest: the dynamic problem', 1935f). He came to see that the crucial issues turned on the working of the labour market, on the role of money and on expectation formation. On the first of these he was by 1962 quite clear: the market for labour cannot be treated like the market for commodities. I have already quoted a number of his remarks in support of that contention. But it is in any case difficult to see how anyone living in the world can deny it. The idea of wages moving so as instantaneously to clear labour markets is recognized as absurd by everyone. It is more difficult to deny the contention that the 'errors' due to this postulate are in practice significant. Of course they were in 1932 or in the early Thatcher years. But in more normal times more precise investigations are needed. One needs to study the nature of the 'long-run relation' between employers and employed, one needs to take account of the role of heterogeneity of the labour force and of course of trade unions. Much of the investigation has taken place in recent years and is not yet concluded. Hicks saw the problems clearly but left them only partially resolved.

On the other hand he fully understood Keynes's distinction between a change in the money wage in one sector and a change in money wages as a whole. A view has grown up that Keynes postulated rigid money wages; he did not. He argued that flexible money wages were a costly and uncertain route to equilibrium (Hahn and Solow 1986). Suppose money wages *were* fixed and let us agree that this fixity is the cause of unemployment. Reduce them all by *k* per cent. Suppose that the gods are kind and that everyone holds with certainty that they will stay at the same level. Then we know by simple appeal to homogeneity that employment will be higher in the new equilibrium only by the workings of 'real cash balance effects'. But that same equilibrium is reachable at the old money wage and a higher nominal money stock. Not only that but you do not need the above implausible expectational assumptions to assert this. For with money wages constant and unemployment (sufficiently high), prices will not move much. This simple argument was as clear to Hicks as it by now should be to others, and he expounded it with all the required refinements. Since he was always aware of the need for process analysis he understood why the expectational assumptions were crucial to the advocates of flexible wages.

Monetary theory also occupied him throughout his life. His 'A suggestion for simplifying the theory of money' (1935b) quickly became famous but did not dig very deeply into the nature of the services money performed. This failing was repaired in his later work, perhaps most satisfactorily in the second lecture in *The Crisis in Keynesian Economics* although it was preceded in some penetrating analysis in 'The Two Triads' in *Critical Essays in Monetary Theory*. In *The Crisis* lecture he is particularly interesting on liquidity: 'liquidity is not a property of a single choice; it is a matter of a sequence of choices, a related sequence' (p. 38). He goes on: 'So it is not sufficient, in liquidity theory to make a single dichotomy between the known and the unknown. There is a further category, of things which are unknown now, but will become known in time' (p. 39). After that the analysis proceeds in masterly fashion. It has since been followed by others (e.g. Jones and Ostroy 1984; Hahn 1989) in a more formal, and less accessible, manner.

Hicks never mentions 'conditional probabilities' for instance, but is plainly using the concept. He does not engage in dynamic programming in a stochastic environment with transaction costs but reports the common-sense results such a programme would yield. In short, this is a virtuoso display in what I called the British tradition. It also makes extremely important points: the role of liquidity (flexibility) in the responsiveness of investment to interest rates, the usefulness of a distinction between 'auto-finance' and 'overdraft finance' of businesses when studying monetary policy and the role of the banking system in the latter under both kinds of business finance. This essay has opened up a new and important field for investigation. For instance, to mention only one, the explanation for good, i.e. almost perfect, and very imperfect or 'closed' markets and the welfare implications of this. These questions turn very much on liquidity in Hicks's sense as can be seen by the splendid work of Diamond (1984).

As far as Keynesian monetary analysis was concerned Hicks seems to have preferred the *Treatise*. He thought that Keynes in the *General Theory* had over-played the speculative motive (although he agrees that this motive can frustrate monetary policy as it did in the UK immediately after the war). He also considered Keynes to have been at fault in not stressing the virtue of liquidity in times of inflationary pressure, although he recognizes that that was understandable in the early 1930s. On the whole one gains the impression that Hicks did not regard a policy of stimulating investment by lower interest rates as very promising, particularly when times were already 'bad'. On the quantity equation and on 'Monetarism' he has no systematically expounded theory. But he had completed a book on monetary theory just before his death and I have not yet seen it. My guess is that he would have regarded any mechanical monetarist exercise with scepticism.

In any case it was clear to him that Keynes's own theory did not exclude the possibility of full-blown monetarist doctrines. It was also clear to Keynes (*How to Pay for the War*, 1940). What both contended, however, in my view correctly, is that the relation between the money stock and the price and money wage level depended on the state of the economy. In other words the T in $MV = PT$ cannot always be held to be given by its steady-state value and indeed it is not clear that it can ever be properly so taken. Nor can V be taken as a constant, partly for the reasons Hicks gives in his discussion of liquidity preference but also because innovations in transaction and insurance technologies occur and change it. It does not reflect well on us that there has been so much argument here on the wrong issues. We should have agreed at the outset that the disagreements concerned the *ad hoc* assumption that economies are typically in, or rapidly converge to, a unique steady-state equilibrium (in which of course *all* markets clear at rationally expected prices).

On the more highly theoretical aspects of monetary theory Hicks wrote little or not at all. He attempted a theoretical history (1969a) of the origin of money which contains much good sense. But he never, in any of his writings, provided a *Value and Capital*-like 'appendix' in which monetary and Walrasian General Equilibrium Theory were fully integrated. As far as I know, the work of Arrow–Debreu never tempted him to speculate on 'existence' problems for monetary economies or to consider how monetary phenomena were related to 'missing markets'. He accepted the sequential structure of markets as obvious fact and not in need of explanation. The British tradition once again! Whether it is here to be censured or not I cannot decide.

His difficulties with expectations I have already discussed. Like Keynes, he recognized how the present hung upon the expected future and this is the important insight. Lindahl and other Swedes were there before either of them but it is perhaps Hicks who made the most sustained attempt to impose orderly thinking.

IV

In the 1960s and 1970s Hicks was naturally affected by what was happening in growth and capital theory. He wrote *Capital and Growth* (1965a) and *Capital and Time* (1973d) and a number of articles. This is a part of Hicks's work I do not propose to discuss in detail. This is only partly due to the fact that the time allotted to me for this piece does not permit the extensive re-reading required. The other reason is that while, as usual, I have admired what he had to say, I have done so less on this topic than on the many others which he made his own.

The capital and growth books seem often to have been written with the aim of clearing his own mind. They are none the worse for that. But his difficulties were not always those of his typical reader and the pace is often somewhat slow. I do not think that here he ever gave us as authoritative and definitive an account of capital theory as that provided by Bliss (1975). McKenzie (1963) and Radner (1961) had a more secure understanding of the turnpike. Debreu (1960), Gorman (1968) and Koopmans (1960) had a deeper insight into intertemporal utility questions. The fact is that many topics here are technical and that Hicks's comparative advantage was in a more informal mixture of technicalities and economics. Of course, his work was distinguished, the exposition often masterly, but it was, at least in my judgement, not Hicks at his most formidable and innovative.

When I reviewed *Capital and Growth* I was enthusiastic about its expositional merits and praised its insights. I noted 'the clarity of exposition, the lucidity of thought and the transmutation of matters of high technique into ordinary language'. But I also drew attention to the absence of references and to a lack of 'many novel conclusions'. Looking back now I think it must be judged as an excellent text for its time. The Hicks of *Value and Capital* was stirring but does not truly emerge. He had his hands full with assimilating largely technical stuff into the British tradition as well as looking over his shoulder at what Robinson, Kaldor and others were saying.

One can detect a renewed interest in growth theory now but one which is more concerned with making much that was taken as exogenous in the past as a proper subject for economic explanation. Arrow and Kaldor were bolder than Hicks in these matters. As for capital theory, I shall perhaps unwisely claim that it is now settled. It is pre-eminently a subject fit for mathematical treatment. For instance, the possibility of perfect aggregation must be, and has been, settled mathematically (Gorman 1968). Double switching, the average period of production and the meaning, if any, of the return to abstinence are all matters which can be put precisely and understood with a little mathematics. Here literary treatments or treatments by arithmetical example etc. have led to much unnecessary noise. Hicks, as far as I can ascertain, never mentioned Malinvaud's famous paper (1953). But that is where modern capital theory starts.

Not everything that Hicks wrote can be judged of fundamental importance, but he wrote more that can be so judged than is given to most scholars. *Value and Capital* is the crown of his achievement, but his work in monetary theory and on Keynesian matters are of the highest order. A time may come when his citation index becomes small, but only because so much of what he wrote will have become identified with the subject of economics itself.

REFERENCES

Allen, R. G. D. and Hicks, J. R. (1934) 'A reconsideration of the theory of value', *Economica*, new series, 1: 52–76, 196–219.

Bliss, C. J. (1975) *Capital Theory and the Distribution of Income*, Amsterdam: North-Holland.

Debreu, G. (1960) 'Topological methods in cardinal utility theory', in K. J. Arrow, S. Karlin and P. Suppes (eds) *Mathematical Methods in the Social Sciences*, Stanford, CA: Stanford University Press.

Diamond, P. (1984) *A Search Equilibrium Approach to the Micro Foundations of Macroeconomics*, Cambridge, MA: MIT Press.

Evans, G. W. (1989) 'The fragility of sunspots and bubbles', *Journal of Monetary Economics* 23: 297–317.

Friedman, M. (1957) *A Theory of the Consumption Function*, Princeton, NJ: Princeton University Press for the National Bureau of Economic Research.

Gorman, W. M. (1963) 'The aggregation of capital', in J. N. Wolfe (ed.) *Value, Capital and Growth*, Edinburgh: Edinburgh University Press.

—— (1968) 'The structure of utility functions', *Review of Economic Studies* 104, 35 (4): 367–90.

Grandmont, J. M. (1982) 'Temporary general equilibrium theory', in K. Arrow and M. Intriligator (eds) *Handbook of Mathematical Economics*, Amsterdam: North-Holland, vol. 2, pp. 879–922.

—— (1988) Paper presented at Stanford IMSSS seminar.

Hahn, F. H. (1989) 'Liquidity', in B. Friedman and F. H. Hahn (eds) *Handbook of Monetary Economics*, Amsterdam: North-Holland, vol. 1, pp. 63–80.

—— (1991) 'Hicksian themes on stability', in L. W. McKenzie and S. Zamagni (eds) *Value and Capital. Fifty Years Later*, London: Macmillan, pp. 64–83.

—— and Solow, R. M. (1986) 'Is wage flexibility a good thing?' in W. Beckerman (ed.) *Wage Rigidity and Unemployment*, London: Duckworth.

Jones, R. A. and Ostroy, J. M. (1984) 'Flexibility and uncertainty', *Review of Economic Studies* 51 (1): 13–32.

Keynes, J. M. (1940) *How to Pay for the War*, London: Macmillan.

Koopmans, T.C. (1960) 'Stationary ordinal utility and impatience', *Econometrica* 28 (2): 287–310.

Malinvaud, E. (1953) 'Capital accumulation and efficient allocation of resources', *Econometrica* 21 (2): 233–68.

Marcet, A. and Sargent, T. J. (1988) 'Convergence of least square learning in self-referential linear stochastic models', mimeo, Hoover Institute, Stanford.

McFadden, D. (1968) 'On Hicksian stability', in J. N. Wolfe (ed.) *Value, Capital and Growth*, Edinburgh: Edinburgh University Press.

McKenzie, L. W. (1963) 'Turnpike theorems for a generalised Leontief model', *Econometrica* 31 (1–2): 165–80.

Pigou, A. C. (1928) *The Economics of Welfare*, 3rd edn, London: Macmillan.

Radner, R. (1961) 'Paths of economic growth that are optimal with regard only to final states, a turnpike-theorem', *Review of Economic Studies* 28 (2), no. 76: 98–104.

—— (1972) 'Existence of equilibrium of plans, prices and price expectations in a sequence of markets', *Econometrica* 40 (2): 284–304.

Samuelson, P. A. (1941/2) 'The stability of equilibrium', *Econometrica* 9: 97–120; 10: 125.

Solow, R. M. (1984) 'Mr Hicks and the classics', *Oxford Economic Papers*, new series, 36, November supplement: 13–25; reprinted in D. Collard, D. Helm, M. Scott and A. Sen (eds) *Economic Theory and Hicksian Themes*, Oxford: Oxford University Press.

Woodford, M. (1988) 'Learning to live with sunspots', mimeo, Chicago.

3

CAPITAL AND GROWTH

Michio Morishima

I

The economics of Sir John Hicks is no longer the economics of J. R. H. This has often been said. Hicks himself admitted it. With Hicks knighted in 1964, we may reckon that the earlier years of the 1960s form the period of this transition. Hicks's work *Capital and Growth*, published in 1965, is particularly interesting, as it is the most important of his works in this period.

I was privileged to be invited by Hicks to work with him at All Souls College during the academic year 1963–4. The work assigned to me was to read the manuscript of *Capital and Growth* and to comment on it. Over a weekend t, he would write chapter t and I would read chapter $t-1$. Sometimes he would give me a revised version, or even a second revised version of $t-1$ (particularly on the turnpike theorem), so the difference equation was disturbed. Otherwise it worked well.

I still remember vividly the day when he handed to me the manuscript of the chapter where he discussed the idea of the 'flexprice' and 'fixprice' methods. He seemed to be satisfied with the new words he had invented. His cheeks were rosy. He excitedly told me how these concepts would be useful in obtaining a clear perspective on the merits and demerits of various alternative approaches to dynamic economic problems. As he writes at the beginning of that chapter, he had been unhappy with his masterpiece, *Value and Capital*, because he realized that the assumption that price adjusts itself so as to equate supply and demand is very hard to accept with reference to modern manufacturing industry (*Capital and Growth* 1965a: 76). He seems to have started to seek an antithesis of the flexprice general equilibrium theory.

Moreover, it seems to me that Hicks was unhappy with the post-war development of general equilibrium. In one of the notes added in the second edition of *Value and Capital* he expressed his appreciation of Samuelson's stability theory as 'the most important development which has occurred between 1938 and 1946', but he also wrote: 'I still feel that something is wanted which is parallel to *my* dynamic theory, and I miss this in Professor Samuelson's work' (1946b: 336–7, my italics). As for the work establishing the existence of equilibrium, he said he could admire the elegance of the proof, but he added:

Existence, from my point of view, was a part of the hypothesis; I was asking if such a system existed, how would it work? I can understand that for those who are concerned with the defence of 'capitalism', to show the possibility of an arm's length equilibrium (an 'Invisible Hand') is a matter of importance. But that was not, and still is not, my concern.

(*Classics and Moderns* 1983a: 374–5)

It would be unfair to attribute the attitude of keeping equilibrium at arm's length by giving it a mathematical proof to the ideology of those economists involved in this mathematical work. The passages quoted above, however, show without any doubt how Hicks felt irritated and increasingly isolated in the post-war development of mathematical economics. He came to search after a new model that would suit his tastes and interests. *Capital and Growth* (1965a) was the starting point of this expedition. Through his trilogy, *Value and Capital*, *Capital and Growth* and *Capital and Time*, Hicks maintained a clear intention of synthesizing the pre-Keynesian economics of the Böhm-Bawerk–Wicksell–Hayek line with Keynes's economics. In the former the major roles were played by the concepts of the production period and the lifetime of durable capital goods, but full employment was assumed. Keynes, of course, was concerned with unemployment, but neglected the two time-elements of the capital theory. Hicks tackled the problem from the flexprice–fixprice point of view, because it was thought that involuntary unemployment must be closely related to the rigidity of wages. He never looked at the problem from the point of view of Say's law, even though Keynes had insisted on equivalence of the premise of full employment with that of Say's law. As will be seen below in this chapter, this resulted in an unfortunate outcome, namely the true cause of Keynesian unemployment remaining unclear in Hicks's works.

II

Capital and Growth's most important contribution is the proposal of the 'fixprice' method which may be regarded as being conjugate with the conventional 'flexprice' method that was adopted in *Value and Capital*. The terms fixprice and flexprice characterize the methods of analysis applied, rather than being aimed at classifying the type of social economy to be investigated.

The fixprice analysis is carried out on the assumption that prices are fixed exogenously; the economy is adjusted in terms of quantities of commodities. As the method regards prices as constant, all sectors of the economy can easily be aggregated into one sector by using prices as the weights of aggregation. Thus, 'money values become volume index. But its own inner logic, and without any deliberate decision having been taken to slew it in that direction, that model becomes a macro-model. The fixprice method has an inherent tendency to "go macro"' (1965a: 78). On the other hand, the flexprice method based on the assumption that prices are flexibly adjusted so as to establish equilibrium in each market has an inevitable tendency to 'go micro'.

However, where the number n of sectors is very large, the microeconomic analysis cannot produce definite and distinct results. We obtain, as its generally valid conclusion, nothing but a sterile proposition to the effect that everything depends on everything else. In order to obtain some definite conclusions the model has to be aggregated into a quasi-macro model with few sectors. Walras himself derives the laws of price changes in a progressive economy by reducing the number of sectors drastically (Walras 1954). In *Value and Capital* Hicks presents the theory of a group of commodities and shows that the commodities in the group can be treated as if they are a single commodity, so long as their relative prices can be assumed to be unchanged (1946b: 33–4, 312). If this is remembered, the fixprice method is not a novel idea at all; it is no more than an extreme case of this theory of the group of commodities, where the relative prices of all commodities are fixed. We can, in fact, derive the Keynes-type macro-fixprice model from the Hicks-type micro-flexprice model by applying the theory of the group of commodities (cf. Morishima 1953: 12–37).

It seems that as far as *Capital and Growth* is concerned, Hicks has taken both the flexprice and the fixprice methods as being equally applicable to any social economy. It is obvious, however, that if the fixprice method is applied to an economy where prices of commodities fluctuate considerably, the analysis will be subject to enormous error. In the opposite case, where the flexprice method is applied to an economy where prices are stationary, it is obvious that it is going to lead to misunderstanding of the mechanism working in the actual economy. If there is excess demand for a certain commodity in an economy of this kind, the flexprice theory will conclude that the price will be raised, whilst in the actual world the output of the commodity will be expanded and the price kept unchanged. Unless the proper method is chosen, depending on the type of economy, we could be misled and commit a gross error.

It would be unfair to say that Hicks was not aware of this. He does, in fact, point out that the flexprice method is appropriate to the analysis of non-storable commodities, such as Marshall's 'fish'. He nevertheless says that it can be applied to storable commodities, like the products of manufacturing industry, without an essential change in the principle. Concerning the fixprice method too, Hicks was of the opinion that it is applicable to both non-storable and storable markets. In his words: 'The fixprice assumption is more awkward in the case of non-storable than in that of storable commodities; but it is an assumption which even there we can bring ourselves, at least provisionally, to accept' (1965a: 70). We can, therefore, according to Hicks, observe the social economy which has 'fish', manufacturing products and others as having constituents from both extreme points of view, that which regards markets as being all of the flexprice type and that which takes the view they are all of the fixprice type. Hicks has, therefore, two social economic models, respectively constructed on the basis of the flexprice or the fixprice assumption.

III

The second point where I cannot agree with Hicks's views as expressed in *Capital and Growth* is that he dissociates the problem of stock from the flexprice analysis, but associates it with the fixprice analysis, despite proposing them both as methods of dynamic analysis. My own view is that in the flexprice analysis as well the economy has, in a certain sense, to be in a state of temporary stock equilibrium at the end of each period. According to the Hicksian flexprice analysis the dynamic movement of an economy is grasped in terms of a sequence of temporary equilibria. In each period, a temporary equilibrium is established, depending on the stocks of commodities available at the beginning of the period. As long as we are only concerned with a single period, we may regard the initial stocks as given or as environmental data, and need not discuss how they are determined. However, where we intend to approximate to the actual movement of the economy by temporary equilibria obtained sequentially, the successive temporary equilibria must be linked with each other.

In this linkage, the initial stocks of the commodities cannot be regarded as given. Those of period t are the stocks of commodities at the end of period $t - 1$. To obtain these, the analysis of temporary equilibrium of a single period must be extended to include a temporary equilibrium stock analysis. The end-of-period stocks are not given arbitrarily but are determined by economic agents at a point where stocks are composed in a temporarily most preferable way. Consequently, we have to say that there must be a temporary equilibrium analysis of stocks compatible with the flexprice theory. It is a weak point of *Value and Capital* that it lacks a stock analysis that can play the role of that link (cf. Morishima 1950, 1992).

This is true not only for Hicks's flexprice temporary equilibrium analysis but also for what he calls the method of Marshall in *Capital and Growth*. This belongs to what Hicks called the 'static method in dynamic theory', according to which a process of change 'is divided into steps, or stages, which are analysed separately, and then (as best we may) fitted together' (1965a: 30). 'Much of the work can be done on a *representative* single period; this single-period analysis is always a first step. But it is never the only step in a dynamic theory, some means of linkage between successive single periods must also be provided' (1965a: 31). The stocks of commodities carried over after production and consumption in one period to the next connect these two and through this linkage future states of affairs are linked with the state of affairs in the current period. When economic agents are concerned with dynamic decisions of consumption and production over several periods, they are implicitly choosing stocks of commodities at the end of each period. This problem of optimum stocks is left obscure and is not examined explicitly in *Value and Capital*, but it was discussed in *Capital and Growth*, though only in relation to the fixprice model.

It seems, in fact, that Hicks considered the division into flow and stock irrelevant to the flexprice analysis. In his words:

> The supply and the demand that are equated, in the single period of Temporary Equilibrium Theory, may (and probably will) contain stock carried over, partly from new production; demand is partly a demand for use, partly a demand for carry-forward ... The analysis does not require that stock and flow should be separated into compartments. It is not the case that there is one stock equilibrium and one flow equilibrium. There is one 'stock-flow' equilibrium of the single-period; and that is all.
>
> (1965a: 85)

It is true that this may be the case for circulating capital goods such as materials, or storable consumption goods. However, there are two related but separate markets for each of the fixed capital goods and consumer durables, one for the services related to the commodity and the other for the commodity itself, in which two different prices are determined. Nevertheless, these two markets are not completely independent of each other; the prices (or rental) of services of a commodity must be equal, in equilibrium, to the rate of interest times the price of the commodity, provided that, for simplicity, we ignore its depreciation and insurance. Where the rate of interest is determined elsewhere, these *two* markets have only one price as a variable regulating demand and supply in the two markets. There must be an additional variable in order for them to be in equilibrium simultaneously.

This is where Say's law is introduced in the flexprice model. In his model of capital formation and credit, Walras regarded the investment that is the demand for the durable commodity as a variable (Walras 1954: 267–312). This means that there is no *ex ante* investment function and the demand is flexibly created wherever there is a supply of any magnitude (Say's law). This resolves any problem of overdeterminacy. It is none the less entirely unsatisfactory to use Say's law as a *deus ex machina* and, once we reject it, as we should do, then the flexprice model has no general equilibrium unless we assume a very tricky investment function.

This was pointed out by Keynes, using a macroeconomic model: his verdict was that there is involuntary unemployment where and only where Say's law does not hold. As the law is a strange and unrealistic proposition, involuntary unemployment is a universal phenomenon. Although Hicks obviously tried in *Value and Capital* to give an interpretation of Keynes's *General Theory* using the framework of the general equilibrium system, he failed to reproduce involuntary unemployment because he failed to distinguish between the stock markets for durable commodities and the flow market for their services, and thus to discuss the Say's law problem. Hicks instead admits in *Capital and Growth*, 'In Keynesian terms, the Temporary Equilibrium Theory is a Full-Employment Theory' (1965a: 74). However, it is clear that neither the concept of stock equilibrium nor Say's law are peculiar to the macro-fixprice analysis. They play an important role in either macro or micro analysis, regardless of whether we choose the fixprice or the flexprice method. Keynes, in any case, is right to identify full employment with Say's law, regardless of whether we adopt the macro aggregate approach or the micro general equilibrium approach.

IV

Throughout the following we rule out Say's law, meaning that we do not generally have full employment. Under such circumstances economists would argue that the wage rate will decline. The supply of labour will then diminish, while demand for it will increase. If the wage rate declines sufficiently, full employment will be realized; alternatively unemployment remains and the wage w will fall to zero. According to this view, unemployment is possible only where w is zero. In this case labour is free; any employer can employ labour without payment because labour is abundant.

However, this neo-classical rule of free goods cannot be applied to labour because no one works if he or she receives only zero wages regardless of his/her acceptance of employment. This implies that the downwards movement of the wage rate must be stopped somewhere before it reaches zero, even though full employment may not be realized. Therefore, given that Say's law is negated, the labour market originally assumed to be of the flexprice type must be transformed into one of a fixprice type, or at least a quasi-fixprice type, since at some point the wage rate loses its downwards flexibility.

Neither Keynesian economics nor conventional neo-classical theory can explain where the wage rate will lose its downwards flexibility. In order for economists to be able to do this, economic theory must be refashioned into a multi-disciplinary subject. It needs to be more institutional, sociological and historical, because the level of wages at which workers will resist fiercely further cuts will depend on the institutional set-up as well as on sociological and historical circumstances. In the early years of capitalism when the working class was politically and socially weak, the wage rate became rigid at the subsistence level, even though, as Marx noted, it differed from country to country, depending on the historical circumstances of the society. In more advanced societies, in which the working class is provided with greater social power relative to employers, the wage rate will become rigid downwards at a level higher than subsistence. It is a common observation at the present time that female wages relative to those of male workers become higher as gender equality movement advances and women become socially more powerful. The distribution of power among social classes fluctuates in line with the general trend such that it becomes more favourable to the working class over time. In developed societies the public will support a high minimum wage rate as being reasonable. The concept of the genuinely flexprice labour market turns out to be impossible.[1]

The cornerstone of the economy will thus become rigid. Moreover, the markets for capital goods and consumer durables are also rigid, because demand for these commodities is not perfectly flexible, since Say's law does not hold. The rigidity of factor prices reduces the flexibility of the cost of production and, hence, the prices of the products.

We must then deal with the problem of how to sustain the life of unemployed workers while they have no wage income. Either trade unions have to help their unemployed members or the state has to arrange a social security system for the general public. The economy then contains organizations whose behaviour cannot be explained by the principle of utility or profit maximization, and because of those institutions the price mechanism does not work in its pure flexprice manner. In addition, entrepreneurs' demand for capital goods and consumers' demand for consumer durables usually needs financial help (loans or mortgages) from banks. Banks, therefore, are indispensable members of a modern society.

We must now assume that society has individual members, workers, landowners, capitalists, entrepreneurs, bankers, trade unionists, bureaucrats and politicians who in turn form its institutional members, namely firms, banks, trade unions and the government. Whereas Walras has emphasized the role of entrepreneurs as the independent fourth category of *personae* in his drama, it is Hicks's view that members are similar in their rational behaviour. It is well known that he put a strong emphasis on the fact that the Slutsky equation for the firm is very similar to that for the consumer; although the former lacks the income effect term, its substitution terms obey the same rules as the corresponding terms of the consumer's Slutsky equation. In his classic article on the simplification of monetary theory (1935b),[2] he also emphasizes the similarity between individuals and banks. In this he writes, 'Our method [of monetary theory] ... is simply an extension of the ordinary method of value theory.... we ought to regard every individual in the community as being, on a small scale, a bank' (1935b: 57).

However, a bank on a small scale is not a bank, as he later recognizes. It runs its business by applying the 'law of large number' (*A Market Theory of Money*, 1989a: 59). In particular, banks finance entrepreneurs' investment programmes by lending them large amounts, which are made available by credit creation. Only banks can create credit because of their scale. Therefore, even on the abstract level, an economic model consisting of households and firms of the kind discussed in *Value and Capital* will differ in its manner of operation from a model where banks play a positive role. It should be noted that, in spite of its title, *Capital and Growth* does not discuss how capital is allocated among entrepreneurs by banks. Hicks did discuss in the turnpike chapters how the allocation of capital needed to be an efficient one in order for the economy to grow rapidly, but, like other turnpike economists, he ignored the problem of how investment projects are financed by banks. In any case, at least as far as *Capital and Growth* is concerned, his growth theory is entirely non-monetary.

V

After *Capital and Growth* Hicks seems to begin moving towards the construction of a more complex model containing heterogeneous sectors. Fixprice and flexprice, originally words used to characterize the methods of analysis, seem to change into terms aimed at describing features of sectors or markets. Hicks, who thus far has viewed the whole economy as a thoroughbred consisting of *n* homogeneous sectors, either all flexprice or all fixprice, now seems to prefer to see it as a hybrid, i.e. a mixed economy having some flexprice and some fixprice sectors. I am not saying that there was a period in his lifetime during which he worked with such a model. Nevertheless, it seems quite clear that his academic interests turned in that direction during the last 20 years of his life.

In *A Theory of Economic History* Hicks investigated unique historical developments in key sectors, such as commercialized agriculture, manufacturing industry and labour market. This work was further developed in his last book, *A Market Theory of Money*, referred to already. On the basis of my conversations with him I may safely say that he did not like these works to be characterized as, say, Weberian. I interpret this as demonstrating his intention of using the results of *A Theory of Economic History* and *A Market Theory of Money* as foundations for theoretical model building, though this may conceivably include some elements of wishful thinking on my part. In any case, it is clear that in these two books Hicks characterizes agriculture and fishery, producing 'corn' and 'fish' respectively, as flexprice sectors. In the case of fish, which is perishable, there is no particular problem, but in the case of corn, which is durable, there is the problem of dealing with surplus stocks; Hicks considers that they are bought by merchants and carried over to the next day. In this flexprice market there are consumers and merchants on the demand side, bargaining with farmers on the supply side.[3]

The manufacturing industry, on the other hand, is characterized as a fixprice sector. The prices of manufactures are decided and announced by the manufacturers or suppliers. They cannot be changed arbitrarily, at a moment's notice, because fluctuations in a product's price greatly damage the reputation of the producer, unless he is able to justify his revision of the price. As for the labour market, Hicks examines in *A Theory of Economic History* diverse types of institutions historically observed, namely slavery and various alternative forms of the 'free' labour market. Some of these have existed side by side and complemented each other. In *A Market Theory of Money* he distinguishes between solid and fluid employment, and emphasizes that the actual labour market has a dual structure. There is a linkage between the wages for these two kinds of employment. He points out that a rise in wages for the fluid employment will be carried over to those for solid employment, even though unemployment may persist in the 'solid' labour market. He also stresses the importance of the ethical code prevailing among workers and trade unionists. In fact, as he points out, any employer must pay a wage which is at least as good as that paid by his competitors; otherwise he is regarded as an 'unfair' employer. This will to some extent explain the downwards rigidity or stickiness of wages.

If this is the real economy as Hicks perceived it in the later years of his life, the model for analysing it needs to be of a mixed flexprice–fixprice type. The method we adopt should therefore also be a mixed one. Neither the pure flexprice nor the pure fixprice method advocated by Hicks in *Capital and Growth* is appropriate for examining this mixed economy. In this world large-scale manufacturers will find workers from the solid labour market and combine them with materials obtained from markets of the flexprice type. They will sell their products at certain fixprices. On the other hand small-scale manufacturers and farmers get labour from the fluid market. The repercussions of prices generated within such a model will obviously be very different from those in the standard one developed in, say, *Value and Capital*. Although economists agree in saying that the price mechanism is the most essential thing for making the free enterprise system workable, it should be noted that the price mechanism working in the mixed economy will be quite different from the one economists know from their analysis of the pure flexprice model. This is what I believe that Hicks was telling us in his final book, *A Market Theory of Money*.[4]

VI

In spite of this movement towards a general hybrid model of the social economy, Hicks seems, on the other hand, to have adhered elsewhere to his original position, viewing the economy in terms of sectors which are all either of the flexprice or of the fixprice type. In 1985, with some revisions and additions, he published the first part of *Capital and Growth* under a new title, *Methods of Dynamic Economics*, which was the sub-title of Part I of the original version.

He justifies this new edition with the words:

I had long been convinced that it was the First Part of *Capital and Growth* that had the most value. The latter Parts . . . are mostly no more than my own versions of work that had already been done by others. Not much attention has been paid to them; few people have found them interesting. That they have been bound up with Part I may well have reduced the number of readers which it might have had.

(1985a: preface)

My own feeling is that this is a somewhat unfair appraisal of *Capital and Growth*, especially of its Part II. While I was reading the manuscript of the book before its publication, I found the chapters of Part II (except for the final one, on 'Traverse') the most fascinating, and I can confirm that this is also F.H. Hahn's view (Hahn 1966). He praised their content, saying:

The second part of the work ('Growth Equilibrium') is an extremely skillful exposition and analysis of the 'regular progressing' economy, ... The chapters on Choice of Techniques (an examination of the factor-price frontier) and on Factor Shares could not be bettered. They should make it clear to students and others just how technology and saving habits and growth rate combine to allow us to determine the 'balanced' output composition and its accompanying price constellations. I found the diagrams in the Factor Share chapter particularly useful, ... The last chapter of this part ('Traverse') is perhaps not quite as satisfying.

(Hahn 1966: 85–6)

This, I reckon, is the view of the book generally held by economic theorists.

We may accordingly say that the original edition of the book is better than the new one, because that lacks the gems of the former. Hicks gives as the reason for the omission the fact that the chapters of Part II are no more than his restatement and refinement of other persons' works, but the chapters included in the new edition are also no more than his version of the works of amongst others, Adam Smith, Ricardo, Marshall, Keynes and Harrod; the only exception is the chapter on 'The temporary equilibrium method', of which Hicks himself is the author. There seems to be no reason to discriminate between the chapters of Part II and those of Part I except in so far as the maximum number of pages given for one method in Part I is only seventeen (on his own temporary equilibrium method), whilst he allocates 106 pages to the linear growth method, if all relevant chapters in Part II are included. It seems to me, therefore, that there is no compelling reason for bringing out the revised edition, except for Hicks's becoming more and more uneasy about the von Neumann-type model after the publication of *Capital and Growth*.

While Hicks was writing *Capital and Time* he asked me to look up mathematics texts concerning Laplace transformations used in the fundamental theorem of the book. I used the opportunity to point out that production processes in a social economy can be vertically integrated into a single continuous process only in cases where the von Neumann horizontal input and output matrices satisfy certain special conditions.[5] The *Capital and Time* model is no more than a modern version of the Böhm-Bawerk–Wicksell model of roundabout production. It is well known that the vertically integrated production process of this type has to be carried out by operating the production activities at various stages simultaneously. That is to say, in the current period 0, the final stage of production must be executed to produce the final product in period 1; at the same time the second, third, fourth etc. stages from the last have to be operated simultaneously to produce outputs in periods 2, 3, 4 in the future. Corresponding to each stage of the vertically integrated production process there is thus a horizontally disintegrated elementary process. The operations of these elementary processes must be synchronized in order to obtain a time stream of output.

Hicks is concerned in *Capital and Time* with an extension of the Böhm-Bawerk–Wicksell problem so as to accommodate durable capital goods within the framework. This so-called Åkerman problem (Åkerman 1923: 145–80; Wicksell 1934: 258–99) is not particularly difficult if we follow the line proposed by von Neumann. Consider a single capital good i which can serve for $T + 1$ periods. Von Neumann regards the i of age t as being qualitatively different from the i of age s. So the i metamorphosed in its lifetime from the commodity i_0 (i.e. the brand-new capital good i) to the i_1 (the 1-year-old i), then to the i_2 and so on to the i_T. These appear on both sides of von Neumann processes: the i_0 on the input side, then the i_1 on the output side; where the i_1 appears on the input side, then the i_2 will appear on the output side; and so on. This is because if we use a unit of the i_v in production, then we still have a unit of the i_{v+1} after using it for one period. Von Neumann proposed that this remaining capital good i_{v+1} be treated as a joint output of the process which used the i_v. What I suggested to Hicks was that we may be able to construct the *Capital and Time*-type of production process by the vertical integration of von Neumann processes treating durable capital goods in this way.

It is important, however, to see that the converse is not true. A given set of von Neumann processes may not necessarily be expressed by a single vertically integrated production process. This implies that the von Neumann approach is more general than the *Capital and Time* approach. That is, the latter can be equivalent to the former only for a certain class of von Neumann processes, such as those which form a triangular input-coefficient matrix and use no durable capital good, as has been discussed by Böhm-Bawerk and Wicksell. Where there are multiple final outputs, or in the case of machines, say a robot being used for robot production, it is impossible to achieve integration of the whole economy into a single process transforming a time sequence of input of primary factors into a time sequence of output. It is in this light that I have concluded that Parts II and III of *Capital and Growth* are better than *Capital and Time*.

However, Hicks did not take my comment up. His view of von Neumann's approach was instead expressed as follows in *Capital and Time*:

This [the method of von Neumann] is to admit a regular (and high) degree of disintegration. The productive process, in each 'firm', lasts just one period. All of the firm's inputs are acquired at the beginning of the period; and at the end it sells – all it has. There is then a regular market in capital goods (or producers' goods) at all stages of production (in the technical sense); a system of prices is set up, which reflects the state of the general process, at every stage.... The von Neumann method is the extreme of disintegration; there is a complete reference back to the market in every period, a period which can be made as short as we like. Ours, on the other hand, is the extreme of (vertical) integration. There is no 'intermediate' reference back to the market.

(1973d: 5–6)

It is true that there is a price for each good in the von Neumann system. Each process, however, need not form an independent firm; it may be merely a single stage of production within a firm. Outputs of this process are then directly transferred to the next stage in the same firm, without passing through markets. The prices charged for these outputs are not market prices, but internal accounting or efficiency prices. Similarly, the prices of input commodities made available by the previous stage of production of the same firm are efficiency prices. Of course, some of the von Neumann prices are market prices; even though the outputs of a process are transferred to the next stage via the market, this has nothing to do with the vertical integrability of processes. What does matter for the integration is not whether commodities are transferred internally within the organization or externally through markets, but whether or not the input and output coefficient matrices structurally satisfy the conditions for integrability. We thus conclude that Hicks in *Capital and Time* and von Neumann are not at opposite extremes in their approaches to the problem of economic growth, but Hicks's method is actually equivalent to von Neumann's in special cases satisfying the conditions for vertical integrability, failing these Hicks's method is impossible, and we must use von Neumann's.

Despite this, Hicks seems to have preferred his own *Capital and Time* method to von Neumann's. He did, in fact, exclude from *Methods of Dynamic Economics* all the chapters in Parts II and III of *Capital and Growth* (except those on traverse and optimum saving), but added to it a new chapter, 'Traverse again: the Austrian method', which may be regarded as an abridged version of *Capital and Time*. This construction of *Methods of Dynamic Economics* seems to reflect Hicks's own appraisal of the relevant parts of *Capital and Growth* and *Capital and Time*. It is, of course, true that the mathematical formulae used in *Capital and Time* are novel, at least in the field of mathematical economics, while those in *Capital and Growth* are all familiar to us and are at best, as Hicks himself recognizes, no more than his own versions of formulae already used by someone else. In spite of this, it must be said that the *Capital and Time* method is useless in analysing the mixed fixprice–flexprice model mentioned above, while the von Neumann method is suitable, even if with some alterations (Morishima 1992).

It is well known that the von Neumann method established the existence of a balanced growth equilibrium. Hicks regarded the turnpike theorem as the main achievement of the application of von Neumann's theory to the analysis of non-steady states. After mentioning that the turnpike theorem belongs to optimum theory, rather than to positive theory, he emphasized that 'it is in fact in optimum theory that the von Neumann assumption develops its main strengths' (1973d: 10–11). This, however, is a very narrow view of the von Neumann model. As I have discussed before, we can easily remove the assumption of balanced growth and can prove the existence of a temporary (or one period) equilibrium of the *Value and Capital* type within the von Neumann framework. We may, as *Value and Capital* did, view economic fluctuations in terms of the sequence of von Neumann temporary equilibria (Morishima 1969: 133–45). We may, moreover, show that equilibrium over two periods exists. In general, for any value of t there exists a general equilibrium over t periods; and, therefore, as the limit of t tending to infinity we have eternal equilibrium over time, as discussed by Hicks himself and Malinvaud (Morishima 1969: 148–57).

VII

In this section I would like to make some brief comments on a few representative definitions of dynamics which may be useful in highlighting the points observed in the previous sections of this chapter. First, we have the definition which Samuelson has attributed to R. Frisch (Frisch 1935–6: 100–6). Namely, a system is said to be dynamic if its behaviour over time is determined by equations involving 'variables at different points of time' in an 'essential' way (Samuelson 1947: 314). However, though this definition is the most widely accepted, it is too general to distinguish important dynamic economic problems from other less important dynamics. Second, Hicks in *Value and Capital* gave the following definition: 'I call ... Economic dynamics those parts of [economic theory] where every quantity must be dated' (1939a: 115). Although this definition is perfectly appropriate for discussing this specific group of problems, it cannot rule out a certain kind of static analysis. A decision concerning future production plans at a certain point of time is dynamic according to Hicks, but static according to both Frisch and Samuelson.

Hicks's definition was criticized by Harrod, who provided a third one: 'In Dynamics as I conceive it dating is no more necessary than in Statics.... Positive saving which plays such a great role in the *General Theory* is essentially a dynamic concept.... It [the acceleration principle concerning investment] is essentially a dynamic principle' (Harrod 1952: 10–12). This view of Harrod's may be compared with that of Walras, who stated: 'According as the excess of income over consumption in the aggregate is greater or less than the excess of consumption over income in the aggregate, an economy is either progressive or retrogressive' (Walras 1954: 269). Walras classified progress into two categories.

> Every time the production function itself undergoes a change, we have a case of technical progress brought about by science and ... every time the coefficients of production made up of land-services decrease while those made up of capital-services increase without any change in the production function, we have a case of economic progress resulting from saving.
>
> (Walras 1954: 386)

He then abstracts from technical progress and discusses economic progress brought about by saving only.

In *Capital and Growth* Hicks, too, is concerned with a particular kind of dynamic economics, i.e. growth theory, in which, as Harrod and Walras have emphasized, savings and investment play essential roles. In a progressive economy net investment is made in the same amount as the net savings of the society. Since the net savings are positive, real capital is accumulated, so that the economy has more real equipment at the end of the period than it had at the beginning. Moreover, such an economy works completely different from the usual static economy where savings and investment are absent. Except in the unrealistic case where Say's law is satisfied, the net demand for each capital good is not a free variable, but has to satisfy the demand function (or the investment function) of the good. As a result, as Keynes insisted and we have seen in the above, full employment is not generally realized. The equilibrium growth is therefore generally impossible, because we have disequilibrium in the factor market. Unfortunately in *Capital and Growth*, Hicks, like other neo-classical economists, failed to realize this dilemma of growth theory;[6] he often implicitly assumed Say's law.

In relation to this point, a remark on the general equilibrium theory would seem to be relevant. Walras discussed four models of general equilibrium: (1) exchange, (2) production, (3) capital formation and credit and (4) money and circulation. The first two have neither savings nor investments; Say's law and anti-Say's law are therefore irrelevant. These two models have general equilibrium solutions. In the last two, however, durable capital goods exist and savings and investment have crucial roles. Unless Say's law prevails, i.e. unless the investment demand D_k for capital good k is a free variable for each and every k, the systems are both over-determinant. Accordingly, assuming Say's law, Walras ensured the existence of equilibrium for these systems. However, the law is unrealistic, so that we must conclude that there can be no full-employment equilibrium under normal circumstances. Thus we see that the general equilibrium system including savings and investment is very much consistent with Keynes's doctrine. Hicks has never developed this view through any of *Value and Capital*, *Capital and Growth* and *Capital and Time*.

VIII

Parallel with his search for a new paradigm, Hicks, as we have seen, extended his interests to economic history and the history of economic thought. This is not at all surprising because the young Hicks specialized in history (of industrial conciliation and wage determination) (Hicks 1928, 1930b). Hicks's interest in history seems to have become increasingly keen in his last ten years. In January 1987, both my wife and I visited Hicks at his Porch House in Gloucestershire, and I handed him a copy of my working paper 'Ideology and economic activity' (Morishima 1990). It took us two hours to return home. When we got back, the telephone was ringing. It was from Hicks, who told me: 'I wish you had sent me your paper before you came to see me, so that we could have discussed it. All I can now do is to make a few remarks.'

A few days later, I received a beautiful letter on the class division according to education in the West in response to my discussion of its Chinese counterpart in the paper. I quoted it in full in the published version, as I found it so lucid that I could not resist doing so. This kind of keen interest on the part of Sir John seems barely compatible with an interest in the topics on which the young J. R. H. worked.

However, prior to my visit to Porch House on 18 February 1989, which turned out to be our last meeting, Hicks wrote to me concerning his intention of providing a better proof for the proposition he had obtained in his paper 'Elasticity of substitution reconsidered' (1983a). It seems that he had tried but was stuck, so he summarized the point and asked me if I might be able to help. Although I had written a paper on elasticities of substitution (in Japanese) more than 20 years previously, I had completely forgotten its content. I possessed neither an off-print nor the original manuscript. I struggled until late at night to produce at least a note which I could show to him. He himself (especially Sir John rather than J. R. H.) would almost certainly have said 'no' if he had been asked whether an economist should repeatedly work on a subject of this type. He nevertheless loved and took care of the brain children of his youth. He tried to put each member of his old paradigm in an appropriate place in his new paradigm, as his three *Collected Essays* volumes show (1981, 1982a, 1983a). At the end of the meeting, he asked my wife to bring him the box of *Sir John Hicks: Critical Assessments* from his bookshelf, where we found Blackorby and Russell's (1981) article on my substitution paper in Japanese![7]

In *Classics and Moderns* Hicks tells an amusing story:

Years later, when visiting Japan, I was assured that my book had been a set book at Kyoto University since 1943. I was astonished, and asked them how it could have been possible for them to get copies. They reminded me that until December 1941 they could import through America; and then, they said, we captured some in Singapore!

(1983a: 361)

I was one of those students who began economics with *Value and Capital* in Kyoto. My copy, however, was not a POW edition, but a pirate edition produced in Japan. When I was a first-year student, the book was recommended to me by Professor H. Aoyama, who later became my supervisor. I asked him, 'Is *Value and Capital* something which a first year student can read?' He replied, 'You must understand that Hicks's economics is in effect an algebra concerning society. You will be all right if you tackle the book step by step, in exactly the same way you solved algebra problems at middle school.' This frightened me, because I had not been good at maths at middle school. Despite this *Value and Capital* soon became my Bible. Indeed, had I not read it at the end of my impressionable teenage years, I doubt whether I should have come to spend the latter half of my life in this, Hicks's country.

NOTES

1   Takata (cf., for example, 1941) insisted that social power should be recognized in the system of general equilibrium, especially in factor markets.
2   Hicks also emphasizes the similarities between statics and dynamics in *Value and Capital*.
3   Of course, these merchants appear in the market as suppliers on the next day.
4   I must mention that Okun (1981) and Morishima (1984), written prior to *A Market Theory of Money*, are of similar intent and belong in the same category.
5   I was referring to a point more or less similar to one of those discussed later by Burmeister (1974). I kept Hicks's letter and my reply together, separately from other correspondence in case of a possible re-visit to the problem at a later time. In writing this article I searched for them in vain.
6   Cf., for example, Solow (1956: 65–94). In Solow's model there was therefore no investment function, and investment is freely adjusted to savings; full-employment full-capacity growth was therefore possible.
7   The original paper was written as a review article of *Danryokusei no Keizaigaku* ('Economics in terms of elasticities') by Professor Sempei Sawa.

REFERENCES

Åkerman, G. (1923) 'Realkapital und Kapitalzins', *Ekonomisk Tidskrift* 5–6: 145–80.
Blackorby, C. and Russell, R. R. (1981) 'The Morishima elasticity of substitution: symmetry, constancy, separability, and its relationship to the Hicks and Allen elasticities', *Review of Economic Studies*; reprinted in J. C. Wood and R. N. Woods (eds) (1989) *Sir John Hicks: Critical Assessments*, London: Routledge.
Burmeister, E. (1974) 'Synthesizing the Neo-Austrian and alternative approaches to capital theory. A survey', *Journal of Economic Literature* 12: 413–56.

Frisch, R. (1935–6) 'On the notion of equilibrium and disequilibrium', *Review of Economic Studies* 3: 100–6.

Hahn, F. H. (1966) '*Capital and Growth*, by Sir John Hicks', *Economic Journal* 76: 84–7.

Harrod, R. F. (1952) *Towards a Dynamic Economics*, London: Macmillan.

Morishima, M. (1950) *Dogakuteki Keizai Riron* (Dynamic economic theory), Tokyo: Kobundo.

―――― (1953) 'The Hicksian micro-dynamics and the Keynesian macro-dynamics', *Osaka Economic Papers* 2: 12–37.

―――― (1969) *Theory of Economic Growth*, Oxford: Clarendon Press.

―――― (1984) *Economics of Industrial Society*, Cambridge: Cambridge University Press.

―――― (1990) 'Ideology and economic activity', in A. Martinelli and N. J. Smelser (eds) *Economy and Society*, London: SAGE Publications, pp. 51–77.

―――― (1992) *Capital and Credit: A New Formulation of General Equilibrium Theory*, Cambridge: Cambridge University Press.

Okun, A. M. (1981) *Prices and Quantities*, Oxford: Basil Blackwell.

Samuelson, P. A. (1947) *Foundation of Economic Analysis*, Cambridge: Harvard University Press.

Solow, R. M. (1956) 'A contribution to the theory of economic growth', *Quarterly Journal of Economics* 70: 65–94.

Takata, Y. (1941) *Seiryoku Setsu Ronshu* (Essays in the power theory of economics), Tokyo: Nihon Hyoron Sha.

Walras, L. (1954) *Elements of Pure Economics*, Homewood, IL: Richard D. Irwin.

Wicksell, K. (1934) *Lectures on Political Economy*, vol. 1, London: Routledge & Kegan Paul.

4

CAPITAL THEORY

Charles Kennedy

Throughout his working life, which ended only with his death in 1989, Sir John Hicks maintained a strong interest in capital theory. The word 'capital' is used in the title of three of his most important books: *Value and Capital*, *Capital and Growth* and *Capital and Time*. But his interest did not begin with *Value and Capital*, because there was a good deal about capital in his earliest book *The Theory of Wages*, arguably more than is to be found in *Value and Capital* itself.

In the economic literature, going back quite a long way, there are to be discerned two distinct, and apparently rival, approaches to the concept of capital (see, for example, Schumpeter 1954: 898ff.). In the one approach, capital is thought of in physical terms. There are capital goods: buildings, machines and stocks of commodities. In the other approach, capital arises as a result of a process in time. The actual physical capital goods are so-to-speak concealed in the process.

Hicks himself was very well aware of the above dichotomy. In a paper he gave to a seminar at the University of Kent at Canterbury in 1973, but which he did not publish, he put up on the blackboard two lists of economists who should be put in the one category or the other. This is not the place to repeat the full lists, even if I could recall them. Clearly, though, Marshall with his emphasis on 'appliances' should be put in the first or 'realist' category, as Hicks liked to call it. Equally clearly, Böhm-Bawerk and Wicksell should be put in the second category.

Where should we place Hicks in the two lists? And where would he himself have preferred to be placed? The first of these questions is easier to answer than the second. Without a doubt he must appear in both lists. In *The Theory of Wages* and in *Capital and Growth* he used the physical concept of capital. In *The Theory of Wages*, capital was a factor of production that entered into the production function in the same way as labour did. The *elasticity of substitution* between capital and labour, a technical tool that he devised for the purpose of analysing the production function, played a large part in his theory of distributive shares. In *Capital and Growth*, the use of a physical concept of capital is also quite explicit. For part of the book Hicks uses a two-sector model in which the single capital good (tractors) is used both in the production of the consumption good (corn) and in the production of tractors

45

themselves. On the other hand, in *Value and Capital*, and even more explicitly in *Capital and Time*, Hicks is concerned with a process in time. The production function is replaced by a sequence of inputs and outputs.

I think the answer to the second question must be that he would have been happy to appear in both lists. In this connection, the opening paragraph of the preface to *Capital and Time* may be worth quoting in full:

> This is the third book I have written about Capital. *Value and Capital* (1939); *Capital and Growth* (1965); *Capital and Time* (1973). They were not planned as a trilogy. I had no idea when I finished the first, that I would write the second; when I finished the second, that I would write the third. Nor do the later volumes supersede the earlier, save in a few quite limited respects. Capital (I am not the first to discover) is a very large subject, with many aspects; wherever one starts, it is hard to bring more than a few of them into view. It is just as if one were making pictures of a building; though it is the same building, it looks quite different from different angles. As I now realise, I have been walking round my subject, taking different views of it. Though that which is presented here is just another view, it turns out to be quite useful in fitting the others together.
>
> (1973d: v)

It was no doubt the disclaimers in the above paragraph that led Solow in his review of *Capital and Time* in the *Economic Journal* to write: 'I think it is to be regarded as an experiment not as any sort of commitment' (1974: 189).

There is indeed internal evidence for this view. And yet, after one has read *Capital and Time*, one cannot help being left with the impression that Hicks had a *partiality* for his neo-Austrian theory. This is in part perhaps the familiar *partiality* of a parent for the youngest child; sometimes, it must also be said, an over-critical attitude to the elder children. But I believe there is more to it than that. I think Hicks felt that there was more of his own work in *Capital and Time*. Again in the preface to *Capital and Time* he wrote: '*Capital and Growth* is critical and expository, rather than constructive' (1973d: v). On the other hand, parts of *Capital and Time* he regarded as 'a voyage of exploration' (1973d: 10). He made the same kind of claim in the introduction to *Value and Capital*. Thus 'I am almost entirely concerned with novelties. I shall confine myself to those aspects of each subject I treat on which I have something new to say; or at least I shall deal with familiar aspects quite cursorily' (1939a: 1).

II

After these preliminaries it is time to consider Hicks's contribution in more detail. In what follows I shall be mainly, but not exclusively, concerned with

Capital and Growth and *Capital and Time*, since these two books are directly comparable.

In both books, Hicks deals with three main not unrelated themes: first, the properties of the steady state and the comparison of steady states; second, the *traverse* from one steady state to another, after a change in circumstances; and third, the character and consequences of technical progress. We shall consider each of these in turn.

In *Capital and Growth*, Hicks used what he later called the method of sectoral disintegration. There are two sectors, one making capital goods and one making the consumption good. There is an implicit market in capital goods, which can be switched freely from one sector to another. In both sectors, there are fixed input coefficients, for both capital and labour; but as Hicks was at pains to make clear, this is not for technical reasons, but arises as a result of the properties of the steady-state solution. As was already mentioned, for part of his exposition Hicks used a model with one capital good, tractors; but this is not at all essential to the argument, since the model can be generalized with little difficulty to the case of many capital goods. In the precise model, as developed by Hicks in Chapters XII–XV in *Capital and Growth*, there would also appear to be no time-lag in the production functions relating inputs to output.

The main analytical tool used by Hicks in the study of steady-state growth equilibrium is what he later in *Capital and Time* came to call the 'efficiency curve', though in its short life it has had many other names given to it. The curve has a dual purpose. On the pricing side, it represents the function that relates the real wage to the rate of interest. If depreciation is left out of account, this is given by

$$w = \frac{1 - ra}{\beta + r(ab - \beta a)} \tag{4.1}$$

where w is the real wage, r is the rate of interest, a and b are the capital and labour input coefficients in the capital sector and α and β are the capital and labour input coefficients in the consumption sector. (In Hicks's convenient notation, Roman letters always refer to the capital sector and Greek letters to the consumption sector.) The efficiency curve slopes down from the left, a higher real wage being associated with a lower rate of interest.

The great virtue of the efficiency curve is that on the quantity side there is exactly the same functional relationship between the amount of consumption per head (c) and the rate of growth (g), so that we can also write

$$c = \frac{1 - ga}{\beta + g(ab - \beta a)} \tag{4.2}$$

To complete the model, it is necessary to establish a link between the quantity side and the pricing side and this is done by a savings function. The most convenient, and the one that Hicks himself used, is a 'classical' savings function, in which a constant proportion (s) of *profits* is saved. It can then be shown that

$$g = sr \tag{4.3}$$

so that the link between the quantity side and the pricing side is established.

Finally, it has to be decided what to take as the independent variable of the system. Hicks habitually made use of two possibilities. If the real wage is taken as given, as in some classical theories of subsistence wages and in theories of development with unlimited supplies of labour, then r, g and c can be read off the efficiency curve. Alternatively, it is assumed that the labour force is fully employed and grows at a constant rate, in which case the rate of growth will be the independent variable and c, r and w can be read off the efficiency curve. In *Capital and Time*, Hicks later called these two possibilities the fixwage assumption and the full employment assumption.

Equations (4.1) and (4.2) took no account of depreciation. There are really only two feasible ways of introducing depreciation into a *Capital and Growth* model. The first is to assume depreciation by evaporation, in which a constant proportion of the capital stock disappears in each period, without any regard being taken of the age of the capital good. In this case, the same rate of depreciation will enter into the price equation (4.1) and into the quantity equation (4.2). It is not essential that there should be the same rate of depreciation in both sectors.

The alternative is to assume depreciation by 'sudden death'. All tractors are assumed to have a given life, but do not deteriorate in any way before the end of their life. In this case, the rate of provision for depreciation, which will enter into the price equations, will depend on the rate of interest; and the mortality rate of tractors, which will enter into the quantity equation, will depend on the rate of growth.[1]

Both of these specifications of depreciation are highly artificial and unrealistic, and indeed it was the inability to deal with depreciation except 'in a very clumsy fashion' that constituted one of Hicks's two main criticisms of the method of sectoral disintegration (1973d: 5).

All the above analysis was confined to a single technique. If there is a possibility of more than one technique, the one that will be chosen will be that which maximizes the real wage at a given rate of interest or, what comes to the same thing, maximizes the rate of interest at a given real wage. Notice that, since decisions are taken on the basis of profit maximization, it is prices that will determine the choice of technique. It is not necessarily the case that the chosen technique will be the one that maximizes the level of consumption per head for a given rate of growth. This will necessarily be so only if all profits are saved and the rate of growth is equal to the rate of interest.

No doubt the above has been an inadequate summary of Hicks's model of capital and growth in a steady state. It is nevertheless time to turn to his neo-Austrian theory in *Capital and Time*.

In the first place, it is to be made clear in what ways Hicks's neo-Austrian theory differs from the strict Austrian theory of Böhm-Bawerk and Wicksell. It will be remembered that the Austrians had attempted to characterize production as a combination of labour and time. In the simplest case (point-input–point-output) a single input of labour at one date resulted in a single output of the product at a later date, so that the production process had a definite time dimension, which could be called the degree of roundaboutness. The 'capital' employed in the process was regarded as stored-up labour (or in Wicksell's case stored-up labour and land). For a given input of labour, the total capital employed could only be increased if the degree of roundaboutness, the period of production, was increased. It could then be shown that a fall in the rate of interest would favour more roundabout techniques. In the typical example of maturing wine, the wine would be left to mature for a longer period. The Austrian approach would still be viable if there were a sequence of inputs, provided that there was only a single output. The period of production could then be replaced by an average period of production.

Already in *Value and Capital* (1939a: 222ff.), Hicks had seen that the Austrian approach only worked in these special cases, and that it could not be generalized to the case where a sequence of inputs converts into a sequence of outputs; and he repeats his objections in *Capital and Time* (1973d: 8ff.). But, although he rejects the strict Austrian theory for this reason, he takes over from the Austrians the notion that production is a process in time, a process in which for Hicks a sequence of labour inputs converts into a sequence of outputs of a consumption product. Normally he supposes that a process will become unprofitable and therefore terminate after a certain time, though interminable processes are not ruled out.

Although the physical capital goods that may be used during the process are not brought into the open, a figure can be given for the value of capital at any stage during the life of the process. This can be done in two ways, a forward-looking way and a backward-looking way. In the former, the value of capital will be the sum of the properly discounted values of the net outputs during the remaining periods of the process. In the backward-looking way, the capital value at any date will be the capital invested in the process, i.e. the sum of the values of the net inputs (negative net outputs) up to that date, accumulated at the appropriate rate of interest. In disequilibrium conditions, the two measures of capital value will be likely to differ, but they must be the same under conditions of steady-state equilibrium. Typically, since the process of production takes time and at least one input must precede the first output, over the life of a process of finite duration the capital value will at first rise and then decline.

Using the forward-looking valuation method, Hicks then proves a *fundamental theorem*. This is that a fall in the rate of interest will increase the capital values of the process at the beginning of each period of the process except the last period. For convenience, Hicks supposes that inputs and outputs are each 'paid for' at the beginning of the period. It follows that the capital value at the beginning of the last period will be equal to the net output of the last period. This will be unaffected by the fall in the rate of interest, but it must be positive, since otherwise the process would have been terminated earlier; and this is the only condition required for the proof of the theorem. It is quite possible that a fall in the rate of interest may allow a profitable lengthening of the process. In that case, the fundamental theorem will hold *a fortiori*.

The initial capital value of the process at the very beginning of the process can be written

$$k_0 = \sum_{0}^{n} (b_t - wa_t)R^{-t} \tag{4.4}$$

where b_t is the output of the product in period t, a_t is the labour input in period t, w is the real wage and $R = 1 + r$ where r is the rate of interest. k_0 is valued in terms of the consumption product, which is taken to be the numéraire.

In competitive conditions, the technique chosen will be barely viable so that $k_0 = 0$. This condition allows us to establish a functional relationship between w and r. For example, if w were to rise, this would lead to a fall in k_0 below zero. To bring back k_0 to zero, a fall in the rate of interest will be required, which will raise k_0 because of the fundamental theorem. Some care is needed, however. The rise in the real wage could render the final period unprofitable, with a negative net output, in which case the fundamental theorem would not apply. Therefore we have to allow for a possible variation (truncation) in the duration of the process, so that the fundamental theorem can be applied. It can then be established that a rise in the real wage will require a fall in the rate of interest. Hence we obtain an efficiency curve for the technique, which will slope down from left to right throughout its length.

When there is a choice of techniques, the same principle applies as in *Capital and Growth*. The technique will be chosen that maximizes the rate of interest for a given real wage, or that maximizes the real wage for a given rate of interest.

In *Capital and Growth*, as we know, the efficiency curve gave not only the relationship between the real wage and the rate of interest but also the relationship between consumption per head and the rate of growth. When this idea is translated into *Capital and Time* terms, a complication arises. So far as I know, it has not been noticed by commentators on *Capital and Time* that Hicks's own handling of this complication was not entirely satisfactory. It may, therefore, be useful to take the opportunity to consider the complication in some detail, so as to clear the matter up.

The problem arises because it is not just the technique that is determined on the basis of the real wage and the rate of interest, but also the precise

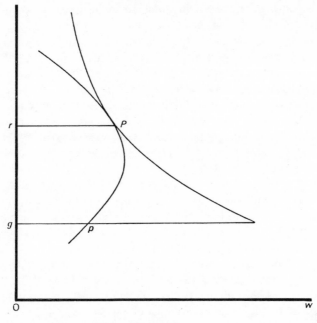

Figure 4.1

duration of the process used in that technique. Hence the curve that we need for relating consumption per head to the rate of growth at the same time as the real wage to the rate of interest will not be the efficiency curve established above which allows the duration to vary. Instead, it will be a *restricted* efficiency curve with duration taken as fixed.

At this point it will be useful to reproduce Hicks's own diagram (1973d: 66) (Figure 4.1). As we know, the unrestricted curve slopes down from left to right throughout its length. For each point on the unrestricted curve there will be a restricted curve, and the unrestricted curve will be the envelope of these restricted curves. Hicks's diagram shows the unrestricted curve and the restricted curve corresponding to the point P. Hicks observes correctly that there is nothing to prevent the restricted curve from turning backwards; and he then asks whether it can turn so far backwards that the point *p* on it lies to the west of P, as he in fact drew in the diagram. The answer he gives is that this could not happen in a steady state, since the social accounts would not come out right. This again is correct. But he then goes on, in the final paragraph of p. 67, to envisage the possibility that there could be techniques with restricted curves behaving in this way, even though such techniques would be inadmissible in a steady state. In this, he is incorrect.

Consider again equation (4.4) with k_0 zero and n taken as fixed. Now,

51

instead of supposing that there is an initial rise in the real wage, let us suppose that there is an initial fall in the rate of interest, with the real wage at first constant. Since the net output of the final period is positive, the fundamental theorem can be applied, so that the fall in the rate of interest will raise k_0 above zero. It then follows that there *must* be a rise in the real wage for k_0 to be brought back to zero. Moreover, this will be true whatever the extent of the initial fall in the rate of interest. It is not precluded that the restricted curve should turn backwards. This would imply that a greater fall in the rate of interest required a lesser rise in the real wage than a smaller fall. What is incontrovertible is that there can be no point on the restricted curve that lies to the south-west of the point P.

Hicks, I thought, took rather lightly the possibility that there could be properly chosen techniques which were yet inadmissible in a steady state. In my own view, this would have constituted a pretty serious objection to his neo-Austrian theory. Fortunately perhaps, this is a debate that need not be pursued; since the situation can never arise.

When one comes to compare the use in a steady state of Hicks's two approaches to capital theory, the striking conclusion is that the results obtained are remarkably similar, in spite of the fact that the concept of capital and the method employed in each case are so very different. In both approaches, efficiency curves can be derived which relate both the real wage to the rate of interest and consumption per head to the rate of growth. This is really all that is needed for the analysis of steady states, once the link between the quantity side and the prices side has been provided by a savings function.

III

It is time to turn to the second main theme of interest to Hicks: traverse from one steady state to another. The need for a traverse can arise either because of technical progress or, more simply, because there is a change in the rate of growth due to a change in the rate of growth of the labour force. The question to be asked is whether the economy can adjust to the new rate of growth whilst retaining full employment of labour. In the simple *Capital and Growth* model with a single capital good, a change in the rate of growth will in general require an adjustment to the total capital–labour ratio, and the question becomes whether this adjustment can be achieved while keeping labour fully employed.

It turns out that the condition for this to be possible is that

$$ab > a\beta \tag{4.5}$$

or, in words, that the capital sector should be relatively more labour intensive than the consumption sector. Hicks attached little importance to this condition, on the grounds that it rested too heavily on the assumption of a single capital good. When there is more than one capital good, there will be more than one capital–labour ratio that will need to be adjusted. Hence the conditions for a full-employment traverse will be more demanding. Hicks deemed it unlikely that all the conditions would be met, but took comfort from the fact that the passage might be made easier by temporary variations in individual factor ratios. It will be remembered that the fixed input coefficients that he used in the development of his model were not *technically* fixed, but fixed only in the context of a steady state.

When he comes to consider the traverse in *Capital and Time*, Hicks finds it necessary to make some drastic assumptions. In the standard case, as he calls it, each process has a simple profile. There is a construction period and a utilization period. No output is produced during the construction period, but in each 'week' of the period there is a constant input of labour. In each 'week' of the utilization period there is a constant (but different) input of labour and a constant output of the product. Hence, per unit of output in the utilization period, we have two labour input coefficients, a_0 for the construction period and a_1 for the utilization period.

It now turns out that the condition for a smooth full-employment passage to a new equilibrium is that

$$a_0 > a_1 \tag{4.6}$$

This condition looks suspiciously like the factor-intensity condition (4.5): they certainly have a similar role to play in the analysis.

In order to shed more light on the matter, it is, I think, instructive to force a *Capital and Growth* tractor–corn model into a process with a simple profile. There is an inconsistency at the outset. If tractors can only be produced by using tractors, we should have to start with some tractors at the beginning whereas in a Hicksian process the first input must be a labour input pure and simple. To get round this difficulty, we have to assume that tractors can be made entirely by hand as well as by using tractors.

The story of our construction period would then run as follows. In the first week, some tractors would be made entirely by hand. In the second week, some of the constant labour force would use these tractors to make tractors, while the rest of the labour would continue to make tractors by hand. This would go on until in the final week all the labour would be working with tractors and none working by hand. (Perhaps we may be allowed to assume that the coefficients are such that this works out exactly without a labour remainder.) Thereafter, the tractors would be applied to the production of corn and the utilization period would begin.

The point of this fairy tale is that it enables us to express the *Capital and Time* coefficients in terms of the *Capital and Growth* ones. In the first place, we have quite directly

$$a_1 = \beta \tag{4.7}$$

The derivation of the expression for a_0 is a little more tricky. In the utilization period, we shall need a tractors per unit of output. The output of tractors in the last week of the construction period, again per unit of product in the utilization period, will be a_0/b. Hence the number of tractors that will be applied to the production of corn per unit of output will be $a \cdot a_0/b + a_0/b$. We then obtain

$$a = \frac{(a + 1)a_0}{b}$$

from which

$$a_0 = \frac{ab}{a + 1} \tag{4.8}$$

If we substitute the expressions (4.7) and (4.8) into the condition (4.6), we obtain

$$ab > (a + 1)\beta \tag{4.9}$$

As can be seen, this condition is virtually the same as the *Capital and Growth* condition (4.5). The fact that 1 is added to a in (4.9) need not worry us unduly, provided the week is short and a is correspondingly large. In fact, Hicks had himself derived the *Capital and Growth* condition (4.5) by means of a limiting process in which the period was shortened and a made to rise indefinitely.

Thus, the similarity between the two conditions is established. But I believe the similarity does not end there. The standard-case assumptions in *Capital and Time* seem to be playing exactly the same role in the analysis as the single-capital-good assumption in *Capital and Growth*: namely the role of reducing the many conditions for a smooth traverse to a single condition. In *Capital and Time*, Hicks does not get very far when he departs from the standard case, but he makes it clear that the conditions for a smooth traverse are more numerous, just as they were in *Capital and Growth* with many capital goods.

To conclude this section of the comparison between *Capital and Growth* and *Capital and Time*, it must be said that Hicks's analogy of the building in the passage from the preface to *Capital and Time* quoted above looks remarkably apt. It is indeed the same building, even though we are viewing it from different angles.

IV

I turn now to the third main theme of interest in Hicks's writings on capital, namely technical progress. It was an interest that dated of course from long before the publication of *Capital and Growth*. In *The Theory of Wages*, Hicks had proposed a classification of inventions. A neutral invention was one which with given factor proportions raised the marginal product of labour in the same proportion as the marginal product of capital. Definitions of (relatively) labour-saving inventions and of (relatively) capital-saving inventions followed naturally from the definition of neutrality.

Hicks also distinguished between two kinds of invention. There were autonomous inventions, which were not expected to have any particular factor-saving bias, and induced inventions, i.e. inventions that were induced by a change in relative factor prices. With the help of these categories, he put forward an explanation of the behaviour over time of distributive shares, which need not be set out here.

The Hicksian notion of induced invention came in for some criticism, notably from Salter (1960). Salter argued that even when labour costs rise, any change that reduces total costs is welcome, and whether this is achieved by saving labour or capital is irrelevant. Salter's objection, however, can hardly be sustained. In so far as the entrepreneur has a choice as to how to apply his expenditures on research and development, it is only common sense that his choice will be influenced by the economic facts, one of which will be the share of labour costs in total costs.

The difficulty about the theory of induced inventions, a difficulty not unrecognized by Hicks at the time, lies elsewhere. When factor proportions have changed as a result of a rise in wages relative to capital costs, it is difficult in principle and impossible in practice to distinguish whether this has occurred because of a substitution of capital for labour with a given production function or because of an induced labour-saving invention. Since the effect is the same in each case, perhaps it does not matter very much whether we can make the distinction or not.

Meanwhile, Harrod had proposed an alternative definition of neutral technical progress. In the Harrod classification, technical progress is neutral if at a constant rate of interest the capital–output ratio remains unchanged. The Harrod definition was particularly appropriate for the theory of growth: for it enabled technical progress, so long as it was Harrod-neutral, to be accommodated within a steady-state growth model.

There is very little analysis of technical progress in *Value and Capital* and not a great deal in *Capital and Growth*. The occasion for the traverse in *Capital and Growth* was a change in the exogenous rate of growth rather than a shift in the efficiency curve as a result of technical progress. There is, however, a section in *Capital and Growth* (1965: 180–2) which considers the effect of technical progress on factor shares. Two kinds of classification are there compared, one of which is the Harrod classification and the second may be described as an amended version of Hicks's own classification in *The Theory of Wages*. In the end, though, what Hicks seems to be after is a classification based on the total effects of technical progress on factor shares and there is little doubt that the Harrod classification is the most appropriate for this purpose.

In *Capital and Time*, the consideration of technical progress is quite extensive. It is undertaken through a comparison of efficiency curves. A technical improvement implies a movement upwards and outwards in the efficiency curve, at least in the neighbourhood of the point given by the initial values of the real wage and the rate of interest. Hicks then suggests the use of an index of improvement in efficiency, which is given by the proportional shift to the right of the efficiency curve; or, in other words, by the proportional increase in the real wage that will be made possible at an unchanged rate of interest. The improvement index, however, will be a function of the actual level of the rate of interest, and Hicks's new classification of technical progress is concerned with the behaviour of the improvement index when the rate of interest changes. If there is a rise in the improvement index when the rate of interest falls, this will be because the cost savings and productivity increases tend to come late in the process: Hicks calls this a case of *forward-biased* improvement. If the improvement index falls when the rate of interest falls, we will have a *backward-biased* improvement.

A *neutral* improvement will be one in which the improvement index is unchanged when the rate of interest changes. Hicks concedes that neutrality of this kind corresponds to Harrod-neutrality. But he is reluctant to identify his proposed classification of improvements with the Harrod classification, because he wants it to be applicable for more general purposes than the study of steady states. Nevertheless, I think we must agree with Solow (1974) that there is at least a correspondence between Hicks's new classification and the Harrod classification, if only because in a steady-state context they come to the same thing.

Also in *Capital and Time*, Hicks returned to the question of substitution and of induced inventions as a response to a rise in wages. Faced with the old difficulty of distinguishing between the two, his preferred solution is to treat every change in technique as an *invention*. In this way, he is able to dispense with the notion of a given spectrum of techniques (technology), which he had come to regard as suspect.

In short, I believe we can discern two tendencies in the development of Hicks's thinking on technical progress, which are not unrelated. First, he has tended to move away from his original classification of inventions towards the Harrod classification. Second, he has tended to abandon the idea of an old-style production function or of a given technology as being too static in conception to be of much use in a dynamic context.

I must admit personally to having some reservations concerning the suitability of the neo-Austrian approach for the analysis of technical progress. This is because in tackling the difficult problems of technical progress we are likely to miss quite a lot that is important if we deny ourselves at least some measure of sectoral disintegration. There are two aspects of an individual invention that may be of importance. The first is its intrinsic character and the second is its sectoral location. Admittedly, one may get involved in identification problems. If an improvement takes the form of the use of some quite new machine in the production of a consumption good, how are we to determine whether this is an improvement in the consumption sector or in the capital sector?[2] Even so, there are other cases which are a good deal more clear-cut.

Take for example one of the most important advances of our time, the so-called 'micro-chip revolution'. Clearly, this is an advance within the capital sector. In itself, it may well have been labour using (capital saving) in character, if one is to judge by the occasional pictures seen on television of people actually fitting the little things into a computer in construction. A far more important aspect of the revolution, however, has been the drastic reduction in the cost of computers. In the first instance, this again will have been capital saving; but the total effect, especially on distributive shares, will have depended on the extent to which computers have been substituted for labour in the production of a host of other goods and services. We are back in a world very close to that of *The Theory of Wages*. By way of contrast, in the longitudinal approach of *Capital and Time*, the two aspects of an invention become inextricably fused within the process.

V

Before attempting a final assessment of Hicks's contribution to capital theory, I ought not to leave unmentioned what might be considered as a fourth major theme of interest. Not only was he concerned with the concept of capital, but he was also intensely interested in the statistical problems of measurement. I shall make no attempt to give an account of his contribution in this regard. His chapter on 'The measurement of capital' in *Capital and Time* is so comprehensive and lucid that it is best left to speak for itself.

VI

It is time now to try to give an assessment of Hicks's contribution to capital theory. Both of his two main models, in *Capital and Growth* and in *Capital and Time*, have their strengths and their weaknesses. Neither can be said to be at all realistic. Hicks's own two reasons for dissatisfaction with the method of sectoral disintegration were that it failed to take account of the time required to build the machines used in the productive process and that depreciation could be dealt with only in a very perfunctory manner.

There is no doubt that the production process does take time, and that the time lags involved in different processes will in general be different. However, this may not constitute an insuperable objection to the method of sectoral disintegration. Morishima has argued that if we are prepared to enlarge our list of goods so as to include fictitious intermediate products, a process of any duration can be thought of as being composed of a number of standardized processes of unit duration (Morishima 1969: 91). Even so, there is no doubt that the neo-Austrian approach deals with the time involved in a productive process in a more direct fashion.

Hicks's point about depreciation is also well taken, especially if depreciation is considered as embracing obsolescence as well as physical wear-and-tear. There is no doubt at all that the neo-Austrian approach can give a much richer and more convincing account of depreciation and obsolescence than the method of sectoral disintegration.

Nevertheless, the neo-Austrian theory has its own weaknesses, the most notable of which is the specification that every process must start with a single input of labour. It is true that Hicks makes it clear, in a characteristically Hicksian passage (1973d: 37), that by labour he does not necessarily mean labour. But I do not frankly think that this helps very much. That there should be just one homogeneous input into a process, whatever it may be, remains a drastic simplification. Moreover the standard case, which Hicks uses in the discussion of the traverse, is a very special case indeed, as he himself readily admits.

The strengths of the two approaches are complementary, and by developing both Hicks has added immensely to our understanding of the subject. Perhaps the way forward will be to attempt to combine the two approaches. An interesting start in this direction has been made by Craven (1975), who takes over the neo-Austrian idea of a process but applies it to a two-sector economy producing tractors and corn. There is a separate process for each sector, and each process uses inputs of tractors as well as of labour.

Not the least of Hicks's achievements in the field of capital theory has been the successful defusion of the controversy – one might almost say conflict – between the Austrians and the 'Realists'. By rejecting what was invalid in the Austrian approach and by developing what was valid, he has so to speak put the Austrians in their proper place. Since Hicks, new students of economics will find the subject of capital much less baffling than it used to be.

In conclusion, it may be appropriate to say a word about his prodigious originality, nowhere seen more strikingly than in his contributions to capital theory. Paradoxically, I do not think he was a great originator. As such, I do not think he is to be compared with Harrod, who is to be found at the beginning of more than one major advance in modern economic theory. Hicks, by contrast, was a great developer. This is not to say that he did not have many inventions to his credit; but his inventions were 'induced' inventions rather than 'autonomous' ones!

To his development work he brought to bear above all a superb technique, firmly based on his mathematical ability. I have always imagined, though without any direct evidence, that he worked out his theories first in terms of mathematics and then, Marshall-like, translated them into lucid prose and into diagrams. He brought to bear also a knowledge of the history of economic thought that was both wide and deep, so that he was never at a loss to find something that was worth developing.

Matthews in his memorial address reprinted in this volume has paid tribute to the width of his interests outside of economics, notably his knowledge of Italian and of Italian literature. Hicks must be unique among British economists in having inserted a reference to Boccaccio into one of his works (1973d: 12–13). In short, Hicks was something of a polymath. It may be of some comfort to us lesser beings to know that there were two skills that he never mastered: he never learnt to swim and he never drove a car. Both of these accomplishments he left to his wife Ursula.

NOTES

1   See Kennedy (1973). There is a minor blemish in Hicks's treatment of depreciation in *Capital and Growth*. He used the same symbol for depreciation in both the price and quantity equations, but wrongly claimed that this would not involve him in the assumption of depreciation by evaporation.

2   Hicks always insisted that a change of technique required the respecification of the capital good. While this is no doubt realistic in the vast majority of cases, I am not sure that, as a matter of analytical policy, he was wise to insist on it at the outset. In principle, he was not averse to treating the simplest case first; and the simplest case of a technical improvement is the discovery of some improved method of utilizing existing factors of production. My own preferred approach would be to work out the consequences of an improvement of this kind in a sectorally disintegrated model, before going on to tackle the problems raised by the respecification of the capital good.

REFERENCES

Craven, John (1975) 'Capital theory and the process of production', *Economica* 42: 283–91.

Kennedy, Charles (1973) The death-rate of tractors and the rate of depreciation', *Oxford Economic Papers* 25: 57–9.

Morishima, Michio (1969) *Theory of Economic Growth*, Oxford, Clarendon Press.

Salter, W. E. G. (1960) *Productivity and Technical Change*, Cambridge: Cambridge University Press.

Schumpeter, Joseph A. (1954) *History of Economic Analysis*, Oxford: Oxford University Press.

Solow, Robert M. (1974) 'Review of Hicks: *Capital and Time*', *Economic Journal* 84: 189–92.

5

THE THEORY OF WAGES
REVISITED

Kurt W. Rothschild

I A BOOK AND ITS FATE

The beginnings of the 1930s were – looking back from today – not a very propitious moment for entering the arena of theoretical economics with fundamental treatises. While the theoretical world (though certainly not the real world) seemed to have accomplished a state of stability and order – Cannan could still plead in 1933 for a greater engagement of professional economists in spending their time in assisting the public 'to grasp the bare elements of economic science' (Cannan 1933: 367–8) – it was in fact at the eve of major revolutions which had been developing underground before but only broke out fully after 1932: the 'imperfect competition revolution' of Joan Robinson and Edward Chamberlin, the 'Keynesian revolution' and – last but not least – the attempts at dynamisation of the Swedish school. Writing at the watershed between these two periods without being integrated into one of the 'inner circles' of the underground movements involved the risk of being 'out of date' (or at least out of discussion) soon and for good.

Two important theoretical treatises appeared in those critical days written by two young economists residing at the London School of Economics (LSE): F. A. Hayek's *Prices and Production* in 1931 (translated from the German *Preise und Produktion* published in the same year) and John Hicks's *The Theory of Wages* in 1932. Both books felt the blow of the following 'revolutions', but they suffered different fates. Though Hayek's book could go into a second (revised) edition in 1935 just before Keynes's *General Theory* came out, it soon 'fell out of grace' without a proper chance of return. Hicks's *Theory* – his first book by the way – went through a different experience. And that for several reasons.

Though *The Theory of Wages* went out of print within 10 years after its publication it was not reprinted because Hicks himself moved quickly with the new times and became an early critic of the 'old-fashioned' parts of his book. As early as 1935 he published an article followed by another in 1936[1] in which he rethought, revised and partly rejected certain portions of his book going so far as to disown one chapter (Chapter IX on 'Wage regulation and unemployment') *completely*. Instead of defending his book by hook or by crook he started to point out liberally its weaknesses (a talent which Hicks maintained throughout his life) so that by the end of the 1930s he 'reached a point when I should have been happy if it could be forgotten' (Hicks 1963b: 311). But just because the weak points had been conceded the book had a chance for survival owing to its undeniable qualities. Not only had Hicks presented and developed traditional viewpoints which kept their (partial) validity in such a clear and consistent manner that Schumpeter could recommend, in his *History of Economic Analysis*, Hicks's *Theory of Wages* as a particularly useful source for understanding the classical treatment of income distribution and technological progress (Schumpeter 1954: 679); but the book also contained several sections with important and original innovations (to be discussed later) which proved fruitful for later research not only in wage and distribution theory but also in other fields.

Thus, following an increased demand Hicks finally agreed to a revised edition of his book which came out more than 30 years after its first edition (1963b) with three reprints following in quick succession. But instead of revising the old text Hicks decided on a different course. In a first part of the new edition the original text is given without any changes (partly also in order to enable users to refer to the non-available first edition), and to this he added a second part containing (1) the lengthy and critical review of the book which G.F. Shove, already aware of the new things coming up in Cambridge, wrote in the 1933 volume of *The Economic Journal*; (2) the two critical articles by Hicks (1935f and 1936c) mentioned before; and (3) an eighty-page commentary in which Hicks looks back on his 'juvenile opus' from a 1963 perspective. When we consider Hicks's *Theory of Wages* today we can see it as the original treatise or as a starting point for the development of many of Hicks's ideas over the span of 30 years. Both these perspectives will be taken up (and mixed) in the following pages. References to the original work, to the two later articles, as well as references to Shove and Hicks's 1963 comments will all be given by page numbers of the revised 1963 edition.

II LABOUR ECONOMIST – ECONOMIC THEORIST

Wages, labour markets, trade unions etc. can be and are approached from two rather different angles: either as a field for applying the analysis and 'laws' of general economic theory with labour services seen as goods and wages as prices, or by stressing the specificities of the labour market and its institutions and taking one's clues from this platform. That there are reasons for such a split can be seen by the fact that we accept without particular surprise the existence of specialists who call themselves 'labour economists' while we would be rather puzzled if we met coat economists, flower economists etc. There is no fundamental necessity that these two approaches should clash: they could very well be regarded as different aspects of one and the same problem whose results could be combined and mutually adjusted. In practice, however, differences in stress and perspective remain even in those cases where the other side is not neglected altogether. A classical example of these differences was the famous exchange of views between the labour economist Richard Lester and the 'pure' theorist Fritz Machlup in the pages of the *American Economic Review* of 1946.

Hicks came to write his *Theory of Wages* as a *theorist* via *labour economist*. At the end of his studies in Oxford he regarded himself 'as a labour economist, not a theoretical economist at all' (Hicks 1963b: 306). His Oxford thesis dealt with 'Skilled and unskilled wages in the building and engineering trades', and this was followed by predominantly descriptive articles dealing with industrial relations themes. Interest in theory was only stirred at the LSE from 1929 onwards under the influence of Robbins and (later) Hayek. As Hicks relates: 'I had just three years in which to learn my economic theory [drawing mainly on Marshall, Pareto and continental literature] to apply to labour problems' (Hicks 1963b: 306).

But Hicks's conversion to economic theorist was profound. His past as a labour economist was not completely forgotten when he wrote his *Theory of Wages*. It shows up in historical and descriptive sections and in numerous realistic and common-sense observations which prevented the book from becoming isolated from reality. It could thus serve to some extent as a direct stimulus for economic policy debates. But as far as the main thrust of the book is concerned it was a clear and almost complete change-over to a general theory approach. The first sentence of the book is revealing: 'The theory of the determination of wages in a free market is *simply* a special case of the general theory of value' (Hicks 1963b: 1; my italics). This assumption is, in my view, the original sin of a considerable segment of past and present literature in the field of wages and labour markets, and it did – as we shall see – mar some arguments and conclusions in Hicks's book. Even then it was mitigated to some extent by the aforementioned after-effects of Hicks's past as a labour economist which led to occasional modifications of the 'hard' theoretical results such as, for instance, references to the role of custom or ideas about 'fairness' in the determination of wages and wage structures (Hicks 1963b: 79–80). But even where such modifications turn up they are usually played down *vis-à-vis* the dominant forces of the basic theoretical frame, not unlike the way in which Böhm-Bawerk argued in his famous essay on *Macht oder ökonomisches Gesetz.*[2]

Later, however, Hicks moved – under the impression of new theoretical insights and changing real events – considerably in the direction of attributing greater weight to the specificities of the labour market and the role of non-economic elements. In 1955, the same year in which Barbara Wooton published her important book *Social Foundations of Wage Policy* (stressing the role of customary and non-economic elements in wage bargaining and wage determination), Hicks in his Presidential Address to Section F of the British Association on 'Economic Foundations of Wage Policy', said

It has never been the general rule that wage-rates have been determined simply and solely by supply and demand. Even on pure grounds of efficiency it is desirable that the wage which is offered should be acceptable, acceptable both to the worker himself and those with whom he is to work. There has in consequence always been room for wages to be influenced by non-economic forces – whether by custom ... or by any other principle which affects what the parties to the wage-bargain think to be *just* or *right*. Economic forces do affect wages, but only when they are strong enough to overcome the *social* forces ... We get no sensible answers (to our questions) if we persist in treating them as pure problems of economics, in a narrow sense.

(Hicks 1955b: 390, 393)

It is also characteristic that in his commentary to the second edition in 1963, Hicks tried to defend himself against some criticisms by stating that he still adheres to the statement with which he *'began the whole book'* which he then quotes as

The need for a special theory of wages only arises because both the supply of labour, and the demand for it, and the way in which demand and supply interact on the labour market, have certain peculiar properties, which make it impossible to apply to labour the ordinary theory of commodity value without some further consideration.

(Hicks 1963b: 316)

This, however, was *not* the *beginning* of the book, but the second sentence. The first referred to the 'simple' supply–demand statement mentioned above.[3] This was now discreetly dropped. The idea of the labour market being a *special market*, hinted at in the 1932 edition and then coming to increasing prominence later on, found even stronger social *and* economic underpinnings in Hicks's later interests in monetary economies and 'fixprice' markets of which the labour market is a particular specimen.[4]

III MARGINAL PRODUCTIVITY

The demand–supply credo which headed Hicks's *Theory of Wages* as a programmatic statement in 1932 was not quite upheld in the book. While the demand side certainly got its share, supply remained rather neglected. Though a special chapter was devoted to supply questions (Chapter V, 'Individual supply of labour'), it appears rather late on the agenda and relies more on fragmentary observation, good common sense, *obiter dicta* etc. than on consistent theoretical and empirical analysis. This is rightly criticized by Shove in his remarkably extensive and deep review essay of 1933 where he stressed that this neglect of supply-side influences both on the general level of wages and the distribution of labour between industries means 'that [the] book is less comprehensive and less ambitious than its title and its preface might seem to imply' (Hicks 1963b: 252). This criticism was gracefully acknowledged by Hicks in the second edition where he particularly rejects as 'foolish' his earlier remarks that the distribution of the population between occupations is a problem of the theory of wages, 'but it is one of the easiest problems of the whole theory' (Hicks 1963b: 319).

To some extent this shortcoming of saying little on supply-side forces can be excused because this had been a general feature of wage theory after the classical period. Only more recently have theoretical and empirical analyses begun to pay more attention to these questions. However, disregarding the question of any 'guilt' of Hicks in this respect the fact remains that the whole theoretical weight of his analysis was concentrated on the demand side. Marginal productivity, the subject of the first chapter ('Marginal productivity and the demand for labour'), thus obtained a pivotal role and provides a backbone throughout the entire book.

In making marginal productivity the central factor in his explanation of labour demand and – building on this (with labour supply, full competition and profit maximization taken as given) – also for wage determination, Hicks was, of course, firmly rooted in a widely accepted tradition which was not only dominant at the time, but survived in Keynes's *General Theory* (at least for periods of full employment) and continues to play a role *in the logic* of neo-classical theory right up to this day, despite the fact that its real importance is regarded more cautiously in view of the complexities and institutional characteristics of the labour market even in circles which are in sympathy with neo-classical microeconomics.[5] In view of these circumstances it is not surprising that Hicks (in 1932) could not offer anything sensational or original in this well-covered field of marginal productivity principles. As Shove commented somewhat dryly the value of these beginning chapters 'is mainly pedagogic' and they should 'prove a serviceable adjunct to the ordinary textbooks' (Hicks 1963b: 252).

But a bit more than this can be said on this first section. First, good pedagogy in itself is an important art if it is to be connected *creatively* with scientific presentation. That Hicks was a master in this art is already very much in evidence in this first major work of his and shows up clearly in his presentation of marginal productivity. Following Marshall in banning all mathematical proofs to the appendix and on top of it renouncing (for whatever reasons?) diagrammatic treatments, Hicks manages to give a lucid as well as an analytically satisfactory account of the assumptions, interconnections and consequences of the basic marginal productivity model and (in later chapters) of its ramifications and numerous applications.[6]

Second, Hicks was better than most of his contemporaries in distinguishing more clearly between two quite different influences on marginal productivity in a static society (on which he concentrated *exclusively* in Chapter I): (1) *scale* of output and (2) methods of production (factor proportions). Even when Hicks had become rather critical of 'that terrible first chapter' (Hicks 1963b: 321) he still defended 'the "scale-proportions" approach [as] the best way of constructing a theory of the demand for labour' (p. 322), because this permits him to show more clearly the *different* ways in which a more plentiful (or cheaper) factor gets absorbed through expansion and substitution processes.

But there are also weak points. Some of them – like questions of monetary and dynamic factors – were later taken up by Hicks himself and will be treated later. But there was a more fundamental weakness which was not fully overcome even in Hicks's later contributions. It is connected with what has been said earlier about the victory of the economic theorist over the labour economist. Notwithstanding Hicks's repeated references to the gap between theory and its rigid assumptions on the one hand, and reality with its numerous frictions, lags and modifications on the other, he is always drawn towards an attempt to make the theory a strongly *deterministic* element which – in later chapters – should give him the basis for 'powerful' answers. Thus while Hicks readily admits that 'a long road has to be traveled before this abstract proposition can be used in the explanation of real events' (Hicks 1963b: 10), that no general equality between marginal productivity and wages can be expected 'for the real labour market is scarcely ever in equilibrium' (p. 18), and so on and so forth, he nevertheless regards the 'Law of marginal productivity' as 'the most fundamental principle of the theory of wages' (p. 9), which he defends with great care against several possible counter-arguments in order to keep the road to 'determinate' equilibrium solutions open. Even when dealing with a dynamic economy, where changes and frictions take place all the time, Hicks tries to defend the marginal productivity wage by looking at the very long run, as

the wage a man would ultimately receive if the fundamental conditions of equilibrium – the number of people in the market, their tastes, their ability to labour, and the property they possess – were made eternal as they exist at the moment, and the process of settling down followed to its furthest limits.

(Hicks 1963b: 86)

This respect for marginal productivity as the *guiding attractor* for wages was helped – in the case of Hicks as well as of other writers – by a concentration on static models and perfect competition. Though Hicks has something, but not much, to say on imperfect competition in goods and labour markets and also on monopsony (without using that term), he tries to avoid these themes because they do not fit so well into the picture, and allowing for them could only be achieved 'at the cost of wrecking completely any simplicity which it has been possible to import into the following arguments' (Hicks 1963b: 114). Of course, in 1932 the imperfect competition revolution was only in its beginning and could be overlooked or disregarded. But it is interesting that later on, when Hicks looked back more critically on his treatment of marginal productivity in the light of the 'revolutions' caused by Joan Robinson and Keynes, he remarked (in 1963) that after 1932 'I was . . . an almost whole-hearted Keynesian; but was by no means a whole-hearted Imperfect Competitionist' (Hicks 1963b: 310). One cannot help feeling that even then his aversion to take imperfect competition – so important in labour markets – fully into account rested on the same reasons which he spelt out more fully and directly in his *Value and Capital*, where he threw out imperfect competition because he feared that its acceptance would cause the 'wreckage of the greater part of economic theory' (Hicks 1939a: 84).[7]

IV SUBSTITUTION, DISTRIBUTION, CAPITAL

While it could be said that Hicks was following traditional tracks in the presentation of marginal productivity – though adding accuracy and individual style – he certainly contributed new ideas and vistas in later chapters of the book. To these belong a greater awareness of the problems created by dynamics, uncertainty, expectations, bargaining etc. than was usual in theoretic discussions of the time. The passages dealing with these themes pointed the way to future developments both in Hicks's thinking and in economic theory in general.

Some of these considerations, going beyond the static frame of the work, will come up as we go along. At the present stage I only want to point out that the *Theory of Wages* saw the birth of a new analytical tool which has become a mainstay in economic research: the concept of 'elasticity of substitution'. Hicks developed it in his endeavour to go beyond an explanation of wage levels on the basis of demand and supply and to deal with the interesting question of wages as a share in the distribution of incomes. In the same way as the American economist Paul Douglas, in his contemporary *Theory of Wages*, Hicks worked with the idea of a homogeneous production function (of the Cobb–Douglas type) though he did not spell out its aspects in all the theoretical and empirical detail which characterized Douglas's work. But with the concept of 'elasticity of substitution' he had found a 'new rule, involving a new definition . . . a measure of the ease with which the varying factor can be substituted for others' (Hicks 1963b: 117).

Though a definition is, of course, no explanation the use of the new tool greatly helped Hicks and later writers to tackle the problems of population growth, technological change, changes in relative factor prices and their influence on relative shares in a more satisfactory manner, and this approach was soon extended to other areas of economic theory. Hicks's achievement in presenting this method is in no way belittled by the fact that the same idea was developed independently in a slightly different form by Joan Robinson at the same time (in the context of ordinary demand theory). 'Multiple discoveries' are a not uncommon experience in the development of economic theory, and the confrontation of Hicks's and Robinson's formulation triggered off very interesting and fruitful debates on the elasticity of substitution in the pages of the *Review of Economic Studies* in subsequent years, in which the *crème de la crème* of economic theorists took part: Machlup, Sweezy, Lerner, Kahn, Tarshis, Meade, Pigou, Champernowne. Hicks rightly remained proud of this early piece of analytical innovation. As late as 1977 when he looked back at his 'first theoretical achievements' he mentions elasticity of substitution (1932b), substitution and income effects (1934a) and the idea of a liquidity spectrum (1935b), and then adds: 'I still feel [it] to be some of my best work' (Kregel 1988: 1).

The elasticity of substitution concept permitted Hicks to give continuity and consistency to the treatment of relative shares under varying influences (relative prices, varying factor supplies etc.) and to introduce sharper classifications (e.g. labour saving, capital saving, neutral inventions). The conclusions regarding actual distributional trends and possibilities suffered from the rigid assumptional restrictions to which the new tool was sub-ordinated. This was immediately criticized by Shove who, after congratulat-ing Hicks on the 'very pretty contribution to pure theory', raises doubts whether Hicks's special cases and generalizations (under pure competition etc.) can be regarded as more than a first approximation (Hicks 1963b: 261). In his 1936 article on 'Distribution and economic progress: a revised version', Hicks concedes these criticisms and admits that he had been too rash in jumping from micro (firm) to macro (community) level and that important complications resulting from the introduction of several production factors (more than two), increasing returns, imperfect competition, capital main-tenance, international trade etc., had not been considered. The chapter on distribution, he said, has 'become seriously out of date ... [but is] probably not much misleading' (Hicks 1963b: 286). This is followed by short attempts to consider what complications are introduced by the neglected elements. It is not surprising that the previous results about relative shares become less clear-cut and unique. Hicks's conclusion that the problems are 'very intricate, and any simple theory is only a simplification' (Hicks 1963b: 302) is probably as relevant today as it was when it was written more than half a century ago.

One aspect remains to be mentioned almost as a curiosity. With Hicks being an outstanding thinker in the field of capital theory it is surprising – though understandable in view of the period – that the treatment of capital falls completely flat in the distribution chapter and elsewhere. Capital is treated simply as a 'factor of production' whose supply can be increased through saving or reduced through 'consumption' and these changes are dependent on wage developments and wage/profit ratios which in turn influence the marginal productivities of both factors. There are a few remarks on capital theory, partly tucked away in a footnote (Hicks 1963b: 17), resting strongly on Hayekian and Böhm-Bawerkian ideas; but on the whole the treatment deliberately excludes a special consideration of capital problems.

Following Shove's criticisms in this respect ('Unfortunately "capital" is not defined and we are not told how quantities of it are to be measured' (Hicks 1963b: 264)), Hicks, in his 1935 paper on 'Wages and interest: the dynamic problem', tries partly to defend and partly to repair his position by pointing out the lack of a satisfactory *dynamic* theory of capital which would be needed in wage theory and then makes an attempt to provide in as simple a way as possible a first approach to a dynamic capital theory. This is not the place to go into the details of this attempt (which Hicks himself later regarded as inadequate), but it deserves to be mentioned that in this context Hicks developed for the first time techniques which later became so important in his *Value and Capital*: the sequence of 'weeks' with 'Monday' decisions under uncertain expectations and temporary equilibrium. Also the important concept of 'elasticity of expectations' is already visible in nucleus (Hicks 1963b: 278–9), though the term itself is not used. Later on, in his commentary to the revised edition of the *Theory of Wages* (1963b) Hicks – with *Value and Capital* behind him – adds a few critical remarks on capital (Hicks 1963b: 342–8) which go far beyond the earlier considerations, touching such difficulties as heterogeneity of capital, valuation problems, depreciation and utilization measures etc. Some of these remarks provided interesting hints for the emerging capital theory controversy.

V REAL AND MONEY WAGES

The 'datedness' of the *Theory of Wages* as a child of the pre-Keynesian era is perhaps clearest visible in its almost complete fixation on real wages. Marginal productivity is most of the time narrowed down in two ways: the neglect of imperfect competition leads to equating marginal *physical* productivity (instead of marginal *revenue* productivity) with wages, and the neglect of the monetary element leads to the reduction of wages to real wages thus resulting in the simple equilibrium equation 'wage = marginal productivity'. This equation dominates Hicks (particularly 1932): not only the 'pure' theory but also the larger part of his more applied chapters where he deals with the history of wage movements and with trade union influence (to be dealt with in the next section).

Hicks was, of course, aware that 'in nearly every thinkable monetary system, the kind of process we have been examining would itself have reactions on the monetary machine; and these would have further repercussions on the "real" process'. But then he continues:

[P]erhaps the writer will be excused if he decides that, for the present, these repercussions lie outside the Theory of Wages. If economic science was fortunate enough to possess generally accepted principles on the broad subject which underlies this problem – the effect of monetary policy on the structure of production – then we could apply these principles to our particular problem ... However, the relation of Prices and Production is today perhaps the most hotly contested issue in all economic theory. There is thus no *via media*; either we must avoid the subject or plunge into it at considerable length. And here it is obviously necessary to take the first alternative.

(Hicks 1963b: 212)

Whether we 'excuse' Hicks for this fatal simplification or not, there are at least good reasons for *explaining* it. To some extent this has already been done: writing in 1932 meant coming in at the worst possible moment as far as the problem of dealing with a *monetary* economy was concerned. The old world seemed still intact and the theoretical 'revolution' was only in its beginnings. As far as it could be sensed at all at the time the LSE was certainly not the place for it. Shove, living in the 'hot' atmosphere of Cambridge, was of course already on a different road. He wrote in 1933,

It is not possible to separate the 'real process' from 'its monetary reactions' ... when we are dealing with *all-round* changes in wages ... Monetary reactions are not simply 'repercussions of' the process set up by the change, they *are* the process and must occupy a central position in any analysis of it.

(Hicks 1963b: 266-7)

This was not the world in which Hicks lived in 1932. As he described it later, it was a 'Hayekian atmosphere' in which he was working, and the book was written 'in a state of monstrous ignorance about everything monetary' (Hicks 1963b: 355). In this 'ignorance' he 'trusted in the "dichotomy" between real and monetary theory', subscribing to a 'caricature' of the quantity theory of money in which 'the Quantity of Money (M) and its income-velocity (V) are *entirely* determined by monetary causes, which are quite separate from the real causes which determine relative prices. It follows that the money value of total income, since it equals MV, is also determined by monetary causes' (Hicks 1963b: 355-6). It is obvious that with such a perspective the distinction between real and money wages receded into the background.

But if Hicks was 'behind' on monetary matters in 1932 he was also a quick learner. Even before the appearance of Keynes's *General Theory*, Hicks's interest turned to monetary theory and he found his own access to liquidity (asset) aspects of money as early as 1935 in his paper on 'A suggestion for simplifying the theory of money' (Hicks 1935b). The change-over to Keynes's analysis of a *monetary* economy was then much quicker and easier for Hicks than for many other economists. The macroeconomic interrelationships between money wage movements, monetary changes and interest rates and their repercussions on inflation, real wages and foreign trade destroy some of the simple conclusions which emerged from the 'pure' *Theory of*

Wages. This was one of the reasons why Hicks was not keen to have his book reprinted after 1936.

The full change of perspective became visible, long before the critical appraisal in the second edition of the *Theory of Wages*, in Hicks's Presidential Address to the British Association in 1955, where he states that

> since 1931, wages questions have been closely associated with mone-
> tary questions; it is even true that the *general* level of wages has become
> a monetary question. So long as wages were being determined within
> a *given* monetary framework, there was some sense in saying that there
> was an 'equilibrium wage', a wage that was in line with the monetary
> conditions that were laid down from outside. But the world we now live
> in is one in which the monetary system has become relatively elastic, so
> that it can accommodate itself to changes in wages, rather than the other
> way about ... It is hardly an exaggeration to say that instead of being
> on a Gold Standard, we are on a Labour Standard.
>
> (Hicks 1955b: 391)

VI TRADE UNIONS, BARGAINING, UNEMPLOYMENT

The *Theory of Wages* with its eleven chapters is divided into two parts: Part I, 'The free market', and Part II, 'The regulation of wages'. While both parts contain a mixture of theoretical analysis, empirical–historical remarks and policy considerations, it is the second part where problems of wage policy and particularly trade union policy are treated more extensively. And it is in these chapters that the confrontation of Hicks the economic theorist with Hicks the labour economist becomes particularly visible.

As far as the theoretical side is concerned two points deserve to be stressed. On the one hand, although Hicks had started off with pure competition he was realistic enough to acknowledge the importance of institutional factors whose inclusion in the theoretical framework he regarded as desirable. It would be too much to say that he succeeded in doing this (who has?), but he made a remarkable pioneering effort in presenting a simple bargaining model which tries to show the process of wage determination under conditions of collective bargaining and strike possibilities.

By a juxtaposition of the respective costs of a strike on the one hand and a concession on the other as seen by the employers and trade unions respectively, he constructs an 'employer's concession curve' and a 'union's resistance curve' where 'acceptable' wages are a function of expected strike duration.[8] Though the model was rather simple, taking into account only rather definite strike expectations and leaving in doubt the question of the 'determinacy' of the bargaining process,[9] it was an important step forward – 10 years before game theory started a more sophisticated attack – in pointing to the need of taking notice of strategic action in non-competitive environments. It is true that Hicks was not the first and only one in the field. Two years before the *Theory of Wages* Zeuthen had published his equally pioneering work *Problems of Monopoly and Economic Warfare*, which offers a superior attempt of dealing with the bargaining problem by stressing aspects of uncertainty regarding the opponent's plans and thus allowing for bluff and other negotiation tactics. But Zeuthen's work remained outside mainstream economics and was certainly unknown to Hicks when he wrote his *Theory*.[10] The priority of Zeuthen (as far as the *problem*, not the *model*, is concerned) does not diminish the pioneering aspect of Hicks's work.

While the bargaining excursion presented a modification or even a break away from the rigid equilibrium mechanisms of competition-plus-marginal productivity theory, the latter remained extremely dominant in most of the remaining theoretical considerations regarding trade union or state action to regulate (real) wages. There seems practically to be no room for 'artificially' high wages, i.e. wages running ahead of *technologically* determined increases in marginal productivity. With meticulous neo-classical care it is shown how the combined play of full competition, mobility, substitutability of capital plus dangers of 'capital consumption', foreign competition etc. leave practically no room for 'artificial' shifts between profits and wages. Wage-induced efficiency effects might soften the impact, but these can only be of minor importance. In the end and in the long run the 'unjustified' wage demands must either be defeated or lead to lasting (or even deteriorating) unemployment. Marginal productivity plays the tune.

This was at least the picture as it presented itself to Hicks in 1932 when he was – as he later reported – under the spell of Robbins' circle at the LSE with its strong belief in competition, free markets and equilibrium. 'I was willing', he writes later, 'to apply this doctrine, even to the labour market; though there I had some reservations, which survive in some chapters of *Wages*. My *Wages* book, however, is in its main lines thoroughly "neo-classical"' (Kregel 1988: 3). It was this stance leading to marginal productivity acting as a strait-jacket which caused Hicks to conclude in 1932: 'The *Theory of Wages*, as elaborated in this book, has not proved a cheerful subject' (Hicks 1963b: 232). Perhaps it would not have been a more cheerful, but certainly a different, book if he had written it two years later when he 'had realised that I had separated myself from the faith in the free market which had been dominant among my colleagues' (Kregel 1988: 4).

The 'reservations' which Hicks mentions in the above quotation occur directly or indirectly in numerous remarks and observations on labour market problems in which the labour economist wrestles with the theorist and makes his own contributions (sometimes 'dressed up' so as to fit better into the theoretic picture). In these parts one can find quite a number of passages which – though using a different terminology – contain many hints and insights which have become prominent in more modern labour market research. Without going into detail let me just mention a few of them.

Implicit contracts are indicated when Hicks points out that employers may refrain from reducing wages in bad times in order to avoid 'the disadvantages of worsened relations and a possible exodus of good workmen' (Hicks 1963b: 52); efficiency wages come to one's mind when he deals with the possibilities of higher efficiency following higher wages (pp. 94, 208); and though 'hysteresis' certainly was not a fashionable word 60 years ago, the fact itself is there when Hicks writes that 'once unemployment has appeared to any appreciable degree, it is itself a factor diminishing efficiency ... This means that the cost of employing these men at the imposed level of wages is raised' (p. 210). Considerable space is provided for what is called 'regular markets' and 'casual markets' (pp. 63–74), a distinction which has close links with the modern theories of segmented labour markets. Thus we are told that, in 'regular markets', experience of working for a particular employer is of importance, continuity of contracts is in the interest of both sides and wages tend to be rigid; in 'casual markets' on the other hand we meet fluctuating demand for labour, workers who are attached to a trade but not to a particular firm and conditions which are very competitive with a steady supply of 'normal' unemployment. This leads 'to the familiar fact that while it is very easy to become a casual labourer, it is much more difficult to stop being one.... The casual labourer has often acquired habits which diminish his usefulness to the employer of regular labour' (p. 69). These are primary and secondary employments alright!

VII CONCLUSION

This chapter has dealt with a number of aspects of Hicks's *Theory of Wages* and some of his later views referring to it from today's perspective. It was impossible to touch all elements of the book that would deserve consideration. But I hope that some of the more important points have been sufficiently covered to give an impression of the book, the author and his development. *The Theory of Wages* is – even after 60 years – still a readable and – over wide sections – an interesting book. Written at a watershed in the history of economic doctrine it shows how a gifted young scholar gives an excellent account of the accomplishments of the past while at the same time trying to develop new tools and to look (very tentatively) into the future. The most fascinating aspect of the story, however, is the alertness and speed with which Hicks managed in the wake of new experiences and theoretical developments to become his own critic and to shed the outdated elements of his 'youthful' work by changing its assumptions and structures in the light of the changed perspectives to whose developments he himself had contributed so much in his later works.

NOTES

1 Hicks (1935f, 1936c); reprinted in Hicks (1963b).
2 Thus, after talking of custom and other non-economic influences, Hicks continues: 'But although this appears to be the motive for a very large proportion of wage changes, it is not their real reason. These rules of fairness and justice are simply rough-and-ready guides whereby the working of supply and demand is anticipated' (Hicks 1963b: 80).
3 See p. 62.
4 See on this the remarks of Laidler's review essay ('Hicks and the classics') of Hicks's last book *A Market Theory of Money* (Laidler 1990: 484–5).
5 Thus in 1951 Paul Samuelson said

> I fear that when the economic theorist turns to the general problem of wage determination and labor economics, his voice becomes muted and his speech halting. If he is honest with himself, he must confess to a tremendous amount of uncertainty and self-doubt concerning even the most basic and elementary parts of the subject.
>
> (1951: 312)

6 As Christopher Bliss rightly remarks: 'Hicks writes beautifully, in a style that is very correct from the formal point of view yet almost conversational in its flow and ease' (Bliss 1987: 645).
7 It is also interesting that in his 1963 commentary Hicks does not mention works by Wooton, Kaldor and others who had been particularly doubtful about the qualities and uses of marginal productivity analysis. Kaldor's sentence at the end of his famous distribution article comes to one's mind: 'I am not sure where "marginal productivity" comes in in all this' (Kaldor 1955/6: 100).
8 This bargaining model is, by the way, the only case in the whole book where Hicks uses a diagram.
9 See on this Shackle (1957: 299–305).
10 Even when he discovered Zeuthen's book later on he 'did not get much out of it' on a first reading (Hicks 1963b: 351), because of the unconventionality of the approach.

REFERENCES

Bliss, C. (1987) 'Hicks, John Richard' in: J. Eatwell, M. Milgate and P. Newman (eds), *The New Palgrave: A Dictionary of Economics*, vol. 2, London: Macmillan.
Cannan, E. (1933) 'The need for simpler economics', *Economic Journal* 43: 365–78.
Douglas, P. (1934) *The Theory of Wages*, New York: Kelly.
Hayek, F. A. (1931) *Prices and Production*, London: Routledge & Kegan Paul.
Kaldor, N. (1955/6) 'Alternative theories of distribution', *Review of Economic Studies* 23: 83–100.
Kregel, J. (1988) *Recollections of Eminent Economists*, vol. 1, London: Macmillan.
Laidler, D. (1990) 'Hicks and the classics', *Journal of Monetary Economics*, 25: 481–9.
Lester, R. A. (1946) 'Shortcomings of marginal analysis for wage–employment problems', *American Economic Review* 36: 63–82.
Machlup, F. (1946) 'Marginal analysis and empirical research', *American Economic Review* 36: 547–54.
Samuelson, P. A. (1951) 'Economic theory and wages', in D. McCord Wright (ed.)

The Impact of the Union: Eight Economic Theorists Evaluate the Labour Union Movement, Harcourt: Brace, pp. 312–42.

Schumpeter, J. (1954) *History of Economic Analysis*, London: Allen & Unwin.

Shackle, G. (1957) 'The nature of the bargaining process', in J. T. Dunlop (ed.) *The Theory of Wage Determination*, London: Macmillan, pp. 292–314.

Shove, G. F. (1933) 'Review of "The Theory of Wages"', *Economic Journal* 43: 460–72; Reprinted in Hicks (1963) *The Theory of Wages*, 2nd edn (with reprint and commentary), London: Macmillan, pp. 249–67.

Wooton, B. (1955) *The Social Foundations of Wage Policy*, London: Allen & Unwin.

Zeuthen, F. (1930) *Problems of Monopoly and Economic Warfare*, London: Routledge.

6

A REFORMULATION AND EXTENSION OF HICKSIAN DYNAMICS

Richard M. Goodwin

With his book *A Contribution to the Theory of the Trade Cycle*, John Hicks (1950a) provided a monumental and eminently successful formulation not only of cycle analysis but also of economic dynamics in a wider sense. Of the great merits of the work, I am personally exceptionally aware, since I had been working on the same lines for about a decade but had not yet published my own efforts. The rapid and deserved success of the book spoiled the market for my own work!

Economic dynamics is a difficult and extensive topic, since it involves aspects of the whole of economics, i.e. output, value, distribution and money, and also the study of these elements in successive motion over time. Hicks had all the right qualities for performing the task successfully: he carefully consulted the major works in the field, evaluating them perceptively and combining them into a new unity – a unity which not only improved them but also produced a new view which converted cycles into cyclical growth, thus sketching out the future course of analysis.

The 1930s had yielded little growth but a great deal of unemployment, so, as Marx tells us, this determined the nature of dynamical theorizing – cycles without growth. Then Hicks, reshaping these theories, developed a model of the cycle which always ended up higher than it had begun and thus perceptively established the theoretical stance appropriate to the post-war era of unprecedented growth with only modest unemployment. He based his analysis on three central figures: Keynes for the multiplier, J. M. Clark for the acceleration principle and Harrod for the role of growth. He laid out the multiplier dynamically, as Kahn had originally stated it but which Keynes had disastrously telescoped into a static form. In doing this he helpfully demonstrated that the use of simple lags does not fundamentally alter the results of a distributed lag. From Clark he took the acceleration principle but was careful to emphasize the asymmetry between the accumulation and decumulation of durable goods. Having admitted this, he did not, in my view, face the drastic effect of this on the quite unrealistic implied length of any depressed phase. Finally, he accepted as possible, but not probable, Roy Harrod's adumbration of the regularly progressive economy (Hicks 1949c). He quite correctly noted that a growth model, being unstable itself, means that any slight deviation would generate progressive departure from the steady-state growth path.

To put together these three basic constituents, he chose a variant of the Hansen–Samuelson cycle model based on multiplier–accelerator interaction. He followed the common practice of using simple lag analysis, thus arriving at a set of linear difference equations, which he analysed very lucidly in an appendix and, wisely, merely stated the consequences in the text. To achieve a second-order difference equation, he used a single lag for investment demand. This raises the serious problem for justifying the use of a simple lag for dynamical analysis. That there are important finite lags in economics is not in question: the trouble is there are too many of them and they are of very different lengths.

He has a system of linear difference equations and hence is faced with the problem posed in the 1930s: a linear system is either stable and hence will gradually disappear or is unstable and will explode. Frisch proposed the basic solution: the system must be stable, but is kept alive by exogenous shocks which confer the added benefit of yielding irregular behaviour. Hicks wisely rejected the Frisch condition and maintained that the results would be too mild to be of interest since the shocks would be both positive and negative. Contrariwise, Hicks followed Harrod, who had dynamized Keynes by the simple argument that increased investment stimulates demand and that increased demand stimulates investment; this generates an unstable system, which creates no problem since it cannot penetrate the barrier of full employment.

By this ingenious combination of the well-known works of Keynes, Clark and Harrod, Hicks brilliantly created a basic contribution to economic dynamics: the economy, being unstable, will expand until it is stopped by full employment. This means, given the undeniable fact of long-run growth in productivity, that each cycle reaches a higher point than its predecessor. Investment is then halted by the decline of growth, but can only fall to zero gross (or small net negative) investment. Hence, by sheer imagination and careful specification, Hicks created out of familiar pieces a new vision – a simple, clear model of a growth cycle.

His model then vibrates between two barriers or 'constraints', the ceiling of full employment and the floor of zero gross investment. Given the known historical fact that in capitalism productivity has grown steadily in the long run, the peak each time will be higher and the low point some approximately constant proportion of the peak, *ceteris paribus*. Consequently each cycle also generates growth. Anyone familiar with the appropriate mathematical literature will recognize an essential relation to Poincaré's fundamental discovery of the concept of a limit cycle, based on an unstable fixed point with two non-linearities, an upper one and a lower one, corresponding to Hicks's two constraints. Hence one has local instability but global stability, yielding the important explanation of why, however disturbed, the economy persists in oscillation. Though he used only linear analysis, what he was really doing was introducing, in a slightly crude form, non-linear analysis, and doing it in such a way that it essentially included technical progress. Such a model has to be considered a fundamental contribution to economic dynamics.

Two non-linearities are sufficient to generate a limit cycle, but only one is necessary and sufficient, i.e. the full employment barrier. When output has fallen, leaving general excess capacity, there is no reason to invest and the accelerator is dead: it can take 15, 50 or more years for the excess capacity to disappear, so that the cycle would be spending most of its time in depression. What is required is Schumpeter's innovational investment, but that is another story, which Hicks ignores.

What he did analytically was to use the conventional wisdom of resolving economic time series into a given trend, and a cycle independent of it, leaving the irregularities to exogenous effects. But this procedure is open to serious objections. Producers do not think that way, and if they did they would make even greater mistakes than they do. What is required is a unitary analysis of growth in irregular waves. What I propose is a reformulation of Hicks so as to achieve such an organic theory. But to avoid the problem of the slow decay of durable equipment, I shall treat only non-durables, which will, I trust, adequately formulate the essential solution.

It is helpful to formulate the problem in ratios which, being independent of scale, allow the representation of dynamics and growth together. Let u be unit cost of labour (proportional to the share of labour), i.e. $u = a_1 w$, where a_1 is labour per unit of output, and the inverse of productivity, and w is the real wage. Define v as the ratio of employment ℓ to labour force n, so that with y as output, $v = l/n = a_1 y/n$. Labour supply grows steadily, independently of demand, and therefore may be treated as a rent good, like land; its price being determined by scarcity not cost. If the wage is low in relation to productivity, then profit and growth are high, leading, in time, to rising wage rates and thus, in turn, to falling profit and growth rates. This constitutes a self-regulation, feedback mechanism, which is the simplest way to explain the extraordinary fact that labour supply, employment and output have multiplied themselves many times over in a century, without persistent misalignment. Assuming a constant rise in labour productivity, the real wage may rise more rapidly or less rapidly, giving a rising or falling labour cost and share. This will in turn alter the growth rate of output and employment.

For simplicity, all earnings are spent and all profits saved and invested in increased output. Then for dynamical equilibrium with supply equal to demand as in Say's law,

$$(\bar{a} + u_{t+1})y_{t+1} = y_t$$

Earnings depend on the degree of employment (v) so that we may write

$$\frac{\Delta w}{w} = \bar{b}\left(\frac{1}{1 - v} - \bar{c}\right)$$

given a constant growth of productivity $(-\Delta a_1/a_1 = \bar{g}_a)$ and of labour force (g_n). Then

$$\frac{\Delta u}{u} = \frac{\Delta w}{w} + \frac{\Delta a_1}{a_1} = \bar{b}\left(\frac{1}{1 - v_t} - \bar{c}\right) - \bar{g}_a$$

and

$$\frac{\Delta v}{v} = \frac{\Delta l}{l} - \bar{g}_n = \frac{\Delta y}{y} - (\bar{g}_a + \bar{g}_n)$$

with $a, b, c, g_a, g_n > 0$. To see the motion sequentially,

$$\frac{v_{t+1}}{v_t} - 1 = \frac{y_{t+1}}{y_t} - 1 - (\bar{g}_a + \bar{g}_n)$$

Hence

$$v_{t+1} = \left[\frac{1}{\bar{a} + u_{t+1}} - (g_a + g_n)\right]v_t$$

and

$$u_{t+1} = \left[1 + \bar{b}\left(\frac{1}{1 - v_t} - \bar{c}\right) - \bar{g}_a\right]u_t$$

Taking the time unit as one year, Figure 6.1 gives for plausible parameters the trajectory in state space. There is evidently a roughly constant periodicity which is moderately stable dynamically. Figure 6.2 shows what is not evident in Figure 6.1, that a non-linear difference equation system produces endogenously erratic behaviour. One sees that each cycle is slightly different: from a simple statistical analysis one could not predict turning points, rates of growth or decline precisely.

In Figure 6.3 the variables are simulated just over two complete cycles covering 26 years. It demonstrates that the single system generates both growth and cycle, with each cycle being moderately different from the other: each peak is different, each trough also, and no two depressions are alike. The long-run average of this system is steady-state growth at 3 per cent; it grows on the average enough to pay a 2 per cent increase each year in real earnings

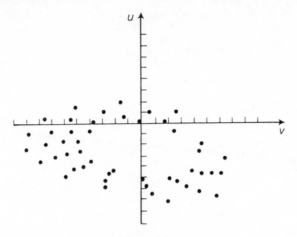

Figure 6.1

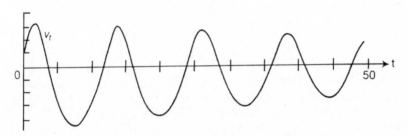

Figure 6.2

and to provide employment for 1 per cent more employees. Thus some of the time the economy is growing faster than 3 per cent and at other times necessarily less; and similarly with wages, part of the time above 2 per cent to be balanced by less than 2 per cent at other times.

The growth rate equals the profit rate, which is first too high and then too low. With a perfect capital market this would be the behaviour of the rate of interest and the return on investment. Thus all that elaborate, traditional capital theory is unnecessary and gives faulty answers. This is, of course, a system with no durable capital goods, which von Neumann treats as joint products. Durable goods complicate the problem and also help to obscure certain central aspects.

This model is a variant of von Neumann's famous paper demonstrating the existence of a solution to the general equilibrium theory. Von Neumann's system was dynamically unstable; his fixed point growth was an unstable equilibrium, so that the slightest deviation from it would lead to ever further departure. This is serious since an unstable point is the one place no actual

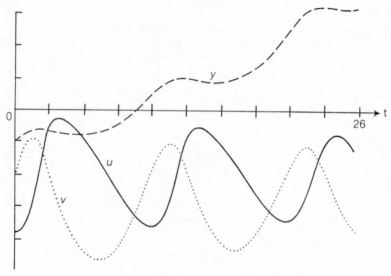

Figure 6.3

system would ever be found. The foregoing model corrects this fault, only to create another. Since it is stable, in the long run it will cease to oscillate. Therefore it cannot, by itself, explain the existence of cycles.

What is required is a stable, but not asymptotically stable system, i.e. a discrete limit cycle, a closed region within which the system will remain forever unless disturbed. What is required is a system which is unstable around its fixed point (equilibrium steady-state growth) and hence will grow in its amplitude of oscillation, but which is stable in its outer region and will experience diminishing amplitude there. A high employment rate v means a high growth rate of wage cost or wage share and a low v means a low one. A high growth rate of wages means a deceleration of growth and leads to a decline in the employment rate: the resulting low v means a low growth rate of wages and restores growth and ultimately brings us back to a high v.

To illustrate clearly the nature of the problem, consider the simplest formulation, i.e. in dimensionless form and in deviations from equilibrium growth. The system in matrix form is

$$\begin{Bmatrix} v_{t+1}/v_t \\ u_{t+1}/u_t \end{Bmatrix} = \begin{Bmatrix} a(1.0 - v_t) & -1.0 \\ +3.2258 & 0 \end{Bmatrix} \begin{Bmatrix} v_t \\ u_t \end{Bmatrix}$$

where a is the unique parameter open to choice and v_{t+1}/v_t and u_{t+1}/u_t each represent unity plus growth rate. The off-diagonal terms being of opposite sign, the system will oscillate. The dynamical stability is determined by the trace (sum of diagonal terms). The one diagonal term is positive for small v around equilibrium: this produces instability with a growing amplitude. For large v the term becomes negative making the system stable with a diminishing cycle of growth rates; thus there is only one non-linearity.

Consequently between the two regions there must be a barrier since no stable point can ever coincide with an unstable one. In differential equations this takes the form of one or more curves enclosing the equilibrium point. For difference equations the situation is more complicated and more interesting, as I shall try to illustrate. Enclosing the equilibrium there must exist at least one bounded, annular ring within which the cyclical limit set must lie. The limit set will cluster but not on a single curve because of the irregularity of non-linear difference equation solutions. Since the solutions are discrete points, the approach to the limit set is not asymptotic but occurs in finite time. By an even greater contrast with continuous time, successive points may jump over the ring from outside to inside, but once within the band appear never to emerge.

By considering a series of values for the parameter a, one discovers first a stable cycle leading to a unique equilibrium, fixed point. Then for a higher value the solution becomes a slightly irregular limit set. For a still larger value the limit set becomes sufficiently irregular that it becomes dubious to call it a single closed band. For a small further increase in a one sees that the limit set is imploding inward towards the fixed point. The next step is a completely chaotic attracting region which fills most of the region around the fixed point. Thus one arrives in successive steps to a whole attractive region in which the phase trajectories appear to move in a seemingly random fashion.

Commencing with $a = 2.0$, one has in Figure 6.4 a very stable cycle leading to a fixed point. Increasing a to 2.8 yields a bifurcation to a limit cycle set (Figure 6.5). That such a solution generates a moderate but definite irregularity is shown in Figure 6.6. With a increased to 3.4, Figure 6.7 begins

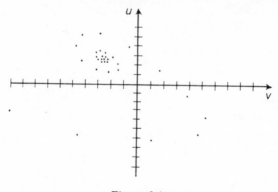

Figure 6.4

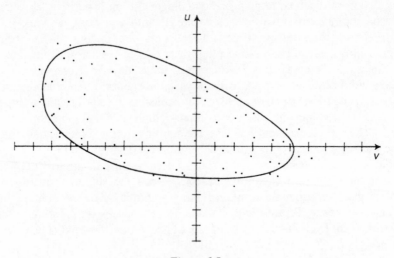

Figure 6.5

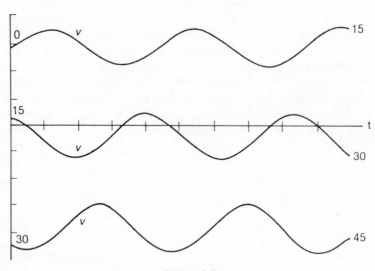

Figure 6.6

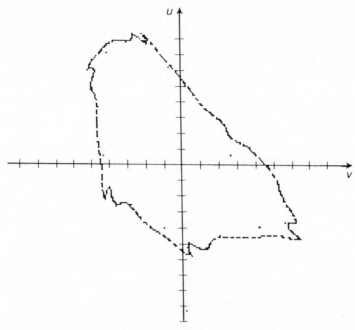

Figure 6.7

to exhibit such a marked irregularity that it is difficult to consider it a single closed band. For $a = 3.5$, it is clear that one can no longer consider the set as contained in any closed band; it is expanding in various ways towards the interior (Figure 6.8). When a is increased to 3.6, there is a full-fledged chaotic attractor: the annular band has simply grown to fill much of the enclosed space (Figure 6.9). The value $a = 4.0$ gives an even more complete filling of the entire region around equilibrium (Figure 6.10). This means, of course, that the corresponding time series is highly erratic or chaotic (Figure 6.11).

Such a system is globally stable not to a fixed point, nor to a fixed motion: rather it is stable to a fixed region within which it moves freely, performing varying degrees of aperiodic, or chaotic, motion. This constitutes a stable 'equilibrium' set of irregular motions. All initial positions outside the defined area will in finite time lead to motions inside the region and they will not exit. Initial positions inside the region give rise to similar motions within the region, never exiting. This is such a stunning generalization of the notion of equilibrium as to negate its original meaning. Such motion if defined, as here, in ratios, can determine an unlimited, chaotic growth path of a somewhat wave-like nature. In this way we have a single, endogenous, unitary theory of erratic cyclical growth of the generic type found in the time series of economic history. One therefore has to assume that there can be two, not one, sources of the familiar irregularity of economic time series.

83

Figure 6.8

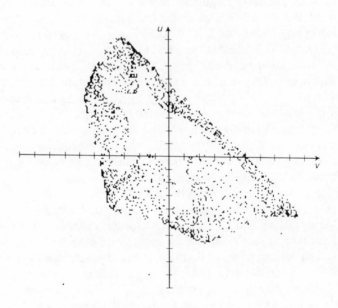

Figure 6.9

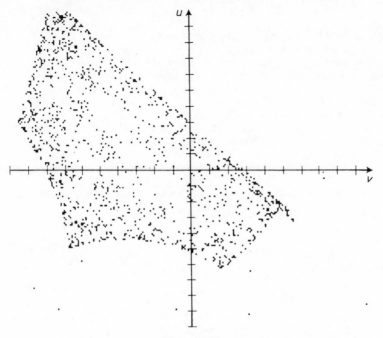

Figure 6.10

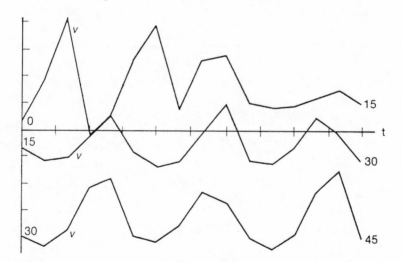

Figure 6.11

BIBLIOGRAPHY

Clark, J. M. (1923) *Studies in the Economics of Overhead Costs*, Chicago, IL: Chicago University Press.

Frisch, R. (1933) 'Propagation problems and impulse problems in dynamic economics', in K. Koch (ed.) *Economic Essays in Honour of Gustav Cassel*, London: Allen & Unwin.

Goodwin, R. M. (1951) 'The non-linear accelerator and the persistence of business cycles', *Econometrica* 19: 1–17.

—— (1967) 'A growth cycle', in C. H. Feinstein (ed.) *Socialism, Capitalism and Economic Growth*, essays presented to Maurice Dobb, Cambridge: Cambridge University Press, pp. 54–8.

—— (1990) *Chaotic Economic Dynamics*, Cambridge: Cambridge University Press.

Harrod, R. F. (1948) *Towards a Dynamic Economics*, London: Macmillan.

7

HICKS ON GENERAL EQUILIBRIUM AND STABILITY

Christopher Bliss

I THE GENERAL EQUILIBRIUM PROBLEM IN GENERAL

It is remarkable how the completion of the task of solving the general equilibrium problem, the great achievement of twentieth-century economic theory, has left many of those who achieved it dissatisfied. In their various ways, several leading general equilibrium theorists searched for something beyond establishing the coherence of the equilibrium concept and proving existence. Why is this?

Kenneth Arrow provides an interesting example which illustrates my point. He seems always to have seen general equilibrium as an idealized view of the market system, useful more for pointing to where real-life markets fail to realize the ideal than for describing reality. This orientation directed his attention to problems of information, market failure and missing markets. Yet Arrow never allowed his readers to think the formal existence problem, what one might call the mathematical issue, unimportant. Mathematical coherence is vital: but it must be the mathematical coherence of the right problem, or the right formalization of an endlessly rich and subtle reality.

Paul Samuelson's position is developed at length in his Ph.D. thesis, subsequently published as *Foundations of Economic Analysis* (Samuelson 1947). His argument may be summarized as follows. The conclusions of economic analysis take the form of comparative static theorems. However, equilibrium conditions, or market clearing conditions, alone do not lead to unambiguous comparative static conclusions. It is when we add the extra information that the system is stable in the region of the equilibrium that we get unambiguous comparative static results. Samuelson called this the *Correspondence Principle*. As he puts it succinctly: 'We find ourselves confronted with this paradox: in order for the comparative-statics analysis to yield fruitful results, we must first develop a theory of dynamics' (1947: 262–3).

The correspondence principle, as Samuelson well understood, is an incomplete answer to the general problem of obtaining definite economic theorems. We have an unambiguous correspondence principle result for the important special case where the solution of the economic system is equivalent to the maximization of a single objective function. In addition, several low-dimension models, where the solution is not equivalent to the maximization of a single objective function, are examined, notably a simple Keynesian model. For the general case there is no correspondence principle, because general stability does not imply anything for comparative statics.

What Samuelson did achieve – and here examples are sufficient to tell us everything – was to show how different dynamics may imply different comparative statics. He argues against Hicks's formulation of the stability condition for a multi-market system, showing the 'partial equilibrium' stability conditions examined by Hicks to be neither necessary nor sufficient for his own 'true dynamic' stability. I shall return to Hicks's discussion of stability below, since one of my main contributions in this paper, which like any review of a master's work must reach beyond reviewing what has already been achieved, is to examine the issue of general equilibrium stability from a new angle.

Kirman (1989) provides a modern and highly sophisticated statement of the view that general equilibrium theory is unsatisfactory. He draws on results of Sonnenschein and Debreu which roughly say that the information that certain demand and supply functions come from a well-behaved general equilibrium system – possibly with a continuum of agents – implies almost nothing beyond the fundamental properties of continuity, boundedness and Walras's law, the same properties which enable us to show existence via a fixed point theorem.

This conclusion is similar to the kind of refined unbelief at which a sophisticated theologian might arrive following years of study and meditation. An ontological God exists but, except for the knowledge that he (or she) exists, nothing else can be known of it. To put it more directly, the emptiness of general equilibrium theory has become a theorem of general equilibrium theory.

II THE EXISTENCE PROBLEM

That Hicks's knowledge of mathematics exceeded that of Walras did not rebound to his advantage when it came to the discussion of the existence problem. Walras perceived a serious problem for which he sought a *computational* solution. Hicks, on the other hand, had studied linear mathematics and convinced himself that equation and variable counting would take care of existence; and he was wrong. Equation and variable counting is not of much use at all for non-linear, non-negative prices, the canonical general equilibrium problem. Unfortunately, neither is the type of computational approach which Walras looked at. However, computation can be helpful (see Scarf 1967), but it is not computation that can be interpreted meaningfully as the market groping for an equilibrium.

What Hicks writes, when he comments on the work of Walras in *Value and Capital*, is most revealing of his view of the canonical general equilibrium problem:

> in spite of these merits, it is clear that many economists (perhaps most, even those who have studied Walras seriously) have felt in the end a certain sterility about his approach. It is true, they would say, that Walras does give one a picture of the whole system; but it is a very distant picture, and hardly amounts to more than an assurance that things will work themselves out somehow, though it is not very clear how they will work themselves out.
>
> (1939a: 60)

The modern general equilibrium theorists thought that they were doing rather more than giving 'a picture of the whole system'; they proved a deep mathematical existence result – equivalent to Brouwer's fixed point theorem. Hicks drew back from a strictly mathematical approach. One might say that *Value and Capital* does everything except prove existence. It shows how the individual agents, firms and households, maximize, how their budget constraints are determined and how profit distribution plays an essential role. In his overall vision Hicks is ahead of Walras, who was surely his starting point. Yet he has much less than an existence proof. Did he believe that equation and variable counting is all that is needed? It is odd how *Value and Capital*, which is sophisticated in many ways, becomes excessively informal at the point at which a mathematical dam buster is needed.

John von Neumann, whose reading in economics was haphazard, could not have appreciated how far ahead of most of his contemporaries was Hicks in his vision of how a general equilibrium system should be constructed. Equally he could not fail to appreciate what seemed to him staggeringly sloppy mathematics. Morgenstern (1976) reports him saying the following:

> You know, Oskar, if these books are unearthed sometime a few hundred years hence, people will not believe that they were written in our time. Rather they will think that they are contemporary with Newton, so primitive is their mathematics. Economics is simply still a million miles away from the state in which an advanced science is, such as physics.

In one respect Hicks and Walras are close together. They both lack a clear sense that there is a mathematical existence problem. They view the problem as one of writing out a set of equations that characterize the system and could be solved in principle. It is an engineer's standard approach (Walras was trained as an engineer). Asked whether a bridge would fall down in a high wind, the engineer does not typically ask whether the bridge exists, although showing that it could not stand even in no wind might be taken to imply that.

If the bridge is known to stand, the engineer may calculate the stresses in its members to help his understanding, but difficulties with those calculations will not bring down the bridge.

Similarly, Walras saw himself as looking for a solution for market prices which 'the market solves empirically'. He had a particular view of how the market could solve what is undoubtedly a complex problem. The idea that a process of 'groping' (*tâtonnement*) would guide the market to equilibrium is perhaps Walras's greatest contribution to economic theory. Indeed it is not unreasonable to ask whether groping is not itself the basis of an existence proof. If groping can only cease when an equilibrium has been found, a demonstration that groping must converge to a constant price vector would imply existence. Nothing comes of this idea, for reasons which I make precise below, but it is not too fanciful to imagine that Walras specially, and even Hicks, may have had a similar picture in their minds.

III COMPARATIVE STATICS

This is the area where Hicks's own contribution is most powerful and where at the time he was ahead of any other economist. His was the first ever examination of the comparative static issue in a general equilibrium context. Cournot and others had established the comparative statics method. They worked it, however, using small-scale or partial-equilibrium models. Yet formally the question of what happens to the fish market if there is a shift in favour of the demand for fish, and the question of what happens to the whole economy if there is a shift in favour of the demand for fish, share as formal problems more in common than separates them.

The general equilibrium comparative statics problem, it goes without saying, is more complex, from the mathematical point of view, than is a simple single market case. Hicks kept the connection clear by considering a process of successive relaxation of more prices (*Value and Capital*, 1939a: mathematical appendix to chs 16–17). Thus, to stay with the case of an increase in the demand for fish, we first hold all other prices constant and show how a rise in the price of fish will follow the increase in demand. This change will disrupt demand–supply equality in, generally, all other markets. Now allow one other price to adjust, say the price of chicken, conceived here as a close substitute for fish. If the demand increase for fish took the form of a shift in demand from goods in general towards fish, with only a small effect on the demand for any particular good, then the small decrease in the demand for chicken which was part of the general shift in demand will be swamped by the increase in the demand for chicken brought about by the substitution effect when the price of fish increases. Hence, when the price of chicken is allowed to rise, there is a further increase in the demand for fish and a consequent extra rise in its price. And so on.

Hicks solved this problem in terms of the sign patterns of Jacobian determinants, obtaining necessary conditions to keep what he called the 'substitutes for substitutes' problem under control. We can recognize the substitutes for substitutes problem as the opposite of *diagonal dominance* (see Arrow and Hahn 1971: 233), and Hicks's discussion is fully connected with the modern general equilibrium theory, the development of which greatly reflected his influence.

On one view Hicks's method, with which he examined comparative static changes as the outcome of a sequence of steps, is just an analytical device, but Hicks made much more of it. What started as a means of examining comparative static changes became the basis for one of Hicks's great ideas: *temporary equilibrium*. We meet the concept in Chapter X, which significantly locates itself, as French would put it, in Part IV of *Value and Capital*, the section entitled 'The working of the dynamic system'. A simple special case of an equilibrium is the equilibrium which every economy reaches, without necessarily finding the right prices, when prices which can adjust move so as to clear markets and agents somehow accommodate to the rationing or unsold excess supply which will characterize other markets, say by running down or adding to stocks.

This corresponds to the partial price adjustment exercises which Hicks developed for comparative statics. His great insight was to see that exactly similar principles operate for an intertemporal system with missing forward markets. This fitted beautifully into Hicks's overall vision according to which, just as with Samuelson, the way to understand statics is to examine dynamics. The comparative statics conditions which Hicks obtained depend on 'stability', defined by him in a special way to correspond to the same alternating sign conditions on the determinants of Jacobian matrices. It is special, admittedly, but a powerful approach.

IV THE STABILITY QUESTION

Walras's specification of the stability problem is found in Appendix I of Walras (1954). Confronting the problem of how to treat price of adjustment in a system of n interrelated markets, he tries to proceed with a partial equilibrium approach, which allows a diagrammatic treatment, but clearly perceives the fundamental problem for this method, that price changes in one market will disrupt, in general, equilibrium in all other markets. He proposes a daring solution to this difficulty:

> It is quite true that in determining the price of (C), we may destroy the equilibrium with respect to (B), that in determining the price of (D), we may destroy the equilibrium both with respect to (B) and with respect to (C), and so forth. But since the determination of the prices of (C), (D) ... will, on the whole, entail certain compensating effects on the relationship between the demand and offer of (B), in all probability

equilibrium will be approximated more and more closely at each successive step in the groping process.

(Walras 1954: 470)

This seems impossibly imprecise, but note two points. First, as remarked above, the convergence of groping and solving for general equilibrium are closely identified in this argument. Second, the argument makes its own difficulties clear: it is the effects of one market price on another market that create problems for the argument. This suggests that an assumption is being made and that it might be made precise, and such is indeed the case. The required assumption is again diagonal dominance, which defines one of the most important special cases which permit the definite stability results, with comparative statics, which general equilibrium reasoning usually denies us.

The stability method which Hicks adopted was a similar extension of his approach to comparative statics. It was based on the idea of successive freeing of prices. Yet the two cases are dissimilar. A simple shock, say an increase in the demand for fish again, is naturally asymmetric. It affects a particular market at first hand, after which its knock-on effects work themselves through other markets until, in a fully independent system, all markets are affected.

Hicks tried to treat stability similarly, but there is a fundamental difference. Stability is not naturally treated by an asymmetrical model. What Hicks did is to consider whether each market in turn will be stable in the sense that excess demand as a function of own price will be downward sloping *when all other prices are continuously adjusted so as to clear other markets*. In one sense there is nothing asymmetrical about this definition. If we require each market to satisfy the same condition, there can surely be no strict asymmetry involved. Yet by assuming implicitly that other prices adjust faster than the price in the market under consideration, we in effect treat each market asymmetrically when we treat it.

From a general point of view it looks, must be, is, quite special. Samuelson showed that the conditions involved were neither necessary nor sufficient for what he called *true dynamical stability*. This means that the simultaneous differential equations in prices defined by

$$\dot{p} = Ax^i(p) \qquad (7.1)$$

where p is a vector of prices, $\dot{p}$ is the vector of time rates of change of prices, $x(p)$ is the vector of excess demands for goods and A is a diagonal matrix of positive scalars which shows the responsiveness of prices in various markets to excess demands, should be stable in the usual sense. For simplicity of exposition, the issue of free goods is ignored here, which omission is corrected below.

This conclusion is bad for Hicks but not as unambiguously disappointing as it might at first seem. True, Samuelson's formulation is unquestionably symmetric and general. However, that is too general to give definite comparative static results. Hicks's approach is strictly equivalent to a partial equilibrium approach, as it corresponds to general equilibrium cases in which partial equilibrium analysis is valid, as McFadden (1968) shows, and with the special case there comes some usable comparative statics. This is much like another way of stating the emptiness of the general equilibrium analysis theorem discussed above.

V HOW DO UNSTABLE ECONOMIES BEHAVE?

Should a general equilibrium system be unstable, what will happen? Economists have sometimes written as if instability is equivalent to the state of the system charging away to a boundary, like a ball rolling to the edge of, and then off, a table. Where, however, the state of the general equilibrium system is characterized by a vector of non-negative prices normalized to lie in a simplex, that cannot happen. The price vector wanders in an enclosed and bounded space. It may arrive at the boundary of the simplex, when one or more prices take the value zero, but this is not of great significance. Even an equilibrium may be on the boundary. Like any bounded sequence, the values of an infinite sequence of normalized prices must have limit points.

Furthermore, if the differential equations that drive prices are mildly well behaved, the system can never revisit a point without repeatedly revisiting that point, and similarly revisiting a complete cycle which will include that point. Then prices would cycle indefinitely without approaching an equilibrium. We might even count such a cycle as a kind of equilibrium, because the system has ceased to wander; where wandering is counted as constantly visiting new points. Again, and obviously by extension, the system might have a set of limit points which constitute a cycle. One might even be tempted to call a system which eventually cycles, or which cycles in its limit points, *quasi-stable*, and boldly hypothesize that any general equilibrium system is quasi-stable.

This line would be quite mistaken, however. The behaviour of prices may well be *chaotic*. This would mean in an extreme case that every point in the simplex would be a limit point of some time path, and the economy would be quasi-stable only in the trivial sense that it would explore the simplex endlessly, always visiting new points and eventually approaching arbitrarily close to any given point. Obviously, the limit points might be a much more restricted set, and yet too full to count as a cycle in any useful sense.

If prices adjust according to a rule which does not keep prices in the simplex but respects the sign constraint that each price should be non-negative, then, because demands are homogeneous of degree one, the economy behaves as if prices were constantly renormalized to keep them in the simplex. Consider, for example, the values ε^i defined by

$$\varepsilon^i = \alpha^i x^i(p) \qquad \text{if } x^i(p) \geq 0 \text{ or } p^i > 0 \tag{7.2}$$

$$\varepsilon^i = 0 \qquad \text{otherwise.} \tag{7.3}$$

This is derived from (7.1) above, setting $A = I$, but also taking care of zero prices and excess supplies. The standard *tâtonnement* price adjustment rule may then be expressed in the form

$$\dot{p}^i = \varepsilon^i. \tag{7.4}$$

This rule does not hold the sum of the elements of p constant; i.e. does not keep p in the simplex. However, p remains a non-negative vector and as such has a *projection to the simplex* obtained by renormalizing its elements to sum to 1. This projection vector may then travel through the simplex, converging to point or cycle, or wandering chaotically.

The implication is that in some cases groping is a hopeless way of seeking out a general equilibrium. One might call this the dynamic analogue of the emptiness of general equilibrium theorem, which originated as a comparative statics result. Chaos undermines the fundamental idea that individual markets could 'know how to' look for equilibrium. One of the most basic and simplest ideas of economics, that raising prices in markets where there is excess demand and lowering them where there is excess supply, turns out not to work.

The conclusion is nihilistic and discouraging. Global planning mechanisms may find an equilibrium. Yet hardly anyone anymore believes in global planning: the ideal model of planning has become a market-mimicking decentralization, which would be subject to the same difficulties as the *tâtonnement*. General equilibrium theory ends by telling us that an equilibrium must exist, that it may be nearly impossible to find it and that no definite comparative statics results may constrain what happens when it is perturbed.

VI CONCLUDING REMARKS

John Hicks has often been seen as a pioneer of general equilibrium theory, as a man who showed the way down paths which others pursued further and to greater effect. There is some truth in this view. Hicks applied calculus and linear mathematics to a problem which needed topology for its root existence result, and non-linear differential equation theory for stability analysis. To that extent Hicks was a primitive pioneer whose methods were later superseded. Yet, by accident perhaps, one could hardly argue that it was the result of prophetic power, Hicks did most of the general equilibrium theory worth doing.

An exact existence proof would be an exception to that view. The existence theorem is important not just because it tells us that an equilibrium exists; more importantly *it shows us what we are assuming when we suppose that an equilibrium does exist*. It tells us, for instance, what we need to obtain continuous demand and supply functions. In this area Hicks left too much unanalysed. The calculus and linear mathematics was not enough to achieve what can usefully be done.

In every other respect what Hicks did is pretty much what we have. He treated general equilibrium as a kind of precisely worked partial equilibrium analysis, which looks terribly special, but is more or less what we have to assume to obtain definite results. The validity of partial equilibrium analysis and unambiguous partial equilibrium theory are one and the same, as Hicks showed and as fuller and more careful later analysis largely confirms. Stability of the general equilibrium market process, again, turns on the special, the very special, case. And what type of case that is Hicks had already made clear. We have it now more fully and richly displayed, with gross substitutability and diagonal dominance. Yet the basic ideas fall out of the pages of *Value and Capital*. Beyond that lie many results but the general equilibrium theory road soon gets rough and its path eventually chaotic.

BIBLIOGRAPHY

Arrow, A. J. and Hahn, F. H. (1971) *General Competitive Analysis*, Amsterdam: North-Holland.

Debreu, G. (1975) 'Excess demand functions', *Journal of Mathematical Economics* 1: 15–23.

Hahn, F. H. (1981) 'General equilibrium theory', in D. Bell and I. Kristol (eds) *The Crisis in Economic Theory*, New York: Basic Books.

———— (1990) 'John Hicks the theorist', *Economic Journal* 100: 528–38.

Kirman, A. (1989) 'The intrinsic limits of modern economic theory: the emperor has no clothes', *Economic Journal*, supplement, 99: 126–39.

Morgenstern, O. (1976) 'The collaboration between Oskar Morgenstern and John von Neumann on the theory of games', *Journal of Economic Literature* XIV (3): 805–16.

McFadden, D. (1968) 'On Hicksian Stability', in J. N. Wolfe (ed.) *Value, Capital and Growth: Papers in honour of Sir John Hicks*, Edinburgh: Edinburgh University Press.

Samuelson, P. A. (1947) *Foundations of Economic Analysis*, Cambridge: Harvard University Press.

Scarf, H. (1967) 'On the computation of equilibrium prices', in W. Fellner and C. A. Hall (eds) *Ten Economic Studies in the Tradition of Irving Fisher*, New York: Wiley.

Sonnenschein, H. (1972) 'Market excess demand functions', *Econometrica* 40: 549–63.

Walras, L. (1954) *Elements of Pure Economics*, trans. William Jaffe, London: Allen & Unwin.

8

HICKSIAN WELFARE ECONOMICS

John S. Chipman

INTRODUCTION

'Welfare economics', according to Hicks (1975c: 326), 'is itself a critique'. While I would not describe the subject this way, it is an apt description of the present chapter. I review Hicks's contributions to welfare economics under four main headings, corresponding to his four main contributions to the subject. Except for the second section, the titles correspond to those of Hicks's essays.

The first section, on the 'Foundations of welfare economics' (1939f), offers a critical examination of the compensation principle as the underpinning of the subject and suggests that some other approaches hinted at by Hicks might form a fruitful alternative, or at least a supplement, notably the abandonment of statics in favour of an intertemporal framework in which uncertainty plays a crucial role. The existing static models cannot distinguish between 'equality of opportunity' and 'equality of outcome', and therefore are incapable of addressing one of the most important policy issues of our time.

The second section takes as its title a combination of Hicks's 'Valuation of social income' (1940a) and 'Measurement of real income' (1958a) and Samuelson's 'Evaluation of real national income' (1950), namely 'Measurement of real national income'. Most of the discussion, however, is devoted to Hicks's last contribution to welfare economics, 'The scope and status of welfare economics' (1975c). Here I challenge Hicks's assumption that one can find support in Smith and Ricardo for a 'cost approach' in place of a 'utility approach' to the measurement of either welfare or productivity. To do this I enter a long digression on the history from Quesnay to Pigou of the concepts of wealth and productivity and attempts to measure them in accordance with a system of national accounting. I find that a frankly utilitarian approach to the measurement of welfare and productivity is unavoidable, and that it is high time that economists abandoned the perceived constraint that measures of welfare must necessarily be linear homogeneous functions. On the other hand I suggest that it may be possible to justify such linear price-weighted averages but only if empirically supported restrictions on the technology and individual preferences are explicitly taken into account.

The third section is a critique of Hicks's celebrated 'Rehabilitation of consumers' surplus' (1941b). Here I show in detail that the tool of consumers' surplus can be very treacherous and misleading, and that it is just as easy – in most cases, actually easier – to work with an exact welfare measure rather than an approximative one in order to evaluate the effects of alternative systems of excise taxes.

The fourth and final section takes as its title the revised (1981) version of Hicks's three papers in which he developed the concepts of compensating and equivalent variation, in their price as well as quantity versions, which he called 'the four consumer's surpluses' – except that I have moved the apostrophe so as to permit discussion of the conditions under which one may extend these binary measures of welfare change from the individual to the community. I come out as a champion of Hicks's equivalent variation as a universal measure of welfare or 'real social income', but under limited conditions and with stringent precautions as to its interpretation or possible misinterpretation.

1 THE FOUNDATIONS OF WELFARE ECONOMICS

In making his case for the scientific respectability of the 'new welfare economics' (1939f: 698), Hicks defined the problem in the following terms (p. 699):

> the subject-matter of our study is something which is defined relatively to its purpose. We are ... like archaeologists, comparing flint instruments made by man for a purpose, one of whose functions must be to compare the relative efficiency of these implements ...
>
> The task of examining the efficiency – in this sense – of any given economic organisation is thus one which we should like to regard as an integral part of economics.

Hicks at once admitted that there was a problem in defining a 'purpose', and therefore the concept of 'efficiency', in a society with heterogeneous individuals. He saw three possible approaches to this problem. Efficiency of one state of the economy relative to another could be defined as: (i) the degree to which the society attains objectives that the investigator considers good for it; (ii) an increase in some index obtained by aggregating individual welfares; or (iii) the possibility of Pareto improvement provided compensation payments are allowed for.

Hicks dismissed definition (i) as 'unscientific' and 'the way of the prophet and the social reformer, not of the economist' (p. 700); however, just as the archaeologist uses his or her own judgement as to whether a particular implement might be more or less conducive to the survival of its wielder – and this judgement might have empirical support and command wide agreement among archaeologists – so might an economic historian be entitled to pass judgement on the suitability of a nation's institutions to its long-run viability. The recent collapse of the Soviet Union and its neighbouring satellites could provide part of the historical evidence supporting a concept of efficiency formulated by the investigator.

Hicks likewise cast approach (ii) aside, having been thoroughly convinced by Robbins (1938) that the possibility of interpersonal comparisons of utility 'rested upon ethical principle rather than upon scientific demonstration' (p. 637), but parted with Robbins in his reluctance to invoke value judgements and make them explicit.

This left approach (iii), which he accepted from Kaldor (1939). Harrod (1938) and Robbins (1938) had both argued that the repeal of the Corn Laws could be justified only on the ground that the harm to the landlords would be outweighed by the benefit to the rest of the community; Kaldor (1939) instead argued that it was enough to show that the rest of the community *could* compensate the landlords out of their gains so as to leave them no worse off than before, and still enjoy a net benefit. It is interesting to note that such an argument had already been advanced by John Stuart Mill more than a century earlier (1825: 400–1). First Mill distinguished between the redistributive effect of the Corn Laws and the deadweight loss:

> That corn which could be obtained abroad, in exchange for the produce of the labour of 100 men, is compelled to be produced at home, by that of 120, 130, or 140; the labour of 20, 30, or 40 men in every 100 is expended in pure waste, and all which they might have produced is entirely lost to the community. The consumer is taxed, not only to give a higher rent to the landlord, but to indemnify the farmer for producing, at a great expense, that corn which might be obtained from abroad at a comparatively small one.

He went on to formulate the compensation principle:

> If the landlords were to require, that the whole people of Great Britain should contribute a certain sum annually in direct taxes for their benefit, who is there that would not raise his voice against so impudent a demand? Yet this would surely be a much more modest request, than that, in order to put a certain annual number of pounds sterling into their pockets, the people of Great Britain should consent to pay three, four, or five times as many.
>
> We seriously purpose, therefore, as a great improvement on the present system, that this indirect tax should be commuted for a direct one; which, if it still gave an undue advantage to the landlords, would, at least, give them this advantage at a smaller cost to the public: or that the landlords should make an estimate of their probable losses from the

repeal of the Corn Laws, and found upon it a claim to compensation. Some, indeed, may question how far they who, for their own emolument, imposed one of the worst taxes upon their countrymen, are entitled to compensation for renouncing advantages which they never ought to have enjoyed. It would be better, however, to have a repeal of the Corn Laws, even clogged by a compensation, than not to have it at all; and if this were our only alternative, no one could complain of a change, by which, though an enormous amount of evil would be prevented, no one would lose.

Unfortunately this line of argument did not reappear in Mill's *Principles*, which contained only the reasoning that free trade would make available 'a more ample supply of the commodities it wants, for the same labour and capital; or the same supply, for less labour and capital, leaving the surplus disposable to produce other things' (1848: vol. II, book III, ch. XVII, §4, p. 116).

Mill went on (1826: 374n) to propose a measure of the consumer's loss:[1]

The annual consumption of wheat in this country is estimated at fourteen or fifteen millions of quarters. The rise occasioned by our Corn Laws in the average price is shown ... to be about 10s. per quarter, viz. from 50s. to 60s. The Corn Laws are, therefore, equivalent to a tax of seven millions, or seven millions and a half, upon the consumer.

Mill did not specify his units in the last sentence, but it may be assumed that they were pounds sterling (20 shillings); thus, rather inexplicably, Mill implicitly assumed that demand was perfectly inelastic. Subject to this blemish, however, Mill's measure was the same as Marshall's subsequent measure of gross loss of consumers' surplus; but under these assumptions the 'revenues' from this 'tax' (i.e. the gains of the landlords) would be exactly the same as the gross loss of consumers' surplus, and there would be no net loss of revenue to the community – contrary to Mill's claim. Mill therefore came very close to but fell short of developing an accurate quantitative underpinning to his compensation argument.

The compensation principle was developed by Pareto (1894) and Barone (1908), but it seems clear that they got the idea from Marshall (1890). The principle was quite explicit in Dupuit (1844); Hotelling (1938) was presumably influenced by both Dupuit and Marshall. Kaldor (1939) presented the compensation principle as an original idea; while he may have been influenced by the 1935 English translation of Barone (1908), Bergson (1938: 329) – who analysed Pareto's and Barone's arguments – apparently did not notice that they were based on the compensation principle. It is thus quite strange that an idea that was independently rediscovered many times was also quickly forgotten – until Hicks (1939f) seized upon Kaldor's idea and made it the central principle of the 'new welfare economics'.

The distinctive feature of the Kaldor–Hicks approach was that the mere possibility of Pareto improvement if compensation is paid was enough to qualify a policy as 'sound', even if compensation was not actually paid. It is what Samuelson (1947: 250–1) characterized as the ''twere better' principle. The difficulties in Hicks's argument are apparent in the following passage (1939f: 711–12):

> I do not contend that there is any ground for saying that compensation ought always to be given; whether or not compensation should be given in any particular case is a question of distribution, upon which there cannot be identity of interest, and so there cannot be any generally acceptable principle. This being so, it will often happen in some particular case that the economist will find himself not at all anxious for compensation to be given; but his personal feeling in that direction will be based either upon the non-economic ground that the persons damaged do not deserve much consideration, or upon the only quasi-economic ground that the loss inflicted on them is nothing but the materialisation of a risk they may be expected to have allowed for. Nevertheless we must expect that there will be many other cases where the redistribution, resulting from a sound measure carried through without compensation, would be regarded by him as deplorable; and then, if he considers the measure in isolation from the question of compensation, he will pay no more than lip-service to its productive efficiency, and probably reject it in practice. From this it is only a step to the state of mind which judges measures solely by reference to their distributive justice, without reference to their bearing on efficiency. If measures making for efficiency are to have a fair chance, it is extremely desirable that they should be freed from distributive complications as much as possible.

It seems to me that this argument is quite insufficient to justify 'sound' measures, and that additional considerations must be introduced. It seems to state that a succession of measures to improve efficiency could constitute 'sound' policy even if each one should reduce aggregate welfare from a utilitarian point of view. I shall consider the problem from two standpoints: (i) that of long-run dynamics; and (ii) that of behaviour under risk.

From the long-run point of view, a very interesting argument was presented by Senior (1828: Lecture II). Senior observed that the public favoured technological improvements even though these caused hardships to some groups, yet it resisted the movement to free trade which was no different in principle from technological improvement. He defended both on the following grounds (pp. 58–9):

> In this case, as in the last, there will be partial individual suffering, as well as partial individual benefit. In both cases, besides the partial

suffering and the partial benefit, is the general benefit to the whole community. A benefit which will be permanent, while both the gain and the loss to peculiar classes of producers will pass away.

That is, while either technological change or trade liberalization will have positive and negative effects on factors in inelastic supply, once the present generation is replaced by a new one whose members are not bound to a single occupation, all will gain. And this gain, according to Senior, will be permanent, available to all future generations. If we can accept this as a correct empirical assessment of the effects of trade liberalization, then from a utilitarian point of view the proper way to pose the issue is not to compare the current hardships simply with the current benefits, but the current hardships with the present and future benefits. When the prosperity of all future generations is weighed in the balance against the hardship of only certain members of the current generation, the proposed change will be reckoned as beneficial by a much wider class of utilitarian value judgements than when only the current generation is considered. Of course, an inter-temporal compensationist argument could also be invoked; the government will be justified in incurring a budget deficit to compensate those harmed by a measure that increases economic efficiency, since future generations can amortize the debt out of the efficiency gains.

Unfortunately, however, the presumption made by Senior need not be valid. From the point of view of modern trade theory, a fall in real wages that might result from trade liberalization (via the 1942 Stolper–Samuelson theorem) would be permanent if factor endowments remained unchanged, and (because of the factor-price equalization theorem) would not necessarily be alleviated by a fall in population (including emigration) unless this fall were sufficient to cause the country to give up production of the import-competing good and specialize in the export good. In the many-commodity–many-factor version of the Samuelson theory (1953), if at the initial factor endowments real wages were to become permanently lowered for some types of unskilled labour, a solution would be for the successors of the unskilled workers to acquire the skills needed to maintain real wages at their previous level, and either for the country to cease production of goods that use unskilled labour relatively intensively, or for labour-saving machinery to replace the unskilled labour in these industries. In either case the efficiency gains would have to be sufficient to finance the training costs and the research and development. Formally, therefore, in order to make the case for unrestricted (and uncompensated) free trade in an intertemporal framework, one would need to take account of long-run changes in the country's technology and factor endowments that could be expected to be brought about by trade liberalization, or that would be required in order to permit long-run Pareto improvement.

The second argument, regarding risk, was hinted at by Hicks in the above passage as well as in an interesting footnote (1939f: 711n). Senior also had something interesting to say along these lines (1828: 60–1):

> I am aware ... that in the existing state of knowledge and feeling in this country, any attempt to apply at once to foreign commerce the principles on which we act, and that as a matter of course, in our internal trade, would be unsuccessful. We have been accustomed in our internal trade to see every improvement accompanied by individual suffering, but we have also been accustomed to consider the general benefit as over-balancing the partial injury, and at once to stifle complaints by replying, "these are the ordinary chances of trade; when your manufacture was introduced you injured somebody else, and if we were to prohibit or restrict whatever interferes with existing interests, we must remain stationary forever."
>
> Unfortunately the prejudices of the mercantile theory have prevented the application of this reasoning to foreign commerce.

It might be argued that wages tend to be higher in 'progressive' industries – i.e. industries subject to substantial technological improvement – than in more stationary industries, to allow for the greater risk of unemployment in the former. It is well known that land that is subject to floods or other natural disasters is cheaper than land with little risk, the difference reflecting the risk premium; those who knowingly purchase such land already receive their compensation. Government policies to assist victims of such disasters, if known to be habitual, could be expected to reduce the risk premium and increase the value of such land. Likewise, comprehensive unemployment insurance could be expected to reduce wage differentials between progressive and stationary industries. In Senior's case, it may be argued that workers had become accustomed to the riskiness of industrial employment and took this risk into account when choosing their occupation; but that they had reason to believe that protectionist policies would remain in force, with the result that there was no risk premium in wages in import-competing industries to compensate them for injuries they would sustain if free trade were introduced. In such cases it is misleading to reason only on the basis of final outcomes. For example, an egalitarian who reasoned on such a basis would find it necessary to advocate that the winners at the roulette table should be required to compensate the losers; but this would be equivalent to outlawing gambling, even though it is a voluntary activity.

Hicks (1939f) threw out a number of interesting suggestions concerning the relevance of expectations to the problems of welfare economics. If welfare economics is to make any important advances in the future, it is undoubtedly by pursuing these suggestions and squarely formulating the problem as one of behaviour in risk-taking situations.

2 THE MEASUREMENT OF REAL NATIONAL INCOME

When we speak of the measurement of temperature we understand the relationship between two quite distinct physical phenomena: (1) the feeling of relative hotness or coldness as between different states of the environment, and (2) the height of a column of mercury in a thermometer. The latter is a measure of the former in the sense that the transitive and total relation 'feels at least as hot as', as applied to two states of the environment, is accurately represented by the numerical relation 'is greater than or equal to' implied by the magnitude recorded by the thermometer, so that if $f(x^t)$ is the recorded temperature of the state x^t, then $f(x^2) \geqslant f(x^1)$ if and only if (other things, such as humidity and wind velocity, being equal) state x^2 feels at least as hot as state x^1.

In his seminal paper on the subject, Hicks (1940a: 107–8) stated: 'Professor Pigou is only the leading representative of a long line of economists who have sought in the Social Income an index of economic welfare, of the wealth of nations. We have little choice but to follow in this tradition.' Starting with the case of a single individual, he proceeded to seek in the concept 'social income' a measure of welfare in a more limited sense; not one such that $f(x^2) \geqslant f(x^1)$ if and only if the commodity bundle x^2 is preferred or indifferent to the bundle x^1 (only a utility function would qualify for this task), but one such that, for at least a subset of pairs (x^1, x^2) of bundles, $f(x^2) \geqslant f(x^1)$ implies that x^2 is preferred or indifferent to x^1 (but not necessarily conversely). Following Pigou, he noted that if the bundle of commodities x^t is purchased at prices p^t, and $p^2x^2 \geqslant p^2x^1$, then we are entitled to infer that x^2 is preferred or indifferent to x^1, provided that tastes have not changed between time 1 and time 2 and that commodities omitted from the bundles x^t do not affect preferences. In general, defining the function $f^t(x) = p^tx$, where p^t is the price vector at which the bundle x^t is purchased, we can conclude that for all x such that $f^t(x^t) = p^tx^t \geqslant p^tx = f^t(x)$, it follows that x^t is preferred or indifferent to x.

This choice of function f^t allows only a limited number of comparisons, namely between bundles chosen at prices p^t, i.e. bundles along the Engel curve (income-expansion path) defined by p^t, and bundles cheaper at those prices than the one chosen. To obtain a total ordering of all conceivable bundles one would clearly require a continuum of price vectors p^t. Thus, 'social income', if this term is meant to refer to p^tx, can qualify as a 'measure' only in a very limited sense. And a measure of what? For Pigou (1920: 69–70), the terms 'real income' and 'national dividend' denoted the commodity bundle x itself, or, more generally, an $n \times m$ matrix $X = [x_{ij}]$ of allocations of n commodities among m individuals, where x_{ij} is the amount of commodity j allocated to individual i. Pigou ranked these allocations X according to the relative 'amount of economic satisfaction' enjoyed by a 'representative member of the group' (p. 70). He then considered the problem of devising a measure of this change in satisfaction. If we ignore for a moment the problem of the 'representative member of the group', we can see that the mathematical problem Pigou posed was simply the integrability problem: how to construct a utility function from data on prices and purchases. What Pigou proposed instead was the double criterion $p^2x^2 \geqslant p^2x^1$ and $p^1x^2 \geqslant p^1x^1$ as a partial way of solving the problem. But in his words (p. 74), 'the condition we have laid down does not determine the choice of a measure, but merely fixes the limits within which that choice must lie'. Obviously, such a choice can only be a utility function.

With Hicks, Pigou's concepts underwent a subtle but significant transformation. The term 'social income' refers not to a vector x or matrix X, but to the numerical magnitude $f^t(x) = p^tx$ (where x is the aggregate bundle, i.e. the vector of column sums of X), i.e. to an element of the *range* rather than of the *domain* of the function f^t, and this function is described as 'an index of economic welfare, of the wealth of nations'. If we define X^2RX^1 by $x_i^2R_ix_i^1$, for $i = 1, \ldots, m$ (where x_i^t is the ith row of X^t and R_i means 'is preferred or indifferent to by individual i'), then a homogeneous linear function $f^t(x) = p^tx$ (or perhaps a finite or even infinite set of these) is proposed as an index to represent the above partial ordering among the Xs. This is what Hicks described as 'social income as an index of economic welfare' (1940a: 119). The ordered set $\langle \mathfrak{X}, R \rangle$ consisting of allocations $X \in \mathfrak{X}$ ordered by R, i.e. the domain of f^t, appears to be what Hicks has in mind by the term 'real social income' – a term which seems to be used synonymously with 'welfare'. Thus, in his terminology (although he never juxtaposed the two terms in this way) 'social income' is a 'measure' or 'index' of 'real social income' – a particularly confusing use of words given that nowadays the phrase 'real national income' is universally used to mean what Hicks meant by 'social income' but not 'real social income'. Hicks also used the 'social income' to measure 'production' or 'productivity'; thus, if the domain of f^t is now a set of aggregate quantity vectors x ordered by the usual vector inequality, a function $f^t(x) = p^tx$ is called by Hicks 'the social income as a measure of productivity' (p. 122); more generally, Hicks defined a productivity index over production-possibility sets.

Hicks's principal advance over Pigou was his use of the compensation principle to dispense with the concept of a representative member of the group. He observed (1940: 111) that if $p^2x^2 > p^2x^1$, where x^2 is the column sum of a matrix X^2 whose rows x_i^2 are purchased at prices p^2, then there exists a Pareto-optimal allocation X^1 of x^1 (i.e. an allocation matrix X^1 whose column sums are equal to x^1) such that X^2PX^1 (where P denotes the strict Pareto ordering 'X^2RX^1 and not X^1RX^2'), and hence that there is no allocation X of x^1 such that XRX^2, the latter being Hicks's criterion for an increase in 'real social income'. It will not be necessary (or possible) here to survey the ensuing controversies (covered in Chipman and Moore 1978); it will suffice to mention (i) Kuznets's 1948 critique showing that two situations might each be deemed superior to the other by Hicks's criterion; (ii) Samuelson's masterful 1950 critique showing, among other things, that the inequality $p^2x^2 > p^2x^1$ could occur even though the consumption-possibility set in situation 1 completely contains that of situation 2 (see Chipman and Moore 1978: 563); (iii) Samuelson's assertion (1950: 2) that his 'weak axiom of revealed preference',

$$p^2x^2 > p^2x^1 \quad \text{implies} \quad p^1x^1 < p^1x^2$$

could be shown by examples to be violated for a community, followed by a specific example in Chipman and Moore (1978: 565) in which both inequalities $p^2x^2 > p^2x^1$ and $p^1x^1 > p^1x^2$ could be observed as equilibria; (iv) Gorman's (1955) example, followed by one by Hicks (1956a) himself and a detailed one in Chipman and Moore (1978: 566–7), of intransitivity in this relationship; and finally, (v) the demonstration in Chipman and Moore (1973), re-exposited in Chipman and Moore (1976), that in order for the equilibrium observations

$$p^2x^2 \geqslant p^2x^1 \quad \text{and} \quad p^1x^2 \geqslant p^1x^1$$

to imply that for all allocations of X^1 of x^1 there exists an allocation X^2 of x^2 such that X^2RX^1, it is necessary and sufficient that individual preferences be identical and homothetic. Thus, the subject was brought all the way back to where Pigou had left it; one had to deal after all with a 'representative member of the group'.

Hicks responded to the critical onslaught with a 'revision' (1958a). This time he provided a definition of 'real social income', namely that it 'is made up of flows of different sorts of goods and services' (p. 127); but instead of specifying an ordering among these flows to be represented by an order-preserving index or measure, he stated: 'any method of measuring it implies a rule for establishing an equivalence between goods of different kinds. The simplest rule of equivalence is equivalence of market price....' But this assumes that the 'measure' is necessarily a linear homogeneous function of aggregate quantities. Earlier (p. 126), Hicks stated that 'we have no choice about that', evidently meaning that no government in the future can ever be persuaded to construct an index of 'real national income' that is a nonlinear function of outputs – which does seem an excessively pessimistic assessment. Hicks went on to outline how under the assumption of 'integrated wants' – evidently meaning the existence of a total, transitive ordering of allocations of the Bergson type – it would be possible to define a social utility function with aggregate outputs as arguments.[2] Having understood so well the possibility of constructing a rational index of 'real social income' in this way, Hicks promptly proceeded to demolish the idea (p. 129):

> The arguments which have been advanced against this notion are familiar; it is unnecessary, at this time of day, to go into them in detail.

In the form in which the question of measurable utility arises in this place, it is completely disposed of by the classic demonstration of Pareto: that the ordering of the sets, which is all that is required by the Integration assumption, does not suffice to determine a single Utility function.... The single 'product', utility, is a mere construct; it is inadequately defined to be an object of measurement. The idea of measuring utility, or welfare, as such, is a blind alley.

The type of thinking shown in this passage occurs throughout Hicks's work; at the risk of seeming irreverent I shall call it the 'great Hicksian hangup' (GHH). Presumably any monotone increasing transformation of either the Fahrenheit or Celsius scale would serve equally well for the purpose of indicating the subjective level of heat, yet these are not reasons for disposing of them. Just because measurability of utility is not needed for the purpose of explaining consumer market behaviour, this does not imply that it might not be useful in measuring welfare. What is most astonishing of all about the passage is that it leads one to infer that Hicks was unaware that the Equivalent Variation of which he was the originator is itself an admirable measurable (indirect) utility index.

Hicks went on to argue, most plausibly, 'that there may be some of these measures which are more interesting and appropriate than others' (p. 130). But then he went on:

But these measures ... are not reckoned in terms of utility; they are reckoned in terms of physical commodities, or combinations of commodities. They are not measures of Utility; they are measures of Real Income.

But what on earth is utility a function of if not 'combinations of commodities'? This appears to be a huge quibble. It is all right to have a measure of 'real income' (ordered combinations of commodities), but we are not allowed to call it 'utility'. In fact, however, Hicks went on to develop several measures, similar to his compensating and equivalent variations but expressed as ratios rather than differences, and which he even described as 'utility indices' (pp. 145ff.) – the terminology apparently being permissible since there were more than one of them. Except for the unfortunate expression 'perverse case' (p. 154) to describe the case in which preferences were not identical and homothetic, Hicks's ensuing discussion moved the subject in a promising direction by stressing the need to take account of empirical uniformities in choosing appropriate welfare measures.

In his final contribution to welfare economics, Hicks (1975c) reverted to an idea he had begun to develop in the second part of his 1940 paper: the 'cost approach' as opposed to the 'utility approach' to measuring the real national income. He asked the interesting question: on what basis could Adam Smith and his successors have aggregated different products together in order to define 'the wealth of nations', given that 'they had none of our modern apparatus of Social Accounting at their disposal' (p. 313)? He concluded, quite logically, that it was the labour theory of value. Thus, the way to salvage the theory of measurement of real national income was to formulate it in terms of costs instead of market prices, with emphasis on the national product rather than on economic welfare. He argued that this is in fact how social accounting is actually used (p. 314):

> In the uses which we make of Social Accounting, we are implicitly relying on Ricardo's simplification; we take it for granted in our thinking, though if it were presented to us explicitly, we would certainly reject it. We do not talk about homogeneous labour, but we still think in terms of homogeneous 'resources'. When we propose, by budgetary policy or otherwise, to transfer a part of the National Income from one class to another, or from private to public purposes – and when we think that we can calculate the effect of the transfer just by doing sums – we are in fact thinking in labour theory terms. It is a fraction of the 'homogeneous resources' of the economy that we are proposing to transfer. So we are still, in much of our applied economics, being crypto-Ricardian.

This point is certainly well taken. He then went on to assess the contribution of Pigou (1920; 1932):

> Having ... restored the Classical approach, we can look upon Pigou's ... with different eyes. Pigou was concerned with Production and Distribution, just like the Classics; where he differed from them was that his method of valuation was different. Instead of valuing by cost, he valued by utility – marginal utility. To some extent this was an improvement, but only to some extent. He was less dependent upon factor substitutability, and that was a gain ... But he paid for it by the troubles about inter-personal comparisons ... He also paid for it in other ways. He was obliged to limit the applicability of his analysis ... to that part of the Social Product which is sold to final consumers ... The public sector, and the investment sector, which on the Cost method give no particular trouble, are not at all well handled by the method of Pigou.

There are a number of difficulties with this argument, however. In the first place, in a closed Ricardian economy with competitive markets, marginal utilities are necessarily proportional to labour–output ratios, so the two methods of valuation give exactly the same result. If markets are imperfect, then even if the cost method could be shown to be superior, it would be impractical since data on costs would not be readily available. If markets are perfect but the economy is open and specializing in some products which it exports, Hicks's method would be to use pre-trade rather than post-trade prices; even supposing that data on pre-trade prices were available, this would imply that a country's national product would not increase as a result of a movement from autarky to free trade, even though from standard arguments (cf. Samuelson 1939) such a movement would make possible (with compensation) an improvement in everybody's welfare. Indeed it seems arbitrary not to allow trade itself to be considered as a form of production, with exports as input and imports as output; after all, opportunity costs are costs. As for public expenditures, one can certainly appeal to the 'benefit principle'; and the valuation of investment has been shown by contemporary growth theory to be handled in a perfectly satisfactory way, at least in principle, by means of the Hamiltonian of the optimal-growth problem.

There is, however, a still more fundamental objection to the 'cost approach': it provides no criterion as to which commodities should be included in the national product, and which should be excluded. The physiocrats – whose founder, Quesnay, in fact introduced social accounting to economics in his *Tableau économique* (1764) (cf. Molinier 1958) – excluded all commodities from the national product except agricultural and mineral products. Quesnay recognized that manufacturing added value to the unfinished product, as shown by the price differential (and his method of valuation was based on market prices[3]); but, given his demographic assumption that population would expand or contract so as to keep real wages at the subsistence level – an assumption that was fairly realistic at the time[4] – he argued that this value added was only enough to cover the worker's subsistence.[5] For him the national product represented only the surplus above subsistence, which could come only from rent. Quesnay's mistake was to include the incomes of farm workers, which were presumably also at the subsistence level. Except for this inconsistency, his was a perfectly logical system of national accounting.

Adam Smith (1776; 1786: book IV, ch. IX), who provided a very fine summary of the physiocratic theory, tried to refute its contention that artificers, manufacturers and merchants were 'barren and unproductive' (his translation of *'stérile'*), although agreeing with the physiocrats that menial servants were barren and unproductive (p. 305):

> It seems ... altogether improper to consider artificers, manufacturers, and merchants in the same light as menial servants. The labour of menial servants does not continue the existence of the fund which maintains and employs them. Their maintenance and employment is altogether at the expense of their masters, and the work which they perform is not of a nature to repay that expense. That work consists in services which perish generally in the very instance of their performance, and does not fix or realise itself in any vendible commodity which can replace the value of their wages and maintenance. The labour, on the contrary, of artificers, manufacturers, and merchants, naturally does fix and realise itself in some such vendible commodity. It is upon this

account that ... I have classed artificers, manufacturers, and merchants, among the productive labourers, and menial servants among the barren or unproductive.

In terminology remarkably similar to Hicks's 'real social product' he elaborated by explaining that when the artificer (craftsman) produces his wares and consumes 'corn or other necessaries' to the same value, both are added 'to the real revenue, to the real value of the annual produce of the land and labour of the society', whereas if the 'corn or other necessaries' are instead consumed by a soldier or menial servant, the addition to the social product is only half as much. Carrying his criterion to its logical conclusion Smith stated (book II, ch. III, p. 146) that

> The labour of some of the most respected orders in the society is, like that of menial servants, unproductive of any value, and does not fix or realise itself in any permanent subject or vendible commodity which endures after that labour is past, and for which an equal quantity of labour could afterwards be procured.

Hence, the activities of 'churchmen, lawyers, physicians, men of letters of all kinds [including presumably Smith himself!]; players, buffoons, musicians, opera-singers, opera-dancers, &c' are excluded from the national product on the ground that 'the work of all of them perishes in the very instant of its production'. His concept of production, to some extent similar to that of the physiocrats, was a physical rather than economic one. Like the physiocrats, he pursued a 'value-in-exchange approach' rather than a 'cost approach' to valuation of the elements of the national product. However, in his emphasis on physical durability of the product he betrayed the continuing influence of his *bêtes noires*, the mercantilists, and his approach constituted even a retrogression from the ideas of the physiocrats.[6]

It remained for Jean-Baptiste Say (1814: I, book I, ch. I) to provide a properly *economic* concept of production (p. 3):[7]

> This faculty of certain things to satisfy various human wants, let me call *utility*.
>
> I would say that to create objects that have any kind of utility is to create wealth, since the utility of these things is the principal foundation of their value, and their value is wealth.
>
> But one does not create objects: the mass of materials of which the world is composed cannot increase or decrease. All we can do is to reproduce these materials in another form which makes them suitable for some use that they did not have, or merely to increase the utility they could have. There is then creation, not of matter, but of utility; there is *production*.

Say went on to ask (p. 4) how one could measure this 'degree of utility', and settled on what Smith had called 'value in exchange', or price (in terms of money).

Malthus (1798: 329) stated quite simply that 'it is with some view to the real utility of the produce, that we ought to estimate the productiveness, or unproductiveness of different sorts of labour'. However, he subsequently (1820: 27–8), after sympathetically considering the physiocratic view, accepted Smith's position:

> If we wish to attain any thing like precision in our inquiries, when we treat of wealth, we must narrow the field of inquiry, and draw some line, which will leave us only those objects, the increase or decrease of which is capable of being estimated with more accuracy.
>
> The line, which it seems most natural to draw, is that which separates material from immaterial objects, or those which are capable of accumulation and definite valuation, from those which rarely admit of these processes, and never in such a degree as to afford useful practical conclusions.... I should define wealth to be, those *material* objects which are necessary, useful, or agreeable to mankind.... It may fairly, therefore, I think, be said, that the wealth spoken of, in the science of political economy, is confined to material objects.

This met with Ricardo's approval (1820: 14–15):

> M. Say objects to this division, but I think there is real use in dividing our enquiries about those material objects which are capable of accumulation, and definite valuation, from those which rarely admit of such processes. Mr. Malthus' definition of wealth has in it nothing objectionable; he states it to be those material objects, which are necessary, useful, or agreeable, to mankind.

In this we see that, from the last sentence quoted, Ricardo in principle followed what Hicks would have called a 'utility approach' rather than a 'cost approach' to the selection of items to be included in the national product, but for practical reasons excluded immaterial objects from the national product on the ground that a 'definite valuation' could not be found for them. Why the market price could not be accepted as providing a 'definite valuation' is not entirely clear; presumably it was considered too erratic, being determined by fluctuations in demand and supply. For these services, the labour theory of value presumably did not apply. Had he had a clear conception of marginal utility, he might perhaps have been willing to include services in the national product. As it was, he was willing to include in the national product only those objects that conformed to the labour theory of value. He made this quite clear in the *Principles* (1817: 3):

> In speaking then of commodities, of their exchangeable value, and of the laws which regulate their relative prices, we mean always such

commodities only as can be increased in quantity by the exertion of human industry, and on the production of which competition operates without restraint.

If this be what should be understood by the 'cost approach', it entails excluding from the national product a wide class of commodities whose production costs cannot easily be ascertained.

The French translator of Smith's *Wealth of Nations*, Germain Garnier (1802: vol. V, note XX, p. 173), remarked upon the anomaly that in Smith's system the making of musical instruments was productive but the playing of them was not. Malthus nevertheless defended Smith against this criticism on the ground that the usefulness of the distinction between material and immaterial objects 'is immediately obvious from the facility of giving a definite valuation to the instruments, and the absolute impossibility of giving such a valuation to all the tunes which may be played upon them' (1820: 46). Ricardo's silence on this passage in his *Notes* (1820) may be interpreted as agreement.

John Stuart Mill (1848: book I, ch. III) started out by endorsing Say's notion of production (§1, p. 56):

> Though we cannot create matter, we can cause it to assume properties, by which from having been useless to us it becomes useful. What we produce, or desire to produce, is always, as M. Say rightly terms it, an utility. Labour is not creative of objects, but of utilities.

However, he went on to fall back on Smith's notion of production (§1, p. 57):

> the question which now occupies us could not have been a question at all, if the production of utility were enough to satisfy the notion which mankind have usually formed of productive labour. Production, and productive, are of course elliptical expressions, involving the idea of a something produced, but this something, in common apprehension, I conceive to be, not utility, but Wealth.

He then went on to say (§3, p. 59) that 'it is essential to the idea of wealth to be susceptible of accumulation', hence 'we should regard all labour as productive which is employed in creating permanent utilities ...'. Services are then excluded (p. 62):

> When a tailor makes a coat and sells it, there is a transfer of the price from the customer to the tailor, and a coat besides which did not previously exist; but what is gained by an actor is a mere transfer from the spectator's funds to his, leaving no article of wealth for the spectator's indemnification.... A community, however, may add to its wealth by unproductive labour, at the expense of other communities, ...

and he gave as examples 'the gains of Italian opera singers, German

111

governesses, French ballet dancers, &c.' which add to the wealth of their respective countries and, by implication, drain Britain of its wealth. One cannot avoid suspecting the lingering influence of mercantilist thought as an explanation of the exclusion of services from the national product on the part of Smith, Ricardo, Malthus and Mill.[8] Yet, in view of the association made by Malthus and approved by Ricardo between a product's non-durability and the impossibility of assigning a cost to it, the exclusion of services from the national product seems a reasonable if not inevitable consequence of adopting a 'cost approach' in place of a 'utility approach' to the measurement of real national income. In any case, as we shall see, it has been a historical consequence.

An interesting alternative (or supplementary) explanation was provided by Cannan (1893: ch. I, pp. 11ff.), who observed that the common meaning of 'wealth' at the time was (as it is today) a stock of assets rather than a flow of income, whereas the British classical economists were under the strong influence of the French physiocrats whose concept of wealth (*richesses*), also translated as 'riches', was that of a flow. While it is true that the term 'wealth' is used most frequently by Quesnay in this sense, one can also find passages where wealth can be interpreted as a stock, and his phrase *richesses annuelles* (annual wealth) suggests that he was not unaware of the distinction.[9]

Turgot's work *Reflections on the Formation and Distribution of Wealth* (1766), which apparently greatly influenced Smith (cf. Lundberg 1964),[10] at first employed the term 'wealth' in a way in which the flow interpretation is the only reasonable one (1769: 11, §VII, pp. 24–5; 1889: §VII, p. 53):

> As soon as the husbandman's work produces an excess over his needs, he can, with this surplus which nature accords him as a pure gift over and above the wages he receives for his pains, purchase the work of other members of society. The latter by selling to him gain only their livelihood; but the husbandman garners, in addition to his subsistence, an independent and disposable wealth, which he has not bought and which he sells. He is therefore the unique source of wealth which by its circulation animates all the work of society, because he is the only one whose work produces more than the wages of his work.

And as Böhm-Bawerk (1889: 24–5) pointed out, Turgot (1766) was the first economic writer to explicitly define capital (1769: 12, §LIX, p. 71; 1889: §LVIII, p. 98):

> Whoever ... receives each year more valuables [*valeurs*] than he has a need to consume [*dépenser*], can lay aside this excess and accumulate it: these accumulated valuables [*valeurs accumulées*] are called *capital*.

Towards the end of his essay, however, Turgot employed the term 'wealth' as a stock. First, he defined what may perhaps best be translated as a 'rate of capitalization' or 'number of years' purchase',[11] being the reciprocal of the rate of return, or yield, or 'own-rate of interest' (1769: 12, §LVIII, p. 70; 1889: §LVII, p. 97):

> The current price of land is thus regulated by the ratio of the value of the estate to its income; the number of times the income is contained in the price of the estate is called *the number of years' purchase of the land.*[12]

He then proceeded in a section heading to his definition of wealth (1770: 1, §XC, p. 152; 1889: §XC, p. 135):

> The total wealth of a nation is composed (1) of the net income of all real estate multiplied by the rate of capitalization of land;[13] (2) of the sum of all movable wealth existing in the nation.

The first sentence in the section elaborates as follows: 'Real estate is equivalent in value to a capital stock equal to its annual yield capitalized at the current number of years' purchase for which land will sell.'[14] Since Turgot shows that rates of return tend to equality in different uses, and to equality with the interest rate, this is equivalent to defining the present value of land as the discounted value of its stream of returns at the current interest rate. At any rate this shows that Turgot had a very clear conception of the distinction between as well as the relation between stocks and flows.

Thus it does not seem justifiable to attribute Smith's concept of wealth as a flow exclusively to the physiocrats, and certainly not to Turgot, who used the term in both stock and flow senses. Nevertheless it is probably true that the conflict between Smith's definition and the popular meaning was, as Cannan suggested, at least a contributing factor (in addition to the lingering mercantilist influence) to Smith's omitting services from the national product. However, in Smith's system the accumulated stock would include not only 'stock lent at interest' but also 'stock reserved for immediate consumption', the latter including perishable products such as fresh foodstuffs (1776: book II, ch. IV) – which would hardly be counted in a census of 'wealth'. To be consistent, then, Smith should have either included services or excluded both consumer goods and services from the national product, leaving only investment. As Garnier stated (1802: V, p. 197): 'What marks the progress or decline of a nation is not the type of its consumption, but the proportion existing annually between what it consumes and what it produces.'

Smith's doctrine concerning productive and unproductive labour was fully accepted by Karl Marx (1905); indeed, this doctrine more than any other underlay Marx's concept of surplus value. In his words (1905: 407; 1951: 178): 'Only labour *which is directly transformed into capital is productive.*' And as an illustration (1905: 416; 1951: 186):

> The same kind of labour may be productive or unproductive.
>
> For example, Milton, who wrote *Paradise Lost*, was an unproductive

worker. On the other hand, the writer who turns out factory-made stuff for his publisher is a productive worker.... A singer who sells her song on her own is an unproductive worker. But the same singer, commissioned by an *entrepreneur* to sing in order to make money for him, is a productive worker. For she produces capital.

It seems that the Soviet national income accountants tried their best to implement this doctrine faithfully. Dobb (1948: 266) notes the complaint of a Soviet writer: 'But why, asks the writer, should a gramophone record be included as a material product and not the voice of the singer recorded on the record?' He notes further that 'film stars' salaries were evidently included among the net value created by the cinema industry', presumably because their output was a material product, a film; it may be assumed that stage actors' incomes were excluded for the same reasons already given by J.S. Mill – failure to produce capital, or 'permanent utilities'.

In the later classical period Senior (1836), who was the first to glimpse the principle of diminishing marginal utility (1836: 133; 1850: 11–12), was also almost the lone dissenter against the prevailing Smith–Mill orthodoxy concerning the meaning of productivity. Expanding on an illustration introduced by McCulloch (1825), he explained beautifully (1836: 150; 1850: 52) how 'a servant who carries coal[s] from the cellar to the drawing-room performs precisely the same operation as the miner who raises them from the bottom of the pit to its mouth.' Further: 'The actor sells his exertions themselves. The painter sells not his exertions, but the picture on which those exertions have been employed.' But in failing to meet the objection that the one output was fleeting and the other lasting, he evidently was unsuccessful in persuading his British contemporaries, and Mill left his treatment unaltered through all seven editions of the *Principles*.

It is to Germany that we must look for the first general acceptance of the modern view that services should be considered equally productive with goods.

Roscher wrote (1854: §62, p. 98): 'Most recent writers ... have come to the opinion that all useful work is also economically productive.' He then cited M. Gioja, A. Scialoja, Say, C. Ganilh, G. Hufeland, Hermann (1832: 20ff.), E. G. Wakefield and Senior, and remarked upon the 'surprising retrogression' of J. S. Mill. He summed up his view as follows (§63, pp. 99–100):

Every worker whose output is in reasonable demand and provided with acceptable payment, has laboured productively. He has laboured unproductively only if there is no one who wishes to buy or is able to pay for his output; this case, however, includes the farmer whose corn rots in the granary for want of a market, no less than the author without readers or the singer no one can hear.

It is from Friedrich List, however, that Smith's doctrine came under the sharpest criticism (1841: ch. 12, p. 215; 1991: 142):

> The man who breeds pigs is, according to this school, a productive
> member of the community, but he who educates men is a mere non-
> productive.... A Newton, a Watt, or a Kepler is not so productive as a
> donkey, a horse, or a draught-ox ...

The significance of List's critique lay in his emphasis on human capital. For
(1841: 201; 1991: 133), *'The power of producing wealth* is ... infinitely more
important than *wealth itself*. This productive power is due (1841: 210; 1991:
140) to 'the *mental capital of the present human race'* ('das *geistige Capital
der lebenden Menschheit'*). He scorned exchange-value as a criterion for
measuring wealth; had he, however, had a more rigorous analytic training in
economic theory, he might have realized that human capital could be valued
by the present value of future earnings, just as Turgot had valued land.[15]

Marshall (1890: 116) started out his analysis of production forthrightly
echoing Say:

> Man cannot create material things. When he is said to produce material
> things, he really only produces utilities. In the mental and moral world
> indeed he may produce new ideas. But in the physical world, all that he
> can do is either to re-arrange matter so as to make it more useful, ... or
> to put it in the way of being made more useful by nature ...

He even added to the list of anomalies implied by Smith's definition, namely
(p. 120n) 'that a singer in an opera is unproductive, that the printer of the
tickets of admission to the opera is productive; while the usher who shows
people to their places is unproductive, unless he happens to sell programmes,
and then he is productive.' But then, like Mill before him, he proceeded to
capitulate to the Smithian definition, on the grounds that (pp. 117–18) 'an
almost unbroken tradition compels us to regard the central notion of the word
as relating to the provision of the wants for the future rather than those of the
present', explaining that 'the true interest of a country is generally advanced
by the subordination of the desire for immediate luxuries [e.g. opera
performances?] to the attainment of those more solid and lasting resources
[e.g. tickets to opera performances?] which will assist industry in its future
work'. However, he redeemed himself later on in his definition of national
income by saying that (p. 560)

> The labour and capital of the country, acting on its natural resources,
> produce annually a certain Net aggregate of commodities, material and
> immaterial, including services of all kinds. This is the true net annual
> revenue of the country, or as we may say the NATIONAL DIVIDEND.

But this definition left uncertain whether the national dividend was a vector
or a scalar; and if the latter, how the aggregation should be performed.

This question was also debated by Smith's followers; it was posed as the problem of finding a *measure* of 'national wealth' or 'riches', these terms being understood as denoting a flow rather than a stock, and a vector (although the mathematical concept of course was lacking) rather than a scalar. That there were difficulties in adopting the current national product, whether nominal or measured in wage units, as a measure of national wealth, was soon perceived by Lauderdale (1804), Ricardo (1817), Malthus (1827) and others, but they posed the problem in some misleading ways. Lauderdale's main thesis was that, save for exceptional cases, public wealth was not conterminous with the aggregate of 'individual riches'. For example, an increase in the supply of one commodity could cause a more than proportionate fall in its price and thus a fall in aggregate 'individual riches', whereas it would necessarily cause an increase in public wealth. In effect, he ranked public wealth by a partial ordering of the vectors of total quantities available (more of any commodity is better), and measured aggregate private riches by nominal national income. He found only one case in which the two rankings would agree: that in which there was a proportionate increase in the supply of all commodities, accompanied by a proportionate increase in the money supply (p. 105):

> The conclusion is therefore inevitable, that there exists only one case, and that a very improbable one, – (to wit, when the quantity and the demand for any commodity are proportionately increased, and funds at the same time are created for the acquisition of the increased quantity, as well as the satisfaction of the increased demand), – in which an increase in the mass of individual riches produces a similar effect on the wealth of the nation.

Ricardo, in his chapter on 'Value and riches' (1817, ch. XVIII), followed Lauderdale quite closely but adhered rigidly to his own labour theory of value. Thus (p. 386),

> From what has been said, it will be seen that the wealth of a country may be increased in two ways: it may be increased by employing a greater proportion of revenue in the maintenance of productive labour, – which will not only add to the quantity, but to the value of the mass of commodities; or it may be increased, without employing any additional quantity of labour, by making the same quantity more productive, – which will add to the abundance, but not to the value of commodities.
>
> In the first case, a country would not only become rich, but the value of its riches would increase. It would become rich by parsimony; by diminishing its expenditure on objects of luxury and enjoyment; and employing those savings in reproduction.
>
> In the second case, ... wealth would increase, but not value.

It should be noted that Ricardo's first method of increasing a country's wealth is based on Smith's distinction between productive and unproductive labour:

people should stop going to the theatre, opera and ballet, and the actors, opera singers and ballet dancers should become factory workers. The second method differs in its conclusion from Lauderdale's example simply in substituting labour value for money value. Like Lauderdale's, Ricardo's concept of wealth was only a partial ordering of commodity bundles (but in Ricardo's case restricted to material goods). As the above passage makes clear, Ricardo expressly denied the possibility of measuring wealth by a weighted aggregate of its components, with weights equal to labour costs (i.e. amounts of labour per unit of output); for, in his second case, a doubling of labour productivity, which would certainly double wealth, would halve all labour costs and leave national income, or 'value' (according to his definition), unchanged. And it certainly never occurred to him to use either base-year or current-year labour costs as common weights in comparing two different situations.

The only discussion I have been able to find in the literature of the classical period of the problem of defining a change in a country's 'wealth' when some outputs rise and others fall, is that of the iconoclast, Samuel Bailey (1825: 166–7):

> If the wealth of two men consisted in one single commodity, then, without entering into the question of exchange or value, we might determine that one was richer than the other, from mere excess of quantity. Even, however, in the simplest imaginable case of this kind, there would necessarily be a superiority of value, if such an idea came at all into question, as well as of wealth . . . .
>
> In all but this very simplest case, it would be impossible to decide with accuracy on the superiority of two individuals in point of riches, except by estimating their value in some common medium. Suppose the individual who possessed the 500 quarters of corn, was worth also 500 yards of cloth, while the other, who had 1000 quarters of corn, possessed only 100 yards of cloth; in what imaginable method could their riches be compared, and the superiority of one over the other be ascertained, except by means of their value, computed in some common medium of estimation, or reduced into one denomination?

While he saw the problem, he did not face up to the difficulties Lauderdale and Ricardo had pointed to, and concluded simply (p. 168): 'Value, therefore, is the only criterion of riches which is left to us.'

Malthus, on the other hand, reached the defeatist but logical conclusion that no measure of wealth is possible (1827: 224–5):

> a proper distinction has seldom been made between the definitions of wealth and value. Though the meanings of these two terms have by no means been considered as the same, yet the characteristics of one of them have been continually allowed to mix themselves with the

characteristics of the other. This appears even in Adam Smith himself. When he says, that a man is rich or poor according to the quantity of the necessaries, conveniences, and luxuries of life which he can command, he gives a most correct definition of wealth; but when he afterwards says, that he is rich or poor according to the quantity of labour which he can command, he evidently confounds wealth with value. The former is a definition of wealth; and of this, or the general power of purchasing, which too much resembles it, there is no measure. The latter is his own definition or expression of real value; and of this the very terms which he uses show that there is a measure.

It seems that Malthus intuitively understood that a partial ordering cannot be represented by a real-valued function unless it is first extended to a total ordering.

This is basically where the history of the subject stood (except, as we shall see, for the development of the theory of price-index numbers) when Pigou (1920) published his massive *Economics of Welfare*. Pigou made no mention of the previous controversies, but he evidently rejected the classical view concerning services in saying that 'the national dividend is composed ... of a number of objective services, some of which are rendered through commodities while other are rendered direct' (p. 30). On the other hand he agreed with the classics that

> what the community as a whole, or any group within the community, receives from time to time as dividend is not one large parcel of one single thing, but a number of small parcels of different things.... In these circumstances the conception of an increase or decrease in the quantity of dividend or real income accruing to any group is not unambiguous.
>
> (p. 69)

Thus, the 'national dividend', or 'real income', is a vector, or matrix, made up of bundles of commodities (presumably including services) allocated to different, apparently homogeneous, groups. Except for the presumed inclusion of services, this agrees with the concept of 'wealth' or 'riches' adhered to by Smith, Ricardo and Malthus. Pigou proceeded to order the vectors accruing to a group according to the satisfaction of a representative member of the group (p. 70). He then set it as his task to find a *measure* to represent this ordering (pp. 71–2), or rather, a measure of the change in satisfaction from period 1 to period 2. He put forth two measures (p. 73) which we may denote

$$\frac{Y^2 \sum_{i=1}^{n} p_i^1 x_i^1}{Y^1 \sum_{i=1}^{n} p_i^2 x_i^1} \quad \text{and} \quad \frac{Y^2 \sum_{i=1}^{n} p_i^1 x_i^2}{Y^1 \sum_{i=1}^{n} p_i^2 x_i^2}$$

where p_i^t and x_i^t denote the price and quantity of commodity i in period t and $Y^t = \sum_{i=1}^n p_i^t x_i^t$ denotes nominal income in period t. The first may be written as a ratio,

$$\frac{Y^2/\sum_{i=1}^n p_i^2 x_i^1}{Y^1/\sum_{i=1}^n p_i^1 x_i^1} = \frac{\sum_{i=1}^n p_i^2 x_i^2}{\sum_{i=1}^n p_i^2 x_i^1}$$

of the two nominal incomes each deflated by a Laspeyres price index, or, more naturally, as a ratio of two Paasche quantity indices. The second of Pigou's measures may likewise be written as a ratio,

$$\frac{Y^2/\sum_{i=1}^n p_i^2 x_i^2}{Y^1/\sum_{i=1}^n p_i^1 x_i^2} = \frac{\sum_{i=1}^n p_i^1 x_i^2}{\sum_{i=1}^n p_i^1 x_i^1}$$

of the two nominal incomes each deflated by a Paasche price index, or, more naturally, as a ratio of two Laspeyres quantity indices. Pigou then noted that if both ratios exceed unity then, assuming that the group acts as a rational unit,

> the fact that in the second period it chooses the form C_2 [i.e. the vector x^2] proves that what it purchases ... yields it more satisfaction than it could get from a collection of the form C_1 ... A fortiori, therefore, its purchase in the second period yields it more satisfaction than it did get from the actual collection of the form C_1 which it did purchase in the first period.

Actually, this follows just from the first of the two ratios exceeding unity. Pigou argued similarly that if both ratios fell short of unity, bundle x^1 would be (to use Samuelson's later terminology) revealed superior to bundle x^2.

Pigou assumed away a lot by postulating that the group could be treated as a single rational unit; nevertheless it is clear that his contribution represented an enormous advance in the subject. His treatment in terms of price indices instead of the more natural quantity indices may be attributed to the fact that the theory of the former had become quite well developed at the time, having been synthesized by its major contributor Fisher (1922) only two years later, to whom we owe (following Walsh 1901: 99) the appellations of the respective price indices of Laspeyres (1864, 1871) and Paasche (1874). Pigou admitted (1920: 74) that 'the condition we have laid down does not determine the choice of a measure, but merely fixes the limits within which that choice must lie', which implicitly assumes that a single acceptable measure is possible. Of course, such a measure could only be provided by a utility function, as Samuelson and others were later to show.

Let us return to the passage in Hicks which set off this long digression (1975c: 313):

There is of course no question that the flow of wealth is production; things are produced, and it is in these products that the flow of wealth consists. But the things that are produced are heterogeneous; it is not obvious that we can take them together and reduce them to a common 'stuff'. *It is already implied in the classical approach that for essential purposes we can take them together. We can represent them by a flow of wealth, which is so far homogeneous that it can be greater or less.*[16] It was the study of this flow of wealth which the Classics called *Political Economy.*

How did Adam Smith and his successors come to think in this way? They had none of our modern apparatus of Social Accounting at their disposal; theory came first, and our Social Accounting is an application of it. The origin, surely was analogy – analogy with business experience. The products of a business may be heterogeneous, but they are reduced to a common measure by being valued in terms of money.

As we have seen, there is no textual justification for the two italicized sentences above. According to Adam Smith (1776: book I, ch. V; 1889: 13), 'Every man is rich or poor according to the degree in which he can afford to enjoy the necessaries, conveniences, and amusements of human life'. Unless one believes that every term defined in economics must be representable by a real number, it is hard to see how one can jump to the inference that the term 'wealth' must denote some real-valued function of 'the necessaries, conveniences, and amusements of human life'. It is true, as Malthus observed, that Smith later provided a contradictory definition of wealth as the amount of labour that a person can command; but both Ricardo and Malthus pounced on Smith for this confusion between 'wealth' (a vector) and 'value' (a scalar). 'Many of the errors in political economy', said Ricardo (1817: 379), 'have arisen from errors on this subject, from considering an increase of riches, and an increase of value, as meaning the same thing, and from unfounded notions as to what constituted a standard of value'.

To summarize, without appealing to preferences we have no basis for deciding which products to include in the 'social income' and which to exclude. And it does not help to fall back on 'productivity' or 'efficiency' as the phenomenon to be measured in place of 'real social income', since as Say noted and all the classics agreed, production means creation of utility. Without consulting preferences, we have no basis for excluding pollution from the list of outputs in the definition of productive efficiency, or indeed for considering it to be a negative contributor to efficiency. It may finally be added that the assumption of constant costs, combined with the criterion of efficiency, by no means avoids the types of internal inconsistencies that beset the use of the double-index criterion as an indicator of improvement. The examples of intransitivities in these criteria (see Example 3 of Chipman and Moore 1978: 566–8) may readily be extended to this case.

Hicks's strategic retreat to the 'cost approach' has thus failed of its object. Can anything be salvaged from it? I think something can. If in making intertemporal comparisons one assumes that the only possible technological improvements (or retrogressions) are uniform percentage changes in all industries, so that labour becomes more productive in whatever it does, then our flat production-possibility surfaces will necessarily be parallel hyperplanes. In that case, the ordering induced by either the compensation principle or the criterion of efficiency is simply that of set-inclusion among production-possibility sets; and no assumptions need be made concerning similarity of preferences. This is an extreme case; but it is possible that real-world production-possibility surfaces are quite flat (i.e. have low Gaussian curvature), and that technical change makes them tilt very little. In this case we may require *some* similarity of preferences, but not necessarily a great deal, to avoid intransitivities. Under these circumstances the standard national-income measures may provide a fairly good approximation to an ideal utilitarian measure for a wide range of value judgements. This would seem to be the only viable approach to salvaging standard national-income comparisons.

There seems to be little empirical information available about the shape of production-possibility frontiers. However, an investigation by Johnson (1966) suggests that they may be quite flat. In analysing the simple two-commodity–two-factor case with Cobb–Douglas production functions he found that, except in the case of very extreme differences in factor intensities as between the two industries, 'even quite marked differences in the relative labor intensity of the two industries ... are insufficient to make the transformation curve depart markedly from a straight line' (p. 697). He continued:

> It may be, therefore, that the constant cost assumptions of Ricardo, Graham, and the Leontief model are quite reasonable approximations for most practical purposes, and that the effort that has been devoted to refining the Heckscher–Ohlin model and investigating its complexities has been concerned with phenomena of trivial practical importance.

Keeping in mind also that in order to construct examples of intransitivities it is necessary to assume very marked differences in tastes among different individuals, it is to these empirical restrictions that one must look if one is to have any hope of justifying the conventional measures of real national income.

3 THE REHABILITATION OF CONSUMERS' SURPLUS

One of Hicks's most influential contributions was his bold attempt to rehabilitate the concept of consumer's (and consumers') surplus. Here the great ordinalist found it indispensable to adopt a cardinal money measure of utility in order to derive useful propositions in welfare economics. The need for this was perceived to be two-fold. (1) In partial-equilibrium analysis of the effects of monopoly or of an excise tax in a particular industry, there was a need to compare the pecuniary gains of the monopolist or the government with the non-pecuniary losses of the consumer. The need to make these types of comparisons is of course what has been at the basis of the appeal of the concept of consumer's surplus since its introduction by Dupuit and Marshall. (2) Since welfare economics deals with a collection of consumers, the natural unit of measurement to use in analysing needed compensation payments among individuals is the monetary one. I shall deal in this section with Hicks's concern with the first of these needs. His 1941 paper, which is the subject of this section, was devoted to a rehabilitation of the Marshallian concept; the next and final section will deal with his further contributions (1942d, 1943d, 1946a) expanding on the concept of compensating variation introduced in *Value and Capital* (1939a), including his attention to the second of the above needs.

I shall take up only a particular example analysed by Hicks, that of the effect of an excise tax imposed on a particular commodity. And in order to avoid having to deal with the troublesome concept of 'producers' surplus', I shall assume that factors of production are in fixed total supply and perfectly mobile among industries, and that firms operate under constant returns to scale. Following Hicks, the analysis is limited to the two-commodity case. As a further simplification I shall assume that there is a single factor of production, labour, and that consumers all have identical preferences of the 'parallel' form

$$U(x_1, x_2) = 2\sqrt{(\gamma x_1)} + x_2 \qquad \gamma > 0 \tag{8.1}$$

in the interior of the positive quadrant. This implies that for disposable incomes Y satisfying $Y > \gamma p_2^2/p_1$, where p_1 and p_2 are the market prices of the two commodities, the demand functions have the form

$$x_1 = h_1(p_1, p_2, Y) = \gamma\left(\frac{p_2}{p_1}\right)^2$$

$$x_2 = h_2(p_1, p_2, Y) = \frac{Y}{p_2} - \gamma\frac{p_2}{p_1}. \tag{8.2}$$

Substituting these into the utility function (8.1) we obtain the indirect utility function

$$V(p_1, p_2, Y) = \gamma\frac{p_2}{p_1} + \frac{Y}{p_2}. \tag{8.3}$$

Letting l denote the labour endowment and b_j the fixed amount of labour needed to produce a unit of commodity j, labour is allocated to the two industries according to

$$b_1 y_1 + b_2 y_2 = l \tag{8.4}$$

where y_j is the output of commodity j. Unit production costs are wb_1 and wb_2 in the two industries, where w is the wage rate. Letting t_j denote the *ad valorem* excise tax rate on commodity j, the market price of commodity j is given by

$$p_j = (1 + t_j)wb_j \qquad j = 1, 2. \tag{8.5}$$

Tax revenues, $R(t_1, t_2)$, which are assumed to be disbursed to consumers in lump-sum fashion, are obtained by solving the equation

$$R(t_1, t_2) = \sum_{j=1}^{2} t_j w b_j h_j [(1 + t_1)wb_1, (1 + t_2)wb_2, wl + R(t_1, t_2)]$$

$$= t_1 w \gamma \frac{(1 + t_2)^2 b_2^2}{(1 + t_1)^2 b_1}$$

$$+ t_2 w b_2 \frac{wl + R(t_1, t_2)}{(1 + t_2)wb_2} - \gamma \frac{(1 + t_2)b_2}{(1 + t_1)b_1} \tag{8.6}$$

to obtain with straightforward calculations

$$R(t_1, t_2) = t_2 wl + w\gamma \frac{b_2^2 (1 + t_2)^2}{b_1 (1 + t_1)^2}(t_1 - t_2). \tag{8.7}$$

Tax revenues in the two industries separately are therefore given by

$$R_1(t_1, t_2) = t_1 w\gamma \frac{(1 + t_2)^2 b_2^2}{(1 + t_1)^2 b_1}$$

$$R_2(t_1, t_2) = t_2 w \left[l - \gamma \frac{(1 + t_2)^2 b_2^2}{(1 + t_1)^2 b_1} \right] \tag{8.8}$$

and disposable income is given by

$$Y(t_1, t_2) = wl + R(t_1, t_2)$$

$$= (1 + t_2)wl + \gamma \frac{wb_2^2 (1 + t_2)^2}{b_1 (1 + t_1)^2}(t_1 - t_2). \tag{8.9}$$

Finally, we may define social welfare as a function of the two tax rates by

$$W(t_1,t_2) = V\left[(1 + t_1)wb_1, (1 + t_2)wb_2, (1 + t_2)wl \right.$$

$$\left. + \gamma \frac{wb_2^2 (1 + t_2)^2}{b_1 (1 + t_1)^2}(t_1 - t_2) \right]$$

$$= \frac{l}{b_2} + \gamma \frac{b_2}{b_1}\frac{1 + t_2}{(1 + t_1)^2}(1 + 2t_1 - t_2). \qquad (8.10)$$

From this we may obtain the change in welfare starting from zero taxes and going to two arbitrary tax rates:

$$W(t_1,t_2) - W(0,0) = -\gamma \frac{b_2 (t_1 - t_2)^2}{b_1 (1 + t_1)^2}.$$

Note that, in accordance with Frisch's (1939) correction of Hotelling's (1938) theorem, $W(t,t) = W(0,0)$ for all $t > 0$. Thus Dupuit's dictum (1844: 369, 374), stressed by Hotelling (1938) and Hicks (1941b), that the welfare loss is of the order of the square of the tax rate, should be replaced by the dictum that it varies as the square of the *difference* between the two tax rates. Likewise we may suppose that one tax rate is already positive and the other is to be raised from the zero level:

$$W(t_1,t_2) - W(0,t_2) = \gamma \frac{b_2 (1 + t_2)t_1}{b_1 (1 + t_1)^2}(t_1 t_2 + 2t_2 - t_1). \qquad (8.11)$$

This is positive for $t_1 < t_2$. Similarly,

$$W(t_1,t_2) - W(t_1,0) = \gamma \frac{b_2}{b_1}\frac{t_2}{(1 + t_1)^2}(2t_1 - t_2) \qquad (8.12)$$

which is positive whenever $t_2 < t_1$.

Now let us see how the welfare effects of an excise tax on commodity 1 are evaluated by means of Marshallian consumers' surplus analysis. Denote the budget triple $B = (p_1,p_2,Y)$ and let $B(\xi) = [p_1(\xi),p_2(\xi),Y(\xi)]$ be a polygonal path connecting

$$B(0) = [wb_1, (1 + t_2)wb_2, wl + R(0,t_2)]$$

and

$$B(1) = [(1 + t_1)wb_1, (1 + t_2)wb_2, wl + R(t_1,t_2)]$$

for $0 \leq \xi \leq 1$, where $t_1 > 0$ and $t_2 \geq 0$. That is, we wish to consider the welfare effects of an *ad valorem* tax t_1 on commodity 1 when an *ad valorem* tax of t_2 (possibly zero) is already in force on commodity 2. The change in indirect utility can be represented by the line integral

$$V[B(1)] - V[B(0)] = \sum_{j=1}^{2} \int_{0}^{1} \frac{\partial}{\partial p_j} V[B(\xi)] dp_j(\xi)$$

$$+ \int_{0}^{1} \frac{\partial}{\partial Y} V[B(\xi)] dY(\xi)$$

$$= - \sum_{j=1}^{2} \int_{0}^{1} \frac{\partial V[B(\xi)]}{\partial Y} h_j[B(\xi)] dp_j(\xi)$$

$$+ \int_{0}^{1} \frac{\partial V[B(\xi)]}{\partial Y} dY(\xi) \tag{8.13}$$

the last equation following from Antonelli's partial differential equation. Now, *if* the marginal utility of income depends only upon p_2, *and* p_2 is constant, then $dp_2(\xi)$ may be set equal to zero and the expression $\partial V[B(\xi)]/\partial Y$ may be factored out of the remaining integrals to give

$$V[B(1)] - V[B(0)]$$

$$= \frac{\partial V[B(\xi)]}{\partial Y} \left\{ - \int_{0}^{1} h_1[p_1(\xi), p_2, Y(\xi)] dp_1(\xi) + Y(1) - Y(0) \right\}.$$
$$\tag{8.14}$$

In the above model, the dependence of the marginal utility of income on the price of commodity 2 alone is assured by the special 'parallel' form of the indirect utility function (8.3), yielding $\partial V/\partial Y = 1/p_2$. Second, constancy of the price of commodity 2 is assured by taking the single factor labour as numéraire and setting the wage rate w constant; with a constant tax rate on commodity 2 the nominal price of commodity 2 must remain constant (see equation (8.5)). Third, since factor income is constant (the supply of labour being inelastic by hypothesis, and the wage rate being the numéraire), the change in disposable income is necessarily equal to the change in tax revenues.[17]

The term in braces in (8.14) is of course the consumers' surplus. In the present model it is calculated as follows:

$$- \int_{0}^{1} h_1[p_1(\xi), p_2, Y(\xi)] dp_1(\xi) + Y(1) - Y(0)$$

$$= - \int_{wb_1}^{(1+t_1)wb_1} \frac{\gamma(1 + t_2)^2 b_2^2 w^2}{p_1^2} dp_1 + R(t_1, t_2) - R(0, t_2)$$

$$= \frac{\gamma(1 + t_2)^2 wb_2^2}{b_1} \left\{ \frac{-t_1}{1 + t_1} + \frac{t_1}{(1 + t_1)^2} \right.$$

$$\left. + t_2 \left[1 - \frac{1}{(1 + t_1)^2} \right] \right\}. \tag{8.15}$$

(This agrees, as of course it should, with (8.11) after multiplication by the constant marginal utility of income $1/[(1 + t_2)wb_2]$.) The first term in braces corresponds to the gross change in consumers' surplus excluding transfers of tax revenues. The second and third terms correspond respectively to the changes in tax revenues in the two industries. Note that the third term is necessarily positive if t_1 and t_2 are both positive; i.e. if an excise tax is already in force in industry 2, an excise tax imposed on industry 1 will not only produce revenues from industry 1 but will also increase the revenues collected from industry 2 at the old tax rate t_2. In conventional consumers' surplus analysis this additional effect on tax revenues is not taken into account; implicitly, tax rates on other commodities are assumed to be zero.

The easiest way to see that if $t_2 > 0$ an excise tax on commodity 1 must increase the revenue collected from industry 2, is to note that since consumption is equal to production, the allocation equation (8.4) applies to the x_j as well as to the y_j. The demands for the two commodities (and therefore the supplies) as functions of the tax rates are

$$x_1(t_1, t_2) = \gamma \frac{(1 + t_2)^2 b_2^2}{(1 + t_1)^2 b_1^2}$$

and

$$x_2(t_1, t_2) = \frac{1}{b_2} - \gamma \frac{(1 + t_2)^2 b_2}{(1 + t_1)^2 b_1}. \tag{8.16}$$

Hence the equilibrium quantity of either commodity varies inversely with the tax rate on that commodity.

An illustration is given in Figure 8.1 corresponding to the example

$$b_1 = \tfrac{1}{3}, b_2 = \tfrac{2}{3}, l = 10, w = 1, t_2 = \tfrac{1}{2}.$$

It is assumed that with a 50 per cent tax rate already in force on commodity 2, a 50 per cent tax rate is introduced on commodity 1. The initial prices are $p_1 = wb_1 = \tfrac{1}{3}$ and $p_2 = (1 + t_2)wb_2 = 1$, hence the demand curve for commodity 1 is given by $x_1 = 1/p_2^2$, which cuts the initial supply curve $p_1 = \tfrac{1}{3}$ at $x_1(0, t_2) = 9$ and the supply curve including the tax, $p_1 = (1 + t_2)wb_1 = \tfrac{1}{2}$, at $x_1(t_2, t_2) = 4$. The gross loss of consumers' surplus is shown by the area ABCDE which is equal to -1 in accordance with the first term of

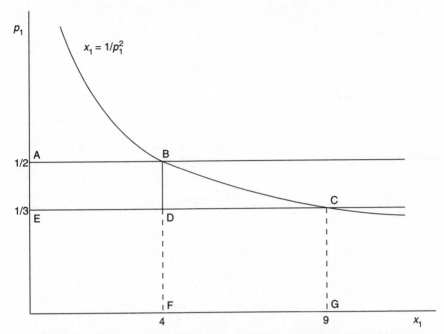

Figure 8.1 Net loss of consumer's surplus, BCD, resulting from an excise tax on commodity 1, ignoring the effect on tax revenues from industry 2

(8.15), while the revenues collected from industry 1 are given by the rectangle ABDE which has area $\frac{2}{3}$ in accordance with the second term of (8.15). Thus, the net loss of consumers' surplus is given by the triangle BCD with area $\frac{1}{3}$, according to Marshallian theory.[18] But this neglects the effects of the excise tax on commodity 1 on revenues from industry 2. In Figure 8.2 are shown the demand curve

$$x_2 = h_2[wb_1, p_2, wl + R(0, t_2)] = \frac{13.5}{p_2} - 3p_2$$

for commodity 2 when commodity 1 is not taxed and revenue is obtained only from commodity 2, and the shifted demand curve

$$x_2 = h_2[(1 + t_2)wb_1, p_2, wl + R(t_2, t_2)] = \frac{15}{p_2} - 2p_2$$

resulting from both the substitution and income effect of the imposition of the tax on commodity 1. The supply curves $p_2 = \frac{2}{3}$ and $p_2 = 1$ correspond to the unit production costs of commodity 2 before and after imposition of the tax on commodity 2. The cum-tax supply curve intersects the demand curves at

127

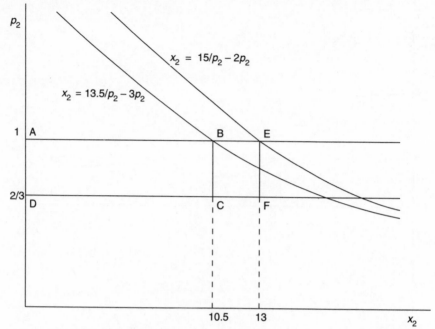

Figure 8.2 Gain in tax revenues from industry 2, BEFC, resulting from imposition of excise tax on commodity 1

B and E respectively, at amounts 10.5 and 13 of commodity 2. Consequently the tax revenues collected from industry 2 were ABCD, or $3\frac{1}{2}$, before the tax was imposed on commodity 1, and AEFD, or $4\frac{1}{3}$, afterwards – a difference of $\frac{5}{6}$, which is the area of the rectangle BEFC and corresponds to the third term of (8.15). This area exceeds the area, $\frac{1}{3}$, of the triangle BDC of Figure 8.1. The grand net increment in consumers' surplus is therefore $-1 + \frac{2}{3} + \frac{5}{6} = \frac{1}{2}$, which is positive, rather than negative as the traditional Marshallian analysis would lead one to believe.

A similar analysis may be undertaken of the welfare effects of an *ad valorem* excise tax on commodity 2. In comparing two budgets $B(0) = (wb_1, wb_2, wl)$ and $B(1) = [wb_1, (1 + t_2)wb_2, wl + R(0, t_2)]$, an exact analysis in terms of line integrals is given by

$$V[B(1)] - V[B(0)] = \sum_{j=1}^{2} \int_0^1 \frac{\partial V[B(\xi)]}{\partial p_j} \mathrm{d}p_j(\xi) + \int_0^1 \frac{\partial V[B(\xi)]}{\partial Y} \mathrm{d}Y(\xi)$$

$$= -\int_0^1 \frac{\partial V[B(\xi)]}{\partial Y} h_2[B(\xi)]\mathrm{d}p_2(\xi)$$

$$+ \int_0^1 \frac{\partial V[B(\xi)]}{\partial Y} dY(\xi)$$

$$= - \int_0^1 \frac{1}{p_2(\xi)} \left[\frac{Y(\xi)}{p_2(\xi)} - \frac{p_2(\xi)}{p_1(\xi)} \right] dp_2(\xi)$$

$$+ \int_0^1 \frac{1}{p_2(\xi)} dY(\xi).$$

Choosing the polygonal path

$$p_1(\xi) = wb_1 \qquad \text{for } 0 \leqslant \xi \leqslant 1$$

$$p_2(\xi) = \begin{cases} (1 + t_2)^{2\xi} wb_2 & \text{for } 0 \leqslant \xi \leqslant \tfrac{1}{2} \\ (1 + t_2)wb_2 & \text{for } \tfrac{1}{2} \leqslant \xi \leqslant 1 \end{cases}$$

$$Y(\xi) = \begin{cases} wl & \text{for } 0 \leqslant \xi \leqslant \tfrac{1}{2} \\ wl + (2\xi - 1)R(0, t_2) & \text{for } \tfrac{1}{2} \leqslant \xi \leqslant 1 \end{cases}$$

we see that the marginal utility of income (evaluated at $\xi = 1$) can be factored out of the second integral as

$$\int_0^1 \frac{1}{p_2(\xi)} dY(\xi) = \int_{\frac{1}{2}}^1 \frac{1}{p_2(1)} R(0, t_2) 2d\xi = \frac{R(0, t_2)}{p_2(1)}.$$

Consequently, the appropriate expression for comparing the gross welfare loss (the negative of the first integral) with the increased tax revenues is

$$p_2(1) \int_0^1 \frac{1}{p_2(\xi)} h_2[B(\xi)] dp_2(\xi)$$

$$= (1 + t_2)wb_2 \int_0^{\frac{1}{2}} \left[\frac{Y(\xi)}{p_2(\xi)^2} - \gamma \frac{1}{p_1(0)} \right] dp_2(\xi) \qquad (8.17)$$

which evaluates to

$$E(0, t_2) = wlt_2 - \gamma \frac{wb_2^2}{b_1} (1 + t_2)t_2. \qquad (8.18)$$

Comparing this with the tax revenues (see (8.7)),

$$R(0, t_2) = wlt_2 - \gamma \frac{wb_2^2}{b_1} (1 + t_2)^2 t_2 \qquad (8.19)$$

we see that the net loss is

129

$$L(0, t_2) \equiv E(0, t_2) - R(0, t_2) = \gamma(b_2/b_1)(1 + t_2)t_2^2 \qquad (8.20)$$

in agreement with (8.12). The procedure adopted in consumers' surplus analysis is, however, to use the expression

$$\int_0^1 h_2[B(\xi)]dp_2(\xi) = \int_0^{\frac{1}{2}}\left[\frac{Y(\xi)}{p_2(\xi)} - \gamma\frac{p_2(\xi)}{p_1(\xi)}\right]dp_2(\xi) \qquad (8.21)$$

in place of (8.17). Integrating along the indicated path we find that this evaluates to

$$S(0, t_2) = wl \log(1 + t_2) - \gamma\frac{wb_2^2}{b_1}(1 + \tfrac{1}{2}t_2)t_2. \qquad (8.22)$$

The corresponding inexact measure of net loss is then

$$N(0, t_2) \equiv S(0, t_2) - R(0, t_2)$$

$$= 10[\log(1 + t_2) - t_2] + 2t_2^2 + \tfrac{4}{3}t_2^3. \qquad (8.23)$$

Table 8.1 gives values in the case of our numerical example of the exact measure (8.18) of gross loss, the inexact one (8.22), their difference

$$D(0, t_2) \equiv E(0, t_2) - S(0, t_2)$$

$$= -wl[\log(1 + t_2) - t_2] - \tfrac{1}{2}\gamma\frac{wb_2^2}{b_1}t_2^2 \qquad (8.24)$$

and the tax revenues (8.19). These are also plotted in Figure 8.3, which shows that both measures of gross loss are increasing concave functions over the interval $0 \leq t_2 \leq 1.5$, and that the inaccuracy of the inexact measure, as measured by (8.24), is an increasing convex function of t_2 in that interval. The tax revenues show the typical shape of the Laffer curve, with maximum revenues at $t_2 = 0.949$. Below the rate $t_2 = 0.895$ the inexact measure is below the revenue line, giving an incorrect indication of net gain from the tax (as in Chipman 1990).

Of course, any diehard user of consumers' surplus analysis will justifiably

Table 8.1 Exact (E) and consumers' surplus (S) measures of gross welfare loss for successive excise tax rates, their difference (D) and the tax revenues (R)

t_2	0.1	0.2	0.3	0.4	0.5	0.6	0.7	0.8	0.9	1.0	1.1	1.2	1.3	1.4	1.5
Exact	0.85	1.68	2.48	3.25	4.00	4.72	5.41	6.08	6.72	7.33	7.92	8.48	9.01	9.52	10.00
Inexact	0.81	1.53	2.16	2.73	3.22	3.66	4.05	4.39	4.68	4.93	5.15	5.33	5.47	5.58	5.66
Difference	0.04	0.15	0.32	0.53	0.78	1.06	1.37	1.70	2.04	2.40	2.77	3.16	3.54	3.94	4.34
Revenues	0.84	1.62	2.32	2.96	3.50	3.95	4.30	4.54	4.67	4.67	4.53	4.26	3.83	3.26	2.50

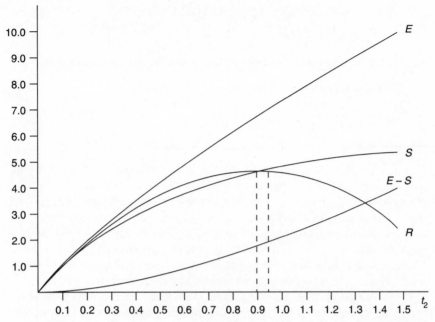

Figure 8.3 Exact (E) and consumers' surplus (S) measures of gross loss from an excise tax t_2 on commodity 2 when there is no tax on commodity 1, together with their difference ($E - S$) and tax revenues (R)

protest that the method cannot show positive gains from an excise tax (even in cases when it should, such as the one analysed above in the case of commodity 1). Indeed, it is the practice in this analysis to ignore income effects. Thus, the devotee will, in place of (8.21), define the gross loss of consumers' surplus (along the given polygonal path) by

$$G(0, t_2) = \int_0^1 h_2[p_1(0), p_2(\xi), Y(0)] \, dp_2(\xi)$$

$$= \int_0^{\frac{1}{2}} \left[\frac{Y(0)}{p_2(\xi)} - \gamma \frac{p_2(\xi)}{p_1(0)} \right] dp_2(\xi)$$

$$= wl \log(1 + t_2) - \tfrac{1}{2}\gamma \frac{wb_2^2}{b_1} t_2(2 + t_2) \qquad (8.25)$$

and define the tax revenues, in place of (8.19), by

$$Q(0, t_2) = t_2 p_2(0) \left[\frac{Y(0)}{p_2(1)} - \gamma \frac{p_2(1)}{p_1(0)} \right]$$

131

$$= \frac{t_2}{1 + t_2} wl - t_2(1 + t_2)\gamma \frac{wb_2^2}{b_1}. \tag{8.26}$$

The net loss in consumers' surplus is then, according to this conception,

$$C(0, t_2) \equiv G(0, t_2) - Q(0, t_2)$$

$$= wl \left[\log(1 + t_2) - \frac{t_2}{1 + t_2} \right] + \tfrac{2}{3} t_2^2. \tag{8.27}$$

This gives us now three measures of net loss: (a) the exact one (8.20); (b) the inexact one (8.23), which erroneously factors out the variable marginal utility of income but correctly takes account of income effects; and (c) the conventional one (8.27), which erroneously factors out the variable marginal utility of income and also ignores income effects. In support of the latter it might be argued that the government hoards or squanders its revenues rather than distributes them to consumers; but in that case it is hard to see how one could count these revenues as a net addition to social welfare. An alternative argument might be that the government distributes the revenues to bureaucrats who spend the funds only on commodity 1 (provided, of course, that there is no excise tax on commodity 1); but in that case, it would be more logical to measure the benefits of the government revenues by the increased consumers' surplus obtained by the bureaucrats from the consumption of commodity 1. Still a third argument might be that the government spends the funds on imported goods; but then unless our country is a very large one, relative prices would no longer be the same; and one would have to allow for sufficient exportation of one of the commodities in order to maintain balanced trade. It is therefore very hard to defend the conventional measure except on the supposition that the income effects will be small. But that they are not small in our example is illustrated in Table 8.2 and Figure 8.4.

The most notable anomaly, already observed in Chipman (1990), is the positive net gain shown by the measure $N(0, t_2)$ in the interval $0 < t_2 < 0.895$. This is due to taking account of the positive impact on demand for commodity 2 of the substantial tax revenues, combined with failure to take account of the

Table 8.2 Exact measure (L) of net welfare loss, inexact consumers' surplus measure (N) of net welfare loss allowing for income effects and conventional consumers' surplus measure (C) of net welfare loss ignoring income effects, for successive excise tax rates t_2

t_2	0.1	0.2	0.3	0.4	0.5	0.6	0.7	0.8	0.9	1.0	1.1	1.2	1.3	1.4	1.5
Exact	0.02	0.10	0.23	0.45	0.75	1.15	1.67	2.30	3.08	4.00	5.08	6.34	7.77	9.41	11.25
Inexact	−0.03	−0.09	−0.16	−0.23	−0.28	−0.29	−0.26	−0.16	0.01	0.27	0.61	1.07	1.64	2.33	3.16
Convent'l	0.05	0.18	0.38	0.61	0.89	1.19	1.52	1.86	2.22	2.60	2.99	3.39	3.80	4.23	4.66

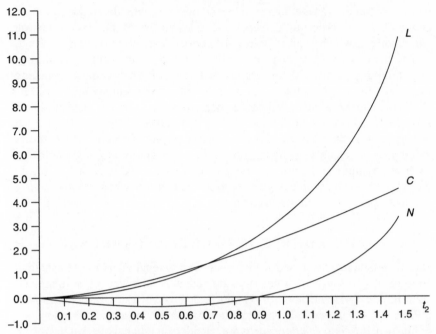

Figure 8.4 Exact measure of net welfare loss (L), inexact consumer's surplus measure allowing for income effects (N), and conventional consumer's surplus measure ignoring income effects (C), resulting from an excise tax t_2 on commodity 2 when commodity 1 is not taxed

declining marginal utility of income. The fact that this measure correctly indicates net loss for higher tax rates is due essentially to the Laffer effect of declining revenues for $t_2 > 0.949$. The conventional measure $C(0,t_2)$ appears to the eye to agree well with the exact measure $L(0,t_2)$ up to their point of intersection $t_2 = 0.625$, but it deviates very substantially at higher tax rates – rates of a magnitude typical of excise taxes on tobacco products and alcoholic beverages. But even in the lower interval, the goodness of approximation depends upon the arbitrary scale along the vertical axis. Clearly, one needs a measuring rod in relation to which this approximation may be judged to be good. And theoretically, comparison of $L(0,t_2)$ and $C(0,t_2)$ is virtually meaningless since the first measure assumes that the tax revenues are distributed to the consumers whereas the second assumes, in effect, that they are not.

This leads us to the fundamental question of the meaning of a particular cardinal measure of utility. When Hicks says (1941b: 114) 'When output has already been contracted below the optimum, a further contraction is very damaging', what does 'very damaging' mean? As Debreu (1960) made clear, a cardinal measure of utility has meaning only if there are at least three objects being compared. We would have to extend the present model to three or more commodities in order to consider the question: with no excise tax on commodity 1, which is preferable, a 10 per cent excise tax on commodity 2, or a 10 per cent excise tax on commodity 3? Or, if a 5 per cent tax is in force on commodity 2 and a 10 per cent tax on commodity 3, is it more damaging to increase the 10 per cent tax by 1 per cent or the 5 per cent tax by 1 per cent? Clearly, in making such delicate comparisons, an order of inaccuracy as shown in Tables 8.1 and 8.2 and Figures 8.3 and 8.4 could easily give the wrong answer: the conventional consumer's surplus measure, which shows successive increments in the tax rate to be increasingly more damaging, is itself increasingly inaccurate as the tax rate increases. One then has to ask: why should one insist on using an approximate measure when it is just as easy – in fact easier – to compute an exact one?

4 THE FOUR CONSUMERS' SURPLUSES

Hicks's article just discussed, which attempted to rehabilitate the Marshallian concept of consumer's surplus, was immediately followed by a significant contribution by Henderson (1941) which analyzed Hicks's earlier treatment (1939a: 38–41) in which Hicks identified Marshall's concept with a new one of his own, the *compensating variation*. Henderson pointed out that they were in fact different. Henderson's paper stimulated Hicks into developing the subject further in a series of papers (1942d, 1943d, 1946a) subsequently merged into one (1981: 114–32).

Hicks's 'four consumer's surpluses' refer to the compensating and equivalent variation – which measure changes in indirect utility resulting from changes in prices or income – and to the analogous measures of changes in direct utility resulting from changes in quantities consumed. If we denote by '$x^1 R x^2$' the relation 'the bundle x^1 is preferred or indifferent to the bundle x^2', and if the individual's demand function is denoted by $x = h(p,Y)$ where p is the vector of prices and Y the individual's income, then the indirect preference relation R^* is defined by '$(p^1,Y^1)R^*(p^2,Y^2)$' if and only if $h(p^1,Y^1)Rh(p^2,Y^2)$'. Using Hurwicz and Uzawa's (1971) *income-compensation function*[19],

$$\mu^*(p;p^0,Y^0) = \min\{Y>0 \mid (p, Y)R^*(p^0, Y^0)\},$$

where the prices p^0 and income Y^0 define an arbitrary 'base budget', we may define the *price-compensating variation* starting from (p^0, Y^0) and ending at (p, Y) by

$$C^*(p, Y; p^0, Y^0) = Y - \mu^*(p; p^0, Y^0)$$

and the corresponding *price-equivalent variation* as

$$E^*(p, Y; p^0, Y^0) = \mu^*(p^0; p, Y) - Y^0$$

(cf. Chipman and Moore 1980). These are the 'dual' concepts; the 'primal' ones may be defined analogously if, following Hicks (1981: 123), we decompose the commodity bundle into $x = (z, y)$ where $z = (x_1, \ldots, x_{n-1})$ and $y = x_n$, where commodity n is the numéraire. Then the *numéraire-compensation function* is

$$\mu(z; z^0, y^0) = \min\{y > 0 \mid (z, y) R(z^0, y^0)\},$$

a function which is unfortunately not always well defined, since indifference surfaces may touch the axes. The corresponding *quantity-compensating variation* is, of course,

$$C(z, y; z^0, y^0) = y - \mu(z; z^0, y^0)$$

and the *quantity-equivalent variation* is

$$E(z, y; z^0, y^0) = \mu(z^0; z, y) - y^0.$$

Hicks developed elegant relationships among these four 'consumer's surpluses', but the last two have not caught on in the literature, presumably since as remarked above the function μ is not a satisfactory index of indifference in general.

As opposed to Marshall's concept, Hicks's two concepts of (price)-compensating and (price)-equivalent variation are exact measures of welfare change between two situations. How, then, can they be used in place of Marshall's measure? Unfortunately, Hicks never went on to apply them to precise situations, such as the analysis of welfare effects of an excise tax. But they have been used, and the Marshall measure has been used, by his followers. The main conceptual difficulty is the following: if one is considering two alternative systems of excise taxes in place of the existing one, can one judge between them according to the magnitude of the compensating or equivalent variation? In the case of the compensating variation the answer is in general no, since the comparison between situation 1 and situation 0 uses the situation 1 prices whereas that between situation 2 and situation 0 uses situation 2 prices; i.e. different utility indices are used in the two binary comparisons. On the other hand, in the case of the equivalent variation, situation 0 prices are used to evaluate both situation 1 and situation 2. Unlike the compensating variation, the equivalent variation is itself a valid indirect utility function (cf. Hause 1975; Chipman and Moore 1980). It depends on the perhaps arbitrary choice of base prices p^0; but except for the problem involved in this choice, it is a natural measure of utility. While Hicks himself did not perceive the question in this light, his contribution to welfare economics in developing this concept was very great.

It was shown in Chipman and Moore (1980, 1992) that in order for the compensating variation to be a valid welfare indicator for comparisons of budgets (p, Y) with the same numéraire price, it is necessary and sufficient that preferences be parallel with respect to the numéraire; and that for it to be a valid indicator for comparisons of budgets with the same income, it is necessary and sufficient that preferences be homothetic. This was generalized in Chipman and Moore (1990) to the proposition that for the compensating variation to be a valid indicator of welfare for comparisons of budgets in a submanifold of the budget space defined by a function $\alpha(p) + \beta Y = $ constant, where $\alpha(\cdot)$ is positively homogeneous of degree 1 and β is constant, it is necessary and sufficient that indirect preferences be representable by a function

$$V(p, Y) = \frac{\delta Y - \gamma(p)}{\alpha(p) + \beta Y}$$

where $\gamma(\cdot)$ is positively homogeneous of degree 1 and δ is a constant such that $\delta\beta \neq 0$. This is a generalization of Gorman's (1961) 'polar form'. This is an example of the general principle that fruitful progress in welfare economics requires one to take advantage of empirical restrictions that may be satisfied by the observed data and by consumer preferences.

I now come to the question of the applicability of these tools of analysis to measurement of *social* welfare. Clearly this is the only way their development can be justified. Hicks's only comment on this point appears to be the following important and suggestive one (1942d: 127):

> In the application to Welfare Economics, the general test for a particular reform being an *improvement* is that the gainers should gain sufficiently for them to be able to compensate the losers and still remain gainers on balance. This test would be carried out by striking the balance of the Compensating Variations.

This conjecture, as we may call it, was recently examined by Ruiz-Castillo (1987), who found that the same aggregation problems that beset the double-index criterion in the measurement of real national income also beset the double criterion of summing both the compensating and equivalent variations: namely that individual preferences must be identical and homothetic.

We thus come to the conclusion that the attempt to evaluate social welfare by means of a real-valued function, or even a pair of numerical criteria, necessarily fails unless either (i) stringent assumptions can be accepted concerning consumer preferences, or (ii) certain restrictions on the set of observable prices and incomes can be specified that enable one to relax the above assumptions concerning preferences. In either case the attempt is futile unless such empirical restrictions can be assumed to exist, and use is made of them. This is the principal lesson I have learned from studying welfare economics, and in particular, the works of its great advocate and developer, Sir John Hicks.

NOTES

Work was supported by a Humboldt Research Award for Senior US Scientists. I wish to thank Douglas Irwin for helping me track down an obscure Turgot reference; I was also privileged to see an as yet unpublished manuscript of his which drew my attention to the relevance of the writings of Mill (1825) and Senior (1828).

1 Curiously, this anonymous 1826 paper is not included in Mill (1967), but it is undoubtedly by Mill. The third paragraph on p. 392 starts out, 'We endeavoured, in a former Number [vol. iii, p. 405–8] to form . . .'; this is a reference to the 1825 paper. Likewise, on p. 171 of his anonymous 1827 article, Mill states, 'From the data which we have exhibited in former articles, . . .' and refers in a footnote to 'Westminster Review, Nos. VI. and XII.' The editor of the *Collected Works* (1967: 144n) identifies the first with Mill (1825) but the second with an article by Mill's father, James Mill, on a totally unrelated subject. The omission of the 1826 article from the *Collected Works* is probably due to the fact that Mill himself omitted it from his bibliography (MacMinn *et al.* 1945: 7–8), whether deliberately or inadvertently we cannot know. Bain (1882: 35–6) attributed the 1826 and 1827 articles to Mill, but inexplicably passed over the 1825 article. Fetter (1962: 584) attributed the 1826 article to 'J.S. Mill (probably)', citing Bain and noting the omission from MacMinn, but he evidently overlooked the internal evidence cited above.

2 Actually, to achieve this requires implementation of a rule to distribute incomes optimally (cf. Samuelson 1956; Chipman and Moore 1979), otherwise social utility could not be expressed as a function of *aggregate* quantities consumed. But if preferences are homothetic and representable by utility functions that are homogeneous of degree 1, then the so-called 'shibboleth' rule of constant proportional income distribution fills the bill provided, and only provided, the Bergson–Samuelson social welfare function (with individual utilities as arguments) is of the Eisenberg–Cobb–Douglas type, with exponents equal to the constant distributive shares (see Chipman 1987). See Chipman and Moore (1979: 133–5) for an example of an aggregate social utility function of the Cobb–Douglas type (with aggregate quantities as arguments) that is generated in this way. Jevons (1884) for a long period persuaded the profession that a geometric mean was the best form of price index; why should it not be the most suitable form of quantity index?

3 Cf. Quesnay (1757b: 1958: 526). Quesnay's *valeur vénale* corresponded to Smith's subsequent 'value in exchange'. According to Quesnay (p. 511): 'Without enjoyment and consumption, the goods produced would be useless. It is consumption that makes them exchangeable and sustains their prices; a good price and the amount produced are what form the income or annual wealth of a nation.'

4 According to Quesnay (1767; 1888: 635), 'population always exceeds wealth (*richesses*) under good and bad governments, because propagation has no bounds other than subsistence, and always tends to pass beyond it'. On the other hand, Turgot (1766; 1769: vol. 11, §VI, p. 23; 1889: §VI, p. 52) argued simply, without reference to population pressures, that wages would be brought down to subsistence by competition of the workers.

5 Cf. Quesnay (1757a: 826; 1888: 234; 1958: 496; see also Meek 1962: 73): 'production of industrial products does not increase wealth, since the value of these products increases only by the cost of the subsistence consumed by the workers'.

6 McCulloch justly criticized Smith (p. 146n) by saying:

All sorts of labour should plainly be regarded as productive, which occasion, whether directly or indirectly, the production of a greater amount of value than was expended in carrying them on ... Dr. Smith looks upon every sort of labour as unproductive which does not directly contribute to the production of some material and vendible product that may be stocked and stored up for a shorter or longer period.

See also McCulloch (1825: part IV). McCulloch also faulted Smith for his criticism of the physiocrats (1776; 1889: 305n), pointing out that since Smith was not aware of the theory of rent, 'his refutation of the system of the Economists is far from satisfactory'. The inconsistencies in Smith's arguments were also effectively exposed by Gray (1797), Lauderdale (1804) and Senior (1836). That Smith's emphasis on durability was a throwback to his mercantilist predecessors was remarked upon by Marx (1905: 280–4; 1951: 171–4); in his words (1905: 283; 1951: 173):

> Thus Adam Smith makes the same distinction between commodities and services as the Monetary System did between gold and silver and other commodities.

7 I have provided my own translation in place of Prinsep's (Say 1814; 1844: I, p. 62), which is from the fifth edition (1826: I, pp. 5–7).

8 That independent spirit, Robert Torrens, in spite of adopting Malthus's definition of wealth (1820: 1), devoted the opening section of his last chapter on 'Mercantile industry' (1821: 147–95) to explaining why transportation was productive because it brought goods from places where their [marginal] utility was low to where it was high.

9 An example of the 'stock' interpretation is given by the following (1757a: 830; 1888: 244; 1958: 506; Meek 1962: 82): 'If the cultivator is ruined by the financier, ... wealth, locked up in the financier's coffers, remains barren, or, if it is invested at interest, overburdens the state.'

10 In fact, Lundberg has advanced the hypothesis that the anonymous first (1793) English translator of Turgot's work was none other than Smith himself, who described the work in the introduction (omitted from the 1859 reprint) as 'a work, on the foundation of which was formed, one of the most approved and justly celebrated treatises in the English language, Dr. Adam Smith's Essay on the Wealth of Nations' (Lundberg 1964: 25). However, Groenewegen (1969: 276n) relates that Jacob Viner had informed him of the existence at the Princeton University Library of a periodical (unnamed) containing a pre-1793 serial version of the 1793 translation of Turgot in which either the translator or the publisher described the translator as 'a merchant', which would exclude Smith. See also Viner (1965: 132–8). A letter from Viner to Groenewegen of 5 March, 1969 (a copy of which was kindly furnished to me by Douglas Irwin) clarifies that the periodical was *The Literary [and Biographical] Magazine, and British Review*, vols 6 and 7 (1791), and that the letter of introduction preceding the translation was signed 'Mercator'. Meek (1977: 20n) has stated that he can 'prove incontrovertibly ... that Smith was the author of the famous translation of Turgot's Six Edicts into Sanskrit'. Thus, the issue of the authorship of the 1793 translation still seems far from settled.

11 Cf. Fisher (1906: 194):

> We have considered the rate of interest as the price of capital in terms of income. If we consider reciprocally the price of income in terms of capital, we shall have what is called the 'rate of capitalization.' It is measured in

years, namely the number of years during which there would flow an amount of income equal to the capital.... The concept of "years' purchase" is common in England as applied to land rents. It is evidently interconvertible with the rate of interest. A rate of interest of four per cent indicates a '[twenty-five] years' purchase' or rate of capitalization of twenty-five years.

(I have corrected an evident misprint.) The concept of 'years' purchase' is a very old one, to be found for example in Culpeper's treatise against usury where he points out that a high interest rate will lower the rate of capitalization of land (1621: 7):

> For the high rate of Vsvry makes Land sell so cheape; and the cheape sale of Land is the cause men seeke no more by industry and cost to improve them: and this is plaine both by example, and demonstration; for we see in other Countries, where the vse of money is of a low rate, Lands are generally sold for 30. 40. in some 50. yeeres purchase: And we know by the rule of bargaining, that if the rate of vse were not greater here, then in other Countries; Lands were then as good a penniworth, at twenty yeeres purchase, as they are now at sixeteene: For Lands being the best assurance and securest inheritance, will still beare a rate aboue money ...

Petty (1690) employed the concept to estimate the 'wealth' (a stock) of various countries given data on income. He observed, for example (pp. 67–8), that 'where the Rent of Land is advanced by reason of Multitude of People; there the number of Years purchase, for which the Inheritance may be sold, is also advanced ...'. Newmarch (1863) used a similar method to estimate capital accumulation, using data from income tax returns; he (p. 1382), 'after taking some trouble, arrived at the conclusion that if we multiply by 20, or, what is the same thing, capitalise at 20 years' purchase, or at the rate of 5 per cent. per annum, ... we shall not overstate' the capital accumulation during the period studied; he did not indicate on what basis he arrived at the figure of 20. Giffen (1878, 1889) estimated the total value of capital in Great Britain by multiplying the gross income of different classes of assets by their years' purchase, the latter varying with the durability of the asset; cf. Nicholson (1893: 214–15). Again, he provided no indication as to how he arrived at the different years' purchase. The concept of 'years' purchase' corresponds of course to the 'price–earnings ratio' of stock-market terminology. Fisher's concept was evidently meant to apply to net rather than gross income.

12 The French expression is *le denier du prix des terres*. The word 'denier' can mean 'penny' but in the present context it means the reciprocal of a number, as in the phrase *intérêt au denier vingt* (interest at one in twenty, i.e. at 5 per cent). The rendering given in the first (anonymous) English translation of 1793 (which according to Lundberg 1964 was probably the work of Adam Smith) is 'so many years purchase of the land' (1859: §57, p. 278). However, Sir William Ashley – who in the preface to his 1898 translation of Turgot's work described the 1793 translation as 'a piece of hack-work, done by a man who had little understanding of the course of Turgot's arguments' (pp. x–xi) – translated the above literally as 'the penny of the price of lands' (1898: §LVII, p. 49). Meek's translation (1973: §LVII, p. 149) is 'the number of years' purchase of the land'. Groenewegen (1977) provided a new translation of Turgot's work, but it follows Ashley's closely. The first German translation by Mauvillon (1775: §54, p. 74), like Ashley's that followed it, used the literal translation 'der Pfennig des Preises der Länderein', while the second translation by Dorn (1903: §58, pp. 39–40) finessed

the problem with 'den "denier" des Bodenpreises'.

13　The original reads: 'du revenu net de tous les biens-fonds multiplié par le taux du prix des terres.' The 1793 translation (1859: §91, p. 307) is 'in the clear revenue of all the real estates, multiplied by the rate of the price of land'. The Ashley, Meek and Groenewegen translations respectively read 'of the net revenue of all the estates in land, multiplied by the rate at which land is sold' (1898: §XCI, pp. 86–7), 'of the net revenue of all the landed property multiplied by the rate at which land is sold' (1973: §XCI, p. 174) and 'in the net revenue of all landed estates, multiplied by the rate at which land is sold (1977: §91, p. 88).

14　The original reads 'Les biens-fonds équivalent à un capital égal à leur revenu annuel multiplié par le denier courant auquel les terres se vendent'. The 1793 translation of this reads 'Real estates are equivalent to any capital equal to their annual revenue, multiplied by the current rate at which lands are sold'. The Ashley and Groenewegen translations read 'Estates in land are equivalent to a capital equal to their annual revenue multiplied by the current penny at which lands are sold' (§XCI, 87) and 'Landed estates are equivalent to a capital equal to their revenue multiplied by the current penny at which lands are sold' (§91, p. 88), while Meek's translation reads 'Landed estates are the equivalent of a capital equal to their annual revenue multiplied by the number of years' purchase at which land is currently sold' (§XCI, p. 174).

15　In fact, computations such as these were made long ago by Petty (1690: 32) who multiplied his estimate of personal income by 20, 'the Mass of Mankind being worth Twenty Years purchase as well as Land', to obtain 'the value of the whole People'. A similar computation was made by Nicholson (1891) employing Giffen's (1889) method; he found that the value of human capital in the UK was five times the value of material capital. See also Nicholson (1893: 47, 120).

　　Senior (1836: 132; 1850: 9) also showed an appreciation of the role of human capital in saying 'Health, strength, and knowledge, and the other natural and acquired powers of body and mind, appear to us to be articles of wealth', and noted that (1836: 133; 1850: 10), owing to the institution of slavery, 'If the question whether personal qualities are articles of wealth had been proposed in classical times, it would have appeared too clear for discussion', and that, 'The amount of revenue derived from their exercise in England far exceeds the rental of all the lands in Great Britain'. And Storch (1824: 29–31) pointed out that immaterial goods could be accumulated in the form of human capital, and resold in the form of services of this human capital. Smith himself, whose insight and common sense fortunately exceeded his consistency, classified 'the acquired and useful abilities of all the inhabitants or members of the society' as part of 'fixed capital' (1776: I, p. 335; 1786: 122). In fairness to Mill it must be pointed out that he also included human capital in saying (1848: book I, ch. III, §3, p. 59)

> The skill, and the energy and perseverance, of the artisans of a country, are reckoned part of its wealth, no less than their tools and machinery. According to this definition, we should regard all labour as productive which is employed in creating permanent utilities, whether embodied in human beings, or in any other animate or inanimate objects.

16　My italics.

17　It might be thought that in a more general model, say a closed-economy two-factor–two-commodity Heckscher–Ohlin model, one could hold the price of commodity 2 constant by taking it to the numéraire. However, imposition of an excise tax on commodity 1 would in general lower the production cost (the producer price excluding the tax) of commodity 1 (since resources would be forced out of industry 1 into industry 2) relative to the production cost in industry 2; while this lower production cost would be adequately accounted for by an upward-sloping industry supply curve, it follows from the Stolper–Samuelson theorem that it would have the additional effect of causing a more than proportionate fall in the rental of the factor used intensively in industry 1 and a rise in the rental of the other factor. It could not be expected that these opposite movements of factor incomes would cancel out; therefore the change in total income would have to be accounted for in the term $Y(1) - Y(0)$ of (8.14). But such income changes, and the resulting shift in the industry demand curve, are not accounted for in consumers' surplus analysis.

18   It is of interest to observe that Dupuit (1844) arrived at the same conclusion but with different reasoning. Working with what today we would call an indirect or inverse demand function (in the present example this would be $p_1 = 1/\sqrt{x_1}$), he defined the utility of x_1 as $\int_0^{x_1}(1/\sqrt{x_1})dx_1 = 2\sqrt{x_1}$ (in agreement with the first term of (8.1)), so that the increase in utility from $x_1 = 4$ to $x_1 = 9$ in Figure 8.1 would be represented by the area BCGF. From this he subtracted the 'costs of production', DCGF, to obtain the increase in net utility BCD (1844: 373–4). On the other hand, when he went on to discuss the effects of a tax (pp. 374–5) he used a concept equivalent to Marshall's (1890 (1920: 467n)) which in the present example is $\int_{p_1}^{\infty} p_1^{-2}dp_1 = -\int_{\infty}^{p_1} p_1^{-2}dp_1 = p_1^{-1}$, in agreement with the first term of (8.3).

19   Based on McKenzie's (1957) 'minimum-income function' $M_x(p)$, where $x = h(p^0, Y^0)$.

BIBLIOGRAPHY

[Bailey, S.] (1825) *A Critical Dissertation on the Nature, Measures, and Causes of Value*, London: printed for R. Hunter; reprinted, London School of Economics and Political Science, 1931.

Bain, A. (1882) *John Stuart Mill. A Criticism: With Personal Recollections*, London: Longmans, Green.

Barone, E. (1908) 'Il Ministerio della produzione nello stato colletivista', *Giornale degli Economisti* [2] 37, August: 267–93; October: 391–414. English translation, 'The Ministry of Production in the collectivist state', in F. A. Hayek (ed.) *Collectivist Economic Planning*. London: Routledge & Kegan Paul, 1935, pp. 245–90.

Bergson (Burk), A. (1938) 'A reformulation of certain aspects of welfare economics', *Quarterly Journal of Economics* 52, February: 310–34.

Böhm-Bawerk, E. von (1889) *Positive Theorie des Kapitales*, Innsbruck: Verlag der Wagner'schen Universitäts-Buchhandlung.

Cannan, E. (1893) *A History of the Theories of Production and Distribution in English Political Economy from 1776 to 1848*, London: Rivington, Percival; 3rd edn 1917; reprinted, London: Staples Press, 1953.

Chipman, J. S. (1987) 'When is a fixed income distribution optimal?', in G. R. Feiwel (ed.) *Arrow and the Foundations of the Theory of Economic Policy*, London: Macmillan, pp. 371–81.

——— (1990) 'Marshall's consumer's surplus in modern perspective', in J. K. Whitaker (ed.) *Centenary Essays on Alfred Marshall*, Cambridge: Cambridge University Press, pp. 278–92.

——— and Moore, J. C. (1973) 'Aggregate demand, real national income, and the compensation principle', *International Economic Review* 14, February: 153–81.

——— and ——— (1976) 'Why an increase in GNP need not imply an improvement in potential welfare', *Kyklos* 29 (3): 391–418.

―――― and ―――― (1978) 'The new welfare economics, 1939–1974', *International Economic Review* 19, October: 547–84.

―――― and ―――― (1979) 'On social welfare functions and the aggregation of preferences', *Journal of Economic Theory* 21, August: 111–39.

―――― and ―――― (1980) 'Compensating variation, consumer's surplus, and welfare', *American Economic Review* 70, December: 933–49.

―――― and ―――― (1990) 'Acceptable indicators of welfare change, consumer's surplus analysis, and the Gorman polar form', in J. S. Chipman, D. McFadden and M. K. Richter (eds) *Preferences, Uncertainty, and Optimality. Essays in Honor of Leonid Hurwicz*, Boulder, CO: Westview Press, pp. 68–120.

―――― and ―――― (1992) 'Compensating variation as a measure of welfare change', in W. Neuefeind and R. G. Riezman (eds) *Economic Theory and International Trade: Essays in Memoriam J. Trout Rader*, Berlin, Heidelberg, New York: Springer-Verlag, pp. 93–128.

[Culpeper, T.] (1621) *A Tract against Vsvrie*, London: printed by W.I. for Walter Burre; facsimile reprint, Amsterdam: Theatrum Orbis Terrarum and Norwood, NJ: Walter J. Johnson, 1974.

Debreu, G. (1960) 'Topological methods in cardinal utility theory', in K. J. Arrow, S. Karlin and P. Suppes (eds) *Mathematical Methods in the Social Sciences, 1959*, Stanford, CA: Stanford University Press, pp. 12–26.

Dobb, M. (1948) *Soviet Economic Development since 1917*, New York: International Publishers.

Dupuit, J. (1844) 'De la mesure de l'utilité des travaux publics', *Annales des Ponts et Chaussées, Mémoires et documents relatifs à l'art des constructions et au service de l'ingénieur* [2] 8, 2e semestre: 332–75, and Planche 75: Figs 1–4. English translation, 'On the measurement of the utility of public works', in *International Economic Papers* 2 (1952), 83–110; and K. J. Arrow and T. Scitovsky (eds) *Readings in Welfare Economics*, Homewood, IL: Richard D. Irwin, 1969, pp. 255–83.

Fetter, F. W. (1962) 'Economic articles in the *Westminster Review* and their authors, 1824–51', *Journal of Political Economy* 70, December: 570–96.

Fisher, I. (1906) *The Nature of Capital and Income*, New York: Macmillan.

―――― (1922) *The Making of Index Numbers*, Boston and New York: Houghton Mifflin.

Frisch, R. (1939) 'The Dupuit taxation theorem', *Econometrica* 7, April: 145–50, 156–7.

Garnier, G. (1802) *Recherches sur la nature et les causes de la richesse des nations; par Adam Smith. Traduction nouvelle, avec des notes et observations*, 5 vols, Paris: Chez H. Agasse, Imprimeur-Libraire.

Giffen, R. (1878) 'Recent accumulations of capital in the United Kingdom', *Journal of the Royal Statistical Society* 41, March: 1–31; discussion, 32–9. Article reprinted in R. Giffen, *Essays in Finance*, 3rd edn, London: George Bell; 1882, pp. 161–96.

―――― (1889) *The Growth of Capital*, London: George Bell, facsimile reprint, New York: Augustus M. Kelley, 1970.

Gorman, W. M. (1955) 'The intransitivity of certain criteria used in welfare economics', *Oxford Economic Papers* 7, February: 25–35.

―――― (1961) 'On a class of preference fields', *Metroeconomica* 13, August: 53–6.

[Gray, J.] (1797) *The Essential Principles of the Wealth of Nations*, London: Printed for T. Becket; reprinted, New York: Augustus M. Kelley, 1969.

Groenewegen, P. D. (1969) 'Turgot and Adam Smith', *Scottish Journal of Political Economy* 16, November: 271–87.

——— (1977) *The Economics of A. R. J. Turgot*, The Hague: Martinus Nijhoff.

Harrod, R. F. (1938) 'Scope and method in economics', *Economic Journal* 48, September: 383–412.

Hause, J. C. (1975) 'The theory of welfare cost measurement', *Journal of Political Economy* 83, December: 1145–82.

Henderson, A. (1941) 'Consumer's surplus and the compensating variation', *Review of Economic Studies* 8, February: 117–21.

Hermann, F. B. W. von (1832) *Staatswirtschaftliche Untersuchungen*, Munich: Anton Weber.

Hotelling, H. (1938) 'The general welfare in relation to problems of taxation and of railway and utility rates', *Econometrica* 6, July: 242–69.

Hurwicz, L. and Uzawa, H. (1972) 'On the integrability of demand functions', in J. S. Chipman, L. Hurwicz, M. K. Richter and H. F. Sonnenschein (eds) *Preferences, Utility, and Demand*, New York: Harcourt Brace Jovanovich, pp. 114–48.

Jevons, W. S. (1884) *Investigations in Currency and Finance*, London: Macmillan; facsimile reprint, New York: Augustus M. Kelley, 1964.

Johnson, H. G. (1966) 'Factor market distortions and the shape of the transformation curve', *Econometrica* 34, July: 686–98.

Kaldor, N. (1939) 'Welfare propositions in economics and interpersonal comparisons of utility', *Economic Journal* 49, September: 549–52.

Kuznets, S. (1948) 'On the valuation of social income – reflections on Professor Hicks' article', *Economica* 15, February: 1–16; May: 116–31.

Laspeyres, E. (1864) 'Hamburger Waarenpreise 1851–1863 und die californisch-australischen Goldentdeckungen seit 1848', *Jahrbücher für Nationalökonomie und Statistik* 3: 81–118.

——— (1871) 'Die Berechnung einer mittleren Waarenpreissteigerung', *Jahrbücher für Nationalökonomie und Statistik* 16: 296–314.

Lauderdale, J. Maitland, 8th Earl of (1804) *An Inquiry into the Nature and Origin of Public Wealth*, Edinburgh: printed for Arch. Constable; 2nd edn, Edinburgh: printed for Archibald Constable, 1819; facsimile reprint of 1st edn, New York: Augustus M. Kelley, 1966.

List, F. (1841) *Das Nationale System der Politischen Ökonomie*, Stuttgart and Tübingen: J.C. Cotta. English translation by Sampson S. Lloyd, *The National System of Political Economy*, London: Longmans, Green, 1885; new edition, with an introduction by J. Shield Nicholson, 1904; reprint of 1904 edition, Fairfield, NJ: Augustus M. Kelley, 1991.

Lundberg, I. C. (1964) *Turgot's Unknown Translator*, The Hague: Martinus Nijhoff.

McCulloch, J. R. (1825) *Principles of Political Economy*, 1st edn, reprinted with J. Locke, *Essay on Interest and Value of Money*, London: Alex. Murray, 1870.

McKenzie, L. W. (1957) 'Demand theory without a utility index', *Review of Economic Studies* 24, June: 185–9.

MacMinn, N., Hainds, J. R. and McCrimmon, J. M. (1945) *Bibliography of the Published Writings of John Stuart Mill. Edited from his Manuscript with corrections and notes*, Evanston, IL: Northwestern University.

Malthus, T. R. (1798) *An Essay on the Principle of Population as it affects the Future Improvement of Society*, London: Printed for J. Johnson.

——— (1820) *Principles of Political Economy considered with a view to their Practical Application*, London: John Murray.

——— (1827) *Definitions in Political Economy*, London: John Murray; facsimile reprint, New York: Kelley & Millman, 1954.

Marshall, A. (1890) *Principles of Economics*, London: Macmillan; 2nd edn, 1891; 8th edn, 1920.

Marx, K. (1905) *Theorien über den Mehrwert*, ed. K. Kautsky, vol. I, Stuttgart: Verlag von J. H. W. Dietz. English translation of selections, *Theories of Surplus Value*, London: Lawrence & Wishart, 1951.

Meek, R. L. (1962) *The Economics of Physiocracy*, London: Allen & Unwin; reprinted, Cambridge, MA: Harvard University Press, 1963; and Fairfield, NJ: Augustus M. Kelley, 1993.

—— (1973) *Turgot on Progress, Sociology and Economics*, Cambridge: Cambridge University Press.

—— (1977) *Smith, Marx & After*, London: Chapman and Hall.

[Mill, J. S.] (1825) 'The corn laws', *Westminster Review* 3 (6), April: 394–420; reprinted in J. S. Mill (1967) *Essays on Economics and Society*, ed. J.M. Robson, *Collected Works of John Stuart Mill*, vol. IV, Toronto: University of Toronto Press, pp. 45–70.

—— (1826) 'Corn laws', *Westminster Review* 6 (12), October: 373–404.

—— (1827) 'New corn law', *Westminster Review* 7 (13), January: 169–86; reprinted in J. S. Mill (1967) *Essays on Economics and Society*, ed. J.M. Robson, *Collected Works of John Stuart Mill*, vol. IV, Toronto: University of Toronto Press, pp. 141–59.

Mill, J. S. (1848) *Principles of Political Economy with some of their Applications to Social Philosophy*, London: John W. Parker.

—— (1967) *Essays on Economics and Society*, ed. J. M. Robson *Collected Works of John Stuart Mill*, vol. IV, Toronto: University of Toronto Press.

Molinier, J. (1958) 'Le système de comptabilité nationale de François Quesnay', in *François Quesnay et la Physiocratie*, Paris: Institut National d'Études Démographiques, vol. I, pp. 75–104.

[Newmarch, W.] (1863) 'The annual accumulation of capital in the United Kingdom', *The Economist* 21, 12 December: 1391–83; 19 December: 1411–13.

Nicholson, J. S. (1891) 'The living capital of the United Kingdom', *Economic Journal* 1, March: 95–107.

—— (1893) *Principles of Political Economy*, vol. I, London: Adam and Charles Black.

Oncken, A. (ed.) (1888) *Œuvres économiques et philosophiques de F. Quesnay*, Frankfurt: Joseph Baer, and Paris: Jules Peelman.

P[aasche], H. (1874) 'Ueber die Preisentwicklung der letzten Jahre nach den Hamburger Börsennotirungen', *Jahrbücher für Nationalökonomie und Statistik* 23: 168–78.

Pareto, V. (1894) 'Il massimo di utilità dato dalla libera concorrenza', *Giornale degli Economisti* [2] 9, July: 48–66.

Petty, W. (1690) *Political Arithmetic*, London: printed for Robert Clavel and Hen. Mortlock.

Pigou, A. C. (1920) *The Economics of Welfare*, London: Macmillan; 2nd edn, 1924; 3rd edn, 1929; 4th edn, 1932.

Quesnay, F. (1757a) 'Grains', in D. Diderot (ed.) *Encyclopédie, ou Dictionnaire raisonné des sciences, des arts et des métiers*, vol. 7, Paris: Chez Briasson, David l'aîné, Le Breton, Durand, pp. 812–31; reprinted in A. Oncken (ed.) (1888) *Œuvres économiques et philosophiques de F. Quesnay*, Frankfurt: Joseph Baer, and Paris: Jules Peelman, pp. 193–249; and in *François Quesnay et la Physiocratie*, Paris: Institut National d'Études Démographiques, 1958, vol. II, pp. 459–510.

—— (1757b) 'Hommes', in *François Quesnay et la Physiocratie*, Paris: Institut National d'Études Démographiques, 1958, vol. II, pp. 511–78.

—— (1764) *Tableau économique*, 3rd edn, in M. Kuczynski and R. L. Meek (eds)

Quesnay's Tableau économique, London: Macmillan, and New York: Augustus M. Kelley, 1972.

—— (1767) *Despotisme de la Chine*, in A. Oncken (ed.) (1888) *Œuvres économiques et philosophiques de F. Quesnay*, Frankfurt: Joseph Baer, and Paris: Jules Peelman, pp. 563–660.

Ricardo, D. (1817) *On the Principles of Political Economy, and Taxation*, London: John Murray.

—— (1820) *Notes on Mr. Malthus' work "Principles of Political Economy, considered with a view to their practical application"*, in P. Sraffa (ed.) (1951) *The Works and Correspondence of David Ricardo*, vol. II, Cambridge: Cambridge University Press.

Robbins, L. (1938) 'Interpersonal comparisons of utility: a comment', *Economic Journal* 49, December: 635–41.

Roscher, W. (1854) *Die Grundlagen der Nationalökonomie*, Stuttgart and Tübingen: J. C. Cotta.

Ruiz-Castillo, J. (1987) 'Potential welfare and the sum of individual compensating or equivalent variations', *Journal of Economic Theory* 41, February: 34–53.

Samuelson, P. A. (1939) 'The gains from international trade', *Canadian Journal of Economics and Political Science* 5, May: 195–205.

—— (1947) *Foundations of Economic Analysis*, Cambridge, MA: Harvard University Press.

—— (1950)'Evaluation of real national income', *Oxford Economic Papers* 1, January: 1–29.

—— (1953) 'Prices of factors and goods in general equilibrium', *Review of Economic Studies* 21: 1–20.

—— (1956) 'Social indifference curves', *Quarterly Journal of Economics* 70, February: 1–22.

Say, J.-B. (1814) 'Traité d'économie politique, 2nd edn, 2 vols, Paris: Chez Antoine-Augustin Renouard; 5th edn, 3 vols, Paris: Chez Rapilly, Libraire, 1826. English translation by C.R. Prinsep, *A Treatise on Political Economy*, from the 4th and 5th edns, Philadelphia: Gregg & Elliot, 1844; facsimile reprint, New York: Augustus M. Kelley, 1964.

Senior, N. W. (1828) *Three Lectures on the Transmission of the Precious Metals from Country to Country and the Mercantile Theory of Wealth*, London: John Murray.

—— (1836) *Political Economy*, in *Enclyclopædia Metropolitana*, vol. VI, pp. 129–224; 2nd edn, London: John Joseph Griffin, and Glasgow: Richard Griffin, 1850.

Smith, A. (1776) *An Inquiry into the Nature and Causes of the Wealth of Nations*, 2 vols, London: printed for W. Strahan and T. Cadell; 1863 reprint of 4th (1786) edition, ed. J. R. McCulloch; reprinted, Edinburgh: Adam and Charles Black, 1889.

Stolper, W. and Samuelson, P. A. (1942) 'Protection and real wages', *Review of Economic Studies* 9, November: 58–73.

Storch, H. F. von (1824) *Cours d'économie politique*, vol. V, *Considérations sur la nature du revenu national*, Paris: Bossange Père, Libraire; Bossange Frères, Libraires.

Torrens, R. (1821) *An Essay on the Production of Wealth*, London: printed for Longman, Hurst, Rees, Orme and Brown; reprinted, New York: Augustus M. Kelley, 1965.

Turgot, A. R. J. (1766) *Réflexions sur la formation et la distribution des richesses*. Adulterized version (with unauthorized changes by P.S. DuPont de Nemours), *Ephémérides du citoyen*, 1769, Tome 11: 14–56; 1769, Tome 12: 31–98; 1770,

Tome 1: 113–173. Second version (no place, no publisher), 1788. Original version as reconstructed by G. Schelle, in L. Robineau (ed.) *Turgot. Administration et Œuvres économiques*, Paris: Guillaumin, c1889, pp. 46–148. Anonymous English translation, *Reflections on the Formation and Distribution of Wealth*, London: printed by E. Spragg, for J. Good, John Anderson and W. Richardson, 1793; reprinted in J. R. McCulloch (ed.) *A Select Collection of Scarce and Valuable Tracts*, London: printed by Lord Overstone for distribution to his friends, 1859, pp. 241–317. English translation by W. J. Ashley, *Reflections on the Formation and the Distribution of Riches*, New York: Macmillan, 1898; facsimile reprint, New York: Augustus M. Kelley, 1971. English translations by Meek (1973) and Groenewegen (1977). German translation by J. Mauvillon, *Untersuchung über die Natur und den Ursprung der Reichthümer und ihrer Verteilung*, Lemgo: Meyersche Buchhandlung, 1775. German translation by V. Dorn, *Betrachtungen über die Bildung und die Verteilung des Reichtums*, Jena: Gustav Fischer, 1903.

Vartia, Y. O. (1983) 'Efficient methods of measuring welfare change and compensated income in terms of ordinary demand functions', *Econometrica* 51, January: 79–98.

Viner, J. (1965) 'Guide to John Rae's *Life of Adam Smith*', in J. Rae, *Life of Adam Smith* (London: Macmillan, 1895), New York: Augustus M. Kelley, pp. 1–145.

Walsh, C. M. (1901) *The Measurement of General Exchange-Value*, New York: Macmillan.

9

HICKS, KEYNES AND MARSHALL

Axel Leijonhufvud

I

Did John Hicks's 'Suggested interpretation' neutralize Keynes's revolution or divert it off the 'right' track? It is perhaps too much to say that this is a much debated question. But it is at least one on which a great many economists have made very definite (and quite contradictory) pronouncements. The issues surrounding the IS–LM model and its influence on the development of macroeconomics will not exhaust the Hicks-and-Keynes subject, but they are at the very least central to it, and this chapter will be confined to them.

The range of pronouncements on whether IS–LM did Keynes rough justice stretches approximately from the vehement denials of Richard Kahn and Joan Robinson to the less energetic but none the less staunch affirmations of Robert Solow and Paul Samuelson. Hicks was himself rather ambivalent over his 'potted version' (1967: VII) of Keynes which had 'succeeded, perhaps only too well' (1982a: 100), but when he came to explain why he had become increasingly dissatisfied with it over the years (1980a), his reasons turned out to have almost nothing to do with the issues over which others were contending.

My own position somewhere in the middle of all of this will seem one of almost contrived truculence: there is no hiding the fact that I do not agree with any of the above – not even with Keynes. The 'income-expenditure theory' criticized in my 1968 book was, of course, basically the mainstream macroeconomics descended from Hicks's 1937[1] paper via Franco Modigliani's almost equally influential 1944 contribution. This troubled me a great deal both then and later, because of my affection and admiration for the two men: I had been a student of Modigliani's at Northwestern and always felt very much a student of Hicks's, even years before he became a close friend. Sir John was not particularly appreciative of my attempt many years later to spell out my views of 'what was the matter with IS–LM' in rather painstaking detail, although he had liked the earlier book well enough.[2] In this chapter, I shall try to restate my earlier position from a somewhat different perspective in the hope of being more persuasive. But, in taking up the matter one more time, I cannot claim his support.

II

In going back over a development that is now more than 50 years old, what are we trying to accomplish? There are (at least) two objectives that we may pursue by excursion into the history of a scientific field. One, of course, is the 'straight' historical one of trying to understand the actual course that the field has taken. This requires us to recreate the intellectual situations of the past as accurately as possible and then to try to understand how they were understood by the protagonists. The most common (but not inevitable) product of this approach is a piece of 'Whig' history, i.e. history told as monotonic progress towards the present state of the arts. The other approach is most likely motivated by disaffection with the present state of the arts and its objective is to find an alternative to what happened. Here one attempts to discern what never happened but could fruitfully have happened, had the influential figures of the field seen the issues a bit differently and come to some different decision. The past is then viewed anachronistically from the present and it is being recalled for the ulterior purpose of furnishing arguments for one side or the other in some present controversy. This approach is certainly not whigish and its credentials as history may be in doubt. While not uniformly respectable, it is none the less an often useful type of intellectual endeavour that should not be spurned. This chapter will use both.

It is useful to think of the history of our subject as forming a decision tree.[3] Major economists force their contemporaries to face choices – choices of what to ask, what to assume, what to regard as evidence and what methods and models to employ – and persuade the profession or some faction of it to follow the choice they make. The path that any particular school has followed traces a sequence of such decisions. Many of the choices faced in such a sequence were not anticipated by the founder to which we trace the development in question, but were created by subsequent contributors; some of the decisions made we may judge to have been 'wrong' in hindsight.

At one time the great works of the past had alternative futures, in the sense that they opened up a range of theoretical possibilities that was narrowed down only later. This was certainly true in exceptional measure of the *General Theory*. But it has been true as well of the influential corpus of theoretical work that Hicks created in the 1930s. The analytical choices of subsequent authors have determined how we have come to understand these works later.

Readers eventually wrest control of great works away from their authors. To try to decide which later construction was *the one* that Keynes 'really meant' is in all probability not a useful exercise. To raise the question most probably means to pose a false choice. We should not suppose that Keynes was uniquely capable of 'logical closure', i.e. of fully anticipating *all* the logical possibilities later found in the theoretical structure he had outlined.[4] It is likely that he 'really meant' *none* of the theories or models later evolved from that difficult book. His untimely death left us with little commentary by

Keynes himself on the directions that Keynesianism took.[5] In his case, the more useful exercise is to try to regain a sense of the contemporary *indeterminacy* of the future consequences of his ideas.[6]

With Hicks, the situation is different. Hicks the Elder had to live with the pervasive influence of the contributions of Hicks the Younger and we have his commentaries over many years on what others had made of his ideas and on what points he himself had changed his mind.

III

Over recent decades, we have become used to the neo-Keynesians railing against the neo-classical establishment for having emasculated Keynes, the revolutionary leader, and – especially around Cambridge – making Hicks the neo-classical goat of the story. But originally, in 1937, the relationship of Hicks and Keynes was of course quite different.

Keynes was the establishment figure. It goes without saying that Hicks was basically unknown outside the small economics profession, while Keynes was a well-known public figure. Within economics, Keynes was not only the author of a number of well-known works but also the long-time editor of the *Economic Journal*. He was a major representative of the dominant Marshallian tradition in Cambridge. It was from this tradition that he had to wage his own 'struggle to escape'.

John Hicks, 20 years younger, could not possibly have seen the intellectual situation in such terms. Far from indoctrinated in a particular analytical tradition, he had the inestimable benefit of not having been trained in economics at all. Outwardly shy and burdened by a bothersome stammer, he had an absolutely firm inner confidence in his own intellectual capabilities and no inclination to bow to authorities. When it came to learning economic theory, he set about it as a task of creating a personal synthesis, making up his own mind through wide and eclectic reading about what were the best elements, how they might be improved and how they might fit together. The personal synthesis of economic theory that he was building had far more of Lausanne, Chicago, Vienna and Stockholm than of Cambridge in it.

In *A Market Theory of Money*, his last, posthumously appearing book, Hicks comments on the differences in outlook between himself and Keynes more than 50 years earlier:

> I have .. .come to feel sure that when Keynes spoke of 'classical' theory it was Marshall's he had in mind. He had learned and then taught in the school of economics that Marshall had founded at Cambridge; it was the doctrine that he himself had been teaching that he was now deliberately casting off.

> (Hicks 1989a: 72)

And in the accompanying footnote:

So it was that when Keynes saw it ['Mr. Keynes and the classics'], though he found my version of his own theory fairly acceptable ..., he insisted that I had got the 'classics' all wrong. My 'classical' was much more primitive than his 'classical' theory. I now regard this as evidence that his 'classic' was Marshall. Though when I wrote that piece I had been teaching for some months in Cambridge ...; my background was still what I had learned in my years at LSE.

What difference does it make whether Keynes's 'classics' were Marshallians or not? What could be so 'much more *primitive*' about Pareto, Knight or the Austrians – the people from whom Hicks had learned his microtheory? This retrospective judgement of his contrasts curiously with the state of theory at the time it was penned: the legacies of Lausanne, Chicago and Vienna are clearly still with us but that of Marshall appears spent and lost.

The issue, I believe, is the treatment of time and the problem inheres in the tension between theory as explanation of historical process and theory conceived as the pure logic of efficient allocation. Hicks wrestled with this problem through his entire career. One can see him grappling with it almost constantly for 60 years,[7] never finding a thoroughly adequate solution – but also never letting go of the problem. He *had to* grapple with it for his aim throughout was to use pure theory to understand history.

In his recent appreciation of John Hicks, William Baumol (1990) perceptively focused in on exactly this aspect of his work. Hicks's youthful contributions up through the *Theory of Wages*, Baumol notes, were historical and institutional rather than mathematical-theoretical in nature. In his old age, he liked *A Theory of Economic History* best of all his books. Was he, in the words of Baumol's title, a 'theorist *malgré lui*'?

John Hicks would hardly have thought so. But Baumol has a point none the less, for the theoretical tools for which Hicks is above all remembered were forged for the purpose of explaining historical *processes*, i.e. typically for analysing the movement of an economy *through time*. Three aspects of his theoretical approach as it developed in the 1930s are germane.

IV

First, Hicks's point of departure is *accounting*. The importance that he attached to it comes through very clearly in his little textbook, *The Social Framework*:[8]

> The method of modern economic investigation is the same as the method of all science. Economics studies facts, and seeks to arrange the facts in such ways as make it possible to draw conclusions from them. As always, it is the arrangement which is the delicate operation. Facts, arranged in the right way, speak for themselves; unarranged, they are as dead as mutton.

Theorizing, to Hicks, is not just an exercise in pure logic; it is *about* observed sequences of 'facts'. How the facts should be measured, and how arranged, to be intelligible are questions that are both central and unavoidable in constructing a theory. Hicks's attitude in this respect differs quite markedly from that of the later general equilibrium literature. Conceptual issues relating to the measurement of income, capital, wealth and welfare remained central to his interests throughout his career.[9] Questions about the 'existence' of a general equilibrium, on the other hand, were of no interest to him at all (cf. Punzo 1991).

Second, the thus recorded process is divided into *periods*. The basic idea is to simulate the dynamic process by applying static price and allocation theory to each of these time-slices. The process is supposed to be in static equilibrium *within* each period: prices and quantities are *simultaneously* determined (given the state of expectations); all flows are treated as if constant and the order in which events happen does not matter. At the 'dateline' between periods, the parameters of the static model are to be updated: the net changes in stock-variables are recorded and expectations revised.

Eventually, Hicks came to feel that it may be more or less impossible to define a period length such that the within-period assumptions that have to be made for the IS- and for the LM-schedule make sense at the same time. Simultaneous determination does 'deliberate violence to the *order* in which in the real world (in *any* real world) events occur'.[10] This problem becomes the more acute, the longer the period:[11]

Keynes's [he said] was a 'short-period', a term with connotations derived from Marshall; we shall not go far wrong if we think of it as a year. Mine was an 'ultra-short-period'; I called it a week. Much more can happen in a year than in a week; Keynes has to allow for quite a lot of things to happen. I wanted to avoid so much happening, so that my (flexprice) markets could reflect propensities (and expectations) as they are at the moment. So it was that I made my markets open only on Monday; what actually happened during the ensuing week was not to affect them. This was a very artificial device, not (I would think now) much to be recommended. But the point of it was to exclude the things which might happen, and must disturb the markets, during a period of finite length; and this, . . . is a very real trouble in Keynes.

Third, beginning with the 1934 'Reconsideration', Hicks consistently built on choice-theoretical foundations. In a temporal context, decisions are represented as choices between the future consequences of alternative options. For the individual's opportunity set to be clearly defined, the actions of all other agents need to be known. If the system is closed by assuming that it is in intertemporal general equilibrium, the result is a teleological structure where all decisions are made at the origin of time. Such theory precludes meaningful history. Hicks's *temporary* general equilibrium construction was an attempt to stop short of this logical dead end and preserve the 'story-telling' ability of value theory. But it was not an altogether satisfactory compromise and 50 years after the writing of *Value and Capital* he was still exploring for other avenues of escape. Hicks the Elder had a very clear conception of what would constitute a satisfactory escape:[12]

> One must assume that the people in one's models do not know what is going to happen, and know that they do not know what is going to happen. As in History!

But this commandment would block any intertemporal generalization of choice theory, for it is clear that Hicks meant to preclude not only its deterministic but also its stochastic versions.

V

From the very beginning of the 'Keynes and the classics' debate, the participants have tended to confuse themselves and each other over statics versus dynamics, equilibrium versus change and sequential causation versus simultaneous determination. Part of the problem, at least, has been the use of IS–LM as the framework of the debate, for Hicks's period-analysis is quite different from Marshall's. This is not the place to go into Marshall's method in detail; the following three-part outline sketches my understanding of it.

(i) Of all the great marginalists, Marshall was indeed 'neoclassicist' in actually building on the British Classical school, rather than discarding its legacy. The theoretical conception of the Classics was, to paraphrase Baumol, 'magnificently dynamic' in the sense that it posed (verbally) a set of differential equations of the type: 'The capital stock will grow as long as the rate of profit is positive;' 'Population will grow as long as the wage exceeds the subsistence wage;' 'Growing population will press on the external and internal margins of cultivation and increase the landlords' share of income.' But economics had to wait for Baumol to actually *model* the theory. The Classics themselves, of course, could not handle systems of differential equations but were constrained to assume that their system had the simplest kind of attractor and would thus converge on a stationary state 'in the long run'. Such stationary states were amenable to much simpler analysis.

Marshall's programme should be understood, I believe, as aiming to expand this mode of analysis to situations in which we are 'not all dead'. His underlying theory is also a system of differential equations. Although a good mathematician (with some knowledge of differential equations), he could not handle the analysis of a dynamic system as complex as the one he had in mind. Instead, he had to bail out of the explicit dynamics by the same escape hatch as his predecessors. The behaviour postulates underlying Marshall's short-run supply and demand analysis are adaptive: 'If the market price exceeds his supply price, the producer will increase the rate of output;' 'If demand price exceeds the market price, the consumer will increase the rate of consumption.' Setting these rates of adaptation to zero (in the aggregate), produces the Marshallian static short-run equilibrium.

(ii) There is no choice theory underlying this market model of Marshall's. This has been overlooked, presumably because the behaviour postulates just paraphrased imply 'stopping rules' that are familiar as first-order conditions for the corresponding static choice experiments. But the difference is very significant between, on the one hand, postulating trial-and-error algorithms – in this case, gradient procedures – for locating (or rather, pursuing) local optima in environments that are changing and may be only very imperfectly known and, on the other, asserting global optimization over opportunity sets perfectly known once and for all *ex ante*. It is the difference between Herbert Simon's procedural rationality and substantive rationality. Marshall's procedural rationality does not trap him into the teleological frame of choice theory. His theory, to use terms that Sir John favoured, is firmly 'in time' from the start; it does not pose the ultimately insoluble problem of putting time back into the 'out of time' logical calculus of mutually consistent choices, i.e. the problem of recovering history from general equilibrium.

(iii) At the level of the market, Marshall's theory would produce two differential equations for the time-paths of the price and for the output rate:[13]

$$\left(\frac{dp}{dt}\right)_t = f[q^d(p_t) - q_t] \tag{9.1}$$

$$\left(\frac{dq}{dt}\right)_t = h[p^s(q_t) - p_t] \tag{9.2}$$

Clearly, these two together make a non-linear monster potentially capable of all sorts of complex dynamic behaviour, about which not much could have been said in the 'pre-chaotic' days of Marshall. He tried to cope with the monster in two (not entirely consistent) ways.

In a number of instances he invoked 'reasonably intelligent' behaviour to, as it were, pour oil on the potentially stormy waters. Equations such as the above are driven entirely by past realizations like proper dynamic systems in the physical sciences.[14] Marshall did not have rational expectations to smooth the market's trajectory, but he seems to have realized that forward-looking agents would tend to dampen the oscillatory tendencies that the system would otherwise be likely to exhibit. But this reliance on expectations in Marshall is not a consistent, analytically developed theme; it occurs, rather, in the form of sporadic common-sense observations of the sort on which his later admirers would base their 'it's all in Marshall' claims.

His main strategy for really taming the monster is of course his market day/short-run/long-run scheme. The procedure is familiar to all economists:[15] the endogenous variables are ranked according to their speeds of adjustment; one then investigates the values that the faster moving variables would go to, if the slower ones were actually constant (cf. Leijonhufvud 1968: ch. II). Marshall uses this trick to persuade his readers that his market process always goes to nice steady-state attractors – i.e. to points on his static demand and supply schedules. To see how his procedure eliminates non-linear dynamic behaviour, note how 'hog cycles' are eliminated by the twin assumptions that (a) each market day, the market price will move *fast* so as to reveal to producers the demand price for that day's aggregate output,[16] and (b) that the output adjustments of individual firms to discrepancies between this market price and their respective supply prices will be *slow* and gradual. *Natura non facit saltum* is not just an innocuous motto. Here it is an article of faith!

The pastor may have had less faith than he preached to the congregation. Marshall's sundry warnings about relying on the mathematics of his own models have often been made fun of by later generations more confident in the power and efficacy of the calculus. In a memorable joke of Bob Solow's, 'Alfred Marshall seems to have felt that, at every step of a mathematical deduction, a little truth leaked out'. But Marshall had every reason to keep his fingers crossed, for he knew that the simple and transparent mathematics of his comparative statics rested on a swamp of ill-understood non-linear dynamics!

On his first reading of the *General Theory*, for the 1936 *Economic Journal* review, Hicks (1982a: 86) saw Keynes as using a period-analysis closely related to the temporary equilibrium method which he himself had been working on for some time:

> Once the missing element – anticipations – is added, equilibrium analysis can be used, not only in the remote stationary conditions to which many economists have found themselves driven back, but even in the real world, even in the real world in 'disequilibrium'.
> This is the general method of this book; it may be reckoned the first of Mr. Keynes's discoveries.

The two methods were *not quite* the same. Decades later, Hicks was to explain in detail how they differed.[17] But by then he had also come to realize that underlying the superficial similarities in modelling were more fundamental differences in theoretical conception. Theory in the Marshallian tradition was 'in time'; theory in the Walrasian tradition was not.

VI

At this point a consciously anachronistic perspective may help. I propose that we conceive of the economy as a complex adaptive system to be modelled as a modern massively parallel computer. The task of the machine is to compute and period-by-period to recompute the allocation of resources, prices and the distribution of incomes.[18] In the simplest model the computer operates at just two hierarchical levels. Individual agents calculate their own activities, processing information that to a large extent is local rather than global in character. These computations are done in parallel. Markets compile the results and iterate to find their respective 'partial' equilibria and these results in turn feed back into agents' calculations. The market computations too are distributed. The system works without a central processor and macro-aggregates, such as gross national product (GNP), are statistical artifacts not computed anywhere.

In such a model, both agents and markets are represented by algorithms. The network of linked algorithms produces a system of prices and a corresponding allocation of resources which are constantly updated as the system adapts to exogenous perturbations.

One of the reasons for using the computer metaphor in this way is that the notion of 'parallelism' is more helpful than that of 'simultaneity' in thinking through many of the issues of the Keynesian debate. Moreover, the linkages between processors that would have to be programmed for the 'machine' to work provides us with a notion of that *sequential causality*[19] which escapes us in analysing what goes on within the 'week' or within the 'year' (as the case may be) of a period model. We may now apply this conception to the 'Keynes and the classics' debate. I choose to focus on the issues pertaining to the determination of the interest rate.

VII

Consider first the interests of the parties. Kahn and Robinson had the strong conviction that the interest rate mechanism could *never* work so as to co-ordinate saving and investment. To them, it was a central tenet of Cambridge faith (among the faithful) that 'I determines S, but S does not determine I'. The simultaneity of IS–LM solutions make nonsense of this, so it must be a heresy.

To Samuelson and Solow the most reasonable and, indeed, most charitable interpretation of Keynes is that he held an aggregative general equilibrium theory with sticky wages. IS–LM, among its other virtues, produces this conclusion and that is good enough. All models have their limitations.

Naturally, as simple a gadget as IS–LM does too. But they are really not worth agonizing about.

Hicks's position was in between these two. He saw clearly that the 'individuality' of Keynes's theory hinged on there being 'conditions under which the interest rate mechanism will not work', and it bothered him that IS–LM would not clearly demonstrate this.[20] But whether the interest rate mechanism will work or not is largely a *within-period* question. The *simultaneity* of the static solutions to period models, be they Hicks's temporary equilibria or his IS–LM equilibria, makes it impossible to address the question. The issue, in the 1930s and 1940s, was liquidity preference versus loanable funds. Hicks addressed it twice and each time came to the conclusion that the two had to be equivalent (cf. Hicks 1936b, 1939a: ch. XII).

The relevant considerations are the following. In using the method of comparative statics, all changes in the values of endogenous variables are 'effects' attributed to the same 'cause', namely, the postulated change in one of the system's parameters. (Applying the method to a 'period model', one may miss the 'effects' of the 'cause' on those slow-moving endogenous variables that are treated as within-period parameters. Constraining the slow movers to constancy will similarly produce some miscalculation of the behaviour of the faster adjusting variables.)[21]

Redoing such an exercise in New Classical fashion, while assuming that the parameter change is public knowledge, the simultaneity of all adjustments becomes instantaneous. All prices are recalculated at once, and all output and consumption rates are reset so that rates of accumulation put the economy on a new equilibrium growth path. Markets should 'open' at the new equilibrium prices and no trading takes place in reaching these prices. Here there are no 'within-period' problems, the period having shrunk to a virtual instant in continuous time, and no awkward period-model approximations.

In neither of these two methods are questions about sequential causality meaningful. The 'order of events' does not matter and talk about 'causal relationships' between the endogenous variables is utter nonsense. But the *reasons* why this is so differ between the two approaches. In the New Classical version, the reason is that the entire system jumps to the new equilibrium in one spasmodic convulsion because everyone *knows* where it is headed. In a Hicksian period-model, one supposes no such thing. Here individual expectations differ as a matter of course and the short-run equilibrium is reached through a process of mutual adaptations in markets – a process which the model suppresses because it is too intricate and complex to model explicitly and, quite possibly, not of sufficient intrinsic interest to be worth the effort.

VIII

Let us now turn back to the economy that is like a massively parallel computer – and imagine it to be run by a 'Marshallian programmer'. Among his various problems, we focus on one, namely that of writing a suitable algorithm for the computation of the interest rate. His point of departure should be some version of (9.1) above:

$$r_{t+1} = f[X(r_t)] + r_t \qquad (9.3)$$

which carries with it two obvious questions: (i) where do we get r_t from and how is it arrived at, and (ii) what excess demand variable should 'govern' the error-correction term $f[...]$?

In a standard rational expectations model, period t opens with all agents having computed the rationally expected equilibrium interest rate contingent on some generally shared information set; everyone's calculation yields the same result, so r_t is established without any transactions taking place.[22] If, moreover, this universally shared rational expectation were based on essentially complete information, the $f[...]$ term would be zero. Since, in this case, each market participant is able correctly to calculate the equilibrium price for himself, feedback from actual market interaction plays no role in arriving at it. There is no work for 'market mechanisms' to do. We are in that land 'beyond supply and demand'.

This, however, is a very special case. If, instead, some relevant information is unavailable to ('unanticipated' by) agents, r_t will be the wrong price. In the absence of any information asymmetries, no one knows that this is so. Something has to happen in the market to bring home to transactors that their information is faulty. Unfolding events must 'activate' the $f[...]$ term.

The more interesting (and normal) case is when information is dispersed and transactors use different models to generate their individual price expectations. In this case, period t would open with a distribution across agents of expected rates (securities prices). We might then think of each agent as making up a set of desired transactions – lending or borrowing, or buying or selling securities – depending on the difference between the market rate at t and the equilibrium rate that he or she expects to emerge.[23] Many of these desired portfolio transactions will be screened out by transactions costs, but the rest will cause a flurry of transactions. For present purposes, it will be convenient (even if artificial) to suppose that r_t in (9.3) is the rate that emerges from this initial flurry of exchanges as reflecting the 'representative expectation' at the beginning of the market period. If this representative expectation is mistaken, the passage of time should, again, activate the error-correcting market mechanism $f[...]$.

What then goes inside the brackets of $f[...]$? Let our Marshallian programmer try two possibilities: (a) the excess demand for money, and (b) the excess supply of securities. The first is the *liquidity preference* (LP) theory and the latter the *loanable funds* (LF) theory of interest determination, as I interpret them, namely as postulating alternative algorithms for the computation of the interest rate, algorithms that come into play whenever activities in the system are not co-ordinated by expectations alone.

What difference does it make? To discriminate between the two hypotheses, one must consider states of the economy such that the excess demands for money and for bonds do not have opposite signs.[24] The Keynesian exercise of a 'decline in the marginal efficiency of capital' provides a convenient example. The entrepreneurs affected will plan to decrease investment and, correspondingly, to reduce the amount of new securities issued (or bank loans raised). Initially, the consumption-saving plans of households are assumed to be unaffected by whatever events caused entrepreneurial expectations to change. The impact effects, therefore, are to create an excess supply for commodities and an excess demand for securities. At this stage of the process, the excess demand for money is still zero.[25] So, we have a test case:

LP When the excess demand for money is zero, the LP version of (9.3) shows that the interest rate will not adjust. Consequently, this interest rate mechanism is obviously incapable of co-ordinating the intertemporal activities of the household and business sectors appropriately.

LF When the excess demand for securities is positive, the LF version of (9.3) would show that interest rates will fall. For the co-ordinated functioning of the system, this is qualitatively the right response. The question becomes whether the rate will fall far enough or whether bear-speculation might make the adjustment stop short.[26]

When the Marshallian programmer tries out the two algorithms he will find that, using the LF alternative, it is possible (but far from inevitable) that the intertemporal price mechanism will solve intertemporal co-ordination problems, but that the LP alternative *never* works.

To Keynes himself, the switch to the LP hypothesis spelled a definite break with 'classical' theory. It meant that saving and investment determined income, rather than the interest rate, and that liquidity preference and the stock of money determined interest, not the price level. It leads directly to the 'Keynesian Cross' – the first encounter with macroeconomics for generations of students – which crystallizes this particular vision of how the self-regulating properties of the market system fail. Here, the intertemporal price is entirely missing from the picture of how consistency of saving and investment plans is brought about. The Cross embodies the previously mentioned proposition that 'investment determines saving, but saving does not determine investment'.[27] The Paradox of Thrift – saving as anti-social activity directed at labour – is another property of the Cross and, as such, also another lemma of the LP hypothesis.

Sir Dennis Robertson fought a long battle against this doctrine and for loanable funds.[28] His fight was to no avail in his lifetime. Yet, in retrospect, he had much the better of it. On this issue, Keynes was wrong and Robertson was right.

Period-analysis did not give Hicks a handle on the distinction between the liquidity preference and loanable funds approaches to interest determination. The inability clearly to delineate the difference between the two and to convey the ideological significance of it runs through the entire IS–LM-based literature. It is perhaps nowhere demonstrated more clearly than in Alvin Hansen's *A Guide to Keynes* (1953), a book that may have done more than any other work to establish Hicks's apparatus as the vehicle for Keynesian theory in the USA, but that entirely fails to come to grips with the macroeconomic issues that were later to separate the Keynesianism of Keynes's Cambridge followers from the neo-classical synthesis of Paul Samuelson and the American 'mainstream' Keynesians (cf. Leijonhufvud 1983: 84–5).

IX

Among the now passé controversies for which IS–LM provided the analytical frame, liquidity preference versus loanable funds seems today the most obscure. (One is tempted to say that it is 'long forgotten', but the truth is that no one any longer remembers how long ago it was forgotten.) But arcane as it may be, it exemplifies issues of both method and substance that, in one guise or another, are still with us.

The discussion above has dealt with the problems of understanding *within-period* processes that are inherent in the Hicksian method. If we were to contrast period-analysis to modern analytical practice, it is instead the *between-periods* treatment that is interesting. It is between periods that the older analysis will slip *unforeseen* news into the account of an economy's evolution. Behaviour in the 'before' and 'after' periods will then not be part of the same optimal planned trajectory. 'As in history!' Stochastic dynamic programming, on the other hand, can do without the artificial discreteness of time but, in never allowing intertemporal optimality to be violated, it banishes history.[29]

The substantive issues have to do with our beliefs about the 'automaticity' of systems of 'free' markets. These beliefs have a curious history that is getting curiouser in our own time. If many pre-Keynesian economists had exaggerated notions of the capabilities of market economies to co-ordinate activities, it was because they relied on the feedback from market interactions to induce individual behaviour adjustments so as to bring supply and demand into line. I interpret Keynes as having demonstrated that reliance on market 'mechanisms' can in some circumstances lead the system astray and make it suffer prolonged co-ordination failures. (I believe he was right about 'effective demand failures' although wrong on the interest rate algorithm.) In the subsequent literature, the Keynesian doctrine hardened into a denial of the capability of market economies 'automatically' to control employment and capital accumulation appropriately. In reaction to this, we got the Monetarist reaffirmation of the belief that market systems will work if not actually interfered with. Out of this reaction, however, grew the New Classical economics in which rational expectations suffice to co-ordinate activities without the need for error-correcting market mechanisms. Arguably, Keynes took markets more seriously than do the New Classicals!

Surely, this story is not finished.

NOTES

1 It is a bit of a historical accident that the profession has for the most part not apportioned credit or blame for IS–LM more widely: Harrod, Reddaway, Meade and Champernowne etc. Cf. Warren Young (1987).

2 Leijonhufvud (1983). This paper was given at the same session of the Florence conference as Hicks's own 'IS–LM': an explanation'. Sir John felt, rather like Solow (1984), that I exercised too energetically with the implicit information assumptions of the model, although he did not suspect me (as did Solow, p. 23) of suggesting 'that macroeconomic policy could usefully be restricted to the production and dissemination of the missing information'.

3 Leijonhufvud, 'Uses of the past', unpublished.

4 For this reason, I do not attach much importance to Keynes's oft-cited approval of Hicks's paper (cf. Keynes 1973:79), although Hicks himself may have overdone his understatement: 'I think I am justified in concluding from that letter that Keynes did not wholly disapprove of what I had made of him' (Hicks 1982a:289).

5 This is of course not to deny the importance of the well-known exchanges that appeared immediately after the book's publication.

6 This means stripping away the theoretical choices made by subsequent Keynesians. Cf. for example, Leijonhufvud (1981:53–4).

7 I have tried to trace this theme through 60 years of his writings in 'Hicks on time and money' (Leijonhufvud 1984).

8 *The Social Framework*, p. 3. The author's outlook is also clearly stated in the preface: 'The greater part of this book is taken up with the study of Social Accounting ... I hope and believe that when a beginner has mastered the substance of this book, he will be able to turn to the theory of value with some idea of what he wants to get from it.'

9 These issues take up most of vol. I of his Collected Essays (1981). Cf., especially, the papers there (re)titled 'Valuation of social income I, II, and III', dating respectively to 1940, 1958 and 1981 and 'Measurement of capital – in theory' and '– in practice', originally written in 1958 and 1969. In the importance that he attached to the conceptual basis of accounting, Hicks was much influenced by Erik Lindahl, as was the case also (and more obviously) with his approach to dynamic analysis.

10 Hicks (1977a: vii). Also quoted and discussed in Leijonhufvud (1984: 32–3).

11 Hicks 'IS–LM: an explanation', as reprinted in Hicks (1982a: 320). The matter is discussed in Leijonhufvud (1984: 35–7).

12 *Economic Perspectives*, p. vii. Also quoted in Leijonhufvud (1984: 44).

13 To more accurately represent Marshall, equation (9.2) should be replaced by a

family of output-adjustment equations, one for each firm, plus an equation for the aggregation of firm output rates. But this refinement would be irrelevant to our present purposes.

14   Economists like to shock physicists with dynamic equations that have future dated right-hand variables and, then, persuade them that this is justified since expectations govern human behaviour. But the physicists are, of course, perfectly right in being shocked by blatantly teleological displays. A properly formulated system has to have expectations formed from past experience and to omit the requisite learning behaviour from the system in order to dazzle one's colleagues is really a rather cheap trick.

15   But the term for it is not. My friend Kumaraswamy Velupillai tells me that this procedure for studying some of the properties of potentially complex non-linear systems was known as *adiabatic transformations* in the older thermodynamics literature. It is all in Marshall!?

16   An assumption which in many cases will not be consistent with 'reasonable intelligence' in price setting.

17   'IS–LM: an explanation' (Hicks 1982a). Cf. also his 'Time in economics', as reprinted in Hicks (1982a esp. 290).

18   Cf. Leijonhufvud (1993) for a further discussion.

19   The term is taken from Hicks (1979g: ch. 7).

20   Hicks (1958a: 143). Note the distinction between 'conditions in which it will not work' and the Kahn-Robinson 'under no conditions will it work'. Cf. Leijonhufvud (1984: 34–5) for Hicks's failure to make his proposition stick.

21   This, of course, amounts to no more than saying that a histogram can only approximate the graph of a continuously varying function.

22   The result is the same also if only a subset of transactors have the most up-to-date information, as long as everyone understands who has and who has not got it.

23   For an explicit model along these lines, cf. Aoki and Leijonhufvud (1988).

24   The proposition that the two excess demands must sum to zero involves of course a false dichotomy.

25   Cf. Leijonhufvud (1984: n. 52, pp. 37–8).

26   Cf. 'The Wicksell connection', in Leijonhufvud (1981).

27   Keynes himself insists on this point both in the General Theory and after. None the less I tend to associate it particularly with Joan Robinson because to her it remained important decades later, long after the great majority of economists had given up trying to make sense of these issues. In several lengthy conversations during the Fall of 1974, I found that whereas she could be persuaded, for the sake of argument at least, to put the capital controversies and wage-push doctrines aside, this proposition was to her the Keynesian bedrock on which her most basic economic convictions were based.

28   Cf. the collection of Robertson's essays (1966) selected by Hicks. Hicks was not much given to editing other people's works. It is a fair inference, I think, that he was in part trying to do Robertson belated justice, having failed originally to see clearly the issues between Robertson and the Cambridge Keynesians.

29   On the question of how much light sunspots will shed on economic history we are still in the dark.

BIBLIOGRAPHY

Aoki, M. and Leijonhufvud, A. (1988) 'The stock-flow analysis of investment', in M. Kohn and S. C. Tsiang (eds) *Finance Constraints, Expectations, and Macroeconomics*, Oxford: Clarendon Press.

Baumol, W. J. (1990) 'Sir John versus the Hicksians, or theorist *malgré lui*', *Journal of Economic Literature* 28: 1708–15.

Coddington, A. (1983) *Keynesian Economics: The Search for First Principles*, London: Allen & Unwin.

Fitoussi, J. P. (ed.) (1983) *Modern Macroeconomic Theory*, Oxford: Basil Blackwell.

Hansen, A. (1953) *A Guide to Keynes*, New York: McGraw-Hill.

Keynes, J. M. (1973) *The Collected Writings of John Maynard Keynes*, London: MacMillan, vol. XIV, pp. 70–79.

Leijonhufvud, A. (1968) *On Keynesian Economics and the Economics of Keynes*, New York and Oxford: Oxford University Press.

—— (1981) *Information and Coordination: Essays in Macroeconomic Theory*, New York and Oxford: Oxford University Press.

—— (1983) 'What was the matter with IS–LM?', in Jean-Paul Fitoussi (ed.) *Modern Macroeconomic Theory: An Overview*, Oxford: Blackwell, pp. 64–90.

—— (1984) 'Hicks on time and money', in D. A. Collard, D. R. Helm, M. F. G. Scott and A. K. Sen (eds) *Economic Theory and Hicksian Themes*, Oxford: Oxford University Press, pp. 26–46.

—— (1987) 'The uses of the past', paper delivered at the annual meeting of the History of Economics Society at Harvard Business School, Boston.

—— (1993) 'Towards a not-too-rational macroeconomics', UCLA Center for Computable Economics Working Paper No. 1.

Modigliani, F. (1944) 'Liquidity preference and the theory of interest and money', *Econometrica* 12: 45–88.

Punzo, L. (1991) 'J.M. Grandmont on money, expectations, and economic dynamics: a discussion', in L. W. McKenzie and S. Zamagni (eds) *Value and Capital, Fifty Years Later*, London: Macmillan, pp.31–7.

Robertson, D. (1966) *Essays in Money and Interest*, selected by Sir John Hicks, London: Fontana Library.

Solow, R. M. (1984) 'Mr. Hicks and the classics', in D. A. Collard, D. R. Helm, M. F. G. Scott and A. K. Sen (eds) *Economic Theory and Hicksian Themes*, Oxford: Oxford University Press, pp. 13–25.

Young, W. (1987) *Interpreting Mr. Keynes*, Cambridge: Polity Press.

10

HICKS'S LATER MONETARY THOUGHT

David W. Laidler

I INTRODUCTION

In his last book, *A Market Theory of Money*, Sir John Hicks treated money as an integral part of the institutional framework within which goods and services are traded, and as something that cannot properly be understood independently of a careful study of that framework. Quite self-consciously, then, he placed himself in a tradition of monetary analysis that seemed to have died out in the 1930s.

There is considerable irony here, because Hicks himself surely stood second only to Keynes in his influence on the monetary economics of that decade. His (1935b) 'Suggestion for simplifying the theory of money' ante-dated the *General Theory* (1936), though not the *Treatise* (1930), as a landmark in the evolution of the theory of liquidity preference. The particular IS–LM version of 'Keynesian economics' which dominated the post-war textbooks, and which provided the analytic framework for much of the monetarist controversy too, was not Hicks's creation alone, but its most influential exposition was his 'Mr. Keynes and the classics'. Whatever Hicks (1937a) may have intended, these two papers helped to set monetary economics moving in what he later came to regard as the wrong direction.

In a sequence of books which began with the *Critical Essays in Monetary Theory* (1967) and continued with *The Crisis in Keynesian Economics* (1974b) and then *A Market Theory of Money* (1989a), Hicks dealt with ideas not just outside, but also critical of, the contemporary mainstream which their author had helped to start flowing. In what follows, I shall describe the salient features of the view of monetary economics which Hicks presented at the end of his life, and although I shall criticize his views on inflation, I shall also argue that certain of Hicks's ideas, notably those that hark back to the classical theory of money, deserve more attention than the profession has so far given them.

II LIQUIDITY PREFERENCE AND IS–LM

The Classical economics which Keynes attacked in the *General Theory* displayed far more variety and intellectual subtlety than he was willing to concede, but it was, nevertheless, an intellectual tradition in trouble. The centerpiece of its monetary analysis was the quantity theory of money, a theory of the behaviour of the general price level, in which a flow of money expenditure (*MV*) interacted with a flow of goods sold (*T*) to generate a determinate value for the price level (*P*). As a theory of the price level, the quantity theory was remarkably successful, but the cycle had been a problem throughout the nineteenth century, and, because financial crises had been one of its regular and highly visible features, monetary economics was expected to say something about it. The quantity theory was pressed into service here too, and in combination with analysis of the Fisher effect of inflation on interest rates it yielded important insights into the influence of price level fluctuations on the stability of credit markets in general and the banking system in particular. These insights lay at the heart of numerous proposals to replace money as a unit of account, notably in credit market transactions, with some more stable indexed standard.[1]

The quantity theory was less successful when it encountered systematic fluctuations in real variables. Classical economics explained output and employment variations in terms of relatively flexible prices interacting with sticky nominal wages to generate systematic variations in the real wage, so the quantity theory had something to offer here, but it was unable to contribute to the understanding of the large fluctuations in the rate of capital accumulation associated with the cycle. A wide variety of non-monetary approaches to this problem were discussed: accelerator effects, contagious waves of business optimism and pessimism, the bunching of innovation and so on. But Classical monetary economists had long been aware that, in addition to providing the economy with means of exchange, banks also acted as financial intermediaries. That is why the conjecture that investment instability stemmed from the failure of the financial system properly to co-ordinate the intertemporal allocation of resources was prominent in pre-Keynesian analysis of the cycle.

Keynesian economics' development of this conjecture, which Leijonhufvud (1981) was later to call 'The Wicksell connection', was crucial in enabling it to supersede Classical monetary economics. Already explicit in the Marshall–Pigou reformulation of the quantity theory in terms of a stock-supply-and-demand-for-nominal-balances framework was the proposition that the rate of return to be earned on assets other than money represented an opportunity cost to holding it. In the work of Lavington (1921) and Keynes (1930), this evolved towards the idea that the demand for money should be treated as a component of a more general theory of portfolio choice. Hicks (1935b) and Keynes (1936) brought this development to full fruition and, along with it, proposed the hypothesis that the rate of interest was the price that would equilibrate the supply and demand for money.[2] But if that was the rate of interest's role, how could it simultaneously co-ordinate savings and investment decisions? And if it could not, then what else would? Keynes's answer, of course, was that variations in the level of income and employment provided the alternative equilibrating mechanism.

A form of Keynesian economics soon came to dominate the discipline, for reasons that need no discussion here.[3] What is important in the present context is that money's means of exchange and unit of account roles played no essential part in establishing its key results, but that money's potential as a store of value was absolutely vital. This shift in the focus of monetary theory which Hicks had done much to initiate in 'A suggestion for simplifying the theory of money' (1935b) was given a further push by his IS–LM formalization of Keynes's model (1937a). The vision underlying this formalization, closely related to that of *Value and Capital* (1939a), was the essentially Walrasian one of a system of interconnected markets in simultaneous general equilibrium.[4] To be sure the equilibrium itself was not Walrasian, because, in the presence of sticky prices, quantities had to move away from their full-employment values to achieve it. But the fact remained that money had no unique role to play in co-ordinating economic activity in such a world; it was simply one asset among many, the market for which would be equilibrated along with those for everything else.

The immensely destructive potential implicit in formulating monetary economics along Walrasian lines, and hence in divorcing it from the explicit analysis of exchange mechanisms, was not fully realized until the 1970s, when the exponents of the New Classical economics began to take a flexible price version of general equilibrium analysis really seriously as a micro-foundation for their work. That price flexibility ensures intertemporal choices are properly co-ordinated, regardless of whether the demand for money is interest elastic or not, was understood earlier, being fully articulated, for example, by Patinkin (1948); but it was not until the New Classicals began to insist on the assumption of perfect price flexibility and at the same time began to look for an essential role for money to play in such a system in the first place that mainstream monetary economics reached its current impasse, with the inadequacy of both overlapping generations models and those based on an arbitrary cash-in-advance constraint being increasingly recognized even – perhaps particularly would be more accurate – by those who have done most to popularize them. This unsatisfactory state of affairs is the direct consequence of the reformulation of monetary theory in the 1930s which Hicks did so much to promote.

III MARKETS, MONEY AND LIQUIDITY

The above judgement is made with the benefit of hindsight. It was never Hicks's intention to promote the development of anything resembling New Classical economics, and indeed, his work of the 1930s only points in that direction if it is read selectively. *The Theory of Wages* (1932b) is particularly important here. Nowadays remembered mainly for its technical contributions to the analysis of the production function, the book nevertheless displays a concern with the institutional detail of markets which was to re-emerge in Hicks's post-war writings on monetary matters. Though there is much in this vein in the *Critical Essays* and *The Crisis in Keynesian Economics*, Hicks's final book, *A Market Theory of Money*, was more deeply marked by it than his earlier work in this area, and derived much of its originality from this source.

Hicks regarded the Walrasian market as an anomaly, useful for certain exercises in pure theory but positively misleading as a basis for applied work. This general view permeated *A Market Theory of Money*, as did the special case of it, which originated in the *Theory of Wages* and continued in *The Crisis in Keynesian Economics*, and stresses the special nature of the labour market.[5] Hicks always insisted that this is not a continuously recontracting spot market, but one in which transactions involve ongoing relationships between buyers and sellers. In his view, contracts, explicit or implicit, are of the essence there; and they have to satisfy criteria not just of economic efficiency, but also of fairness. That is why it is difficult to negotiate wage bargains, and dangerous to disturb them; it is also why money wages are sticky, or why, to use Hicks's own terminology, the labour market is a 'fixprice' market.[6] But goods markets too were discussed in *A Market Theory of Money*. It was stressed that production and trading take place over real time, so that current prices, of raw materials as much as finished goods, must always be heavily conditioned by expectations about the future. In some cases, typically for commodity inputs, we find formally organized 'flexprice' speculative markets that cope with this problem. In others, which link producers and consumers, ongoing relationships among specific agents lead to 'fixprice' behaviour, just as they do in the labour market.

This view of markets, closely related to that of Arthur Okun (1981), formed the essential background to the monetary theory developed in the second part of *A Market Theory of Money*. Market transactions were there presented as involving three acts: the striking of a bargain, the delivery of some item and the receipt of payment; and in a world where real time passes, it was noted that these are seldom simultaneous. Accounts have to be kept, therefore, and money's numéraire function is primary. Money can appear as a means of exchange at this stage, and historically speaking sometimes has, but transactions can also be completed by exchanging goods of equal value. Where ongoing relationships exist among traders, such exchange does not have to be simultaneous, and leads naturally to the creation of evidences of indebtedness. The latter step was crucial in Hicks's view. Such evidences can be offset against one another as a means of consummating exchanges; and as the range of market transactions is extended, specialized agents develop who will, for a price, either act as guarantors of the debts of others or substitute their own liabilities for them. The acceptance and discounting of bills, the emergence of interest, indeed the very existence of banks and bank money, were thus, for Hicks, the products of market processes. And in due course, he showed how central banking, the emergence of government responsibility for the monetary system, not to mention international monetary arrangements, may all be traced back to these roots.

Now this line of argument was very much in the Classical tradition of Henry Thornton (1802), Walter Bagehot (1873) or Jevons, as was Hicks's insistence that the capacity to act as a store of value is not a distinguishing feature of money. However, because activity in real world markets is spread out over time into an uncertain future, stores of value capable of mitigating the costs of dealing with that uncertainty are desirable, and money, among other assets, has the capacity to satisfy that desire. For Hicks, then, an asset demand for money, or more generally liquidity preference, was also a creation of markets.[7] The liquidity preference theory of the 'Suggestion' (1935b), not to mention the *Treatise* and the *General Theory*, had enabled Keynesian economics to convert conjectures about the failure of the interest rate satisfactorily to co-ordinate intertemporal allocation into the foundation of a coherent macroeconomic theory. In *A Market Theory of Money*, a general-ization of liquidity preference theory was presented as a corollary of an essentially non-Walrasian approach to market and monetary analysis, and provided the bridge between that analysis and the somewhat broader set of propositions about macroeconomic issues which occupied the third and final section of that book.[8]

A long-standing and pervasive characteristic of Hicks's approach to monetary theory was a belief that propositions which are true and relevant in one time and place may not be in another. Hicks had no difficulty in arguing that the monetary economics of Thornton or Jevons was true for their days, but not for the 1930s; and that Keynes's analysis of liquidity preference as a simple choice between money and all other assets fitted the economy of the 1930s, but was now too simple. That is why the analysis of *A Market Theory of Money*, though recognizably descended from Classical monetary theory by way of the *General Theory*, nevertheless differed from both. No plea for a return to the pre-Keynesian quantity theory, and certainly no defence – rather a curt dismissal (1989a: 63, 103) – of monetarism was to be found here. And though Hicks recognized a demand for money *qua* means of exchange in his model, this derives from money's character as a 'running asset', is largely involuntary and is automatically satisfied by a banking system which cannot help but passively create the assets to do so. Liquidity preference, though it is as central to the analysis of *A Market Theory of Money* as to that of the *General Theory*, has nothing to do with anything as simple as the demand for some unique asset that can usefully be called money. Rather it is expressed in the structure of portfolios containing a wide variety of financial assets which may be classified with respect to their ease of convertibility into the economy's means of exchange.

Furthermore, argued Hicks, the financial system of the 1970s and 1980s has almost evolved into a rather complex version of Wicksell's (1898) 'pure credit' economy in which the only instrument of monetary policy is a rate of interest, and in which the liquidity preferences of financial intermediaries, not to mention those of asset holders in general, create premia which separate the rates of interest that the authorities can directly control from those that impinge immediately upon the spending decisions of ultimate borrowers. These premia, moreover, are variable and hard to predict. Their existence hampers the efficiency of the intertemporal allocative mechanism and renders monetary policy unreliable and difficult to implement. This modern variation on an old theme led Hicks to argue that it is difficult nowadays for monetary policy to cope with inflation (rather than, as in the 1930s, with chronic unemployment). For Hicks, inflation was not primarily a monetary phenomenon. And though monetary (i.e. interest rate) policy could stop inflation if used forcefully enough, the costs here were high. In Hicks's view then, it would often be wiser to accommodate inflationary pressures coming from elsewhere without exacerbating them.

IV INFLATION

Though inflation was not discussed at great length in *A Market Theory of Money*, the fact that my major disagreements with Hicks arise here makes it necessary to deal with his ideas about inflation, drawing on some of his earlier writings in the process.

The economic history that motivated Hicks's work was, of course, that of the UK. If we read his work from the 1940s onwards, we find him successively concerned with the problems of reconstructing the post-war economy in the face of a chronic shortage of capital equipment; with the implications of 'full-employment' policies, which were firmly in place by the mid-1950s, for the stability of prices; and, finally, with the explanation of the devastating inflation of the 1970s. The key essay for understanding his approach to the latter two issues was the 1956 'Inflation and the wage structure' (1982a: ch. 16), in which he argued that full-employment policies had effectively put Britain on a 'labour standard' as far as price level behaviour was concerned.

A monetary policy geared to the 'needs of labour' is essentially the same as one linked to the 'needs of trade', so it is not surprising that Hicks recognized that such a policy would be incapable of stabilizing the price level should the latter start to rise as a result of some external shock. In his own words, the system was suited to 'fair weather' but was bound to break down in the face of the harvest failures and energy price increases of the early 1970s, which made it impossible for the real economy to continue to meet the 'needs of labour' on the terms to which labour had become accustomed.

Hicks argued in *The Crisis in Keynesian Economics* (1973b) that British inflation was a cost-push phenomenon brought about by the interaction of real wage rigidity and exogenous real shocks; an inflation that monetary measures were powerless to control at any acceptable cost. Against this I would argue that the stability of the British economy in the 1950s and early 1960s was the result not of fortuitously fair economic weather but of an essentially universal political commitment to the maintenance of a fixed exchange rate on what was then an extremely stable US dollar. Far from being on a labour standard, Britain was on a dollar standard, and just as a commitment to the gold standard rendered any policies based on the real bills doctrine innocuous in the nineteenth century, so in the 1950s and 1960s the dollar standard stifled the inflationary bias inherent in full-employment policies. According to this diagnosis, the roots of British inflation in the 1970s lay partly in the post-1966 policies of the Johnson administration in the USA, which destroyed the stability of the US dollar. Within Britain, and of greater importance for a critique of Hicks's ideas, they lay in the expansionary policies embodied in the 1972 budget and in the breakdown of the commitment to exchange rate stability that culminated in its formal renunciation in that same budget. Though the real shocks of the early 1970s did not help matters, in my view they came long after the real damage had been done.

Now Hicks was never among those who believe inflation to be a minor irritant. His 'The costs of inflation' (1982a: ch. 20) gives a brief account of the costs of inflation in terms of its capacity to undermine social relations, which, among other things, presents the standard welfare cost theorems as little more than analytic trivia. Hicks's perception of inflation as a major social problem, together with his scepticism about the chances of controlling it through monetary means, lent a pessimistic tone to much of his policy-related writings of the 1970s. For the New Classical believer in clearing markets and rational expectations, the monetary cure for inflation presented no real problem: a credible pre-announced policy for the money growth rate would do the trick. As the 1970s and 1980s progressed, things did not work out so easily, and Hicks's pessimism seemed to be justified by experience. Even so I did not then, nor do I now, fully share it.

In particular, much of Hicks's scepticism about the weakness of monetary policy stemmed from his argument that it is impossible for the authorities to conduct open market operations and hence control money growth at high inflation rates (see, for example, 1982a: 262–4). That argument, in my view, rests on a confusion between the interest elasticities of demand for money and for credit. Therefore I have more confidence than did Hicks in our ability to achieve monetary growth targets. Nevertheless, the evidence of the 1980s surely does support Hicks's other contention that the labour market in particular is fixprice in nature and slow to respond to underlying economic forces. Even if the theoretical foundations of this view were not fully developed in his work, and remain so after his death, it seems to me to be unwise to ignore them in assessing the likely consequences of anti-inflation policies.

V CONCLUSIONS

It should be clear that I do not accept Hicks's suggestions as expressed in *A Market Theory of Money*, and as developed more fully in his earlier writings, that inflation is not primarily a monetary phenomenon; that no meaningful aggregate corresponding to the quantity theory's *M* exists in a modern financial system; and that no control can be exerted over the overall level and structure of the banking system's liabilities, except by an indirect route running from the level of interest rates to the behaviour of aggregate demand and prices, and thence through the demand for financial assets to their nominal quantities. I shall not argue these matters further here, however. Whether my resistance on any or all of them is misplaced is not the point that I wish to stress in dealing with the monetary ideas developed by Hicks towards the end of his life. The important point is rather that disagreement about such issues has in the past led many, myself included, to pay insufficient attention to other aspects of what Hicks was trying to tell us.

Hicks was not blameless here. His historical rather than econometric attitude to empirical questions, epitomized in his insistence that, by their very nature, they can be answered in different ways in different times and places, made it very difficult for those of us who set a high value on systematically testing theory against data to engage him in fruitful debate. But as the methodological priorities of monetary economists have shifted away from empirical testing and towards logical rigour and 'sound' micro-foundations, other aspects of Hicks's monetary theory, notably those deriving from Classical economics and having to do with its market theoretic foundations, demand our attention.

Anyone for whom continuously clearing Walrasian markets are the *sine qua non* of any meaningful economics, or who is swayed by arguments based on Walrasian models concerning the essential irrelevance of monetary shocks in generating real economic fluctuations, would do well to consider Hicks's view that money emerges in the first place precisely because markets do not conform to the Walrasian ideal. If that view is correct, it surely creates a presumption that conclusions about money's irrelevance based on Walrasian premises are highly suspect.

Those who already agree with Hicks that useful monetary theory requires non-Walrasian premises might also have something to learn from him. Brunner and Meltzer (1971) have long stressed the information-economizing potential of an economy's adoption of monetary exchange. So too have those who, like Jones (1976) or Kiyotaki and Wright (1989), take a more formal approach to showing how a common means of exchange might emerge in a search economy where trade is characterized by spot transactions between strangers who meet at random. If Hicks was right, and it is permanent, or at least repeated, trading relationships in organized markets which give rise to money, and it is money which in turn permits trade with strangers to begin, then this literature would appear to have some things the wrong way around. It would need a much more rigorous analysis than Hicks gave us in *A Market Theory of Money* to confirm or contradict the usefulness of his specific conjectures about the market theoretic foundations of monetary exchange, but at a time when monetary theory needs all the help it can get, perhaps some of its practitioners might spend a little time investigating the viability of his insights as a starting point for their work.[9]

It is, of course, easier by far to ask for a more rigorous analysis than to provide it. If Hicks, who was a leader in mathematical economics in the 1930s, largely gave up that approach in the post-war period, that was perhaps because the problems he wished to address did not seem to him to be easily amenable to a formal treatment. But that is always how matters look before a theoretical breakthrough; and it is, in any event, unwise to allow our choice of problems for study to be dictated by our current technical capacity rather than by their intrinsic scientific importance.

The success of a version of 'Keynesian economics' based upon the IS–LM model broke the historical continuity of monetary economics by trapping it in a technically tractable Walrasian world in which there was no room for monetary exchange. For more than 20 years Hicks strove to show that this development, which his own earlier work had done so much to promote, was destructive. He also argued that it was possible to look at the advances which monetary theory made in the 1930s in another way, which both exposed their Classical roots and opened up alternative lines of investigation. It would be a happy outcome if the story of Hicks's contributions to monetary economics, which began with his helping to destroy the authority of the Classical tradition, were to end with him posthumously aiding in the restoration of the sub-discipline's continuity with that same tradition.

NOTES

This chapter is a revised version of the author's 'Hicks and the classics', *Journal of Monetary Economics* 25 (June 1990) and incorporates material from his 'John Hicks' *Money, Interest, and Wages* ... A review essay', *Journal of Money, Credit and Banking* 15 (August 1983). The editorial help of Omar Hamouda is gratefully acknowledged, as is the financial support of the Lynde and Harry Bradley Foundation.

1   Including those of Alfred Marshall (1887) and Irving Fisher (1911); the 'Fisher effect', first investigated by Fisher in (1896), was in fact analysed by Marshall

in (1887) and (1890), as Fisher acknowledged. One blemish on Hicks's account of Classical interest theory in *A Market Theory of Money* is his extraordinary assertion in Chapter 9 that Marshall's version of that theory assumed stable prices and that Marshall would not have resorted to the Fisher effect to explain the coexistence of high interest rates with inflation.

2   The internal evidence of Hicks's (1935b) 'Suggestion' makes it clear that he had, at the time of its writing, only a very vague direct acquaintance with these ideas. Their influence on him at this stage was at second hand, through Keynes's (1930) *Treatise*. For a detailed account of Hicks's role in developing liquidity preference theory in the 1930s, see Laidler (1990).

3   In referring to 'a form' of Keynesian economics here, I intend to convey the judgement both that IS–LM analysis does encompass some of the things Keynes intended to say in the *General Theory* and that it omits many others. This essay is not the place to enter into a discussion of 'what Maynard really meant'.

4   Chick (1990) provides an important guide to the monetary content of *Value and Capital*.

5   Of course in 'Suggestion' (1935b) Hicks was not self-conscious about the differences between Walrasian analysis and the type of market mechanisms he dealt with in the institutional sections of *The Theory of Wages*. Walras appears there mainly as a contributor to marginal productivity theory.

6   In some respects this terminology is misleading, because neither here nor in any of his post-war writings does Hicks treat money wages as literally fixed in the manner of old-fashioned textbook expositions of IS–LM. Hicks's 'fixprices' are variable, albeit at intervals and at significant costs.

7   Though Hicks does not explicitly say so, the puzzle of which certain modern monetary theorists make so much, namely that money is held even though dominated in rate of return by other assets, is explained by the fact that the real world markets which generate this observation are not the Walrasian markets of the models which have so much difficulty explaining it.

8   The liquidity preference theory of *A Market Theory of Money*, like its analysis of the transactions demand for money as an 'involuntary demand' for a running asset, was first developed in his 'Two triads' which form the first part of the *Critical Essays* (1967). Hicks later used this analysis where the treatment of inflation in his *Crisis in Keynesian Economics* (1974b) is in most important respects the same as that outlined below. The last section of *A Market Theory of Money* that is to say, contains less original analysis and insight than the first two, but is nevertheless an integral part of the book.

9   That the existence of organized markets should be regarded as an important prerequisite for the emergence of monetary exchange is the principal insight of Clower (1977). I am aware of only one attempt to ground a formal theory of money's origins in credit relationships, that of Arie Arnon (undated).

BIBLIOGRAPHY

Arnon, A. (undated) 'Towards a credit theory of money', mimeo, Department of Economics, University of Pennsylvania, Philadelphia.

Bagehot, W. (1873) *Lombard Street – A Description of the Money Market*, London: H.S. King.

Brunner, K. and Meltzer, A.H. (1971) 'The uses of money: money in the theory of an exchange economy', *American Economic Review* 61, December: 784–805.

Chick, V. (1990) 'On the place of *Value and Capital* in monetary theory, *Greek*

Economic Review 12, Supplement, Autumn: 53–71.

Clower, R.W. (1977) 'The anatomy of monetary theory', *American Economic Review* 67, February: 206–12.

Fisher, I. (1896) 'Appreciation and interest', *Publications of the American Economic Association*, 3rd Series II, August: 331–442.

——— (1911) *The Purchasing Power of Money*, New York: Macmillan.

Jevons, W.S. (1875) *Money and the Mechanism of Exchange*, London: Kegan Paul.

Jones, R.A. (1976) 'The origin and development of media of exchange', *Journal of Political Economy* 84 (1), August: 756–75.

Keynes, J.M. (1930) *A Treatise on Money*, London: Macmillan.

——— (1936) *The General Theory of Employment, Interest and Money*, London: Macmillan.

Kiyotaki, N. and Wright, R. (1989) 'On money as a medium of exchange' *Journal of Political Economy* 97, August: 927–54.

Laidler, D. (1990) 'What was new about liquidity preference theory?' *Greek Economic Review* 12, supplement, Autumn 9–37.

Lavington, F. (1921) *The English Capital Market* London: Methuen.

Leijonhufvud, A. (1981) 'The Wicksell Connection', in A. Leijonhufvud *Information and Co-ordination: Essays in Macroeconomic Theory*, New York and Oxford: Oxford University Press.

Marshall, A. (1887) 'Remedies for fluctuations of general prices', *Contemporary Review*; reprinted in A. C. Pigou (ed.) *Memorials of Alfred Marshall*, London: Macmillan, 1925.

——— (1890) *Principles of Economics*, 1st edn; London: Macmillan.

Miller, M. H. and Orr, D. (1966) 'A model of the demand for money by firms', *Quarterly Journal of Economics* 80: 413–33.

Okun, A. (1981) *Prices and Quantities: A Macroeconomic Analysis*, Washington, DC: The Brookings Institution.

Patinkin, D. (1948) 'Price flexibility and full employment', *American Economic Review* 38, September: 543–64.

——— (1956) *Money, Interest and Prices*, New York: Harper Row; 2nd ed, 1965.

Thornton, H. (1802) *An Enquiry into the Nature and Effects of the Paper Credit of Great Britain*; reprinted, ed. F. A. von Hayek, London: Allen & Unwin, 1939.

Wicksell, K. (1898) *Interest and Prices*, tr. R. F. Kahn, London: Macmillan, 1936.

11

IN TIME WITH HICKS
Probability

O. F. Hamouda and Robin Rowley

Hicks contributed to economic literature for more than 60 years. His evolution from labour economist to monetary economist, pure theorist and historian (with important side excursions to trade cycles, national accounts and various other economic topics) significantly affected all the areas that he touched along his personal journey of discovery. Always, he sought out the major research problems and, always, perhaps because of their inherent complexity and his comprehensive vision, he left some unfinished business for the rest of us to puzzle over. Never dull, his work revealed a high degree of effective scholarship, attentiveness to the clarity of communication and sufficient qualifications to show a lack of definitiveness. Furthermore, as a model for all of us, he retained strong confidence in much of his work, while openly turning away from some weaker parts of it as he identified them, and while suggesting possible amendments to any earlier stance that he subsequently found inadequate. The search for improvement and his awareness of the evolution of ideas persisted to the end, as is evident from his final efforts (Hicks 1989a, 1990b).

One major piece of unfinished business is described in Hicks (1965a: 70) by reference to a potential defect in *Value and Capital* (1939a, 1946b); namely,

> My 1939 analysis has often been criticized ... for its neglect of uncertainty. Far more is known now than was known then about decision-making under uncertainty' (Theory of Games and all that!); what it is that is left out, on the uncertainty side, can now be more accurately defined.

This recognition of an omission and the possibility of dealing with it was typical of Hicks's search for improvement. During his long career, Hicks explored three different approaches to the treatment of uncertainty as characterized by probability measures. The first approach emerged prior to 1933 as Hicks was transformed into an economic theorist at the London School of Economics (LSE) and began to look at the collective risk of a spectrum of financial assets and at their non-stationary contribution to some

174

cyclical phenomena. Another approach fitted his critical appraisal of econometrics and his re-evaluation of partially ordered probabilities during the last decade of his life. The third approach was evident for much of the intermediate phase of Hicks's career as he sought to clarify particular aspects of money and portfolio analysis.

In the brief commentary given below, we review these three approaches to probability in their historical context, and then consider whether any of them is an appropriate means for amending the well-known theoretical framework of *Value and Capital*. After a half century of active attempts by many economists to assess and extend this particular framework, our task to introduce elements of probability should be trivial. However, the task is not as straightforward as one might hope – due to some troublesome aspects of probabilistic concepts and to particular problems in their fashionable use by economists. Here Hicks's reference to the theory of games seems (from a current perspective) to be quite unhelpful. However, we can still draw on his highly developed appreciation of history. We can also note the dilemma of choosing a particular probabilistic conception (with attendant demands for heterogeneous and incomplete awareness, elucidation of values, computability and criteria for rationality of economic agents) when economic theory is so remote from reality. Such limited devices as rational or consistent expectations, simple linear and covariance-stationary stochastic processes to generate the dynamic paths of adjustment by economic agents and special *ad hoc* rules to determine unique solutions in rational expectations models seem inadequate means of resolving our basic problem of dealing with probability. In brief views expressed in this chapter, we offer a few cursory comments on these matters. The whole exercise seems worthwhile in order to provide a sensible forum for exploring some of Hicks's evolving views and for assessing the unfinished business left by him for us to resolve.

Hicks's comment in *Capital and Growth* (1965a) was associated with an assessment of how his temporary-equilibrium method might be affected if uncertainty were introduced. The means and impact of introducing uncertainty were interesting issues, for which he constrained discussion in 1965 by considering only a restrictive and unduly optimistic framework:

> An uncertain expectation ... can be represented (more or less adequately) by a probability distribution; and this (in turn) is *usually* describable by a fairly small number of parameters ... It is insufficient to consider the changes in production (or consumption) plans that result from changes in the prices that are 'expected' as most probable. Attention must also be given to the effects of changes in the confidence with which these values are expected. When these are allowed for, the theory of the 'plan' becomes much more complicated ... But the

temporary equilibrium itself would not appear, *at first sight*, to be much affected.

(p. 70, emphasis added)

Further inspection (Hicks 1965a: 70–5) revealed significant difficulties in this optimistic extension once the consequences of multi-valued expectations, credit barriers, imperfect competition, variations in dynamic flexibility and temporal spillovers were noted. However, Hicks's direct characterization of uncertainty by parameters of a stable probability distribution (which others might associate with 'risk') is clearly consistent with his earlier treatment (from 1935) of portfolio analysis. It retains the separability of some views of perfect competition and leaves obscure the awkward relationship between subjective concepts (like expectation and confidence) and their objective counterparts.

I VARIETIES OF PROBABILITY

Hick's interest in uncertainty seems to have begun when Robbins asked him to lecture on risk, 'starting of course from Knight' (Hicks 1982a: 6). In contrast to Knight (1921), he accepted the validity of using numerical probabilities so we can usually, without much distortion, identify his use of the term 'uncertainty' with a probabilistic construction – irrespective of whether we maintain a Bayesian, frequentist or some other philosophical stance. Hicks's first excursion into uncertainty, as published in 1931, recorded his disagreement with Knight's assertion that unmeasurable 'true' uncertainty (and not 'risk') was the basis for the valid theory of profit. His second excursion appeared 2 years later when he confronted Hayek's view of monetary disturbances and cyclical phenomena. Together, these two early papers present an interesting vision of uncertainty in economics, one that is richer than the narrower approach that was adopted from 1935 onwards in the context of money. This wider vision illustrates the extent of Hicks's knowledge of probability prior to the writing of *Value and Capital*.

Early days

There are some ambiguities and imprecision in Hicks's early accounts of probability. Their occurrence is hardly surprising given the limitations of his background and the incomplete state of probability theory when he wrote. Both of these situational elements must be addressed. It is convenient to begin with a broad classification of probability concepts such as that often put forward by Good (1959, 1965). We should separate 'epistemic' probability, which can be logical, subjective or multi-subjective, from 'physical' probability (intrinsic probability, chance or propensity) which is associated with objective states. Crudely put, Hicks shifts from the internal expectations of economic agents to external or objective market conditions. This unfortunate habit of mixing such internal and external elements foreshadows the troublesome identity of 'subjective' and 'objective' probabilities in familiar accounts of rational expectations models in the 1980s. The habit is quite disturbing since the frequentist notions are mixed with mental constructs that may have only momentary existence. Hicks also made much use of 'laws of large numbers' in asserting the reduction of risk.

Although Jevons, Edgeworth, Bowley and Keynes had explored some important aspects of both probability and statistics by the beginning of the 1930s, the general awareness of such aspects among most economists at that time must have been slight. From a wider perspective, Fisher had begun to explore the use of probabilities as evidence, while Neyman and Pearson were introducing formal procedures for testing hypotheses and recognizing probabilistic elements in routine decision making. The radical transformation of probability mathematics into the forms that we now recognize did not occur until the first years of the 1930s, when Russian mathematicians (such as Kolmogorov and Khintchine) introduced axiomatics and pursued the basic concepts of stochastic processes. (This transformation has been dated by Wegman (1986) on the basis of recollections of Cramer. See, too, the historical review by Maistrov (1974).)

Turning to particular distributions with few parameters (of which the Gaussian or normal distribution is now the most commonly invoked), the clarification of central limit theorems for sums of random variables proceeded rapidly during the 1920s and especially in the early 1930s, as surveyed by Le Cam (1986). Within this historical context, it is likely that Hicks drew primarily on older, less precise, sources. His frequent reliance on the law of large numbers may stem from a brief contact with the traditional or non-modern development, which was earlier described by Keynes (1921: ch. 28) and owes much to Poisson and Quetelet. As Keynes and more recently Good (1986) suggest, this traditional view of universal laws involved more than simple empirical observations of relative frequencies so Hicks's mixture of probability concepts is possibly consistent with earlier practices. With very little effort, we can see Hicks's papers of 1931 and 1933 as markedly conditioned by their historical context (see Hamouda 1993: 14).

The treatment by Hicks (1931c) of profits in relation to risk or uncertainty is surprising in several respects. Although heavily influenced by Knight and the earlier commentaries that he cites, Hicks added novelty in two significant ways. First, he brings together frequency distributions of expected returns for groups, collective portfolios and average risks. Second, he stresses potential reduction of risk due to scale effects (associated with variations due to the combination of operations or activities). For his analysis, he begins by assuming 'objective chances' for returns to economic operations, where chance is some occurrence ratio. The simple averaging of such returns from contemporaneous, separate operations is linked to 'some grouping and some setting-off' in the sense that we now attribute to portfolios. On a larger scale, the combination of operations is somehow explored in 'a simple application of the law of large numbers', which seems to resemble the familiar result that the variance of an average of approximately independent random variables from a common distribution is reduced as the number of constituent random variables increases!

Beyond the inclusion of static and individual risks, Hicks presents frequency curves for groups (explicitly borrowing here from earlier work by Pigou, *Economics of Welfare*). These frequency curves differ among groups and they may not be either symmetric or stationary. Hicks also retains some notion of competition in relation to prices when, in an extraordinary manner, he introduces functionals in their theoretical determination. Prices are assumed to depend on the *whole* of these frequency curves – with the result that overall supply and demand are fundamentally affected by the shape of curves and, hence, the nature of any equilibrium is much more complicated than the intersection of shifting curves. We feel that in the widest representation, the curves are clearly *not* limited to the simple mean-variance characteristics that came to dominate the later literature on portfolio analysis, including that of Hicks. Finally, Hicks adopts a narrower vision. He notes what we now term 'certainty equivalents' and indicates the Bernoulli approach to diminishing marginal utility for stochastic returns, with a brief recognition of the phenomenon that we now refer to as a potential taste for gambling. Arrow (1986: S390) has reminded us that the English marginalists, Hicks's mentors, 'were aware of Bernoulli's expected-utility theory of behaviour under uncertainty (probably from Todhunter's *History of the Theory of Probability*) but used it only in a qualitative and gingerly way'.

In the second paper (Hicks 1933b), the impact of Hayek's arrival at the LSE is clear but again novelty emerges in the perceived non-stationarity of uncertainty over the duration of the trade cycle. Here, we discover that 'banking is of course no more than the application of the law of large numbers to the reduction ... of risk' (p. 34), that 'monetary theory, in the strictest sense, falls outside equilibrium theory' (p. 35) and that velocity of circulation is a risk phenomenon. For our purposes, the principal ingredient is the spectrum of assets, ordered according to their relative degrees of risk, which are subject to 'frequent and significant' (p. 36) general shifts over the cycle. This balance-sheet approach to money, which permits some liquidity preference, means that probabilities – to the extent that they are physical rather than epistemic – are linked to historical conditions. Thus probabilities must be dated and they may not be wholly reversible (although Hicks's cycles occur around some norm) so ergodicity and other comfortable features of stable distributions or stochastic processes are lost. In language of the later Hicks and traditional Keynesians, the probabilities are essentially *in time* with the problems of abstraction and topicality still to be resolved.

Narrower characterizations

Hicks has often contrasted monetary theory with economic theory in terms of their relative levels of abstraction. For example, Hicks (1967e: 156) asserts that

> Monetary theory is less abstract than most economic theory; it cannot avoid a relation to reality, which in other economic theory is sometimes missing. It belongs to monetary history, in a way that economic theory does not always belong to economic history.

Topicality of monetary phenomena is prompted both by the pressures of particular episodes or experiences and by the irreversible evolution of financial institutions and instruments in response to changing economic conditions, either passively or in response to regulatory influences. Thus it is difficult to explain why Hicks's usual approach to probability during the period extending from his paper in 1935 to his efforts clarifying money three decades later is so stationary and limited. The risk characteristics of asset portfolios and of money within the general spectrum of financial assets are generally identified only with a few parameters from probability distributions, the intertemporal evolution of which are not clarified.

Within this approach, time is sliced into momentary segments, days perhaps, and then choice is defined without a truly dynamic perspective. This method, convenient and readily assimilated, is much narrower than that of the earlier two papers of 1931 and 1933, although the analytical treatment of momentary portfolio choices is somewhat enhanced. The dynamic programming of such choices, which seemed to be called for in a changing stochastic environment, is essentially subordinated to the momentary shifts into and away from liquidity. In particular, the episodic transformations of history and the impact of cyclical phenomena are downplayed because of the crude probabilistic approach. This method, therefore, is still profoundly abstract as the probabilistic framework ignores, in most significant respects, the process of history in favour of a series of unco-ordinated snapshots – a major problem if we want to use this method, for example, to extend the dynamic format of *Value and Capital* toward reality by acknowledging more uncertainty. Clearly most of the contingency-claim models in recent years also share this problem by ignoring dynamic linkages, the existence of some temporal asymmetries and progressive innovation in response to economic influences. Their probabilistic bases are also either too separable for individual participants or underspecified, except as abstract parables.

The structure of the portfolio approach is sketched in Hicks (1935b, 1962a, 1967, 1977a; see also Hamouda 1993: 173–7). Any probability distribution for the collective return of a group of assets is simply represented in terms of a few parameters. Hicks (1935b: 69), for example, began with 'a mean value, and some appropriate measure of dispersion', but he later, in 1977, added an additional parameter for potential skewness, when his doubts concerning the ubiquitous generality of normality became focused. As explained by Hicks (1977a: 166) in a curious passage:

> [In 1967] I followed what has become the conventional approach, supposing that the 'prospect' of each available investment could be expressed in terms of the first two moments of a probability distribution ... I did this, in spite of feeling that many of the 'prospects' involved in actual business decisions are *by no means normally distributed*, but are highly skewed ... I therefore extended my discussion to take account of skewness; but I made no pretence that the extension was satisfactory.

> (Emphasis added)

During the first four decades of his research, Hicks revealed other shifts of focus. These involved both the primary conceptions of probability and views concerning the appropriateness of the common Bernoulli specification for rational choice – as re-expressed in theory of games and in popular expositions by Friedman, Savage and others. Against such changes we can set his persistent reliance on some variant of the 'law of large numbers' to reduce risk and a constant desire to use marginalist calculations, at least in some descriptive sense.

From the beginning of his concern with uncertainty, Hicks stressed both utilities (or preferences) and probabilities so it is somewhat surprising that he took so long to be aware of the major contribution of Ramsey (1931) to the theory of subjective probability, especially since Hicks read so widely and was alert to developments in many areas of economics. Gradually, the relationships between probabilities and reality in his published research grew more attenuated over time. In 1935, 'objective facts' were assumed by Hicks to permit the estimation of risks, which were then bound up with 'subjective preference for much or little risk-bearing' (1967: 72). However, as different concepts of probability flourished in economics, objective elements were supplanted by subjective probabilities, which 'can have no existence except in the mind of the chooser' (Hicks 1967: 20). The ultimate reversal occurred when Hicks (1977a: 166–76) put forward a more conciliatory attitude to the Bernoulli format, markedly at odds with particular views expressed by him throughout his earlier career (e.g. in the mathematical appendix to Hicks (1962a)). Despite these shifts of emphasis, there were two lines of development – both of which maintained the drastic simplicity of probability characterizations for expected returns. One of these developments was the gradual change from physical probabilities (and, perhaps, from explicit frequentist concepts) to epistemic probabilities, while the other development involved the criteria for defining individual rationality in marginalist calculations (irrespective of whether probabilities were based on observation, prior reasoning or normative views).

The two lines of development, clearly part of an evolving climate of dominant intellectual fashions, were interconnected in two respects. First, they involved the search for reasonable axioms to govern both subjective probabilistic weights and utility measures. Second, they raised awkward questions of measurability or cardinality. Both connections continue to perplex us. (See the responses to the recent survey by Fishburn (1986).) As always, Hicks took an independent path, conditioned by his own values. He responded to some changes in the dominant intellectual climate (although he did not embrace many of the mathematical ones), while resisting the attractions of other changes. While the flexibility and general tone of his early work fits comfortably with the efforts of contemporaries such as Lange (1944) and Hart (1947, 1949), his later work was a little more combative when he responded to comments by Arrow (1965) and resisted the steady assimilation of Savage's axioms and other developments. Even now, a consensus has still not emerged for the best specifications of criteria for rational choice (even within the narrow range of familiar approaches to normative rational choice) in uncertain economic environments. Recent reappraisals of Savage's axioms and related matters reveal an unresolved dispute, which is being revitalized as younger scholars take up the mantle of Allais and clarify the potential sources of apparently paradoxical choice. Despite the evident ambiguities and imprecisions of this area of research, we can at least say that Hicks's belated criticism of ubiquitous normality was a severe blow to the method of simple characterizations of probability.

Incomplete orderings

While practical statisticians explored probabilities to yield evidence or to guide choices when hypotheses conflict, Hicks and many other economists have, in essence, only used probabilities or the language of uncertainty for description or for the recounting of parables (wise theoretical stories). Irrespective of what type of theory (monetary or economic in Hicks's dichotomy) is being considered, the connections between 'risks' and both the physical probabilities and subjective weights of economic agents have always been tenuous. Aspects of computability, vagueness, framing or status-quo biases and regret must cloud the identification of most popular theories with stochastic ingredients and real situations. Similarly, the intransitivity of choices and potential occurrence of preference reversals affect the practicality of some utility concepts. The shift from physical probabilities and relative frequencies to their subjective counterparts is thus symbolic rather than operational. Experience and experiment have seldom fed 'pure' theory! The rhetoric of 'laws of large numbers' and other statistical theorems far outstrips the context of economic models, which rely on 'representative individuals' or some other fictional characters.

Towards the middle of the 1970s, Hicks's dependence on complete probability distributions began to weaken. He questioned the need to provide the comprehensive information that underlies any use of weighted averages such as a mathematical expectation and variance. Instead, he turned to incomplete orderings of probabilities, which had earlier been stressed by Keynes (1921). At the same time, the mature Hicks also turned to methodological issues that appraised economics as a discipline in relation to both history and science. Thus we can find, in Hicks (1979g, 1983a, 1984b), a new approach to probability. This new approach is incompatible with the calculus of certainty equivalents and mean-variance formulations. As expressed by Hicks, probabilities do 'not have to be numerical' (Hicks, 1979g: 114) and rationality is defined in a non-unique way as occurring when events fall within some preconceived bounds (i.e. in language reminiscent of Shackle, the economic agent is not surprised). Mathematical manipulations are severely restricted in this approach although they may not be eliminated as mathematicians clarify various concepts of fuzziness. Within statistics, some scope for effective analysis in this context has been explored, most noticeably by Good.

The step toward qualified rationality, incompleteness and partial ignorance is a simple one for economists to take if they accept an honest assertion by Pratt (1986: 498):

> No sensible person ever really thought the probability and utility assessments preexist in anyone's mind, or that probabilities could or should be assessed directly and then checked for consistency, or that they would be naturally consistent.

Individual economic agents might indeed assign a partial ordering to probabilities, and orders of these subjective probabilities could differ among individuals when they seek a means of agreeing on a collective choice. (Some references to Good's attempts at modelling inference in this particular situation are provided in Good (1981), while Lindley et al. (1979) illustrate the limited reconciliation of incoherent personal assessments of probabilities.) If applied and theoretical statisticians are prepared to deal with these awkward corners away from the simple tractability of conventional approaches to probability, economists should also explore outside the safety set that is provided by completeness, simplicity, separability and stationarity. Perhaps the treatment of incomplete orderings in economics is long overdue and Hicks was encouraging us to widen our explorations.

For Hicks, the latest shift in his attitude to uncertainty returned him to his initial disagreement with Knight, in which issues of measurability were so prominent. To what extent is Knight's uncertainty different from the modest incomplete ordering of Hicks? The shift contemplated by Hicks brought a strengthening of the attention given to historical episodes at the cost of theoretical generality. Hicks (1969a: 3), considering historical questions, distinguished between those 'which can usefully be discussed in terms of the notion of statistical uniformity, and those which cannot'. Partial orderings of probabilities in economic models seem more consistent with the latter type of question – even though some economic theorists might argue, as did Hicks (1969a: 4) himself, somewhat earlier, that 'Economics is rather specially concerned with such "statistical" behaviour' and 'Whenever our interest is in general phenomena, theory (economic or other social theory) may be relevant; otherwise usually not'.

II ABSTRACTION, EVIDENCE AND ECONOMIC THEORY

The complex interrelationships of economic theory with various degrees of abstraction and with forms of evidence in the presence of uncertainty are troublesome. These interrelationships are at the heart of the difficulties that we experience in seeking to provide suitable guidelines to modify the deterministic framework of *Value and Capital*. We suggest that the choice of probability concept to be embodied in the revised framework must be neither idiosyncratic (where the theorist pursues any concept without an appraisal of its contextual suitability) nor simply instrumental (where theoretical predictions have an excessive influence on model premises). Rational expectations in the post-Muth sense seem both idiosyncratic and instrumental. They require normality and linearity, while the criterion of mean-square-error optimality makes too many demands on the practical availability of information. These expectations abstract from many important features of economic agents and their markets so the rational expectations models may not be meaningfully connected with concepts of uncertainty such as the 'real world' knows them.

Hicks, as a methodologist, tried to deal with the interplay of abstraction and evidence – again leaving unfinished business for the rest of us to resolve. Two recent comments illustrate his concern:

> We are told that 'when theory and fact come into conflict, it is theory, not fact, that must give way.' It is very doubtful how far that dictum applies to economics. Our theories ... are not that sort of theory; but it is also true that our facts are not that sort of fact.
>
> (1983a: 371–2)

> The facts which we study are not permanent, or repeatable, like our facts of the natural sciences; they change incessantly, and change without repetition ... [As] a general rule, it is not our business as economists to come close. We are trying to detect general patterns amid the mass of absorbing detail; shapes that repeat among the details that do not repeat ... In order to analyse we must simplify and cut down.
>
> (1976e: 245)

The anti-empirical tone of these views, briefly summarized by Helm (1984: 123), may leave the specification of uncertainty without clear bases. Should choices for uncertainty be realistic? Should we resort to instrumental assumptions that are remote from reality but convenient for the story being told (like Aesop's fables)? What details of uncertain environments should we retain and from what details should we abstract? Can the desire to focus on general patterns indicate what probabilistic concepts we should seek to apply? Does anything go?

Looking back over the professional literature that appeared during the 60 years of Hicks's career, we see that such questions were seldom addressed. Instead, the familiar symbols of our probability distributions generally lack situational (historical and realistic) clarification. From some vague and generous deity, sequences of theories permit every economic agent to be frequently assigned a complete, subjective, distribution of risk – costlessly obtained and accurately elucidated, without any recognition of incoherence or inconsistency, and somehow connected to the objective facts or premises of a given model. Although elegant as a theoretical representation, it is tempting to view the result of relying on such procedures as disappointing, unless one simply cares for the pursuit of an intellectual game. Whether this view reflects a valid indictment of theoretical developments involving uncertainty or, rather, a misunderstanding of the benefits that stem from the pursuit of 'pure' knowledge from abstract models is difficult to judge. Perhaps, in contrast to Hicks, we do not need to 'simplify and cut down' but rather to build up from realistic concepts of probability. Hicks (1979g: 107) suggested:

> The probabilities of 'states of the world' that are formally used by economists, as for instance in portfolio theory, cannot be interpreted in terms of random experiments. Probability, in economics, must mean something wider. It need not, indeed should not, be so wide as to be irrational. Economic decisions are based on imperfect evidence, but they are based on some evidence. And they have a definite relation to the evidence they are based on.

If economic decisions are indeed based on evidence, then perhaps we should also insist that the theoretical representations of probability concepts used in economic models are based on real evidence (see Hamouda 1993: 247–55).

Turning more specifically to the potential modification of *Value and Capital*, we can identify the difficulties that will seriously affect attempts to include Hicks's three approaches to probability in general equilibrium models. First, the selection of criteria for individual rationality of economic agents in such models have become much more diverse. Some practical issues – such as those of computability and cognitive biases, for example – can no longer be ignored to the extent that they were in 1939. (See the symposium on 'The behavioral foundations of economic theory', reported in the *Journal of Business* (October 1986).) The simplicity of *Value and Capital* is lost and we will struggle in vain to replace the former prominent outcomes, such as Pareto efficiency, by their stochastic counterparts. Second, any firm dependence on non-measurable sets for probability leads to a form of satisficing (or non-surprising) behaviour rather than to the familiar marginal calculations of deterministic optimality. Third, when the dynamic constraints that affect actions of economic agents in theoretical models reflect the disparities between subjective probabilities and the realized values of corresponding economic variables (not as white noise), we cannot focus only on a few distributional parameters and retain myopic behaviour. Fourth, the meaning of equilibria in these stochastic models will be less clear and we may depend more on simulative experiments than on analytical solutions and mathematical theorems. Finally, the inclusion of the non-stationarity of Hicks's first approach to uncertainty from 1931 to 1933 and of his subsequent stress of particular historical shift imply probabilities that will exhibit state dependency and some 'fixing' in time, both of which are far away from the simple deterministic framework from 1939.

We are left with much to do. In terms of the well-known Chinese proverb, we are condemned to live in interesting time. Our successors will surely thank us if we can resolve at least a few problems with uncertainty. Hicks will continue to serve as a source of gentle inspiration as we re-assess the contents of his research and go on to areas that he resisted. His deep commitment to a search for improvement and to the persistent questioning of entrenched views should guide our efforts.

REFERENCES

Arrow, K. J. (1965) *Aspects of the Theory of Risk-Bearing*, Helsinki: Yrjö Jahnsson in säätio.

⸺ (1986) 'Rationality of self and others in an economic system', *Journal of Business* 59: S384–99.

Fishburn, P. C. (1986) 'The axioms of subjective probability', *Statistical Science* 1: 335–99 (with discussion).

Good, I. J. (1959) 'Kinds of probability', *Sciences* 129: 443–7.

⸺ (1965) *The Estimation of Probabilities: An Essay on Modern Bayesian Methods*, Cambridge, MA: MIT Press, ch. 2.

⸺ (1981) 'Some logic and history of hypothesis testing', in J.C. Pitt (ed.) *Philosophy in Economics*, Dordrecht: Reidel, pp. 149–74.

⸺ (1986) 'Some statistical applications of Poisson's work', *Statistical Science* 1: 157–80.

Hamouda, O. F. (1993) *John R. Hicks. The Economist's Economist*, Oxford: Blackwell.

Hart, A. G. (1947) 'Keynes' analysis of expectations and uncertainty', in S. E. Harris (ed.) *The New Economics: Keynes' Influence on Theory and Public Policy*, New York: Knopf, ch. 31.

⸺ (1949) 'Assets, liquidity, and investment', *American Economic Review* 39: 171–81.

Helm, D. (1984) 'Predictions and causes: a comparison of Friedman and Hicks on method', in D. A. Collard, D. R. Helm, M. F. G. Scott and A. K. Sen (eds) *Economic Theory and Hicksian Themes*, Oxford: Clarendon Press, pp. 118–34.

Keynes, J. M. (1921), *A Treatise on Probability*, London: Macmillan.

Knight, F. H. (1921) *Risk, Uncertainty and Profit*, Chicago, IL: University of Chicago Press; reprinted in 1971.

Lange, O. (1944) 'Uncertainty', in *Price Flexibility and Employment*, Bloomington, IN: Principia Press, ch. 6.

Le Cam, L. (1986) 'The Central Limit Theorem around 1935', *Statistical Science* 1: 78–96.

Lindley, D. V., Tversky, A. and Brown, R. V. (1979) 'On the reconciliation of probability assessments', *Journal of the Royal Statistical Society* 142: 146–80.

Maistrov, L. E. (1974) *Probability Theory: A Historical Sketch*, New York: Academic Press.

Pratt, J. W. (1986) 'Comment', on G. Shafer, (1986) 'Savage Revisited', *Statistical Science* 1: 463–501, pp. 498–9.

Ramsey, F. P. (1931) 'Truth and probability', *Foundations of Mathematics and Other Logical Essays*, London: Humanities Press.

Wegman, E. J. (1986) 'Some personal recollections of Harold Cramer on the development of statistics and probability', *Statistical Science* 1: 528–35.

12

RISK AND UNCERTAINTY

John D. Hey

As pointed out by the editors of this volume, in a letter to me elaborating on their kind invitation to contribute to this volume, 'the theory of risk was one of Sir John's main preoccupations'. One of his first theoretical studies was his 1931 *Economica* article 'Uncertainty and profit', and the last chapter of his last book, completed just before he passed away, was 'Risk and uncertainty', an appendix to his 1989 *A Market Theory of Money*. In between, he returned to the subject on many occasions, especially in 'The theory of portfolio selection' (in his 1967 *Critical Essays in Monetary Theory*) and 'The disaster point in risk theory' (in his 1977 *Economic Perspectives*).

The modern, mainstream approach to risk and uncertainty is intellectually strongly intertwined with the modern, mainstream approach to probability. Hicks, however, in keeping with others of his 'generation', typically kept the two subjects rather separate. I shall follow his lead, and confine my attention here to Hicks's work on risk and uncertainty, leaving the elucidation of Hicks's views on probability in the capable hands of Professors Hamouda and Rowley. It is probably true to say, however, that where Hicks ventured into formal, mathematical analysis of economic problems involved with risk and uncertainty, his implicit or explicit view on the appropriate characterization of the underlying risk and uncertainty was that adopted by the modern, mainstream approach: to the effect that risk and uncertainty are inter-changeable terms applicable to situations in which non-certainty can be described in terms of objective or subjective probability distributions. However, in his frequent forays into verbal evaluations of the complications introduced into economic analysis by the existence of risk and uncertainty, Hicks often revealed a rather less rigid characterization. Such issues are explored in Professors Hamouda and Rowley's chapter.

In his more informal writings, Hicks repeatedly returned to two interrelated questions concerned with the consideration of situations involving risk and uncertainty: 'how do people react to such risk and uncertainty?'; 'how might such risk and uncertainty be reduced?' This latter question was a particular concern in his writings on historical and institutional matters; for example, in his 1969 book *A Theory of Economic History*, he examined the evolution of the mercantile economy partly in terms of the development of institutional and commercial arrangements for the reduction of risk – which he clearly regarded as being potentially a formidable obstacle to growth in trade. So, on page 59, for example, he discusses the establishment of legal and quasi-legal institutions, 'institutions for the protection of property and contract', the 'development of particular forms of contract, such as insurance and hedging'; and the development of key trading centres whose existence allows 'risks on both sides' (of a trade) to be reduced. Elsewhere in this book (p. 79) he elaborates on one key aspect of these risk reduction measures, namely the growth of insurance, and draws attention to the 'law of large numbers' which makes such insurance both possible and desirable.

This concern – with institutional methods for *reducing* the incidence of risk and uncertainty – is clearly motivated in Hicks's writing by his verbal and mathematical analysis of the effect of such risk and uncertainty on behaviour and welfare. By and large, his analysis proceeded in two stages: first, he argued that economic agents perceived risk and uncertainty in terms of an (objective or subjective) probability distribution of some appropriate random variable. Second, recognizing that, even though this in itself was an enormous (and perhaps unwarranted) simplification, the complexity of a probability distribution was too great to be handled, he argued that this in turn needed to be simplified dramatically. In various writings (some of which I shall discuss later) he agonized long and hard about how great a simplification was necessary. He almost always thought in terms of *moments* of the distribution, and there was no difficulty about the most important of these – namely the *mean*, or expectation, of the distribution. Indeed, he argued in many writings that the gist of the relevant economic problem could be captured in terms of this single moment, and that nothing of much importance would be lost by neglecting higher moments. But, in other writings, he recognized the crucial role of such higher moments. So, for example, on page 73 of his 1985 *Methods of Dynamic Economics*, he argues:

> An uncertain expectation ... can be represented (more or less adequately) by a probability distribution, and this (in turn) is usually describable by a fairly small number of parameters. These may be the ordinary statistical parameters (mean value, variance, and so on); or it may be that there are others more appropriate to the particular matter in hand. The important thing is that an uncertain expectation cannot be adequately described in terms of a single parameter. It is insufficient to consider the changes in ... plans that result from changes ... that are 'expected' as most probable. Attention must also be given to the effects of changes in the confidence with which these values are expected.

However, later in the same chapter, he recognizes the enormous complications in the analysis that might ensue by so doing.

One of Hicks's main strengths as a theorist was his ability to simplify, to abstract away inessentials and to concentrate attention on the key elements of any piece of economic theory. At the same time he was acutely aware of the dangers of excessive simplification – of abstracting away the very essence of the problem with which one was concerned. Hence his continuing tussle to determine the 'correct' set of moments of a probability distribution that was relevant to some given economic problem. Much of the time he worked with either just the first moment, the mean, or just the first two moments, the mean and the standard deviation. (He preferred the latter to the variance – used by others – since the units of the former 'meant something', unlike the units of the latter.) In some of his writings, his analysis of the impact of the dispersion was largely intuitive:

> Even if the most probable price expected to rule at some future date remains unchanged, a person's readiness to adopt a plan ... may be affected, if he becomes less certain about the probability of that price, if the dispersion of possible prices is increased. Generally, one would suppose, an increased dispersion would make him less willing to make plans ... If this is so, an increased dispersion will have the same effect as a reduction of the expected price, in cases where the individual plans to sell, as an increase of the expected price, in cases where he plans to buy.
>
> (*Value and Capital*, 1946b: 125)

Of course, all this has now been formalized by modern theorists, armed with the tools of modern expected utility theory, but, at the time, Hicks's analysis was remarkably advanced. Even more remarkable was the insight shown by his 1931 *Economica* paper 'The theory of uncertainty and profit', one of his earliest publications.

One infers that this was largely motivated by Frank Knight's *Risk, Uncertainty and Profit*, published in 1921: while paying fulsome tribute to Knight's insight into the link between uncertainty and profit, and indeed into the role of uncertainty as the *raison d'être* of profits, Hicks was at pains to demonstrate that one did *not* need to use 'unmeasurable risks', or genuine Knightian uncertainty, to achieve these results. Indeed, according to Hicks, one could work with (subjective or objective) probability distributions and achieve similar results.

In retrospect, the analysis appears crude, and, in places, incomplete (though it is fairly clear that Hicks (1931c) was aware of the lacunae in his analysis – see, for example, footnote 8 on page 178). Nevertheless, it laid the foundation for much important work that was to follow. After some general discussion on the existence of risk and uncertainty, and its reduction through insurance, Hicks moved on to some more formal analysis. Here he used what he termed 'frequency curves' to illustrate uncertainties faced by various economic agents; in modern-day language these are frequency density functions or probability density functions. Hicks distinguished two broad types of such functions: one which resembled a negative exponential distribution, bounded above by some positive value and with the density declining to zero as one moved to lower values; and the other which resembled a bell-shaped, normal distribution. Hicks thought that the former function was more appropriate to a situation in which, for example, 'resources are hired for a fixed payment, but there is a possibility that the payment will not be made (or not made in full) ...', while the latter function was more suited to a situation in which 'resources are exposed to uncertainty, and the reward is to be a share in the net return, *whatever it is* ...', (p. 178, italics in the original).

The scenario which Hicks was considering in this paper was one in which a business man is considering in which of several alternative investments he should put his money. The rewards from any investment are supposed to be risky, with a return schedule characterized by one or other of the two probability density functions discussed above. Hicks considered first the situation in which the lender restricts attention solely to the mean reward under each alternative. If this was the case, Hicks argued, then 'the investor would go to that one where the expectation of reward was higher' (p. 180). As a consequence, 'we should arrive at the interesting conclusion that no net share in the National Dividend was to be attributed to anyone for the bearing of risk'.

Hicks argued that this conclusion was not consistent with the facts since the implication of the assumption that the *mean* of the distribution is the sole factor taken into account by the decision maker means that 'people would be equally ready to invest in an undertaking that promised a safe £100, in one which promised equal chances of £200 or nothing, and in one which promised nine chances of £110 to one of £10'. Hicks concluded that 'it seems fairly safe to say that this is not the case'!

In modern parlance, this leads us to the conclusion that Hicks regarded the assumption of risk neutrality as implausible; judging by the tone of the quotes in the paragraph above it seems fair to infer that he thought that the assumption of risk aversion more plausible. In terms of modern theory, this is characterized through expected utility (rather than expected value) maximization, with a concave (risk-averse) utility function. Hicks arrived at the same conclusion, but by a rather different route: relying on the 'law of diminishing marginal utility' combined with maximization of subjective satisfaction. Though purists would argue that this 'old-fashioned' cardinal utility argument is different from the modern Neumann–Morgenstern cardinal utility argument, the spirit of the explanation is quite clearly the same.

So Hicks arrived at expected utility maximization and concave utility functions, leading to the conclusion that the mean of a probability distribution was not the sole criterion used by a decision maker in deciding between two alternative distributions. Clearly, higher moments were also potentially important; though Hicks did not go into detail in this early article. He did, however, return to the topic on several future occasions. I shall do likewise.

Hicks also realized that a globally concave utility function could lead to difficulties – especially when it came to explaining gambling behaviour. For he realized that such a utility function implied that such an agent 'would never be willing to give even £1 for a 1/1000 chance of winning £1,000'. Unless, of course, he consciously or unconsciously overestimated the chances of winning; this he termed the 'gambling over-estimate'. It would appear that gambling and gamblers rather disconcerted Hicks; at times he seemed to want to exclude such behaviour from the realms of economic analysis. For example, in his 1962 Presidential Address to the Royal Economic Society, published as 'Liquidity' in the 1962 *Economic Journal*, he remarks: 'To expect consistency in gambling is futile, for gambling is a rest from consistency'!

So the 1931 paper leads us to some key notions of modern treatments of risk and uncertainty: subjective or objective probability assessments; expected utility maximization; concave utility functions; risk premia. Some comparative static exercises also are there: some specifically (the effect of a rightward shift in some probability distribution); others rather vaguely. It was left to the later articles to make the latter more specific.

Much of Hicks's later work implementing these skeletal notions was in the field of portfolio selection. He returned to this theme on a number of occasions, but clearly had difficulty in deciding on the most appropriate implementation. Part of this difficulty was sheer algebraic complexity; e.g. in his chapter on 'The pure theory of portfolio selection' in his 1967 *Critical Essays in Monetary Theory*, he remarks that 'it only gives manageable results ... if we take the utility function ... in a very simple form ...' (p. 106). But another part of his difficulty was that 'in its simplest form it ... gives results that are not acceptable' (p. 106). He never did seem to resolve these difficulties to his own satisfaction; but nevertheless his writings gave great insights.

I shall discuss his various contributions to the theory of portfolio selection in three main sections: first, I shall discuss his 'mean, standard deviation' approach which underpins much of the analysis in 'The pure theory of portfolio selection' and 'Liquidity'; I shall then discuss his extensions to this analysis achieved through the incorporation of skewness; finally, after examining the reasons for some unhappiness he felt at using the basic (and extended) 'mean, standard deviation' approach, I shall turn to his material using an expected-utility-based constant relative risk aversion approach which brought him into apparent conflict with Professor Arrow, but which also brought him to his 'disaster point' concept which he clearly regarded as having great potential – even though his death stopped him from exploiting it to the full.

His 'mean, standard deviation' approach to portfolio choice is nowadays a familiar one, though this was not the case when Hicks first wrote on the topic. His analysis (in 'The pure theory of portfolio selection') began with a two-dimensional diagram with the *mean* return (denoted by E) on a portfolio along the horizontal axis, and with the standard deviation (denoted by S) *down* the vertical axis. (The latter he did because S is a *disutility*, and he wanted indifference curves in his diagram to have the conventional shape.) I shall return to the indifference curves in due course, but for the moment I shall concentrate on the *budget constraint* in this diagram. Typically, Hicks built up his analysis in stages, beginning with the set of absolutely safe securities (those with zero standard deviation) and hence defining the *best* such absolutely safe security (the one with the highest expected value) which determined the point on the budget constraint on the horizontal axis, on the assumption of a fixed sum of money to allocate to the portfolio. Hicks then introduced a risky security (one with a positive standard deviation) and argued that, for this to be considered for inclusion in the optimal portfolio, it must have a higher mean value than the best absolutely safe security. If so, its mean and standard deviation define a point in our two-dimensional diagram for the case when the entire portfolio is put in this single risky asset. Points on the straight line between that point and the point on the horizontal axis on the budget constraint are also points on the budget constraint – representing portfolios consisting of both the best absolutely safe security and the risky security.

Hicks then introduced a second risky security, whose return may or not be correlated with the return on the first risky security. Through elementary algebra, Hicks derived the extension to the budget constraint implied by the addition of this further asset, and showed that it is inevitably curved, rather than linear. Moreover, it is concave, guaranteeing a unique point of tangency with the assumed-convex indifference curves. Further risky assets were added in a similar fashion leading to an overall concave budget constraint (except for a linear portion linking the best absolutely safe security to the risky security whose excess return over the absolutely safe security was highest relative to its own standard deviation). Hicks then carried out a number of comparative static exercises concerning the effect of changes in the means and standard deviations of the various securities, as well as changes in the correlations between them. Much of what he found is now part of the lore of portfolio analysis.

However, Hicks was not completely satisfied. This was partly for reasons, which I shall come to shortly, connected with the utility function lying behind the 'mean, standard deviation' indifference map assumed in the above analysis. But it was also partly because he 'had an obstinate feeling that it does not go far enough. Why should the first and second moments of the probability distribution be all that we must take into account?' (1967: 117–18). He illustrated his concern with a simple example:

> There is one portfolio which offers a 90 per cent chance of an outcome of 4, and a 10 per cent chance of an outcome of 14; the mean value of the prospect is 5, and the standard deviation is 3. There is another which

offers a 90 per cent chance of 6 and 10 per cent chance of –4; the mean value is again 5, and the standard deviation again 3. It is implied in (E, S) ['mean, standard deviation'] theory that the investor would be indifferent between these two outcomes, which are skewed in opposite ways. But it is not by any means obvious that we are justified in assuming that he would be indifferent, though it is not easy to say straight off which would be preferred. Though the two prospects are equally *uncertain*, common parlance would surely say that one was more *risky* than the other.

(p. 118, italics in the original)

Recall that this was written before Rothschild and Stiglitz formalized a particular definition of riskiness, based on modern expected utility theory. But it does open our minds once again to alternative ideas about riskiness.

Hicks, of course, was getting at *skewness*; he took as his measure the cube root of the third moment around the mean (which is measured in the same units as the mean E and standard deviation S). He denoted this by Q. For reasons which are not altogether obvious, he began by confining attention to cases in which Q was negative, i.e. in which the distribution was negatively skewed. He then went on to consider the shape of the indifference map in (E, S, Q) space – not, it should be emphasized, from the perspective of expected utility theory, but rather from the perspective of intuitive reasonableness. He first argued that (for Q negative) its marginal utility would be positive – so as a distribution got less negatively skewed its attractiveness increased. Furthermore he assumed that the marginal utility of Q would be diminishing, implying that the attractiveness increased at a decreasing rate. Finally, he assumed that the marginal utility approached zero in the vicinity of Q equal to zero.

Hicks then amended his graphical analysis of indifference curves in (E, S) to include this third dimension. He extended his algebraic analysis similarly, coming up with some insightful results on the impact of skewness on optimal portfolio choice. Almost inevitably, this involved him in a consideration of securities with *positive* skewness $(Q > 0)$. These he called *speculative* securities, as distinct from *risky* securities (i.e. those with $Q < 0$). This particular nomenclature appears to have disappeared from modern economics – which is a pity, since Hicks's analysis showed how a 'speculative security (if it exists) will have a strong tendency to draw investment to itself, for once the rising part of its curve can become effective, it will be extremely powerful' (1967: 123).

Hicks's incorporation of skewness adds significantly to 'mean, standard deviation' analysis. Unfortunately, he did not take the analysis very far, nor indeed the analysis of the further incorporation of *kurtosis* (the fourth moment of the distribution) on which he speculated at the end of 'The pure theory of portfolio selection'.

Possibly one reason for his not doing so was his unease about the 'expected utility' foundation for 'mean, standard deviation' analysis. At that time he recognized that two possible routes from expected utility theory to mean, standard deviation analysis were as follows: first, through the assumption that all relevant probability distributions could be describable simply in terms of their means and standard deviations (as if, for example, all distributions were normal); and second, through the assumption of a quadratic utility function. He did not seem too keen on the first of these (possibly because returns on securities are more likely to be lognormally distributed); nor was he much keener on the second, as Section IV of 'The pure theory of portfolio selection' makes clear. His first objection was the by-now familiar criticism of the properties of a quadratic utility function which displays risk aversion: sooner or later, marginal utility becomes negative. He adds a second objection, which 'though it is no less of a mare's nest, it is of somewhat greater economic interest' (1967: 116).

Suppose, for convenience, that the return on the safe asset is zero, and the initial equilibrium for an investor is on the linear part of the budget constraint – i.e. on the line, discussed above, joining the point on the horizontal axis representing total investment in the safe asset to the point representing total investment in the asset with the highest excess return over the safe asset relative to its standard deviation. Now suppose that the investor's capital is doubled or tripled. This extends the straight line segment of the budget line, though its slope is unaltered. This means that the investor's optimal point is unchanged. This can be achieved only by putting all the extra capital in the safe asset. To Hicks 'this is obvious nonsense'!

Hicks returned to portfolio choice theory in 'The disaster point in risk theory', Chapter 8 of his 1977 *Economic Perspectives*, in which he repeats his dissatisfaction with the 'mean, standard deviation' approach, whether supplemented or not through the incorporation of skewness. One guesses that he was somewhat nettled by an apparent disagreement with Professor Arrow, though he acknowledges intellectual stimulation from Professors J.L. Ford and S.C. Tsiang.

In this chapter, Hicks is at pains to develop a theory of portfolio selection based centrally on expected utility analysis, preferably combining plausible assumptions about the utility function with plausible conclusions about portfolio choice. He began with the latter. He thought it would be desirable if one could end up at a situation where the proportions of the portfolio held in the various different securities were *independent* of the size of the portfolio: so that, for example, a doubling of the size of the portfolio would lead to a doubling in the holdings of each and every security. His argument, which I am tempted to reproduce here, but which can be found both in 'The disaster point in risk theory' and in the appendix 'risk and uncertainty' of his 1989 *A Market Theory of Money*, is a splendid example of his lucid thinking. A modern-day theorist would spoil the elegance of Hicks's prose by asserting, quite rightly, that the desired result would follow from the assumption of *constant relative risk aversion*. This guarantees that the scale of a problem does not affect the distribution of the risk. Constant relative risk aversion is specified by

$$- x \frac{U''(x)}{U'(x)} = \alpha \qquad (12.1)$$

since the left-hand side is the Arrow–Pratt index of relative risk aversion. Here, I slightly depart from Hicks in using x to denote the terminal wealth and $U(.)$ to denote the investor's Neumann–Morgenstern utility function.

Integrating (12.1) twice we get

$$U(x) = \begin{array}{lll} B + A \ln x & \text{if } \alpha = 1 & (12.2) \\ B + A x^{1-\alpha} & \text{if } 0 < \alpha < 1 \text{ or } \alpha > 1 & (12.3) \\ B + Ax & \text{if } \alpha = 0 & (12.4) \end{array}$$

Equation (12.4) is the uninteresting case of a risk-neutral agent; so I ignore it. Hicks ignored also equation (12.2), on the grounds that 'though it was the case that was specially considered by Bernouilli, [it] needs for our purpose no special attention' (1977a: 168). He concentrated on equation (12.3), examining specially the restrictions on the parameters A, B and α.

For marginal utility to be positive everywhere (it is assumed that x is non-negative) we require $A(1 - \alpha)$ to be positive. For marginal utility to be diminishing (i.e. for our investor to be risk averse) we further require α to be positive. B can be anything. That still leaves open two possibilities:

(A) $\alpha < 1, A > 0$ and   (B) $\alpha > 1, A < 0$

It is here where his apparent dispute with Professor Arrow emerged.

In both cases (A) and (B), the utility function given by (12.3) is *unbounded*: in case (A) $U(x) \to \infty$ as $x \to \infty$; in case (B) $U(x) \to -\infty$ as $x \to 0$. (Recall that we are assuming that x, the return on the portfolio, is non-negative.) Now there is a very famous theorem in Arrow's *Aspects of the Theory of Risk Bearing* (1965), reproduced on page 69 of Arrow's *Essays in the Theory of Risk Bearing* (1970), which states that 'any utility function which satisfies the conditions of the Expected Utility Theorem must be bounded both from above and from below'. Hicks was happy to go along with part of this, but not all. In particular, he was happy to agree that the utility function should be bounded above. The rationale for this result has its roots in the famous St Petersburg paradox: which states that any risk-neutral individual (i.e. an individual who cares only about the expected return from any prospect) would be willing to pay any finite amount, however large, in order to buy a bet which yielded £2^i with probability 2^{-i} ($i = 1, 2, \ldots$). A way round this particular version of the paradox is to assume that the individual is a risk-averse expected utility maximizer; in which case the individual would be willing to pay only a finite sum for the privilege of buying the bet.

For example, a logarithmic utility function does the trick.

However, it was then realized that a logarithmic utility function was unbounded above, and therefore that an individual with such a utility function would be prone to a variant of the St Petersburg paradox: consider, for example, a bet that pays £exp(2^i) with probability $2^{-i}(i = 1, 2, \ldots)$. This has expected utility, for an individual with a logarithmic utility function $U(x) = \ln x$, of

$$\sum_{i=1}^{\infty} 2^{-i} \ln[\exp(2^i)] = \sum_{i=1}^{\infty} 1$$

which is infinite. So this individual should be willing to pay any finite amount, however large, for the privilege of buying this bet. Again, this seems paradoxical.

A similar argument can be used for *any* utility function that is unbounded above. In other words, for an expected utility maximizer with a utility function which is unbounded above, one can always construct a risky bet which has infinite expected utility for this individual, and for which, therefore, the individual should be willing to pay any finite amount, however large. (There are various objections to such paradoxes, most eloquently expounded in Samuelson (1977), but I leave these to one side.)

The other half of Arrow's theorem, and the one to which Hicks objected, proceeds along similar lines, *mutatis mutandis*. Here the argument is that for an expected utility maximizer with a utility function which is unbounded *below*, one can always construct a risky bet which has an expected utility of *minus* infinity. The individual would then pay an infinite amount to get rid of it – *if he had it in the first place*. Although Hicks did not explicitly state this, I feel that it is the italicized phrase to which he objected, for one cannot presume that the individual holds such a bet in the first place. So the key question is: can we trap such an individual into some such paradox, starting from an initial position of certainty or starting from a decision problem in which he can avoid the potential fate of infinitely negative utility?

Hicks thought not, and I agree. Suppose then that our individual has a utility function given by equation (12.3),

$$U(x) = B + Ax^{1-\alpha}$$

where A is negative and α is greater than 1. As x approaches plus infinity, $U(x)$ approaches its upper bound of B; and as x approaches zero, $U(x)$ approaches minus infinity.

Consider now the portfolio choice problem: our individual has capital K to allocate among n securities. x_j is the amount invested in the jth security ($\sum_{j=1}^{n} x_j = K$). I follow Hicks in assuming that there are m 'states of the world', or 'eventualities' as he rather less pompously preferred them to be called, with the return on one unit of capital invested in the jth security being a_{ij} in the ith state of the world. The as are known by the investor, as are the probabilities $p_1, \ldots, p_m$ ($\sum_{i=1}^{n} p_i = 1$) of the m states of the world. Thus given an allocation x_j ($j = 1, \ldots, n$) the return in the ith state of the world is $\sum_{j=1}^{n} a_{ij} x_j$, and so the expected utility to our investor is

$$\text{EU} = \sum_{i=1}^{m} p_i U \left(\sum_{j=1}^{n} a_{ij} x_j \right) \tag{12.5}$$

Now, for simplicity, I assume that each p_i is strictly positive. (This enables me to ignore questions about the consequences of multiplying zero by infinity, and hence rather philosophical questions about expected utility when there is a zero probability of getting a utility of minus infinity.) So the crucial question is whether our individual can avoid getting *any* of the $U(\sum_{j=1}^{n} a_{ij} x_j)$ terms equal to minus infinity; i.e. whether our individual can avoid getting *any* of the

$$\sum_{j=1}^{n} a_{ij} x_j \qquad i = 1, \ldots, m \tag{12.6}$$

terms equal to zero.

This is straightforwardly answered: some of the a_{ij} will be strictly positive; some *may* be zero. Each of the expressions in (12.6) will therefore be strictly positive as long as the investor does not put the whole of his capital into a security (or a set of securities) which has zero return in some (feasible) state of the world. As Hicks put it more eloquently than I:

> He may put some of his capital into such an investment; but so long as the rest is put into investments where there is no such possibility, he is not undertaking a finite possibility of total loss, over his whole portfolio. We all know about the gambler who stakes his last shirt on a wager, but if we are looking for a standard case of investment behaviour, it need not incommode us if such extreme cases of gambling are excluded from it. There is nothing to stop the investor, whose behaviour is included, having 'a bit of a flutter' with a *part* of his capital.
>
> (1977a: 170)

Hicks was right. The utility function (12.3) is perfectly sensible in the context of this portfolio choice problem. Moreover, it leads to elegant results about the actual composition of the portfolio choice and its dependence on the various distributions and the risk aversion parameter α. Moreover, it paves the way for a further refinement to which Hicks accorded considerable importance. This refinement proceeds as follows.

The utility function (12.3) has a *disaster point* (Hicks's terminology) when x becomes zero. But why, asks Hicks, should the disaster point be at zero? Disaster may well set in at some finite value c (> 0). To incorporate this, we modify (12.3) to become

$$U(x) = B + A(x - c)^{1-\alpha} \tag{12.7}$$

where, once again, A is negative and α is greater than 1. Utility now becomes negatively infinite at $x = c$, and this now becomes the disaster point. Everything proceeds as before, except that the unit outcomes become $a_{ij} - c/k$. To avoid disaster now, the investor must avoid putting the whole of his capital in any security for which some of the $a_{ij} - c/k$ are negative or zero. As Hicks put it:

> The investor will thus tend to avoid securities which have these low a_{ij}
> – securities that is, which have a very bad outcome in some even-
> tualities. He will avoid such risky securities. He will 'play for safety' as
> he gets poorer, or as he gets nearer to his disaster point.

(173)

This line of argument led Hicks into believing that c/k was a better indicator of risk aversion than the exponent α. Recall that α is the (Arrow–Pratt) index of relative risk aversion, and is one of the key risk aversion indexes used by modern expected utility theorists. (The others being the absolute risk aversion index and the partial risk aversion index.) True, α has an impact on the optimal portfolio choice – so that, for example, individuals with higher values of α (i.e. those more risk averse) will invest, *ceteris paribus*, more heavily in less risky securities. But c/k captures some other dimension of risk aversion which is not really captured by the Arrow–Pratt relative risk aversion index. It captures the notion that a key component of risk is the possibility of ending up bankrupt – beyond Hicks's disaster point. So a more risk-averse individual in this sense is one for whom the disaster point c/k is larger. The key difference between these two indexes is clear: the Arrow–Pratt measure captures the curvature of the utility function whilst the Hicksian index (c/k) captures the prominence of the point at which disaster strikes – and utility becomes negatively infinite. Modern-day theorists have perhaps concentrated too much on the former and too little on the latter – to the detriment of economics.

Hicks returned to his *disaster point* in the appendix 'Risk and uncertainty' of his final book *A Market Theory of Money*. In this he also returned to Knight and partly recanted his earlier views on Knight's writing. I referred to these in the early pages of this chapter. Hicks, it will be recalled, was somewhat dismissive of Knight's 'unmeasurable risks'. However, in the closing stages of his life he writes that 'I would now attach much more importance to it [unmeasurable risk] than I did in my first contribution to the subject ['Uncertainty and profit'] written under his influence not much more than ten years after his book appeared' (1989a: 142).

He then went on to propose a combination of the Knightian distinction, between measurable and non-measurable risky choices, and his own distinc-tion, between risky choices and non-risky choices. Here, by a risky choice, he meant one that involved the *possibility* of disaster (i.e. an outcome beyond the disaster point). So Hicks proposed a four-way classification of risks:

1   measurable risky choices;
2   non-measurable risky choices;
3   measurable non-risky choices;
4   non-measurable non-risky choices.

Under (1) there are circumstances which might be mitigated by some form of insurance; under (2) we have the 'true uncertainty' of Knight; under (3) we have, for example, the purchase of lottery tickets; and under (4) we have situations such as the 'ordinary running of a business'. Category (3) is the one most-beloved of modern-day theorists.

The problem, of course, remains that we have very little theory to guide us as to behaviour in the non-measurable risks cases ((2) and (4)). There is a little, but it is dwarfed by the expected utility paradigm apparatus.

As far as Hicks's risky cases are concerned, there is a problem – if the possibility of the disastrous outcome cannot be avoided. (Note that it usually could be in the portfolio choice cases considered above.) If this possibility cannot be avoided whatever the decision maker does, then the expected utility to the decision maker is minus infinity whatever the decision maker does. Expected utility, therefore, is no longer a guide to choice.

It is sad that Hicks is not around to tell us where to go from here.

REFERENCES

Arrow, K. J. (1965) *Aspects of the Theory of Risk Bearing*, Helsinki: Yrjö Jahnsson in säätio.
——— (1970) *Essays in the Theory of Risk Bearing*, Amsterdam: North-Holland.
Samuelson, P. A. (1977) 'St Petersburg paradoxes: defanged, dissected and historically described', *Journal of Economic Literature* 15: 24–55.

13

EMPLOYMENT AND MACHINERY

Harald Hagemann

I INTRODUCTION

By the late 1960s Hicks had clearly become fascinated by the *Ricardo machinery effect*, i.e. the employment consequences of the introduction of a different, more 'mechanized' method of production. Hicks came to the defence of what he regarded as the central message of Ricardo's analysis of the machinery question: there are important cases in which the introduction of a new type of machinery might reduce both real output and employment in the short run, the harmful effect might persist for quite a time, but the increased investment caused by higher profits due to the increased efficiency of the new production process should eventually lead to a path of output and employment which is above that one which could have been achieved with the old production process.[1]

In the new Chapter 31, 'On machinery', in the third edition of his *Principles*, Ricardo retracted his previous position that the introduction of machinery benefits all classes in society and instead concluded '[t]hat the opinion entertained by the labouring class, that the employment of machinery is frequently detrimental to their interests, is not founded on prejudice and error, but is conformable to the correct principles of political economy' (Ricardo 1951: 392). This chapter, which according to Sraffa (1951: LVII) marked the 'most revolutionary change', had impressed both friends and foes and set the stage for later debates of the employment effects of mechanization which has become known as the compensation controversy. Starting from Ricardo's contemporaries like McCulloch, who was shocked by Ricardo's change of mind, it has always drawn the attention of economists whatever their school or generation. While Marx elaborated Ricardo's arguments pro displacement, Schumpeter concentrated on those pro compensation. The list includes John Stuart Mill as well as Wicksell, who criticized Ricardo for neglecting that wage reductions, caused by the diminished demand for labour after the introduction of new machinery, would lead to the reabsorption of displaced workers (see Wicksell 1906; 1934: 133–44). Hicks praised Ricardo for his 'candour and courage; he followed his reasoning where it led him, not just where he (or his friends) wanted it to go' (1969a: 151). As the whole modern debate on technological unemployment, which came up against the background of the microelectronics revolution and higher unemployment rates since the mid-1970s, has shown, the pronouncement which Schumpeter made shortly before his death, that 'the controversy that went on throughout the nineteenth century and beyond, mainly in the form of argument pro and con "compensation", is dead and buried' (Schumpeter 1954: 684), has been proved wrong.[2] Ironically, Schumpeter made his statement with reference to Hicks's theory of wages and the advancement of the new and better techniques to classify technical progress that it contained.

Hicks has not been the last of many great economists who have been attracted by Ricardo's chapter on machinery. In his *Path of Economic Growth*, Lowe (1976) characteristically starts his investigation of the macroeconomic consequences of technological change and of the necessary conditions for bringing an economy back to an equilibrium growth path from Ricardo's analysis of the machinery problem. Most recently Samuelson (1988, 1989) has set out to vindicate Ricardo's propositions that machinery can hurt wages and reduce output and employment. Samuelson's exposition contains numerical examples that lead to a new long-run equilibrium position with unemployed labour, i.e. to *permanent* technological unemployment. In Ricardo's numerical example, the economy takes off from a stationary state equilibrium and the evolution of the gross and net produce is calculated for three successive periods, depicting the effects of the construction and utilization of machinery on aggregate output (Ricardo 1951: 388–90). There is, however, no indication that the economy will arrive at another uniquely determined equilibrium, i.e. the subsequent development of profits, investment, output and employment is largely left in the dark. For that reason Ricardo's example can be regarded as an 'early and rude type of traverse analysis' (see Kurz 1984) which contains a capital shortage theory of *temporary* technological unemployment. According to Ricardo's view capital accumulation and output expansion will in the long run act as a compensating factor to the initial displacement effect of machinery. This has been fully grasped by Hicks who in the late 1960s set out to accomplish Ricardo's traverse analysis.

With the historical and theoretical analysis of the impact of industrialism on the labour market, Hicks made another intensive effort to answer a question which had preoccupied his mind from the early 1930s onwards: is progress beneficial to labour? In particular two issues have to be addressed, namely the impact of technological change on employment and on the distribution of income. The introduction of a new type of machinery might initially reduce the demand for labour and/or the absolute level of real wages. Whereas certain types of innovations could harm workers in the *short run*, Hicks leaves no doubt that without the tremendous increase in productive power, due to the introduction of new technologies, the rise in real wages in the *long run* could not have occurred.

In the context of Hicks's analysis of the machinery question four important streams of development flow together.

1 Whereas abstract theoretical reasoning had been a hallmark of the younger Hicks, as comes out best in his *Value and Capital*, the older Hicks stressed the relationship between economic history and economic theory as of fundamental methodological significance. He not only had a deep sense of the historical origins and time-related character of economic models, thereby also identifying their intrinsic limits, but also made ample use of the materials of economic history and the history of economic thought as necessary tools in the process of economic theorizing.[3]

2 An important characteristic of the historical process is the irreversibility of time. Hicks grappled with an adequate treatment of time in economic theory for almost six decades.[4] It is therefore no surprise that many of the theoretical concepts for which Hicks is best remembered were shaped for the purpose of analyzing the movement of an economy through time. According to Hicks the evolution of disequilibrium over time is the central subject of macroeconomic theory. In particular, Hicks has pointed out the relevance of the time dimension in analyzing the compensation process. The take-up of a new technology is a time-intensive process; it is historical and no longer logical time in the sense of Joan Robinson which matters. Especially because of the deficient modelling of time, Hicks (see 1977a: 190) soon became dissatisfied with the embryonic theory of traverse (caused by a once-for-all rise in the exogenously given rate of growth of labour supply) which he analysed in Chapter 16 of *Capital and Growth* on the basis of a two-sectoral fixed coefficient model, and switched over to a neo-Austrian model in *Capital and Time* to analyse the problem of a traverse caused by a change in technology.[5] The older Hicks of *Capital and Time* who was concerned with the working out of processes over historical time was a pioneer in the field of traverse analysis, which he developed to answer the question of the impact of technological change on employment (and the distribution of income) in both the short and the long run.

3 Throughout his life Hicks kept a deep interest in capital theory. 'Capital is a very large subject, with many aspects; wherever one starts, it is hard to bring more than a few of them into view' (1973d: V). Hicks made numerous attempts to take different views of this subject which is in the centre of his famous trilogy *Value and Capital*, *Capital and Growth* and *Capital and Time*.[6] The older Hicks revealed a preference for his youngest child, thus emphasizing the potential of capital theory for evaluating the impact of accumulation on the labour market. Hicks's primary target is to achieve the construction of a theory of an economy which is not on a balanced growth path but has in the past been in equilibrium which at time 0 is disturbed by a change in one of the determinants of growth such as technical progress. The investigation of

the macroeconomic consequences of such 'impulses'[7] is at the centre of Hicks's analysis of the traverse, which is the easiest part of skiing but one of the most challenging problems of economics. For an economy experiencing such an impulse its own history matters, which, most importantly, is reflected in the inherited capital stock. The existing stock of fixed capital goods implies a structural barrier to short-term responses when an impulse is given by an innovation. The dynamic traverse from one steady growth path to another necessarily involves a change in the whole quantity structure of the economy, especially the rebuilding of the capital stock.

4 Hicks's traverse analysis is based on a *neo-Austrian* representation of production structures. 'A "steady state" theory is out of time; but an "Austrian" theory is in time. It is in time that it belongs' (Hicks 1983a: 109). The most important element which Hicks took over from the Austrians was not subjectivism but the idea that production is a process in time with strong intertemporal complementarities. Time is the essence of capital in Hicks's neo-Austrian approach and enters production in a twofold way: as duration of the process by which the labour inputs are converted into consumption goods and in the sense of intertemporal joint production of final output at different dates, a sequence generated by the fixed capital goods. Capital is an expression of sequential production. Hicks's *neo*-Austrian theory, in treating fixed capital goods, is different from that of the *old* Austrians who dealt only with working capital and could thus work only with a production process of the flow input-*point* output type. Since Hicks regarded capital goods to be the source of a whole stream of final consumption goods at different dates, i.e. he considered productive processes to be of the *flow* output type, Hicks explicitly abandoned typically Austrian concepts like Böhm-Bawerk's construction of the period of production. Moreover, he also neglected concepts like the greater productivity of more roundabout methods of production and the underestimation of future needs (the positive rate of time preference) and thus the determination of the rate of interest.[8] The sole but decisive Austrian elements in Hicks's theory, therefore, are the focusing on the time structure of the production process and the special treatment of capital goods as intermediate products in a vertical model.

It was one of Hayek's major contributions to have shown the importance of the temporal structure of production processes for cyclical fluctuations. Hicks repeatedly pointed out how much he had been influenced by Hayek in whose seminar at the London School of Economics he participated between 1931 and 1935.[9] In particular Hayek had introduced him to the work of Wicksell, who had linked Böhm-Bawerk with Walras, and had made Hicks think of the productive process as a process in time. However, there is a remarkable difference. For Hayek cyclical adjustment problems arise because of monetary factors, like changes in savings behaviour and in particular credit expansion which distorts the system of relative prices. Hicks, on the other hand, always had been sceptical about Hayek's claim that the economy would be in equilibrium if there were no monetary disturbances. Although he took over from Hayek the idea that the impact of an impulse on the real structure of production is most important, it is very clear for Hicks that, unlike in Hayek, the divergence from a steady-state path and the dynamic adjustment process are not caused by monetary but by real factors like technological change.

> Where ... I do not go along with him [Hayek] is in the view that the disturbances in question have a monetary origin. He had not emancipated himself from the delusion ... that with money removed 'in a state of barter' everything would somehow fit. One of my objects in writing this book has been to kill that delusion. It could only arise because the theory of the barter economy had been insufficiently worked out. There has been no money in my model; yet it has plenty of adjustment difficulties. It is not true that by getting rid of money, one is automatically in 'equilibrium' – whether that equilibrium is conceived of as a stationary state (Wicksell), a perfect foresight economy (Hayek) or any kind of steady state. Monetary disorders may indeed be superimposed upon other disorders; but the other disorders are more fundamental.
>
> (Hicks 1973d: 133–4)[10]

Thus it becomes clear that Hicks's neo-Austrian model is designed as a barter-type economy in which money is at best the medium of exchange. It therefore cannot be granted 'that some anti-Say's law prevails, as in Keynes's *General Theory* model' (Morishima 1989: 185). Since Hicks's neo-Austrian theory has nothing to say about the problems of a monetary economy, it cannot take account of Keynesian unemployment but it can allow for the employment consequences of a physical restructuring of capital due to increased mechanization, i.e. technological unemployment. Hence Hicks's finding that the introduction of improved machinery may lead to a temporary contraction in output, and in employment, in the early phase of the traverse does not, in itself, contradict Say's law of markets. It is manifest that this type of 'neo-Austrian' theory is as much inspired by Ricardo[11] as by Böhm-Bawerk and Hayek, a fact openly admitted by Hicks (1985a: 156): 'So where we have come to, on this Austrian route, is close to Ricardo.... to his latest insights, which he did not live to follow up. The Austrian method is indeed a Classical method.'[12]

II THE NEO-AUSTRIAN VISION OF THE PRODUCTION PROCESS

At the heart of Hicks's neo-Austrian theory of capital lies his conception of the production process which is completely integrated vertically. Only a series of dated quantities of labour are visible as inputs, whilst only a series of dated quantities of a particular final product which is assumed to be a consumption good are visible as outputs. Labour is assumed to be the only original and homogenous input. 'Capital goods are simply stages in the process of production' (Hicks 1973d: 5), i.e. they are regarded as intermediate products which do not appear explicitly but are implied and produced within each process of "maturing" of original inputs into the final product. The fixed capital goods, which disappear from view in the neo-Austrian theory,[13] can be dealt with again if we translate the Hicksian approach back into the von Neumann–Sraffa framework.[14] We follow Hicks in distinguishing between the *construction phase* and the *utilization phase* of machines. The construction phase can stretch over n periods and thus bring about $n - 1$ intermediate products on the way to producing the fixed capital good. It is an essential characteristic of Hicks's neo-Austrian model that the first intermediate product is produced solely with the use of the direct labour, i.e. what Ricardo (1951: 53) called 'unassisted labour'. It is combined with direct labour at the next stage of production to produce the second intermediate product and so on, until finally at the end of the construction phase the fixed capital good appears. Thereafter the fixed capital good is operated by means of further direct labour inputs to produce a sequence of dated quantities of the consumer good in the following T periods of the utilization phase. With wages paid *ex post* there is no basic product in Hicks's model, i.e. the production process is thought of as being uni-directional rather than circular as in the von Neumann–Sraffa–Leontief model.

Setting the output quantities of the intermediate products at the various stages of production in the construction phase equal to unity, and assuming that at the end of the production process there are neither scrap values nor shut-down costs, we get the following *system of equilibrium prices and book values*:

$$
\begin{aligned}
& wa_1 && = p_1 \\
(1+r)p_1 &+ wa_2 && = p_2 \\
(1+r)p_2 &+ wa_3 && = p_3 \qquad\qquad \textit{construction phase}\\
&\ \ \vdots \\
(1+r)p_{n-1} &+ wa_n && = p_{n_0}
\end{aligned}
$$

$$
\begin{aligned}
(1+r)p_{n_0} &+ wa_{b_0} && = b_0 p_b + p_{n_1} \\
(1+r)p_{n_1} &+ wa_{b_1} && = b_1 p_b + p_{n_2} \qquad \textit{utilization phase}\\
&\ \ \vdots \\
(1+r)p_{n_{T-1}} &+ wa_{b_{T-1}} && = b_{T-1} p_b
\end{aligned}
$$

(13.1)

where a_i $(i = 1, 2, \ldots, n)$ denotes the input of direct labour needed to produce one unit of the ith means of production and a_{b_t} $(t = 0, 1, \ldots, T-1)$ denotes the input of direct labour which together with the t period old fixed capital good is needed to produce the quantity b_t of the consumer good; $p_1, \ldots, p_{n-1}$ are the (accounting) prices of the intermediate products which are necessary in the production of the fixed capital good, p_{n_t} is the book value of the t period old machine, p_b the price of the consumption good, w the wage rate and r the rate of profits. With the consumption good as the *numéraire* ($p_b = 1$), and the wage rate exogenously given, the price system is closed.

Whereas system (13.1) allows for the possibility of the return of the same truncation period, i.e. reswitching of the same process length,[15] this is excluded in the 'standard case' which forms the basis for the traverse analysis in *Capital and Time*. As usual, Hicks resorted to simplifying assumptions and accessible mathematics for his voyage of exploration. All production processes considered have the simple profile of a labour input a_0 during the single construction period 0 in which no consumption output is produced, and a labour input a_1 per unit of output in each of the n periods of the utilization phase of the machine. For this special case of constant efficiency the price system reduces to

$$
\begin{aligned}
wa_0 &= p_{n_0} \\
(1+r)\, p_{n_0} + wa_1 &= 1 + p_{n_1} \\
(1+r)\, p_2 + wa_1 &= 1 + p_{n_2} \\
&\vdots \\
(1+r)\, p_{n-1} + wa_1 &= 1
\end{aligned}
\tag{13.2}
$$

Hicks's main analytical tool is the efficiency curve (serving the dual purpose of the wage–profit curve and consumption–growth curve under the conditions of the duality theorem) which is derived by equating the present value of the production process to zero.

$$
-wa_0 + \sum_{t=1}^{n} (1 - a_1 w)(1 + r)^{-t} = 0.
\tag{13.3}
$$

The starting point of Hicks's new classification concept of technological change is the w–r relationship which follows from this equation (see Hicks 1973d: 85):

$$
\frac{1}{w} = a_1 + a_0 r_n
\tag{13.4}
$$

with

$$
r_n = r + d = \frac{r}{1 - \{1/(1 + r)\}^n}
\tag{13.5}
$$

where r_n denotes the gross rate of profits and d the depreciation rate. Equation (13.4) can be interpreted as a cost equation with a_1 as the running costs and $a_0 r_n$ as the sum of interest and depreciation on the construction costs. Since the consumption good serves as numéraire, it follows that $1/w$ is the price of the consumption good expressed in terms of wage-units (labour commanded concept).

III HICKS'S NEW CLASSIFICATION OF TECHNOLOGICAL CHANGE

Hicks assumes that the economy originally is on a steady-state growth path which is disturbed by technological change which makes new process(es) available. This poses the problem of choice of technique, i.e. the question of whether the new production process is more profitable than the old one used in the initial equilibrium. The criterion for the investment decision is Hicks's new *index of improvement in efficiency* $I(r)$.

Denoting the coefficients of the old production process and the corresponding prices by an asterisk and assuming the gross rate of profits $r_n = r_n{}^*$ as exogenously given, the new production process is more profitable than the old one if it is possible to pay a higher wage, i.e. if

$$I(r) = \frac{w}{w^*} = \frac{a_1^* + a_0^* r_n}{a_1 + a_0 r_n} > 1. \tag{13.6}$$

$I(r)$ must always lie between the two cost ratios $h = a_0^*/a_0$ and $H = a_1^*/a_1$.

$H > 1$ indicates a saving in utilizational or running costs, whereas $h > 1$ indicates a saving in constructional costs. In contrast to these two indices h and H, which are determined by technical coefficients alone, the index of improvement in efficiency in general depends also on distributional parameters, i.e. the price system.

The change in the time pattern of labour inputs plays the crucial role in the new classification of technological change developed by Hicks, who distinguishes three kinds of innovation:

1 a neutral or unbiased innovation with $h = H = I(r)$;
2 a forward-biased innovation with $H > h$; and
3 a backward-biased innovation with $h > H$.

In general it holds that in cases of a non-neutral or biased innovation, $I(r)$ depends on income distribution. But this does not lead to complications for weakly biased innovations. With both cost indices h and H and therefore also $I(r)$ greater than unity a weakly biased innovation will always be chosen. Things are more complicated in cases of strongly biased innovations when the introduction of the new production process depends on the rate of profits.[16]

The distinction between a weakly and a strongly forward-biased innovation is of particular importance. It is the latter which gives rise to the Ricardo machinery effect. If $H > 1 > h$, then the construction costs of the new technique are higher before a saving in labour inputs can be obtained during the utilization phase of the machine. In the range of low rates of profits the strongly forward-biased innovation has the lower costs of production. With a higher rate of profits the higher construction costs of the new technique get a higher weight and start to dominate the lower running costs from the switchpoint rate of profits onwards, i.e. the old process is more profitable than the new one.

Hicks investigated two different types of traverse: the *fixwage path* along which employment is variable and the *full employment path* along which the wage rate is variable. In the former case the price system of the economy is closed by an exogenously given real wage and the development of the quantity variables depends on the savings function which serves as the link between the price and the quantity system. In the latter, flexprice, case the system is closed on the quantity side by the exogenously given rate of growth of labour supply. Again, the savings function plays a crucial role since, via savings behaviour and the growth–profit relationship resulting from it, the rate of profits and thereby all other price variables are determined. The wage rate now is a variable which complicates the adjustment problem since, contrary to the fixwage traverse, additional secondary changes of technique *within* the new technology arise as a consequence of changes in distribution during the traverse.

IV   THE FIXWAGE PATH

With an exogenously given real wage the optimal technique remains the same unless there is a change in technology, by which new processes become available that were not available before. Since the wage is fixed, the new optimal technique will continue to be dominant throughout the traverse. Thus there is no more than a single switch from the old technique which was chosen on the original steady-state path to the new technique, the consequence of Hicks's assumption that there is only a *single* change in technology. By assumption labour supply is completely elastic at the given real wage, a situation which is empirically significant in the early phase of a country's industrialization process when the agricultural sector (and a rapidly increasing population) serves as a supplier of labour and as an employment buffer for the industrial sector. The real wage rate is determined by labour productivity in the agricultural sector, as in Lewis-type models. The presence of this subsistence sector impedes the increase of the wage rate for industrial workers. As long as there is an unlimited supply of labour from the agricultural sector an increase of labour productivity in this sector is the precondition for an increase of wages for industrial workers. In such an economy the question of full employment is not raised, but the question of the determination of the employment volume is. However, there is an analogous concept which Hicks calls *full performance*, an assumption which is equivalent to full capacity utilization of the capital stock which, as we know, is not explicitly dealt with in the neo-Austrian model. At full performance, which describes also an equilibrium between I and S, activity is limited by saving. The assumption about saving is crucial, therefore, for the determination of output and employment on the adjustment path.

Hicks distinguished three phases of the traverse which is started by a process innovation.

1 The first phase is the *preparatory phase*, consisting of period 1 in the standard case, during which employment is unchanged, but new machines are constructed, though still not producing any consumption goods.

2 Then the *early phase* occurs, during which both old and new machines produce final output. During this early phase, which lasts from periods 2 to $n + 1$ and which is in the very centre of Hicks's traverse analysis, the share of consumption goods produced by machines of the old type is decreasing more and more. With the beginning of the early phase the growth path of the economy changes. The time paths of employment and output heavily depend on the parameter h, i.e. the relation of constructional labour between the old and the new technique. With $h \geq 1$, employment and consumption output grow faster than on the reference path, i.e. the old steady-state path on which the economy would have remained without the change in technology. If, however, the innovation is strongly forward biased, i.e. $h < 1$, output and employment first fall compared with the reference path,[17] and it may take several periods before they recover to and rise above the reference level.

3 In the *late phase*, starting with period $n + 2$, all consumption goods are produced by new machines. Nevertheless, the adjustment process has not come to an end with the scrapping of the last old machines. However, Hicks was not very much interested in the late phase when the question of *convergence* of the traverse to a new equilibrium path comes up. He considered the convergence problem to be of minor importance only, as convergence would take a long time during which various kinds of new phenomena could occur (a second innovation for example). In the same line is the rationale given by Zamagni for 'the substantial irrelevance of the problem of convergence as such':

> Indeed, the rate at which technologies, endowments, and institutional constraints change is so rapid in modern times, relative to the rate at which an economy adjusts to any set of underlying institutional and structural factors, that any inherent convergence tendencies are of very secondary importance and interest.

> (1984: 148)

While this argument is plausible with regard to 'real' growth processes, as is Zamagni's emphasis on the advantage of traverse analysis to inform us about the short-run and medium-run effects of technological change compared with stability analysis, it is problematical from a methodological point of view. In his investigation of traverse processes Hicks used a steady-state growth path as a starting point and as a reference path. This, however, logically requires that convergence of traverse paths to a new equilibrium path can be assured.[18]

For the development of the output and employment volume during the early phase of the traverse, Hicks's core phase, the assumption about savings behaviour, especially savings out of profits, is most important. While he assumed a classical saving function with $0 = s_w < s_r < 1$ for the steady state – which on the basis of the savings-equals-investment postulate leads to $g = s_r r$ as the link between the quantity and the price system of the economy – Hicks made the *Q-assumption* for the study of the traverse, i.e. he assumes that consumption out of profits (the 'take-out' Q_T) is unaffected by the change in technology.[19] This has an important consequence. The assumption that all additional profits resulting from the change to the new, more efficient production process are saved and invested (whereby gross investment is increased during the whole early phase compared with the reference path), is most favourable for a successful compensation process. The greater the part of the additional profits consumed and the earlier this happens, the more the increase in employment and output weakens.

With the 'classical' or Ricardian assumption of an exogenously given wage rate,[20] employment varies positively with saving. Hicks's fixwage traverse is a kind of wage fund theory of employment. Given that a number of processes are already operating using up the wage fund determines the number of starts of new processes. The introduction of a strongly forward-biased innovation is the most complex and interesting case. It is profitable when the savings in running costs dominate, but during the constructional period of the new machines at first a higher input of labour is required. This implies that in the second year of the traverse a smaller number of (new) machines is available for the production of consumption goods compared with the same period on the reference path. The number of workers who are producing consumption goods with the machines of the new technique decreases even more because of the saving in utilizational labour. Although this saving in running costs implies an increase in profits which supposedly are completely invested in the constructional department of the economy, the *existence of temporary technological unemployment* is inevitable.

Hicks's fixwage model provides almost an exact replica of Ricardo's assumptions and shows that the introduction of machinery has an adverse effect on employment in the short run only in the case of 'strongly forward-biased' innovations, a case which is similar to the one discussed by Ricardo, namely an increase in mechanization, i.e. the use of more fixed capital in order

210

to economize on circulating capital. However, Violi (1984a, b) has shown that all types of innovations can lead to temporary unemployment when neo-Austrian production processes with more general profiles are considered (although the case of a strong forward bias combined with a lengthened construction period is the one that leads to it with highest probability) and that the crucial condition for technological unemployment to occur is not the specific form of the innovation but the effect on the development of the 'gross produce', a point that was already grasped by Ricardo.

V THE FULL EMPLOYMENT PATH

While employment is a variable in the fixwage model, in the flexprice model the level of employment on the adjustment path is bound to move as it would have done in the old steady state, i.e. on the reference path. But the real wage now is a variable, with the consequence that wage changes can alter the most profitable technique along the traverse. This complicates the analysis of the dynamic behaviour of an economy during the adjustment path considerably, for, even with only one innovational shock to occur, one can no longer confine oneself to the analysis of the effect of a single technical change. In general we have to distinguish between changes in technique as the consequence of innovations, i.e. additional pages in the 'book of blueprints' ('*autonomous*' technical changes in the language of Hicks), and changes in technique (or better the choice of another technique) within a given or constant technology because of changes in income distribution ('*induced*' technical changes). Accordingly, Hicks divided his analysis of the full employment traverse into two parts.

At first he abstracted from the complications of induced innovations and concentrated on the effects of the first autonomous change in technique because of the process innovation. Since a change in technique incorporates a change in labour input coefficients, it implies in general the necessity of a *sectoral reallocation of labour*, i.e. a change in the percentage of total employment between the constructional and utilizational department of the economy. The only exception constitutes the case of a neutral innovation $h = H > 1$ where saving in utilizational labour is proportional to saving in constructional labour. The new machines produced by the constructional workers in the first year of the traverse have a greater output capacity so that in the second year the output of consumer goods increases proportional to the increase in the number of new machines. The increase in final output continues up to the end of the early phase, i.e. with the end of the lifetime of the last old machines, when the new equilibrium growth path is reached because of a balanced age structure of the capital stock.

This is not the case either with a backward-biased or with a forward-biased innovation. Since employment in the constructional department plays a key

211

role for the full employment traverse, a short look at the watershed case of a forward-biased innovation with $h = 1$ might be useful. In the first year of the traverse there is no change except the fact that constructional workers now produce the same number of new machines as they had produced of the old type before. As a consequence, in the second period consumption output remains constant (contrary to the case of a neutral innovation) but a shift of workers into the constructional department has to take place because the new machines require less utilizational labour. 'Technological unemployment' occurring in the machine-using industry is matched by an equal and opposite change in the demand for labour in the machine-making industry, i.e. by a transfer of displaced workers. The effect is that from the third period onwards, more new machines exist which have to be manned to produce consumer goods. Therefore there is an increase in labour demand in the machine-using industry which dampens the original displacement effect but cannot dominate it as long as the condition $a_0 > a_1$ is fulfilled.[21]

The problems involved are even more complicated in the case of a strongly forward-biased innovation $H > 1 > h$, in which an influx of workers into the constructional department is necessary already in the first period to maintain output capacity. With the existing constraint on the labour supply side, this could only be managed by a withdrawal of workers from the utilizational department, where they are yet still needed to produce consumption goods with the old machines. In other words, under the assumption that capacities are fully utilized in the initial situation, the introduction of a strongly forward-biased innovation at the beginning is inevitably connected with an *absolute reduction in the production of consumption goods*. This could have implied negative effects on employment if the wage rate has not been temporarily reduced. Or, as Hicks put it, '[I]f final output (consumption output) is reduced, someone must economize' (1977a: 189).[22] This sag in wages, when current output is the only source from which wages are paid, corresponds to the temporary loss of employment on the fixwage traverse in the Ricardo machinery case.

Due to the uneven age structure of the real capital stock existing at the beginning of the late phase, the economy has not yet fully adjusted to a new steady-state path. The same holds for backward-biased innovations which supply the mirror picture to forward ones with regard to the reallocation of workers between the two departments of the economy necessary for the maintenance of full employment. Again, a secondary effect exists which opposes the primary one. Because of the withdrawal of workers from construction during the early phase of the traverse, the number of new machines decreases relatively, with the consequence of an inevitable decline in the production of consumption goods. This becomes the more possible the stronger the innovation is backward biased. On balance, during the early periods of the traverse dissaving dominates whereas later on the opposite movement of a saving and investment process is required. Hicks therefore came to the result that 'the forward bias does better in the long run than in the short; while the backward bias does better in the short run than in the long' (1973d: 108).

In the case of the full employment traverse all quantity variables are determined by the exogenously given rate of growth of labour supply and the technical conditions of production. With the employment of labour and the technique given, *production* and *distribution* are entirely separated, i.e. the distribution of income does not influence the amount of final consumption goods. But an assumption about saving behaviour is necessary to determine the development of the rate of profits and the real wage in time, and thus also the distribution of the final product. The situation becomes much more complicated when secondary changes of technique as a consequence of changes in distribution are taking place during the adjustment process. Both production and distribution are now related to the saving propensities which influence the choice of the optimal technique. If the new technology consists not only of one technique but of a whole spectrum of non-inferior techniques with intersecting wage–profit curves, changes in the distribution parameters during the adjustment process can lead to secondary (induced) changes of technique within a given technology along the full employment path. Hicks dealt with these additional changes of the dominant technique during the course of the traverse in his chapter on 'Substitution' – 'the principal impulse chapter' (Hicks 1977a: 195).

Since the take-up of a new technology is a time-intensive process, the choice of technique out of long-run equilibrium depends not only on the current real wage (and the current rate of profits) but also on entrepreneurial expectations about the future development of the real wage. Thus the problem of expectations becomes of crucial importance for the flexprice model, because it is the expected values of the real wage and the rate of profits which determine the (expected) present value of a production process, i.e. the choice of technique and, with more complex efficiency profiles than in Hicks's 'standard case', also the optimal truncation period. In general, the choice of cost-minimizing or profit-maximizing technique involves the choice of the economic lifetime of a fixed capital good as well as the 'planned' degree of capital utilization. Hicks made the assumption of *static expectations*, 'that, when the decision to adopt a particular technique for *new* processes is taken, the current wage is expected to remain unchanged' (1973d: 56). Since these expectations are wrong, the adjustment path being chosen is not an optimum path. Hicks saw the unrealistic nature of his assumption but 'nevertheless ma[d]e use of the "static expectations" assumption, since it probably throws as much light on actual processes of development as we can expect to get from our general approach' (1973d: 56).

The primary effect of an innovation is to raise the rate of profits. Via increased savings and investment there is a tendency to raise the demand for constructional labour. With total employment being limited by the growth of

213

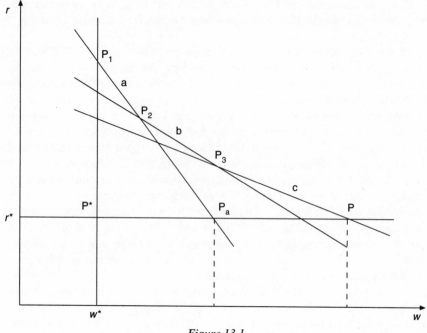

Figure 13.1

the labour force, i.e. with labour being the 'scarce' factor, sooner or later the wage rate rises. Hicks pointed to

> a sequence ... which depends on three effects. The first runs from wages to choice of technique; the second from choice of technique to productivity (B/A); the third from productivity to wages. The first and second depend on the techniques (the parameters of the techniques); but the third is quite different, for it depends on saving. With any reasonable assumption about saving, a rise in productivity will lead to a rise in wages.
>
> (1973d: 111)

Given a spectrum of techniques within the new technology, the rise in wages results in switches to techniques which are more profitable at higher wage rates. These induced changes in techniques can best be shown diagrammatically.[23]

In Figure 13.1 wage–profit curves of three non-inferior techniques within the new technology are shown which follow from equation (13.3) or (13.4) and transform into straight lines in the case of a 'simple profile'. Point P* (w^*, r^*) denotes the distribution constellation in the initial equilibrium in which the old technique is used. After the innovation at first there is the autonomous change to technique a, because technique a makes possible the highest rate of profits at the ruling wage rate $w*$. Despite the first periods in the case of a strongly forward-biased innovation, this change will lead to an increase in labour productivity and thus to an increase in the real wage. This implies a movement along the efficiency curve of technique a up to the point P_2 in which an induced change to technique b becomes profitable for the investing entrepreneur.

The induced change comes in as an attempt to arrest the fall in the rate of profits. The further movements follow the efficiency frontier of the new technology until the new equilibrium is reached at P. If there had been no substitution, i.e. technique a had been maintained throughout, the final equilibrium would have been at P_a, instead of P. So the effect of substitution is that it slows the rise in real wages that accompany technical improvements but stretches the rise over time so that a larger rise is ultimately achieved. The factor (labour) against which substitution takes place becomes the ultimate beneficiary of an improvement of technology. Hicks regarded this result as 'an important proposition, perhaps the most important in all this book' (1973d: 115).

But there remain two problems. The first is a methodological one which depends on the fact that there is a missing co-ordinate in the diagram: *time*. The figure is no more than a piece of steady-state analysis and for the study of the traverse that is not good enough. Nothing is said on when the final equilibrium position (or all the other positions on the way) will be reached. So it is possible that the wage on the efficiency curve b is lower at a particular point in time after the switch than it would have been on curve a, when the movement along the new efficiency curve is slower.

Second, Hicks's key assumption of static expectations, while acceptable for the fixwage model where price expectations are fulfilled, is unconvincing for the flexprice model. To assume that while substitution is going on through time and the rate of profits is falling (the wage rate is rising) expectations are always that the current profit rate will be maintained, is a very fragile assumption to make. No wonder that this 'pretty poor piece of ad hockery'[24] came under severe attack. The assumption of static expectations reveals the static character of parts of Hicks's traverse analysis along the neo-Austrian lines. This assumption certainly has to be substituted by more realistic assumptions concerning the formation of expectations on the side of investors which would make traverse problems far more complicated and would throw us back into all the perplexities of the determination of capital accumulation and technical change in the short period when the expected values of future net receipts in an uncertain world play a crucial role. Hicks saw this but did not feel himself able to work it out. However, his traverse analysis is not obsolete but in need of and capable of improvement. But one should not forget that '[i]n summary, the incidence of an invention cannot be easily determined without restrictive assumptions' (Burmeister 1974: 437).

VI WAYS AHEAD

Hicks was not ashamed of making simplifying assumptions like the 'simple profile', the fixwage hypothesis and static expectations, and ended his analysis of the traverse within the neo-Austrian framework with a chapter called 'Ways ahead' which 'was meant as a signal that I was sure I had not finished the job' (1982a: 294). However, most of his Anglo-Saxon fellow economists who found the writings of the young Hicks brilliant and innovative, appreciating his *Value and Capital* as his 'masterpiece', regarded his traverse analysis as troubling and unconvincing and therefore did not follow the path which was trodden by Hicks. While it must be conceded that the work which Hicks produced in his last two decades is more difficult to evaluate because it was not welded into a coherent and technically advanced theory, it cannot be denied that his attempts to cope with the working out of processes over historical time were creative and most fruitful. But the seeds of his later concerns germinated more in France and especially in Italy, his favourite country, where *Capital and Time* was far less coolly received. On the contrary, the Hicksian traverse analysis based on a neo-Austrian, vertically integrated representation of the productive system has stimulated many subsequent writings, a field which is still very flourishing today.[25]

A great deal of work consisted in working out the consequences of a lowering of the strict assumptions of the 'standard case', like the 'simple profile', the same length of the construction and utilization period of all techniques and so on. When the possibility of shortening and lengthening the construction period is taken into account, some interesting business cycle phenomena arise. Hicks himself started with some considerations, coming to results that the lengthening of the construction period has similar effects as the strongly forward-biased innovation in the standard case and that, in general, '[i]t is bound to be impossible, in the face of considerable changes in the construction period of fixed capital, continuously to maintain Full Employment' (1973d: 130). On the full employment traverse lengthening (shortening) leads to great downward (upward) jumps in the rate of starts of new processes in the early phase because the new processes contribute later (earlier) to the final products. These 'jumps' or 'jerks' invoke echo effects later on when the new processes reach the utilization phase and when they are terminated.[26]

Most interestingly, in the case of the fixwage traverse the full performance hypothesis can give rise to negative solutions for the rate of starts during the early phase of the traverse, signalling the incompatibility between the supply with output goods and the input requirements of the processes that have been started earlier and are still operative. This implies also that some of these old processes must be stopped. It cannot be denied that such phenomena of underutilization of the productive capacity that has been built up – which are not the consequence of a lack of effective demand but of certain complementarities of the capital structure, and therefore have properly been termed '*Hayek effects*' (see Zamagni 1984: 143) – can actually occur.

After a structural change a new equilibrium growth path can only be achieved, if ever, when the conversion of the capital stock to the proportions required by the new steady state has been completed. A critical evaluation of the analysis of traverse processes in models with a horizontal representation of productive activities[27] shows that a sectorally disaggregated approach of the Leontief–Sraffa type (of which the three-sectoral Lowe model and the two-sectoral model used by the Hicks of the 1965 vintage are simplified versions) encounters some difficulties when the effects of innovations are to be studied which involve the introduction of *new* capital goods. In models with a horizontal sectoral structure, technological change is not treated as a phenomenon involving changes in the qualitative characteristics of goods and labour but takes the form of a pure reduction of technical coefficients. Thus it is abstracted from the appearance of new, different capital goods. Only innovations which have a quantitative effect are considered. The transmutation of the capital stock is reduced to the achievement of the new physical proportions of the same capital goods which are required by the new steady-state equilibrium after an innovational shock has taken place. This implies that the adjustment of the economy to a new technique is mainly carried out by a reallocation of resources between the different sectors and/or a process of real capital formation.

This kind of traverse analysis in which emphasis is on horizontal transfers between sectors has been heavily criticized by some authors, because the time taken to make the machine is liable to be forgotten and a reshaping of the capital stock in which old machines are scrapped and new and different types of machines have to be produced is neglected.[28]

It is precisely the focus on the adjustment problems caused by the impact of technical innovations that led Hicks to turn away from the two-sectoral model in *Capital and Growth* to a vertical representation of the productive structure in *Capital and Time*. Hicks saw the decisive advantage of the Austrian method in its ability to cope with the important fact that process innovations nearly always involve the introduction of *new* capital goods.

It is here undesirable that these goods should be physically specified, since there is no way of establishing a physical relation between the capital goods that are required in the one technique and those that are required in the other. The only relation that can be established runs in terms of costs, and of capacity to produce final output; and this is precisely what is preserved in an Austrian theory.

(Hicks 1977a: 193)

A similar explanation is given by Pasinetti (1981), who develops his theory of structural change in terms of vertically integrated sectors. While conceding that the input–output model gives more information on the structure of an economy *at any point in time*, Pasinetti points out that, because of the change of input–output coefficients and the 'breaking down' of the interindustry system *over time*, the vertically integrated model is superior for dynamic analysis (see Pasinetti 1981: 109–17). Measuring capital goods in *units of vertically integrated productive capacity* of the final commodity 'has an unambiguous meaning through time, no matter which type of technical change, and how much of it, may occur' (1981: 178).

But there remains a problem. By treating fixed capital as if it were working capital Hicks did not recognize the need for a special machine-tools sector. An important consequence of this proceeding is that in the neo-Austrian model, in contrast to models with a horizontal sectoral structure, the effects of innovation upon industrial structure are not shown. Hicks (1977a: 193) openly admitted this deficiency.

The unsatisfactory treatment of fixed capital goods in the Austrian representation of the production process had already been the main point of critique when Burchardt (1931–2) set out to compare, contrast and combine the two most important alternative ways of conceiving the production process: the schemes of the stationary circular flow in Böhm-Bawerk and Marx. He emphasized that the Austrian way of tracing back the production process to some original factor(s) leaves unexplained the reproduction and expansion requirements of the stock of fixed capital goods. Burchardt recognized that it is a characteristic feature of any modern industrial system that there exists a particular group of fixed capital goods[29] which can be maintained and increased only with the help of a circular process in which these machine tools also act as inputs. The role of these capital goods in industrial production is thus analogous to the role of seed-corn in agricultural production. It is therefore not possible to trace all finished goods technically back to nothing but labour (and land) and to treat fixed capital goods as the output of some intermediate stages of production in the vertical model.

For an elementary (neo-)Austrian process to have a finite duration, not only must there be no basic commodities in the sense of Sraffa, but also there should not exist the slightest degree of circularity in the production process which instead must be organized in a completely hierarchical way. The input matrix A of working capital must be a kind of triangular matrix which is semi-positive under the principal diagonal, where a_{ij} represents the amount of the ith intermediate product needed in the production of one unit of the jth intermediate product.

$$A = \begin{bmatrix} 0 & 0 & 0 & \cdots & 0 & 0 \\ a_{12} & 0 & 0 & \cdots & 0 & 0 \\ a_{13} & a_{23} & 0 & \cdots & 0 & 0 \\ \vdots & \vdots & \vdots & & \vdots & \vdots \\ a_{1n} & a_{2n} & a_{3n} & \cdots & a_{(n-1)n} & 0 \end{bmatrix}$$

The input structure is more general than in system (13.1) because at each stage of production in the construction period not only the intermediate product of the immediately preceding stage but also some or all of the intermediate products of all the previous stages of production can be included, but still A has to be specific of the lower triangular kind. Baldone (1984) has shown conclusively that the absence of this necessary and sufficient condition leads to an indeterminateness of the traverse paths in the vertically integrated neo-Austrian model.

An evaluation of the particular contribution that the horizontal and the vertical approaches have provided to the analysis of the employment consequences of new technologies shows that in many respects the two models are different ways of saying the same thing. Since both approaches enjoy comparative advantages in the analysis of traverses, a complementary (or synthetic) perspective should be encouraged.[30] This complementary perspective was also shared by Hicks who felt that 'it was unwise to commit ourselves, finally, to the one route or to the other' (1973d: 11–12). Consequently, he contributed to the development of both approaches. After giving priority to the Austrian model in the 1970s, in *Methods of Dynamic Economics* Hicks (1985a) again explored both routes in which a productive system can adjust itself when 'horizontal' rigidities (Chapter 13) or 'vertical' rigidities (Chapter 14) are present.

The particular contribution of traverse analysis is its focus on explicitly representing structural rigidities and in the investigation of how such rigidities interact with forces of change to determine the (stage or phase) pattern of structural transformation of an economic system. Lowe's and Hicks's emphasis was on the rigidities which existing capital structures and work in process flows impose on the dynamics of transformation. A similarly important theme is the explicit specification of the rigidities and potentialities of a given stock of human capabilities; skill structures and the resource- and time-consuming process of transforming existing and evolving new skills impose a similar rigidity constraint on the transformation of a productive system as a given stock of capital goods; the difference, however, is the inherent ability of the same human producer to acquire new skills and thus advance the productive potential of the productive system. Capital goods, on the other hand, have to be exchanged with new capital goods or at least combined with new complementary production elements to achieve a similar result.

Finally, two other important directions for future research should be mentioned. Full employment can only be maintained if the economy is able to implement a continuous process of structural reallocation of labour between the different departments, in accordance with the twofold effect of technical progress on labour productivity and the evolution of demand. The integration of the demand aspect of technological change into the theoretical framework is one of the advantages of Pasinetti's (1981) analysis of structural change. The factor ultimately responsible for structural change is technical progress as a result of learning. Increases in productivity lead to increases in per capita income. With increases in real income consumers do not expand their demand for each existing commodity proportionally. When in some sectors the introduction of new technologies causes high rates of growth of productivity which cannot be matched by an adequate increase of demand because some saturation is reached, then a fall of employment in these sectors cannot be avoided. With a growing population, the economy must also enlarge its overall productive capacity continuously. Moreover, with technical progress new products come up. It certainly is one of Pasinetti's most innovative achievements to have shown so clearly the two facets of technological change on the supply side *and* on the demand side and the interaction between the two.

But so far this demand aspect of technological change has not been integrated into traverse analysis. Furthermore, the traverse analysis which had been developed by Hicks with reference to a barter economy, where the current output obtained with the existing productive capacity is always fully matched by final demand at the end of the period, certainly has to be extended to a monetary economy[31] where additional complications, like effective demand failures and Keynesian unemployment, may arise.

NOTES

1 See Hicks (1969a: 148–54, 164–5, 168–71; 1971b; 1973d: chs V, VII–X; and 1977a: 184–90).

2 For the history of the debate see Gourvitch (1940), Lowe (1955) and Kähler's important study (1933) of the displacement of workers by machinery. Kähler's pioneering multi-sectoral analysis of displacement and reabsorption effects which is based on a very advanced embryo of input–output analysis, even today can be regarded as a significant contribution to our understanding of the employment consequences of new technologies. Unfortunately, Kähler's highly original work even in Germany had almost fallen into oblivion for half a century, partly because of its high complexity and its cumbersome arithmetical examples, but also because the political events in Germany in the year 1933, which forced the author to emigrate in the year of publication, marked a deep turning point for the economics profession as well.

3 The role and importance of economic history for Hicks's theoretical analysis is focused upon by Baumol (1990), Scazzieri in his contribution to this volume and Hamouda (1993; ch. 10) who informs us that history had already been Hicks's favourite subject at school and had continued to be his preferred library reading ever since.

4 Hicks's contribution 'Some questions of time in economics' (1976f) to the Festschrift in honour of Georgescu-Roegen is perhaps the best account of why Hicks became increasingly dissatisfied with the axiomatic approach to the pure theory of efficient allocation and the temporal general equilibrium method of *Value and Capital*, as well as the semi-stationary, almost timeless character of the steady-state growth models of *Capital and Growth* as he continued to think about how to deal with essentially dynamic problems.

5   Kennedy's critique (1968) that the earlier analysis did not pay adequate respect to the sequence in time and that Hicks's growth equilibrium method implied that the capital goods produced during a period are themselves used in the production of the output of the period was instrumental for Hicks's switch to a model with a totally different representation of production structure.

6   From his many articles on capital theory his contribution to the Corfu Conference (1960c) and his reflection on ancient and modern capital controversies (1974a) stand up.

7   For a more detailed explanation of the concept of the *impulse*, which is implicit in *A Theory of Economic History* and in *Capital and Time*, see Hicks's Nobel Memorial Lecture 'The mainspring of economic growth' (1973b) and his essay on 'Industrialism' (1977a: ch. II).

8   Faber therefore came to the critical conclusion that 'Hicks has emptied the Austrian theory of capital of its content' (1975: 594).

9   See, for example, Hicks (1967).

10 Hicks's analysis in *Capital and Time* thus is consistent with his earlier theory of the trade cycle where he had already emphasized 'the real (non-monetary) character of the cyclical process' (1950a: 136).

11 It should be noticed that Ricardo, when he approved of Say's law of markets, made reference exclusively to the employment of capital, not to the employment of labour (1951: 290, 296). The machinery chapter is the most telling evidence that Ricardo did not associate Say's law with full employment. Ricardo's version of Say's law differed fundamentally from Keynes's version and the typical neo-classical idea that the validity of Say's law must imply the full employment of labour.

12 It should be emphasised that Hicks (1985b, 1990a) dissociated himself from the neo-Ricardian theory as it had been founded by Sraffa. Although he was 'not wholly out of sympathy' with Sraffa's approach, Hicks saw at least two main differences between Ricardo and Sraffa: Ricardo's model is essentially dynamic whereas Sraffa's is not, industries in Ricardo are fully integrated whereas production in Sraffa is fully interlinked.

13 'The intermediate goods are *spurlos versenkt* inside the process' (Solow 1974: 189).

14 For the interpretation of Hicks's neo-Austrian model as a special case of the von Neumann–Sraffa model see Burmeister (1974), Hagemann and Kurz (1976), Schefold (1980) and Morishima's contribution to this volume.

15 For greater details see Hagemann and Kurz (1976).

16 For a graphical representation of the choice-of-technique problem in cases of strongly biased innovations see Hicks (1973d: 87) and Faber (1979: 172–3).

17 Contrary to Hicks's exposition (1973d: 91–5), consumption output and employment may decrease further, beyond the first period of the early phase, before thereafter they rise steadily and more rapidly than on the reference path.

18 See Gozzi and Zamagni (1982), Violi (1984b) and Malinvaud (1986) for the fact that convergence of the traverse path to a new steady-state path compatible with the new technique can be assured only under very special conditions.

19 The fact that Hicks made two different savings assumptions, a 'classical' one for the steady state and a 'superclassical' or 'golden age' one for the traverse, is backed by Burmeister who emphasizes that 'The assumption that saving is a constant proportion of profit income ... is a dangerous assumption to make about an economy out of steady-state equilibrium with changing prices. For ... it has been proved that the dynamic behaviour of an economy with many capital goods is significantly altered provided not all capital gains are saved' (1974: 429).

20 This also means that the rate of profits and, with $g = s_r r$, the growth rate must be higher in the new equilibrium than on the reference path.
21 Without this necessary as well as sufficient condition for full employment during the traverse being fulfilled, an oscillation of the transfer of workers between the two departments would become necessary from period to period. This shows that full employment would be by no means easy to achieve.

The condition $a_0 > a_1$ is similar to the 'Uzawa condition' known from two-sectoral neo-classical growth models. For a detailed discussion of the stability problems in the full employment model see Hicks (1973d: 103–4, 189–90), Burmeister (1974: 437–9), Magnan de Bornier (1980: 51–2) and van Schaik (1976: 294–7).
22 There is a parallel sag in wages in the cases of a traverse to a higher rate of growth of labour supply and a labour-displacing innovation analysed by Lowe (1976), who shows that, in order ultimately to increase the growth rate of consumption output, at first a temporary fall in this growth rate is necessary. Forced or involuntary savings place at disposal the additional means required for accumulation in the early phase of the adjustment process.

The problem has some similarity with the notion that investment priority for the capital-goods sector is a pre-condition for attaining a higher growth rate formalized by Fel'dman during the Soviet industrialization debate in the late 1920s.
23 See Hicks (1973d: 112; 1985a: 155).
24 See Section II of Hahn's contribution to this volume.
25 See, for example, Amendola and Gaffard (1988), Baldone (1984), Baranzini and Scazzieri (1990), Belloc (1980), Gozzi and Zamagni (1982), Magnan de Bornier (1980, 1990), Nardini (1990, 1993), Violi (1984a, b) and Zamagni (1984), which is by no means an exhaustive list.
26 Nardini (1990) has shown that these reinvestment cycles can also occur on a fixwage traverse in a slightly modified Hicksian model.
27 See Lowe (1976) and the discussion in Hagemann (1990, 1992) and Gehrke and Hagemann (1995) for greater details.
28 See, for example, Amendola and Gaffard (1988: ch. 2).
29 Lowe later called these capital goods 'machine tools'.
30 See also Zamagni (1984: 136–7). This complementary perspective is partly realized in the model of Lowe (1976) where all three sectors are divided into four stages representing the successive maturing of natural resources into finished goods. For a closer inspection of Lowe's synthesis of Austrian sequentiality and classical circularity see Gehrke and Hagemann (1995).
31 See Amendola and Gaffard (1988) for a first attempt in that direction.

BIBLIOGRAPHY

Amendola, M. and Gaffard, J.-L. (1988) *The Innovative Choice. An Economic Analysis of the Dynamics of Technology*, Oxford: Basil Blackwell.
Baldone, S. (1984) 'Integrazione Verticale, Struttura Temporale dei Processi Produttivi e Transizione fra le Tecniche', *Economia Politica* 1: 79–105. English translation, 'Vertical integration, the temporal structure of production processes and transition between techniques', in M. Landesmann and R. Scazzieri (eds) (1995) *Dynamics in Production Systems*, Cambridge: Cambridge University Press.
Baranzini, M. and Scazzieri, R. (eds) (1990) *The Economic Theory of Structure and*

Change, Cambridge: Cambridge University Press.

Baumol, W. J. (1990) 'Sir John versus the Hicksians, or theorist malgré lui?' *Journal of Economic Literature* 28: 1708–15.

Beach, E. F. (1971) 'Hicks on Ricardo on machinery', *Economic Journal* 81: 916–22.

Belloc, B. (1980) *Croissance Economique et Adaptation du Capital Productif*, Paris: Economica.

Böhm-Bawerk, E. von (1921) *Positive Theorie des Kapitales* (Kapital und Kapitalzins, 2. Abt.), Jena: Fischer, (1st edn, Innsbruck: Wagner, 1899). Translated as *Capital and Interest*, vols 2 and 3, South Holland, IL: Libertarian Press.

Burchardt, F. A. (1931–2) 'Die Schemata des stationären Kreislaufs bei Böhm-Bawerk und Marx', *Weltwirtschaftliches Archiv* 34: 525–64; 35: 116–76.

Burmeister, E. (1974) 'Synthesizing the Neo-Austrian and alternative approaches to capital theory: a survey', *Journal of Economic Literature* 12: 413–56.

Faber, M. (1975) 'Mehrergiebigkeit und Hicks' neuer Begriff des technischen Wandels', *Kyklos* 28: 574–96. English translation as ch. 9 in M. Faber (1979) *Introduction to Modern Austrian Capital Theory*, Berlin-Heidelberg: Springer.

—————— (1979) *Introduction to Modern Austrian Capital Theory*, Berlin-Heidelberg: Springer.

Gehrke, C. and Hagemann, H. (1995) 'Efficient traverses and bottlenecks: a structural approach', in M. Landesmann and R. Scazzieri (eds) *Dynamics in Production Systems*, Cambridge: Cambridge University Press.

Gourvitch, A. (1940) *Survey of Economic Theory on Technological Change and Employment*, Philadelphia; reprint, New York: Augustus M. Kelley, 1966.

Gozzi, G. and Zamagni, S. (1982) 'Crescita non uniforme e struttura produttiva: un modello di traversa a salario fisso', *Giornale degli Economisti e Annali di Economia* 41: 305–45.

Hagemann, H. (1990) 'The structural theory of economic growth', in M. Baranzini and R. Scazzieri (eds) *The Economic Theory of Structure and Change*, Cambridge: Cambridge University Press, pp. 144–71.

—————— (1992) 'Traverse analysis in a post-classical model', in J. Halevi, D. Laibman and E. J. Nell (eds) *Beyond the Steady State. A Revival of Growth Theory*, London: Macmillan, pp. 235–63.

Hagemann, H. and Kurz, H. D. (1976) 'The return of the same truncation period and reswitching of techniques in neo-Austrian and more general models', *Kyklos* 29: 678–708.

Hamouda, O. F. (1993) *John R. Hicks. The Economist's Economist*, Oxford: Blackwell.

Kähler, A. (1933) *Die Theorie der Arbeiterfreisetzung durch die Maschine*, Greifswald: Julius Abel.

Kennedy, C. (1968) 'Time, interest and the production function', in J. N. Wolfe (ed.) *Value, Capital and Growth. Papers in Honour of Sir John Hicks*, Edinburgh: Edinburgh University Press, pp. 275–90.

Kurz, H. D. (1984) 'Ricardo and Lowe on machinery', *Eastern Economic Journal* 10: 211–29.

Lowe, A. (1955) 'Technological unemployment reexamined', in G. Eisermann (ed.) *Wirtschaft und Kultursystem – Festschrift für Alexander Rüstow*, Stuttgart and Zürich: Eugen Rentsch Verlag, pp. 229–54.

Lowe, A. (1976) *The Path of Economic Growth*, Cambridge: Cambridge University Press.

Magnan de Bornier, J. (1980) *Capital et Déséquilibre de la Croissance*, Paris: Economica.

—————— (1990) 'Vertical integration, growth and sequential change', in M. Baranzini and R. Scazzieri (eds) *The Economic Theory of Structure and Change*, Cambridge: Cambridge University Press, pp. 122–43.

Malinvaud, E. (1986) 'Reflecting on the theory of capital and growth', *Oxford Economic Papers* 38: 367–85.

Meacci, F. (1985) 'Ricardo's chapter on machinery and the theory of capital', in G. A. Caravale (ed.) *The Legacy of Ricardo*, Oxford: Basil Blackwell, pp. 285–302.

Morishima, M. (1989) *Ricardo's Economics. A General Equilibrium Theory of Distribution and Growth*, Cambridge: Cambridge University Press.

Nardini, F. (1990) 'Cycle-trend dynamics in a fixwage neo-Austrian model of traverse', *Structural Change and Economic Dynamics* 1: 165–94.

—— (1993) 'Traverse and convergence in the neo-Austrian model: the case of a distributive shock', *Structural Change and Economic Dynamics* 4: 105–25.

Neisser, H. (1942) '"Permanent" technological unemployment', *American Economic Review* 32: 50–71.

Pasinetti, L. L. (1981) *Structural Change and Economic Growth. A Theoretical Essay on the Dynamics of the Wealth of Nations*, Cambridge: Cambridge University Press.

Ricardo, D. (1951) *On the Principles of Political Economy and Taxation* (1st edn, 1817; 3rd edn, 1821), vol. I of *The Works and Correspondence of David Ricardo*, ed. P. Sraffa with the collaboration of M. Dobb, Cambridge: Cambridge University Press.

Samuelson, P. A. (1988) 'Mathematical vindication of Ricardo on machinery', *Journal of Political Economy* 96: 274–82.

—— (1989), 'Ricardo was right!', *Scandinavian Journal of Economics* 91: 47–62.

Schaik, A. B. T. M. van (1976) *Reproduction and Fixed Capital*, Tilburg: Tilburg University Press.

Schefold, B. (1980) 'Fixed capital as a joint product and the analysis of accumulation with different forms of technical progress', in L. L. Pasinetti (ed.) *Essays on the Theory of Joint Production*, London: Macmillan, pp. 138–217.

Schumpeter, J. A. (1954) *History of Economic Analysis*, London: Allen & Unwin.

Shields, M. P. (1989) 'The machinery question: can technological improvements reduce real output?' *Economica* 56: 215–24.

Solow, R. M. (1974) 'Review of "*Capital and Time*" by J. Hicks', *Economic Journal* 84: 189–92.

Sraffa, P. (1951) 'Introduction' in *The Works and Correspondence of David Ricardo*, vol. I, Cambridge: Cambridge University Press, pp. XIII–LXII.

Violi, R. (1984a) 'I processi dinamici di transizione indotti dall'innovazione tecnologica', *Annali della fondazione Luigi Einaudi*, 53–95.

—— (1984b) 'Sentiero di traversa e convergenza', *Giornale degli Economisti e Annali di Economia* 43: 153–96.

Wicksell, K. (1906) *Lectures on Political Economy*, vol. I, London: Routledge & Kegan Paul, 1934.

Zamagni, S. (1984) 'Ricardo and Hayek effects in a fixwage model of traverse', in D. A. Collard, D. R. Helm, M. F. G. Scott and A. K. Sen (eds) *Economic Theory and Hicksian Themes*, Oxford: Clarendon Press, pp. 135–51.

—— (1991) 'Hicks on capital and growth', *Review of Political Economy* 3: 249–67.

14

ECONOMIC THEORY AND ECONOMIC HISTORY
Perspectives on Hicksian themes
Roberto Scazzieri

I INTRODUCTION

Hicks's contribution to economic scholarship covers a range of perspectives that is seldom found in the lifework of an individual researcher. As a matter of fact, Hicks paid attention to economic decision making but, at the same time, withdrew from the abstract (axiomatic) approach to pure theory and emphasized the importance of accurate description as a field in which innovative conception could emerge. In particular, he stressed the relationship between economic theory and economic history as of fundamental methodological significance, both in identifying the intrinsic limits of economic theorizing and in assessing the relationship between free choice and determinism, i.e. between economic rationality and irreversible processes.

More generally, Hicks belongs to the small group of distinguished economic writers in which the attention for human deliberation and action is not leading to a pure theory of choice, but is instead connected to a theoretical appraisal of human institutions and other relatively persistent structures.

The aim of this essay is to consider the different features of Hicks's work that may be related to his attempt of constructing a theory of economic behaviour in real time. In particular, we shall examine in which way Hicks's attention for time-related phenomena (stocks and flows, fixprice and flexprice, decisions and sequential causality) reflects a general concern for human action as a historical process, i.e. as a set of stage-related decisions and transformations of the 'material' world. Hicks's contribution to economic theory, if considered in its full complexity, appears to be one of the most ambitious attempts carried out to date of building a bridge between theoretical and descriptive accounts of economic behaviour.

In this way, the whole of Hicks's contribution could be considered as providing the building blocks of a theory of economic history, in which a selective utilization of economic models allows for the analytical reconstruction of historically relevant practices under institutionally specific set-ups.[1]

This chapter is organized as follows. Section II considers Hicks's distinction between stocks and flows and its relationship to the conventional (i.e. task-specific) character of methods of dynamic analysis. Section III analyses the relationship between price setting and the nature of business income as a special case of Hicks's own historically oriented selection of economic models. Finally, Section IV examines Hicks's method of sequential causality and considers the linkage between money and the time structure of production as the most critical feature of the Hicksian theory of historical processes.

II   FLOWS, STOCKS AND ECONOMIC DYNAMICS

One important feature of Hicks's approach to dynamic analysis is his distinction between two different ways of considering a process of economic change.[2] A clue to such a distinction is given by the work of economic historians:

> one of the standard ways of writing economic history (particularly practised by political historians in their economic chapters) is to survey the *state* of the economy under consideration, as it was in various historical periods, comparing one state with another.... This is the method of comparative statics. It is when the economic historian tries to throw his work into the form of a narrative that he becomes, in the theoretical sense, dynamic.... Any examination of the work of economic historians will show that a difficult threshold has to be crossed at that point. It is in fact exceedingly difficult to cast economic history into a narrative form without becoming *more* abstract than one has to be on the survey method – greater realism in the matter of time sequence has to be purchased by a higher level of abstraction in most other respects.
>
> (Hicks 1956c in Helm 1984: 201–2)

The methodological issue of the realism of time sequences also comes up in the field of economic theory:

> the historian is baffled by the problem of narrating in a single sequence events that occur successively and those that occur contemporaneously – and even in [economic] theory the analysis of a number of contemporary interacting processes soon proves to be beyond our powers. It is no accident that dynamic theory tends so largely to run in terms of simple aggregative models.
>
> (Hicks 1956c in Helm 1984: 202)

The above framework highlights the possibility of dealing with processes of change in two different but complementary ways. 'For economic dynamics is not only concerned with what happens; it is also concerned with what is planned, or intended, or expected to happen. We do not merely have to deal with one time scale; time reduplicates itself as in a mirror, or in a series of mirrors. Parallel to the real events, which have one course in time, are constantly changing series of planned or expected events, with similar but distinct courses' (Hicks 1956c in Helm 1984: 203).

The two approaches mentioned above may be related to the methods of economic history in the following way. The purposive behaviour of individuals reflects itself in the existence of distinct and interacting sequences of plan formation and realization. On the other hand, the unfolding of real events through historical time makes it possible to introduce a sharp distinction between expected events and actual changes, and to assign a major role in the kind of structural heritage that each time period receives from the past.

In this connection, Hicks emphasizes the importance of accounting methods as means for determining what is fixed and what is allowed to change at any given time when a dynamic process is considered. As a matter of fact, the identification of a *particular* accounting period makes it possible to spell out which descriptive convention is adopted in considering a process of change. For example, if the agricultural year is adopted as the accounting period (as with the physiocrats and the Classical economists), agricultural products are described in terms of flows of finished goods reaching completion at the end of each period. On the other hand, if we assume that the production periods of manufactured goods are different from the (conventional) agricultural period, it would follow that manufactured goods would be described either as *flows* of goods-in-process or as *stocks* of commodity reserves, depending on whether their production period is longer or shorter than the agricultural 'year'.

If we stretch our view beyond the agricultural period, *stocks* of agricultural products may be identified (these would be, for example, quantities of corn completed at the end of period t and not used for consumption or production in the course of period $t + 1$). Similarly, it is possible to identify stocks of the manufactured goods whose production takes more than the agricultural year, if we consider a number of accounting periods whose total length exceeds that of the corresponding manufacturing period. On the other hand, in the case of manufactured goods whose production takes less than the agricultural year, the consideration of more than a single accounting period (of the agricultural type) involves the piling up of greater 'stocks', which may be depleted or not, depending on what is happening on the demand side.

In other words, once a particular accounting period is adopted, the distribution of stocks and flows among productive sectors is also determined within the single accounting period. The consideration of time intervals longer than the accounting period may turn flows into stocks, as with 'long' manufactured goods. However, the stretching of time cannot turn stocks into flows (see the case of 'short' manufactured goods considered above). There is thus an asymmetry that has to do with the irreversibility of time: the stocks of 'short' manufactured goods are the outcome of a process that 'is past, over

227

and done with; it is there and cannot be changed' (Hicks 1976f in Helm 1984: 263–4). The stretching of our time horizon cannot turn existing stocks into flows; it will simply increase the time interval in which stocks may pile up.[3] Hicks's emphasis upon the duality between real events and expected events (see above) provides a first introduction to his own 'theory' of economic history. In particular, it calls attention to the critical role of descriptive frameworks in identifying different patterns of interaction between sequences of plans and sequences of real states. In this connection, Hicks has stressed the importance of business accounting as a conceptual framework especially suited to the investigation of time sequences in which rationality and plan formation may realistically be expected to play only a limited role. As Hicks puts it:

> it is felt (and it is really quite proper to feel) that *explanations* which run so largely in terms of subjective factors (*quantified* subjective factors) are unsatisfactory, because they are so largely incapable of verification. A framework which lays less stress upon such variables keeps us closer to the facts.
>
> (Hicks 1956c in Helm 1984: 207)

If the analysis of processes of change draws upon the conceptual frameworks common in business accounting 'the emphasis upon *ex ante* budgeting' will have to be dropped (Hicks 1956c in Helm 1984: 207). For '[b]usinesses have too little control over their future operations to be able to present formal forward accounts; though they of course make estimates and plans for their own purposes, those estimates are always affected by a high degree of uncertainty' (Hicks 1956c in Helm 1984: 207).

To sum up, stocks and flows may be assigned a critical role in identifying linkages between different accounting periods. In particular, the relationship between equilibrium of stocks and equilibrium of flows makes events within the current period (flows) to influence the maintenance of stock equilibrium:

> if stock equilibrium is to be maintained over the period, the end-stock equilibrium must be constant with what was envisaged at the beginning; if, during the period, there had been a revision of expectations about the further future, the passage from one to the other could not be reduced to the flows that had occurred between them.
>
> (Hicks 1982a in Helm 1984: 215)

This implies that stock equilibrium between two subsequent dates, when expectations are being revised, cannot be maintained unless stocks are also varied. In other words, conditions of flow equilibrium should be satisfied if stock equilibrium is to be maintained, but flow equilibrium is not a *sufficient* condition for stock equilibrium. Flow equilibrium may be associated with stock *disequilibrium* (cumulation or decumulation of stocks) if there is any mismatch between real and expected events within the current period.

In this connection, the asymmetry is worth noting between flows and stocks. Equilibrium of flows is possible under conditions of stock disequilibrium, even if stock equilibrium necessarily implies the equilibrium of flows within the current period. It seems that the position of stocks points to a deeper level of economic reality, i.e. to a level at which current *decisions* do not adequately reflect the state of linkages between subsequent accounting periods. Stocks, particularly in the case of manufacturing firms, represent the objective counterpart of past decisions, which current decisions can only partially modify. As a result, the dynamics of stocks, rather than that of flows, provide a privileged standpoint to the consideration of historical linkages between periods.

The distinction between stocks and flows ultimately reflects our choice of the accounting period (see above). As a result, commodities whose production period is short tend to be associated with the formation of stocks, whereas commodities with a long production period would generally be described by flows if the accounting period is sufficiently long. The structure of the stock–flow network characterizing any given economic system within a certain accounting period depends upon the length of the accounting period and the duration of the production process. In this way, an important linkage is introduced between the time structure of production and dynamic principles such as stock cumulation or decumulation. However, structural specification, in the form of the selection of a convenient unit period, emerges as a critical step in identifying, in each particular situation, the most important historical linkages between periods.[4]

III FIXPRICE, FLEXPRICE AND THE NATURE OF BUSINESS INCOME

The formation of business income and its relationship to accounting practice is considered by Hicks as an important field of investigation in order to highlight the relationship between economic theory and economic history.

As a matter of fact, 'the purpose of income calculations in practical affairs is to give people an indication of the amount which they can consume without impoverishing themselves' (Hicks 1939a in Helm 1984: 49). In the case of business income, its calculation provides a linkage between the stocks existing at the beginning and at the end of each accounting period.[5] In this way the valuation of business income provides an important connection between the past and the future, for variations of stock (capital accumulation or decumulation) will reflect in which way business income (or *profit*) is used in order to modify the structure of claims and liabilities existing at any given time.[6]

For example, a situation of initial and final stock equilibrium would be one in which business income (over and above capital maintenance) is entirely consumed.[7] On the other hand, capital accumulation and decumulation would be associated with initial stock disequilibria (existing stock being less than desired stock in the former case, and more than desired stock in the latter case). Of course, the previous notion of income implies that *negative* income may be defined as what must be taken out from the existing stock in order to cope with a loss. A consequence is that, in this case, capital decumulation will always take place independently of the relationship between existing and desired stock. There is thus an asymmetry with respect to the positive income case, in which income may be either consumed or transformed into a capital increase.

The stock–flow framework makes it possible to consider changes of current variables (such as gains or losses) within a time-structure perspective. This is achieved by linking the definition of a gain or loss with the change in the structure of claims and liabilities that identifies the capital stock of a business firm at any given time. In this way, the level of current variables (gains and losses related to the definition of positive or negative business income) will not be identified unless it is possible to describe two different balance sheets separated by a finite time interval (the accounting period).

The above framework allows for the analysis of a variety of cases, which may be related with different 'carry-over mechanisms', i.e. with different arrangements by which 'events of a first period ... determine the events of its successors' (Hicks 1956c in Helm 1984: 204). In this way, the theory of the single period that concentrates its attention upon 'what happens in that period and what is planned ... to happen in it' (Hicks 1956c in Helm 1984: 204) may be linked with 'continuation theory', whose aim is to consider the relationship between successive periods in terms of sequential causality.[8]

In this connection, Hicks distinguishes between the 'carry-over' mechanisms that may be associated with fixprice and flexprice models respectively. In the former case, prices are considered to be relatively sticky (they cannot vary within the single period), and 'a failure to fulfill plans ... results in an unwanted accumulation or decumulation of stocks (or perhaps in the appearance of "negative stocks" in the sense of unfulfilled orders)' (Hicks 1956c in Helm 1984: 205). As a result,

the determination of prices is held over to be a first step in continuation theory. Prices are determined, in each successive period, largely as a consequence of the discrepancies between supplies and demands which have appeared in the period before.

(Hicks 1956c in Helm 1984: 205)

A characteristic feature of the carry-over mechanism of flexprice models is that, since prices are held to be fixed within the single period, linkages among successive periods are in terms of stock accumulation or decumulation. Continuation theory aims at identifying sequential linkages in terms of the transmission of wanted or unwanted stocks.

A different approach is adopted in flexprice models, such as the one considered in *Value and Capital* (Hicks 1939a). Here, 'prices [are] flexible, so that there could be no unintentional carry-over of stocks; prices could vary within the *single-period*, but the movements of prices within the period (from one part of the period to another) were neglected' (Hicks 1956c in Helm 1984: 205). In this case, on the other hand, prices are allowed to vary with the period, thereby ensuring demand and supply equilibrium in terms of quantity. It follows that continuation theory (the theory of systematic linkages between different accounting periods) would be based upon the comparison of real and expected prices: 'the windfall gaps between expectation and realisation were thrown over on to the price side' (Hicks 1956c in Helm 1984: 205). Differently from what happens with the fixprice model, the 'structural heritage' that is passed over from one period to another reduces, in the flexprice case, to purely subjective elements, and the economist's attention may concentrate upon the relationship between interacting sequences of plan formation and realization without considering 'objective' linkages between subsequent accounting periods.

The alternative theories of continuation implicit in flexprice and fixprice theories respectively reflect two different historical situations, which we may tentatively associate with the technological and market structures of purely exchange and pure production models respectively (on this distinction, see Baranzini and Scazzieri 1986a, b).

Flexprice analysis implicitly assumes an idealized 'pure exchange' economy, in which only two types of commodities may be traded:

(1) perishable goods and personal services, which *could not* be carried over from one period to another; (2) speculatively traded commodities, stocks of which were held by merchants in order to make a profit on the difference between present and future prices.

(Hicks 1956c in Helm 1984: 206)

In this type of situation, there is no unintentional carry-over of stocks, and continuation theory may focus upon purely subjective factors:

it is insisted that the producer will only accumulate stocks if he thinks that the price he will be able to get, by selling them in some future period, will be better (in spite of the costs of holding) than what he could get by selling now; so in this sense the accumulation of stocks is *voluntary*.

(Hicks 1956c in Helm 1984: 13)

A different type of continuation theory would be suitable in a situation in which pricing follows the fixprice procedure. In this case,

demands and supplies do not have to be equal; there is then no equation of demand and supply to determine prices. In describing this model as a flexprice model, it is *not* assumed that prices are unchanging over

231

time, from one single-period to its successor; only that they do not necessarily change whenever there is demand–supply disequilibrium.

(Hicks 1956c in Helm 1984: 213)

Here, demand-and-supply disequilibria within the current period would be reflected in the formation of involuntary stocks of unsold commodities or unfulfilled orders. In other words, the continuation theory of a fixprice economy would be characterized by 'material' linkages between periods (real commodities or claims upon them) rather than by 'psychological' linkages expressing realized or unrealized expectations.

It may be interesting to see how the two different types of continuation theory are related with two distinct approaches to the formation of business income and its dynamic over time.

In a fixprice economy, a mismatch between actual and desired stock at the beginning of the accounting period would be reflected in a process of capital accumulation or decumulation during that period, i.e. (assuming positive business income) in a process by which part of business income is converted into capital stock or part of the existing stock is sold and converted into consumable income. Here, business income may be considered as the flow variable regulating the adjustment process between subsequent states (structures) of the capital stock. A different perspective must be adopted when considering a flexprice economy. In this case, there would be no significant carry-over from one period to another except for purposes of speculation. It follows that gains and losses could be considered as the primary objective of business behaviour, quite independently of the 'structural' evaluation of the capital stock. In other words, business income becomes the critical explanatory variable, and it comes to be identified with reference to flow receipts and payments without considering the structure of the capital account. We may conclude that the flexprice assumption implies a concentration of attention upon the purposive behaviour of economic agents, quite independently of the structural rigidities emerging within the fixprice set-up.

In Hicks's view, flexprice continuation theory presupposes particular historical conditions, in which exchanges only consist of 'perishable goods and personal services' and 'speculatively traded commodities' (see above). On the other hand, fixprice theory considers an institutional set-up in which prices are set by manufacturers and retailers and are not allowed to vary too quickly as a consequence of demand-and-supply disequilibrium. In this type of set-up, 'a model in which quantities bear the brunt of disequilibrium fits most of the facts distinctly better' (Hicks 1956c in Helm 1984: 206).

Manufactured commodities are often produced under conditions in which, contrary to what happened when 'the typical end-products of manufacturing industry [consisted] of objectively standardizable goods, which could be traded on competitive wholesaler markets' (Hicks 1989a: 23),

it is now the producer himself who has to take responsibility for the quality, and usefulness, of what he is selling; for he is selling, at least at the end of the chain, to a consumer who is not an expert.

(Hicks 1989a: 24–5)

Under such circumstances,

arbitrary changes [of price] 'unsettle' the consumer. He may be taking time to decide to buy; so if, when he finally decides, he finds the price has risen against him, his confidence is lost, and the seller's reputation is damaged. And it can happen that there is a similar obstacle to price-reductions; they cast suspicion on the quality of the product, they suggest that something is wrong. Thus the diversified market had a tendency to be what I have called a *fixprice* market, meaning not that prices do not change, but that there is a force which makes for stabilization, operated not by independent speculators, but by the producer himself.

(Hicks 1989a: 25)

To sum up, the flexprice set-up suggests a type of continuation theory that is especially suitable to the modelling of historical cases in which commodities are perishable or speculatively traded. This implies that disequilibria are immediately reflected in price adjustments within the single period, and that there is no carry-over of disequilibrium via the formation of involuntary stocks. The linkage between each period and its successor is based upon the mechanism of expectations formation and realization, and the structure of the capital account of each business firm does not normally operate as a built-in stabilizer (as is the case with fixprice linkages). The above framework is found to be especially relevant in analysing the historical experience of financial firms, or of merchant companies not directly involved in the production process. In both cases, and most clearly for a financial firm, 'nearly all of whose assets are marketable securities' (Hicks 1982a in Helm 1984: 214), the business unit 'can change [her own] assets from one form to another, almost at a moment's notice' (Hicks 1982a in Helm 1984: 214).

The capital account, due to price flexibility, may be taken to be always in equilibrium (actual stock being equal to desired stock virtually at any single point of time). In this way, the distinction between stock equilibrium and flow equilibrium recedes to the background, and flow equilibrium may be considered as a *continuum* along which the firm moves, without any significant time lag, from one stock equilibrium to another.[9]

We may now move to the consideration of the fixprice set-up. The corresponding continuation theory is suitable to the modelling of historical cases in which commodities may normally be stored and the formation, or depletion, of stocks is not generally associated with speculative behaviour. In this case, price adjustment within the single period is impossible (see above), and disequilibria between demand and supply are normally carried over from one period to another by means of involuntary stocks (that may be positive or negative). The connection between subsequent periods is primarily due to the objective existence of involuntary stocks, and the structure of the capital account of a business firm operates as a built-in stabilizer with respect to the agents' behaviour within the current period.

Manufacturing firms may be considered as characteristic examples of a fixprice set-up. In particular, as Hicks points out, 'an industrial business ... must have a large proportion of its assets in forms which make them not at all readily marketable; and even if they could be sold, they could not be replaced in new forms in a hurry' (Hicks 1982a in Helm 1984: 214). As a result, a mismatch between demand and supply within the current period is likely to determine the emergence of stock disequilibrium at the end of the period. In this case, a change in the firm's environment is generally associated with a situation in which 'the goods (and claims) that are listed on [the firm's] balance-sheet are *not* the best out of a range of alternatives' (Hicks 1982a in Helm 1984: 214). The formation of involuntary stocks of unsold commodities or unfulfilled orders would be the rule, so that inspection of a firm's capital account and of its evolution over time is an essential feature in the analysis of a business unit operating within a fixprice set-up. An industrial firm

> will always be, to some extent, in a state of stock disequilibrium. Its endeavours, over time, to right that disequilibrium will be a major aspect of its policy. They will determine the time-path of the induced investment (or disinvestment) that it will undertake.
>
> (Hicks 1982a in Helm 1984: 215)

In other words, 'stock disequilibrium is the engine, or a part of the engine' by which the propagation over time of a given impulse takes place (Hicks, 1982a in Helm 1984: 214).

Alternative methods of price setting reflect the structure of markets, which is in turn related with the real composition and economic function of commodity stocks. In this way, the flexprice–fixprice distinction calls attention to a fundamental theme in Hicks's theory of economic history, i.e. the relationship between freedom of choice and the 'complementarities over time' (Hicks 1939a) that restrict the space of feasible actions within any given time period.[10]

IV MONEY, THE STRUCTURE OF PRODUCTION AND SEQUENTIAL CAUSALITY

The previous sections of this essay have considered alternative types of continuation theory in connection with different assumptions about the price mechanism. In this concluding section, we shall argue that a comprehensive analysis of the relationship between 'free choice' and 'determinism' (i.e. of the conceptual foundation of Hicks's 'theory' of economic history) cannot be undertaken unless production and money are explicitly considered. In the present analytical set-up, the production process may be considered as the unfolding of successive fabrication stages over real time, and money is essentially 'a standard for deferred payments' (Hicks 1989a: 42), i.e. the means by which credit and debit relationships across different time periods may emerge.

As a matter of fact, the analytical features of continuation theory that may be considered when distinct mechanisms of price setting are examined (see above), re-emerge independently of price formation as soon as stocks and flows consist not only of finished final output but also of unfinished commodities (work-in-process) and finished commodities *not yet* used as means of production. In particular, the consideration of an economic system in which a multiplicity of productive units (firms, establishments) interact with each other in terms of a complex division of labour requires the introduction of systematic linkages between different time periods. This is essentially due to the different length of the various partial processes, and to the need to establish a framework within which the mutual commitments to deliver means of production and to acquire finished goods may be enforced.

In this connection, the association between the time structure of the production processes and the emergence of monetary relationships emerges quite clearly. For any production process consisting of a multiplicity of stages would normally require the carry-over of stocks of work-in-process from one time period to another. On the other hand, the different lengths of different partial processes require some form of co-ordination between the accumulation or decumulation of stocks within the different productive units. A clue to this issue may be provided by the consideration of the debit and credit relationships that ensure the consistency of the production network over time. The reason is that the interdependence between short and long production processes requires a device (a convention) by means of which the processes of short duration 'lend' their output (or part of it) to the processes of long duration, making it possible for the latter to be undertaken at all. Such a device may consist in the formation of purchasing power with the sale of the final output of short-lasting processes, and its transfer to the long-lasting processes. The latter may thus be feasible even if no purchasing power gets formed when the work-in-process is carried over from one period to another. In other words, the start of long-lasting processes depends upon the formation of a 'store of value' by means of which the revenue from the sale of the output of 'short' processes is accumulated and carried over from one time period to another. In a symmetric way, the initial purchase of the raw materials needed in long-lasting processes, and the carry-over of work-in-process from one period to another, takes place through a 'deferred payment', which may or may not be associated with the actual transfer of money but necessarily entails the formation of loans (in the sense that the net output of short processes builds up a 'reserve' that supports the life of long processes throughout the time interval in which the final output from long processes is under gestation but not yet delivered).

The coexistence of short and long processes within the production network of a modern economic system requires, in general, the formation of reserves, by means of which processes may be lengthened and payments deferred. Such reserves may be considered both from the real and the monetary points of view. In the former case, they consist of commodities delivered by short processes and permitting the long processes to be undertaken (an instance would be the wage fund considered by the classical economists). In the latter case, reserves consist of 'stored' purchasing power that may be borrowed or lent independently of the physical composition of the real reserves. (An early analysis of the relationship between real and monetary reserves in connection with the time structure of production may be found in Fanno (1931, 1933); see also Scazzieri (1991).)

A production economy based upon a complex division of labour would generally present a split between the short processes delivering goods for direct consumption and the long processes producing instrumental goods (tools, machines). The above argument suggests that there is, for this type of economic system, a specific 'structural' reason why it is likely to acquire features of a monetary economy. This is that money is essentially associated with deferred payments,[11] so that a monetary economy has a built-in *ad hoc* device by means of which the co-ordination between short and long processes may be achieved. The possibility of monetary payments binds together production processes of different durations, so that the net output from short processes may be used to start and maintain long-lasting processes. This may be achieved by considering the net output of short processes as a 'store of wealth' having a monetary expression. In this way, the continuation of a long process through its successive fabrication stages will be made possible by monetary loans to the productive units in which such processes are carried out. It is these loans that provide long processes with the resources needed to maintain the work-in-process under operation for longer than the reproduction requirements of short processes would allow. The operation of a long process requires the availability both of direct consumption goods (wage goods) and of the goods in process themselves. (The latter category includes 'normal stocks of materials, of half-finished and of finished goods'; see Hicks (1969a: 151).) Wage goods are generally produced (and reproduced) by short processes, so that in this case the linkage between short and long processes is based upon the utilization of the wage processes' *net output* in order to maintain long processes. (The 'simultaneous exchange' of finished products between short and long processes is not possible, due to the different lengths of production periods.)

The case of goods in process is remarkably different. For goods in process are generated as internal products within the long processes, so that there is no need for them to be 'bought' when moving from one subperiod to the next.

However, the work-in-process cannot be carried forward unless the corresponding maintenance costs (including fuel, labour and so on) are actually met. The co-ordination between short and long processes appears to be quite different depending on which side we consider. From the point of view of *short processes*, co-ordination takes the form of a real loan of short processes' net output. From the point of view of *long processes*, the latter have to be able to borrow 'liquidity' (financial loan) in order to cope with contingent needs before their output is finished.

The distinction between short and long processes makes liquidity (and the corresponding monetary arrangements) a central feature of productive co-ordination and division of labour, quite independently of the particular financial needs that may be associated with the existence of fixed capital. In this connection, a critical point is whether capital is or is not 'sunk' in some form of investment, 'from which it can only gradually, at the best, be released (Hicks 1969a: 144). Capital may be 'sunk' both when it is embodied in some type of equipment and when it is 'locked' in the work-in-process of a long-lasting productive activity. In either case, 'it is the availability of liquid funds which is crucial' (Hicks 1969a: 144–5), and financial institutions perform an essential role in shifting real resources from one sector to another independently of the physical form that 'liquid resources' originally have.

The monetary form of loans to producers makes it possible to bind short and long processes together, by permitting the storing up of the value of short processes' net output and its utilization under a physical form (direct consumption goods and semi-finished goods) that may be different from the original one. However, real reserves (and real 'deficits') would be the necessary basis upon which monetary linkages between short and long processes may be introduced.

As a result, monetary institutions could provide a critical linkage between different sectors of a productive system. Money emerges here as performing an essentially macroeconomic function, in the sense that it appears to smooth the asymmetries and bottlenecks due to the different time structures of the production processes. In this connection, real stocks and flows within the individual productive units bring about a complex picture in which each production process of given length is associated with a distinct stock–flow relationship, and thus with a particular way of relating the past with the future. On the other hand, the technical relationships among different processes require a co-ordination device, which may operate at the level of decisions by making consistent across a number of different time periods situations that are clearly inconsistent if a shorter time horizon is considered. In this perspective, monetary arrangements may be helpful in order to overcome the 'temporal unevenness' of an interlinked productive system, and also to ensure that the structure of inherited assets existing at any point of time is not an obstacle to the transformation of the output mix and production techniques. As a matter of fact, the existence of a store of value in 'immaterial' form (money) permits intertemporal exchanges purely on the basis of the institutional arrangements regulating the credit–debit relationships. In this way, it emerges that there is an important linkage between money, markets and the organization of production, particularly after a detailed division of labour has been introduced. More specifically, the co-ordination of short and long processes is made easier by the existence of markets for future delivery, and money appears to be an essential institutional device in order to ensure the credibility of commitments taken in that connection. As a result, a new field of research takes shape in which the theory of economic history derives from blending the abstract reconstruction of co-ordination requirements with the analysis of the particular asymmetries and institutional corrections operating in any particular situation.[12]

NOTES

1   In this connection, it is worth recalling Hicks's view of economic theories as 'blinkers', that is as focusing devices useful in interpreting particular features of reality while leaving the rest unexplained. Hicks's conceptual framework identifies analytical tools for the interpretation of economic experience but never assimilates the whole experience with the domain of a particular theory. In this perspective, economic theories may be considered as rational reconstructions of pre-analytical descriptions, and their utilization reflects the particular purposes of the analysis that is carried out. (See Hicks (1976e, 1984b); also Scazzieri (1989), for an elaboration of the view of economic theory as rational reconstruction of pre-theoretical descriptions and beliefs.)

2   Hicks points out that

> [i]f we look for a definition which shall define scope not method and which shall embrace the whole of the field which practice treats as dynamic, the kind of definition to which we must come is fairly obvious. I shall take it to be the theoretical analysis of the *process of economic change*. So defined, the subject includes the study of change in particular markets as well as in the whole economy; and no commitment is made in advance about the method by which the subject is to be examined.
>
> (Hicks 1956c in Helm 1984: 201)

3   Of course, any given stock of a 'short' manufactured good is itself the result of a cumulated flow. We may go back from stock to flow by reducing the length of our accounting period.

4   It is worth noting that the above argument applies not only to the case of the stock–flow distinction, but also to the distinction between *flows* and *funds*. The latter duality reflects objective characteristics of goods from the point of view of their utilization in production or consumption (in general, a factory or a house are funds, whereas oil or raw materials are flows from *this particular point of view*). The stock–flow distinction, on the other hand, refers to the formation of 'reserves' of goods and is not directly linked to their pattern of utilization in consumption or production. The length of the accounting period is related to the distinction between funds and flows in the sense that most funds could be seen as goods with a 'reproduction cycle' longer than the unit period. In general a switch to a shorter accounting period tends to increase the number of funds,

which comes to include a considerable number of reproducible goods (e.g. machinery and human capital). On the other hand, the lengthening of the accounting period reduces the number of funds to that of non-producible goods (e.g. land). A recent treatment of the flow–fund distinction mainly from the point of view of production theory may be found in Georgescu-Roegen (1969, 1971, 1986, 1990). The general issue of structural specification, in connection with the analysis of economic dynamics, is considered in Baranzini and Scazzieri (1990), Landesmann and Scazzieri (1990) and Scazzieri (1990).

5   Here the stock would include 'the evaluation of the existing stock of real capital, and the network of claims and obligations that are built upon it' (Hicks 1956c in Helm 1984: 207).

6   The relationship between business income and the structure of current and capital accounts is also considered in Hicks (1983a). A more general assessment of the relationship between business accounting and economic theory may be found in Hicks (1984b in Baranzini and Scazzieri 1986b: 99).

7   This would of course be the microeconomic counterpart of the classical stationary state.

8   As Hicks puts in *Causality in Economics* (1979g), sequential causality implies that cause precedes effect in a causally relevant way, i.e. in a way that is directly related with the *production* of the effect.

9   The notion of flow equilibrium as a succession of stock equilibria may be considered as an extension (to the extreme flexprice case) of Hicks's own definition of 'flow equilibrium', which seems to have been formulated having a fixprice set-up in mind. According to Hicks, 'if a unit is in stock equilibrium at the beginning of the period, and is still in stock equilibrium at the end, we shall want to say that it is in flow equilibrium during the period' (Hicks 1965a: 89). The extreme flexprice case suggests that a firm that is *continuously* under conditions of stock equilibrium will also meet the conditions of flow equilibrium during the relevant period of observation.

10 It has been argued in this connection that the analysis of the relationship between 'rationality' and 'time' is the most distinctive feature of Hicks's contribution to economic theory (see Meacci 1986).

11 This feature of money is associated with the fact that

> the representative transaction, of sale or purchase, [is] in principle divisible into three parts. The first is the contract between the parties, consisting of a promise to deliver and a promise to pay ...; the second and the third consist of actual delivery, one way and the other. In the case of the spot transaction, all are simultaneous; but they do not need to be simultaneous. If there is any difference in timing, promises precede deliveries; that is the only rule which applies throughout. Delivery of the article may come before it is paid for ...; or it may come after, or partly after ... What remains, in general, immediately after the making of the contract, are on the one hand a debt 'in real terms' from the seller and on the other a debt in money terms from the buyer.
>
> (Hicks 1989a: 42)

12 There is thus a unifying thread linking Hicks's analysis of real markets (1969a) with his attention for the real capital structure (1965a, 1973d, 1977a, 1985a) and for the types of 'continuation theory' suitable in its investigation (see, in particular, Hicks's treatment of liquidity and sequential causality in Hicks (1979g)). Specific features of Hicks's contribution to the theory of economic history are discussed in Bauer (1971) and Gerschenkron (1971).

239

REFERENCES

Amendola, M. and Gaffard, J.-L. (1988) *The Innovative Choice*, Oxford and New York: Basil Blackwell.

Baranzini, M. and Scazzieri, R. (1986a) 'Knowledge in economics. A framework', in M. Baranzini and R. Scazzieri (eds) *Foundations of Economics. Structures of Inquiry and Economic Theory*, Oxford and New York: Basil Blackwell, pp. 1–87.

——— (1986b) *Foundations of Economics. Structures of Inquiry and Economic Theory*, Oxford and New York: Basil Blackwell.

——— (1990), 'Economic structure: analytical perspectives', in M. Baranzini and R. Scazzieri (eds) *The Economic Theory of Structure and Change*, Cambridge: Cambridge University Press, pp. 227–333.

Bauer, P. (1971) 'Economic history as theory-review', *Economica* 38, May: 163–79.

Fanno, M. (1931) 'Cicli di produzione, cicli del credito e fluttuazioni industriali', *Giornale degli Economisti e Rivista di Statistica* LXXI, May: 329–70. English translation as 'Production cycles, credit cycles and industrial fluctuations', *Structural Change and Economic Dynamics* 4 (1993): 403–37.

——— (1932) 'Irrtümer in der Zeit als Ursachen wirtschaftlicher Schwankungen', *Zeitschrift für Nationalökonomie* 4: 25–51.

Georgescu-Roegen, N. (1969) 'Process in farming versus process in manufacturing: a problem of balanced development', in G. U. Papi and C. Nunn (eds) *Economic Problems of Agriculture in Industrial Societies*, London: Macmillan, pp. 497–528.

——— (1971) *The Entropy Law and the Economic Process*, Cambridge, MA: Harvard University Press.

——— (1986) 'Man and production', in M. Baranzini and R. Scazzieri (eds) *Foundations of Economics. Structures of Inquiry and Economic Theory*, Oxford and New York: Basil Blackwell, pp. 247–80.

——— (1990) 'Production process and dynamic economics', in M. Baranzini and R. Scazzieri (eds) *The Economic Theory of Structure and Change*, Cambridge: Cambridge University Press, pp. 198–226.

Gerschenkron, A. (1971) 'Mercator gloriosus', *Economic History Review* 24 (4), November: 653–66.

Helm, D. R. (ed.) (1984) *The Economics of John Hicks*, Oxford: Basil Blackwell.

Landesmann, M. and Scazzieri, R. (1990) 'Specification of structure and economic dynamics', in M. Baranzini and R. Scazzieri (eds) *The Economic Theory of Structure and Change*, Cambridge: Cambridge University Press, pp. 95–121.

Meacci, F. (1986) 'John Hicks: a review of selected works', *Atlantic Economic Journal* XIV (1): 127–30.

Scazzieri, R. (1989) 'Economic theory as rational reconstruction', *Ricerche economiche* XLIII, January–June: 40–56.

——— (1990) 'Vertical integration in economic theory', *Journal of Post Keynesian Economics* 13 (1): 20–46.

——— (1991) 'Flussi, fondi e dinamica economica: riflessioni sul contributo di Marco Fanno', in M. Manfredini Gasparetto (ed.) *Saggi in onore di Marco Fanno*, Padova: Cedam.

15

TIME IN ECONOMICS

Nicholas Georgescu-Roegen

Dear God, Give me time,
...
Give me time to eat,
Give me time to plod,
Give me time to think.

'The Prayer of the Ox'
Carmen Bernos De Gasztold, *Prayers from the Ark*

Time, much more than space, has been the reason for the philosophical, actually metaphysical, torment beginning with that of Heraclitus and Plato, going through many illustrious minds such as John Locke and Immanuel Kant down, in our own era, to Alfred North Whitehead, Henri Bergson and G. L. S. Shackle. Even some natural scientists have not been satisfied with the idea that time is nothing else but that which is measured by a mechanical pointer-reader, a clock. The most vigorous and competent protest came from Sir Arthur Eddington (1928). As we may remember, he argued that time is an element of our cognition much more mysterious than space, a point later accentuated nicely by Robert M. Maclver (1962): 'Time is the greatest of all human mysteries, and whichever way we think about it, we end in an impasse, faced by some great intriguing question to which no answer is forthcoming, since we find no road between the question and its exploration'. On a moment's reflection the reason is evident: we can hold a slice of space between our left and right hands and point out from 'here' to 'here'.

From the struggle that followed Saint Augustine's famous conversation about our cognition of time, Sir Arthur's analysis has emerged as the most important source for that issue. He was first to observe that, contrary to what we generally believe, time is not properly measured by the movement of the hands of a mechanical clock. Its true measure is the amount of the clock's wear-and-tear. Is not the age of a human, for example, shown more apparently by how that person looks physically and mentally than by a birth certificate?

The paramount importance of time for economics comes from the fact that it envelops every human action, actually, all actions of every life bearing structure. Any such structure must produce just like us, the humans, for to live means in the first and last place to produce food and to defend oneself (Georgescu-Roegen 1986).

It is through the universal activity of production that we come to learn the brutal meaning of time for us, although we still say, with Saint Augustine, that we do know time, but we cannot explain what time is in the same way as we can explain what a prime number is.

However, some for whom nature can be described only with help of clocks have found Saint Augustine's dialectical representation of time distasteful. An honour mention should go to Isaac Barrow (1630–1677), a famous divine, an outstanding mathematician and Sir Isaac Newton's teacher and supporter, who claimed in one of mathematical *Lectiones* that Saint Augustine's deliberation is a 'trite Saying', that mathematicians 'ought to have a distinct idea of the meaning of that word "time", otherwise they are Quacks'. He even announced that he was ready to offer a definition 'in the plainest and least ambiguous Expression, avoiding as much as possible all trifling and empty words' (quoted in Capek 1975: 203). But such a definition is still to come. On the other hand, humans have made increasing use of clock-time as mechanical processes have come to dominate economic production.

It is because time is such an elusive notion that it has been possible to treat it lightly, especially in economics. For most of the economic processes the time now is clock-time, in objective barters everything must be measured in some way or other. Yet in economics time enters also in a role that cannot be associated with a clock. Whatever belongs to strictly human manifestation, expectations and innovations, is not tied to the clock. These are uniquely difficult issues that have taxed many economic talents from whom we learned much but not what is the most important, how expectations and innovations are formed and how they appear in the open.

An attractive way to introduce expectations in an analytical representation of the economic process was founded by Sir John Hicks. Being a Marshallian, as he has been par excellence – i.e. being a marvel of an analyst with his feet solidly grounded into the world of hostile facts – his inspiration came from one of Marshall's ideas but is different from it. Marshall, we recall, associated economic time with his famous periods, the short run and the long run of varying lengths determined by the dialectical phases of the economic change. Sir John (1946b: 122) chose instead periods determined by the durations necessary for the usual successive economic operations: one 'day' for the determination of prices on the basis of whatever expectations people may have, one 'week' for preparing production on the basis of those prices and so on down the line, with the logical condition that no phase can be active before its own turn and no price can be changed outside the market day. Expectations are made every day, but are active only on the market day.

Another wondrous vision of the economic change as a true evolution – as an economics exclusively *in* time – is, besides *Das Kapital*, that of J.A. Schumpeter (1934), which he anchored on the uninterrupted, steady production of the human inventing faculty, some of which may turn quasi-periodically into practical innovations. The inestimable merit of that vision is

242

revealed by the fact that 30 years after Schumpeter's original German edition
was published, in 1912, and about 10 years after its English translation came
out, Richard Benedikt Goldschmidt, a first rank German geneticist at
Berkeley University, astounded the biological profession of that epoch by
proposing a theory of biological evolution totally homomorphic with
Schumpeter's theory. Whereas Schumpeter (1934: 81n) argued that economic
evolution is sustained by great, *not small*, innovations, Goldschmidt maintained that biological evolution is punctuated not by the small imperceptible
mutations assumed by Darwin's theory, but by the constant emergence of
monsters, of 'successful monsters', as he put it. Line up as many mail coaches
as you may wish, you will not get a railway engine thereby – as Schumpeter
used to characterize the essence of evolution, whether in biology or in
economics. Add to it another conclusion from Schumpeter's vision, namely
that a railway engine is a 'monster' in respect to a mail coach, and you see
how as an anti-Darwinist Schumpeter anticipated Goldschmidt.

With economists growing increasingly interested in the most esoteric
mathematics just for showing off within the profession (so it seems), the time
factor had been reduced just to a sign, t, deprived of any kinship with clock-
time by the 'equilibrists' – as Sir John (1976f: 139) called them. They are the
thorough economic theorists who on their diagrams move from one equilibrium position to another, to another ..., instantaneously (Georgescu-Roegen
1976: 414f). And since a sign is a sign is a sign ..., which can have any
meaning we may fancy, the gate has been wide opened for endless fanciful
interpretations of it.

Perhaps, the most disturbing anomaly intellectually is the identification of
t also with an index of the changing technological conditions over a given
period of time for some country, any country (Solow 1957). The proposed
aggregate production function of an economy for the period t, during which
it possesses a technical structure indexed also by t, is given by Solow's own
formula (1) (p. 312). In a more adequate form this is

$$Q = F(K, L, H, R; t). \tag{15.1}$$

But explicitly and correctly the production function (15.1) for some year, say
1957, should be written

$$Q_{1957} = F_{1957}(K_{1957}, L_{1957}, H_{1957}, R_{1957}; 1957) \tag{15.2a}$$

where the subscripts show the period over which that production has taken
place. (The other notations are the usual ones for the aggregate factors of
production.)

In his highly considered article, Solow also puts the partial derivative of
(15.1) with respect to time t to a very important use. But I have asked
(Georgescu-Roegen 1992) what meaning may this partial derivative have?
My answer has been: none other than a play-thing with pencil and paper, to
use the famous epithet of Percy Bridgman. Indeed, the mathematical

definition of a derivative (where else may we go for it?) is the limit of an average of a *finite* difference which in the case of (15.2a) would be, for example,

$$\frac{F_{1958} - F_{1957}}{1958 - 1957} \tag{15.2b}$$

which surely is not a *partial* difference since the qualities of most (usually all) factors must have changed from 1957 to 1958, otherwise formula (15.1) would be absolutely idle for any analysis of Heraclitian changes, not only for the economics of development (often 'growth' in standard economics).

In economics we have not been aware, so one may conclude, of the multiple important and ticklish facets of the time factor. Even on the issue of dimensionality economists have failed to be up to the task. A truly important issue of this sort concerns the hoary production function, unchanged since Philip Wicksteed (1894: 4) proposed it in an incomplete definition.

The product being a function of the factors of production we have

$$P = f(a, b, c, \ldots) \tag{15.3}$$

without saying what the factors of production are, what kind of function is f and, above all, what is its relation to time. Production is time in the first place, isn't it?

Little surprise that a concept as that introduced by Wicksteed, now called a production function, has been, still is, handled with unlimited arbitrariness, of which Solow's foregoing proposal is a good illustration. But even in its simple aspect of dimensionality, time has been mistreated. The result is that in standard economics there are two equivalent production functions with two time dimensionalities, 'a double-barrel production function' as I exposed it (Georgescu-Roegen 1992). For a number of prominent standard economists the production function relates stocks used or produced, for others it relates flows with respect to time (Georgescu-Roegen 1970). The failure of realizing the difference between flows and stocks, not only in this particular case, has been so widespread that even Ragnar Frisch was not immune to it (Georgescu-Roegen 1970: 2). The failure may seem innocuous, but it is not. For if any production process can be analytically represented by

$$Q = G(X, Y, \ldots, Z) \tag{15.4a}$$

where the variables are stocks, or indifferently by

$$q = g(x, y, \ldots, z) \tag{15.4b}$$

where they are flows with respect to time of the same factors as in (15.4a), then all production processes must necessarily be indifferent to scale, i.e. with constant returns to scale (Georgescu-Roegen 1970, 1972), which is utterly absurd, as we have been taught by Aristotle, Herbert Spencer and J.B.S. Haldane, as well as by a few others.

The perplexity, responsible also for the holes concerning scale in some standard policy principles, is the inevitable result of the characteristic disinterest of economists (save Adam Smith and Karl Marx) in a step-by-step analysis of the production process in time. There is no denial though that such analysis raises one of the most recalcitrant epistemological issues. How can an actual process be described step by step given that in the primal recognition it strikes the human mind as a thing very complicated where something happens almost continuously at every one of its *points*? In holistic or Gestalt perspective such a concept is dialectical. For a description of any dialectical concepts step by step in time it has come about that we must take a courageous leap, from dialectics to analysis, to see how.

As is natural, we should begin with the basic co-ordinate of the analytical representation, its boundary which completely identifies the process – *no boundary, no process*. And because in analysis *tertium non datur* (*pace* Schumpeter, in analysis one can be either an entrepreneur or not an entrepreneur) the analytical boundary must be a vacuous entity, at any given time during the process any element is either inside or outside it. And it goes without saying that the boundary must have two dimensions, a geographical one and a temporal one, both finite if we wish to use this construction for economic policy. For if, for example, the temporal boundary extended to $+\infty$, we could not make any plans about the end product, and if it started at $-\infty$ it would not be of any use for our policies since we have no jurisdiction over events going back to the beginning of the cosmos.

But the most important effect of that leap is the renunciation of considering all happenings within a process. The boundary just identifies the process, what the process does in time is represented by what happens on the boundary only, by the crossings over it. In the analytical perspective, the only one that can be adopted by economics as a theoretical discipline, there is no way for considering what happens inside a process. We know, for example, that in a glass plant melted glass passes from the furnace into the rolling mills, but that cannot be shown by the analytical representation of such a plant. If we are interested in that particular motion, we must draw another boundary that would divide the plant process into two subprocesses separated at the place of that passage. However, if we continue to divide and divide, in the end the analytical picture looses the very virtue for which it was introduced (Georgescu-Roegen 1970, 1972). That virtue is the underlying reason for the prominent role the terms 'input' and 'output' now have in economics.

That is also why those popular terms are properly defined only by analysis, not by etymology. An input should not be defined implicitly as something we *put in* and an output not as something that is *put out*: etymology does not inform us where is 'out' or 'in'. Analytically, an element is an 'input' if it crosses the boundary over into the process, and an element that crosses the

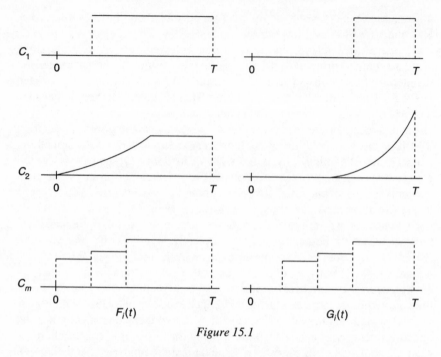

$F_i(t)$ $G_i(t)$

Figure 15.1

boundary from inside to outside is an 'output', which does not mean that it is a simple matter to decide in every actual case whether the element is 'in' or 'out' (Georgescu-Roegen 1970, 1971). With this background, time now enters the picture forcibly through the activity of each element in the process.

To represent that activity analytically, the initial detailed elements could be aggregated, as is the general practice in statistics, in a finite number denoted $C_1, C_2, \ldots, C_n$. The activity of any element, say C_i, may then be represented by two non-decreasing functions $F_i(t)$ and $G_i(t)$, defined over the duration $(0, T)$ of the process, with F being the cumulative input and G the cumulative output of the element of interest during the interval $(0, t)$, $0 \leqslant t \leqslant T$ (Georgescu-Roegen 1970, 1971). The graphs of these functions on one and the same time axis, as in Figure 15.1, show in a striking manner that the production process cannot be represented analytically (which is the most descriptive representation) by a point function, like equations (15.4) above. The analytical representation, although a compromise from dialectics, must still be a Dirichlet function, yet a function of functions

$$Q_0^T(t) = f[R_0^T(t), I_0^T(t), M_0^T(t), W_0^T(t); L_0^T(t), K_0^T(t), H_0^T(t)]$$

(15.4c)

which in mathematics is called a *functional*.

The letters used in here for the notation of the individual functions correspond to the composite element with which the function is associated as follows: Q is the product, L is the Ricardian land, K is the capital equipment, H is the labour force and I are other products, which are the traditional ones. The existence of two other flow elements was brought to light by the analysis step by step in time: first, the natural resources R – contrary to the pronouncement of Robert Solow (1974: 11), the 'world can[*not*] in effect, get along without natural resources' – and second, waste W, that output so completely left out by standard economics that when pollution struck everyone in the face we wondered from where it could come since it had not been in our production function.

Another significant result stemming from the foregoing analysis is that according to their role as participants in the process the elements are divided into *funds* and *flows* (Georgescu-Roegen 1970, 1971). By straightforward definition funds are the elements that go in and come out of the process without any economic alteration. The beau-example of a fund is the Ricardian land, which should have prevented the repeated confusion of fund with stock; land is certainly not a stock as the sugar in your pantry. The fund element was also, we may remember, the pivot of the theory Karl Marx hinged on the constant capital economy which, if we wish to mark the fact, is an indispensable, albeit usually unavowed, underpinning of much of the current economic essays.

I have included capital equipment and human capital in the fund category. The inclusion of capital equipment is justified in the abstract by the existence of a maintenance flow. In all institutions, like in households, a good deal of activity is devoted to keeping every material item clean and in a workable condition. The inclusion of the labour power is justified on the perhaps excusable argument that all humans associated with a production establishment are normally repaired at home. However, my fundamental reason for that composition of the fund category is the economically important common virtue of those funds: they are the agents that transform the input flows into the output flows. They provide services, measured in time-dimensional co-ordinates, say one hundred man-hours provided by a fund of four weavers. Ignoring this truth, a popular fallacy asserts that funds are embedded in the product just as some flow inputs normally are. However, if one finds a fund, a taylor's needle in a new pair of pants, it would certainly be an unpleasant accident.

The distinction between flows and funds has an invaluable role in the analysis of time scarcity, to which I now turn.

What is the relation between a fund and the economy of time in production? Let us first observe that every production is carried out by what I have referred to as an *elementary process*, the process through which every unit or every batch of the product is obtained from its material ingredients. The beau-example is the process by which a single cabinet maker in a shop produces one cabinet after another in time, as portrayed by Figure 15.2(a). It is a system of production in which elementary processes are arranged *in series*

247

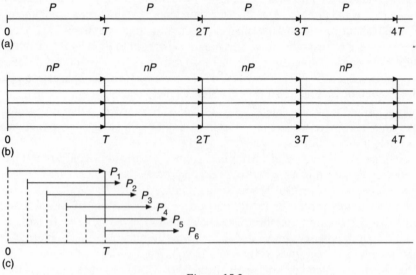

Figure 15.2

(Georgescu-Roegen 1972). So defined, an elementary process is the atom, as it were, of any production plant and can be found out by walking in step with the successive transformations of the input flows from the first transformation to the last. Of course, instructively one could walk in step with an assembly line. And if one takes just a look at a cabinet maker's shop, one will realize, perhaps surprisingly, that not only in that technique but in any other there is some inherent idleness of every fund. As illustrated by that elementary process, every tool remains idle during appreciable time periods, not because of some economic compulsion, but because of the inexorable physical nature of all economic transformations. The point which cannot be sufficiently stressed in connection with this phenomenon is that idleness of funds constitutes a truly pressing economic problem, as almost any husbandman would insist (Georgescu-Roegen 1969, 1970; Betancourt and Clague 1981; Winston 1982; Tani 1986).

There are several ways by which the physically inherent idleness of funds, that loss of time, may be reduced and eventually minimized. The most obvious way would be for the single master to hire another worker who could use the tools when they are not used by him. This solution is subject to some restrictions. The first is the availability of a second well-prepared cabinet maker, an issue that depends on the level of education of the community in respect, one that does not invite my attention on this occasion. But another perhaps unsuspected trouble is that the schedule of the tasks performed by the master may not splice completely with a second identical schedule. To wit, the time when in that schedule the hammer is not used may be smaller than that

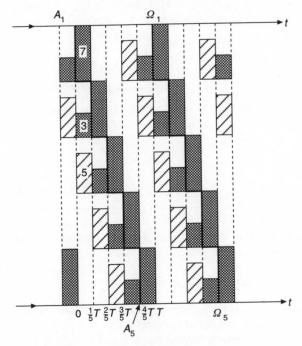

Figure 15.3

necessary to use it in the schedule of the additional worker. However, a theorem says that a sufficient number of some elementary processes can be spliced together provided that the durations of the tasks are commensurable with T, as shown in Figure 15.3 (Georgescu-Roegen 1969: 517). This nice-looking solution also has its hitch, which is that the rate per time of the demand for that product may not be sufficient to absorb the optimal splicing.

Surprise is in order at this juncture because this by-product of the foregoing time analysis not only vindicates theoretically Adam Smith's famous dictum that 'the division of labor is limited by the extent of the market', but it extends its significance to the 'division' of capital, i.e. to the qualitative change of capital equipment (Georgescu-Roegen 1971: 249).

Repelling though the picture of the completely spliced schedules might be, what it actually illustrates is a very important and also highly familiar sight: the FACTORY. The virtue of the factory is that it is the only system of production that does away completely with fund idleness. The open secret is the assembly line, in which one elementary process starts immediately after another such process has begun (Figure 15.2(c)), a condition to which I have referred as a process *in line* (Georgescu-Roegen 1970).

We should expect that the special structure of the factory system should be reflected in some way by the corresponding functional (15.4c), and that is so.

Since the factory system proceeds at a smooth, constant rate with respect to time, all the elements of (15.4c) become linear homogeneous functions of time if $t'=0$ for the time origin of the system.

$$Q(t) = qt \quad R(t) = rt \quad I(t) = it \quad M(t) = mt$$

$$W(t) = wt \quad L(t) = lt \quad K(t) = kt \quad H(t) = ht. \tag{15.5}$$

Each of these functions is now completely determined also by its coefficient, qt by q, rt by r and so forth. The functional (15.4) may thus be replaced by the point function

$$q = g(r, i, m, w; l, k, h) \tag{15.6a}$$

which proves that, of the two point functions (15.4) examined earlier, the correct form is (15.4b). But the functions (15.5) may be defined also by their values $Q^*, R^*, I^*, M^*, W^*, L^*, K^*, H^*$ at the end of the process, i.e. for $t = T$. It would then seem that with the substitution of these co-ordinates in (15.4) we obtain still another point function,

$$Q^* = G(R^*, I^*, M^*, W^*; L^*, K^*, H^*) \tag{15.6b}$$

a sister-function of (15.4a) which confronts us once more with the double-barrel conundrum. However, what may have appeared at first glance as true, is not so. Formula (15.6b) is wrong by incompleteness; it leaves out one important element. This element is the length of time T that the factory system has been open. If we also introduce this co-ordinate into the representation of the factory system we obtain

$$Q^* = J(R^*, I^*, M^*, W^*; L^*, K^*, H^*: T) \tag{15.6c}$$

which must be a homogeneous function of the first degree, since all variables may be multiplied by the same factor without any alteration of J. This finding throws light on the still simmering controversy about constant scale and 'ant-men' operating 'ant-machines'.

It is thus clear that the principle 'double the inputs, double the output' is a free translation of the near-tautology 'double the working time, double the output', which is the teaching of (15.6c), correct but unused for some unknown reason.

On elementary mathematics once fiercely denounced as false (Georgescu-Roegen 1969: 528; 1976: 38), from the homogeneity of J by making $t = 1$ in (15.5) we obtain the identity

$$J(r, i, m, w; l, k, h: 1) = G(r, i, m, w; l, k, h) \tag{15.7}$$

which clears up the habitual blunder that the homogeneity of (15.6c) makes (15.6b) homogeneous too. Identity (15.7) expresses a physical law, not a temporal one like (15.6c). But some misinterpretation of (15.7) is probably responsible for the difficulties surrounding the problems of time in production even when we limit ourselves to dynamical time, as I have done in the previous paragraphs.

The problem raised by fund idleness presents new aspects if it is considered in the economy at large. The most pressing aspect is that some processes which minimize idleness cannot be used in any place at any time whatsoever. These are most of the production processes in husbandry. Nature, the silent partner of man in husbandry, dictates when an agricultural process should start. If in the temperate zone of, say, Europe one does not plough and seed the field with corn in early Spring, one would have no reason for harvesting when the Fall comes. The well-known predicament of the husbandmen is that, because they generally cannot eliminate the idleness of their agricultural machinery, they have to bear in some way or other the interest for that capital fund from planting to harvesting. The composite agricultural activity consists of a number of agricultural units engaged in virtually identical processes during the proper time for some produce.

This situation can be portrayed by some parallel arrows (Figure 15.2(b)), the situation of a process *in parallel* (Georgescu-Roegen 1969, 1970). In such a process the idleness of the individual process is amplified linearly by the number of participants.

In this fact resides the difference of the role of time in processes in manufacture and of processes in farming (Georgescu-Roegen 1969). What is involved is that an elementary manufacturing process can be started virtually at any time of the day, week or year, and in fairly large geographical places. Figure 15.3, which depicts the spliced elementary processes as they are in a factory, makes it clear that a proper factory is like a music box, it starts to produce the instant it opens and it stops to work the instant it is closed.

The old controversy about whether production needs time or not receives thereby a clear answer. Production by factory needs no time: to wit, when an assembly line at an automobile plant starts to move in the morning it may very well happen that a new car would just slide off it. Curious though it may appear, in places with an uniform climate over the year, as is the case on the Island of Bali, where rice is produced by processes in line, people eat the rice that has just been planted, as we could well say. It is because of this special property of the factory, the low average cost due to the total elimination of fund idleness, that now in the USA chickens are no longer raised on chicken farms but in chicken factories, and also in the national diet chicken is no longer 'on Sunday only'. That change, we may remember, triggered the chicken war of yesteryear (Georgescu-Roegen 1971: 253).

Production of commodities from commodities by factories, therefore, needs no time. But production of commodities does not suffice. Obviously, we need also production processes, which are not just a pile of accumulated commodities. It usually takes a great deal of time to transform 'a pile' of commodities into a factory and, we should not forget, also much (occasionally enormous) time to prime thereafter the new production process. Therefore, time is needed in production but only as the Marshallian waiting time, which concerns the waiting for a new production establishment to be readied.

The foregoing paragraphs vindicate what I have submitted earlier, namely that production means in the first place time. However, the portraits of all graphs presented so far are painted mainly by clock-time, hence they fail to reveal what production means for a human. The most inspiring fact I happen to know to bear on this additional issue has been brought to our attention in a strict analysis of the measurability of time by the unsurpassed analyst Paul Samuelson (1976). On that occasion Samuelson exploited the unique case of Evariste Gallois. The story is fairly well known. Gallois, who had thought up a new mathematical theory, the theory of algebraic groups, had only one night to write it, the night before the day he had to fight in a duel (which did kill him). So, he repeatedly scribbled on the margin of his text 'I have no time ... I have no time ...'.

It was not only Gallois who needed more time. As Ross Webber, for example, pointed out, 'One thing managers never have enough of is time'. This almost general, albeit idle, consensus was most eloquently recognized by Richard Zeckhauser (1973) as he argued that 'the ultimate source of [the enjoyment of] utility is the disposition of time'.

Why did Gallois not have enough time? Was it because there are only twenty-four hours in a day, or only twelve in a night, as Lionel Robbins (1948: 15) once justified time scarcity? On that count time should not be scarce at all, there are no less than some 10^{16} nanoseconds in a day! Time is scarce for us only in relation to our tasks (including, of course, the task of just continuing to be alive). A night's time is hardly sufficient for writing the foundation of the modern group theory! Even the ox did not pray to God just for time, for which it could have no use had it no tasks to perform – to eat, to plod, to think. ...

Another story to meditate about: the editorial of *The Sunday Times* (12 December 1976) claimed after the famous black-out of the Atlantic coast that 'We have time. We can at present have more electricity than we need.' But the perspicacious astrophysicist, Sir Fred Hoyle, who had the co-ordinates of the problem on the tips of his fingers, immediately protested that this is 'an error. We do not have time' (Hill and Weingard 1986: 67). All this is economics with time in it.

Possibly, we could have more electricity, but not during the next year, the period supposed by the probably cornucopian optimist, the author of that editorial. And, of course, for any such task we also need some material resources, the production of which (if possible at all) needs additional time, the crucial thread for producing and living. If people from various places of want struggle to immigrate into some highly developed country it is only because a high level of industrialization allows people to have more 'free time', a point on which Karl Marx insisted from his earliest economic attempts (1971: 148f.). Later Mihail Manoilescu (1931) put that issue on the main agenda of foreign trade in a tight engineering argument with a conclusion so obvious – it is preferable to have one's country industrialized to the greatest possible extent – that it has become a popular banality of the economy of social time. That is time, I submit, nay – that is time for any human, I maintain.

Although time emerges clearly as the absolutely necessary factor for the enjoyment of life as well as for maintaining life by production, only one thinker, Hermann Heinrich Gossen, founded an economic theory on the scarcity of lifetime alone. But because he claimed in the preface of his only book (1983)[1] to be the Copernicus of the 'science of pleasure' – as he conceived political economy – preparing for the coming of its Kepler or its Newton, he has been ridiculed day and night, night and day, the 'genialer Idiot' with the euphemism of Werner Sombart (1930: 4). Actually, it is the ridiculers who deserved to be rightfully ridiculed for their opaque minds.

Gossen was a true wizard in dealing with time as the only indispensable factor of economic life, as well as an original and proficient analyst of the way humans distribute their lifetime between pleasures and drudgeries. His contributions to economic theory were not numerous, yet, as William Stanley Jevons (1879: xxxviii) elegantly recognized, they were 'more general and deeper' than his own, i.e. than those of the main forefather of the neoclassical school. Yet the full, albeit completely ignored, truth is that most of Gossen's results pertaining to the economy of time are still much above the present economic lore (Georgescu-Roegen 1983).

The essential problem of the science of pleasure which Gossen set for himself was to find out how 'Man should organize his life so that his total life pleasure becomes a maximum' (Gossen 1983: 5). The problem was already in the air and is a popular one even in the present era, yet the manner in which Gossen addressed is inimitable.

To begin with, let us look at Gossen's first law of utility, which freed from the German bureaucratic style reads: *'If an enjoyment is experienced uninterruptedly, the corresponding intensity of pleasure decreases continuously until satiety is ultimately reached at which point the intensity becomes nil'* (Georgescu-Roegen 1983: lxxx). Compare it with the principle of decreasing marginal utility as formulated in the standard economic literature. For the special case of moral fortune this principle was thought up more than two hundred years ago, in 1738, by the mathematical physicist Daniel Bernoulli, and introduced in the social sciences in an improved enunciation by Jeremy Bentham in 1780. However, Gossen reached his law independently (Georgescu-Roegen 1983: lxxiv–lxxix).

But for appreciating Gossen's most important merit, let us mark the point that no law can be of real importance if it does not have an application outside itself. Thus, until Stanley Jevons first showed how to use the principle of decreasing marginal utility to explain how a person distributes a given amount of money between the satisfactions of all felt wants, that principle was only an adornment of the received political economy. Jevons's own literary success as well as that of all his followers rested on the fact that only money (in a market economy) may satisfy every want. Insulin, for example, satisfies just one.

How to bring together all commodities, insulin and all, is a formidable rub that Gossen overcame in an unusual way. Instead of money he referred all his laws to time, not to clock-time, but to time as felt fleeting by any human being, the nearest to Saint Augustine's comprehension. He conducted his entire analysis of the individual's behaviour in terms of a special concept, enjoyment, one of the acts by which an individual derives pleasure: drinking a cup of coffee, playing a game of tennis, listening to an opera from the television, looking at Mona Lisa in the Louvre and so forth and so on. Second, contrary to our current habit of constantly referring to the amount of pleasure or pain – which brings up the conundrum of what is the bin where those quantities are stored and used later to console the individual for some misfortune – Gossen's essential reasoning uses 'intensity'. As appears from most of his diagrams, where the abscissa always represents the passing of time, Gossen conceived intensity as a feeling over an atom of time, the Whiteheadian 'duration' or Shackle's 'now'. For Gossen, time is not a mathematical continuum, but a dialectical sequence of time-atoms, the term that, as we shall see, he uses in many of his behavioural propositions.

Still another use of enjoyment to express the time factor from a quasi-historical angle is the beau-ideal of Gossenian epistemology of time. It is Gossen's second law, as it should properly be titled.[2] *A similar decrease of the intensity of pleasure takes place if a previous enjoyment is repeated. Not only does the initial intensity of pleasure become smaller but also the duration of the enjoyment becomes shorter, so that satiety is reached sooner. Moreover, the sooner the repetition, the smaller becomes the initial intensity as well as the duration of the enjoyment* (Georgescu-Roegen 1983: lxxx).

On this basis Gossen observed that if one overindulges in what may seem to be the greatest pleasures, one may end with a disastrous result. Louis XV, the King of France, argued Gossen (1983: 17), must have been 'more miserable than the most repressed serf of his kingdom [just because] everything that could produce pleasure ... was offered to him almost without interruption'. But because every enjoyment influences the future ones of the same nature, we must find out which is the optimum enjoyment, i.e. the one which by its inherent recurrence at its specific interval will maximize the sum of pleasure intensities over the presumed life of the individual in question. That problem was one of calculus of variation, similar to but simpler than those that were an almost regular feature of *Econometrica* during the 1930s, for utility or income maximization over time, for which the Euler condition applies. Whether Gossen knew Euler's method or not, he handled that problem in his particular style, a direct, simple approach that bespoke again of his fertile imagination. He observed first that if one would eat, say, filet-mignon at every meal one's pleasure intensity from eating that delicacy would be blunted down next to zero, as shown diagrammatically by Figure 15.4(a).

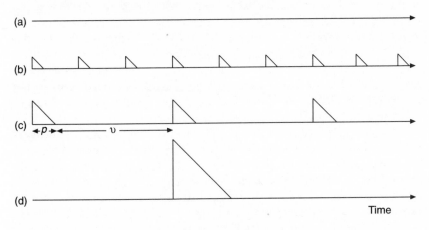

Figure 15.4

And if the same person would eat filet-mignon only once in his life (Figure 15.4(c)), the average intensity of that unique feast would be the greatest possible, but averaging it for the entire life would also come down to zero. Variation between these two zeros should encounter at least one maximum maximorum (Figure 15.4(b)). How strong this idea is may be shown by using it for the extreme possibility of immortal humans. For even an immortal human should seek to use pleasures in such a way that his intensity of pleasure be the greatest possible at every time atom. Gossen's second law works for mortals and immortals.

Continuing to refer everything to his atomic time, Gossen proved the most powerful theorem for consumer behaviour, a model of careful diction, generally but wrongly termed 'Gossen's second law'. *In order to maximize his total pleasure, an individual free to choose between several pleasures but whose time is not sufficient to enjoy all to satiety must proceed as follows: however different the absolute magnitudes of the various pleasures may be, before enjoying the greatest pleasure to satiety he must first satisfy all pleasures in part in such a manner that the magnitude (intensity) of each single pleasure at the moment when its enjoyment is broken off shall be the same for all pleasures* (Gossen 1983: 14). But one theorem of Gossen stands out to prove his unique leaning on time, not on clock-time: *'in order to maximize his life pleasure, man must distribute his time and energy among various pleasures in such a way that for every pleasure the intensity of pleasure of the last atom produced shall be equal to the magnitude* [intensity] *of the discomfort experienced by him at the very last moment of his expenditure of effort'* (Gossen 1983: 53).

From such theorems, which with some variations abound in his volume, Gossen reached the highly familiar formula in current standard economics for the distribution of income when prices of all commodities are given. But he went further and proved that the principle of equality on the margin for all atoms is valid not only for the time of production, but for that of consumption as well. Gossen's conception of an economic system is such that it mirrors the economic life in what it has most properly its own, like the life of those societies which in history lived without any reference to a clock. For those societies time meant simply the feeling of the stream of conscience.

After Gossen, probably because of the general scorn for him, the theory of consumer behaviour moved in different directions. One exception has been G. S. Becker (1965), who in a paper with a title that describes exactly one of the main problems treated by Gossen, but without any reference to Gossen, considered a problem of the distribution of the individual's time between home producing, say barbecuing pork, and leisure. In contrast to Gossen, Becker does not consider separately the time spent on consuming commodities. True, to eat a chocolate bar does not need any home production time, observed Becker, but this point does not deny that to eat a chocolate bar needs some time (Georgescu-Roegen 1983).

As it comes out from what I have said above, time is plurichromatic, it enters in economics in multiple ways, both in production and in life enjoyment. But I have only alluded to that aspect of time that is gauged in its mysterious passing that has led to the peculiar image of history as an agent of change. The journey of a spaceship, say, to Mars certainly takes time, which, as Schumpeter distinguished it, is dynamical time because the phenomena it supports can be reproduced over and over again within very large circumstances. An adage says that history repeats itself, yes there has been one war after another and then another, but the Punic War was surely different, essentially different, from the Gulf War. This is the historical time that Schumpeter (1954) opposed to dynamical time in connection with a still more important distinction – between 'growth', mere accretion and 'development'. Standard economics stops its interest just as the problems turn to what happens in history and why, which means that the essential influence of time on the life of humans is not of the dominion of standard discipline. This is what must have escaped L. A. Boland (1978: 241) when he took to task Sir John Hicks (1976f) together with Shackle (1972) and myself (1971) for having maintained that standard economics is *out of time*.

That lacuna of standard economics has formed the target of many controversies about what economics ought to be. The issue prompted Sir John, almost alone among the contemporary great at that time, to say in his peerless *Value and Capital* (1946b: 116)[3] that 'the economic system has now to be conceived of, not as a network of interdependent markets, but as a process in time'. And he kept fighting for changing standard economics from a discipline '*about* time' – about clock-time – into one '*of* time', of qualitative changes (Hicks 1976f: 139). He pointed his finger straight at the perpetrators of timeless economics, the 'equilibrists' whom I have decried earlier. Sir John overtly disapproved of an economics that represents the macroeconomic changes using a system of differential equations in which time is reduced to a simple algebraic sign t.

Worthy of unparcimonious attention by the economists interested in the problem of time (especially of historical time) is the fact that by now Schumpeter's evolutionary pattern has acquired a great vogue among biological evolutionists (e.g. Levins and Lewontin 1985) who have even adopted the dialectical reasoning that characterized Schumpeter's own epistemology (Georgescu-Roegen 1976: 4). Two particular issues about which Schumpeter delighted to debate dialectically were, first, the difference between small and great innovations and, second, 'where the concept of entrepreneur begins and where it ends'. It is an authoritative sign that historical time, the bed of real change, can be discussed fruitfully only by dialectics.[4] This view has been on the mind of those few economists who have not been content to devise one grandiose (but idle) system of equations after many others. This lesson has been taught in an eloquent way by Sir John saying that 'There is no firm line, on the score of novelty, between shifts that change the technology and shifts that do not' (quoting himself, 1976f: 146).

NOTES

1 The history of Gossen's volume after he published it on commission in 1854 has been sprinkled by several impurities described in Georgescu-Roegen (1983). The only English translation, an excellent work due to Rudolf Blitz, is now available and is given in the bibliography as Gossen (1983).

2 The terms used for the various analytical results of Gossen seem to have been selected to confuse even the most careful students. First, the term 'Gossen's second law' has been, and still is, applied to an old law, the law of satiety. Worst, the same term, law, has been applied even to a Gossen theorem.

3 *Value and Capital* has been my great teacher of analytical economics ever since the first edition came out from the press in 1939. Most of its mathematical appendices are jewels of the economic literature, but the elegance of the appendix to Chapters II and III is inimitable. It is not an accepted form to dedicate something to a literary piece, but if I may be absolved, I would like to dedicate this paper of mine to that appendix.

4 It would be preposterous on my part to think that the dialectical biologists saw the right light after reading my old impassioned entreaty for the necessity of relying on dialectic (opposed to the arithmomorphic) concepts in all scientific domains involving true change, qualitative change, as in any life discipline. That entreaty was a good part of Georgescu-Roegen, *Analytical Economics* (1966), expanded in Georgescu-Roegen (1971). It was quite an old call, preceding the change of mind in biology, none the less I derive immense satisfaction from the fact that my idea has found approval even without any reference to my work. As things stand today with the sociology of science, an adherent to it might say that because, like H.H. Gossen, I have failed to sell my ideas extensively to the scientific public, even to most of my peers, I have not been a genuine scholar. Having no solid stand on which to do so I would not protest the conclusion, but I would fight the logic to my last breath.

BIBLIOGRAPHY
Betancourt, R. and Clague, C. (1981) *Capital Utilization*, Cambridge: Cambridge University Press.

Becker, G. S. (1965) 'A theory of the allocation of time', *Economic Journal* 75: September: 493–517.

Boland, L. A. (1978) 'Time in economics vs. economics in time: the "Hayek problem"' *Canadian Journal of Economics* 11, May: 240–62.

Capek, M. (1975) (ed.) *Concepts of Space and Time*, Dordrecht: Reidel.

Eddington, Sir A. (1928) *The Nature of the Physical World*, Cambridge: Cambridge University Press.

Georgescu-Roegen, N. (1968) 'Utility', in *International Encyclopedia of the Social Sciences*, London: Macmillan and The Free Press, vol. 16, pp. 236–67.

—— (1969) 'Process in farming versus process in manufacturing: a problem of balanced development', in U. Papi and C. Nunn (eds) *Economic Problems of Agriculture in Industrial Societies*, London: Macmillan, pp. 497–528.

—— (1970) 'The economics of production' (1969 Richard T. Ely Lecture), *American Economic Review* 60, May: 1–9.

—— (1971) *The Entropy Law and the Economic Process*, Cambridge, MA: Harvard University Press.

—— (1972) 'Process analysis and the neoclassical theory of production', *American Journal of Agricultural Economics* 54, January: 279–94; reprinted in N. Georgescu-Roegen (1976) *Energy and Economic Myths*, Oxford: Pergamon Press.

—— (1976) 'Dynamic models and economic growth', in G. Schwoediauer (ed.) *Equilibrium and Disequilibrium in Economic Theory*, Dordrecht: Reidel, pp. 413–49; reprinted in N. Georgescu-Roegen (1976) *Energy and Economic Myths*, Oxford: Pergamon Press.

—— (1983) 'Hermann Heinrich Gossen: his life and work in historical perspective', Introduction in H. H. Gossen *The Laws of Human Relations and the Rules of Human Action Derived Therefrom*, tr. R. C. Blitz, Cambridge, MA: MIT Press.

—— (1986) 'Man and production', in M. Baranzini and R. Scazzieri (eds) *Foundations of Economics*, Oxford: Basil Blackwell.

—— (1992) 'Georgescu-Roegen about himself', in M. Szenberg (ed.) *Eminent Economists: Their Life Philosophies*, Cambridge: Cambridge University Press.

Goldschmidt, R. (1940) *The Material Basis of Evolution*, New Haven: Yale University Press.

Gossen, H. H. (1983) *The Laws of Human Relations and the Rules of Human Action Derived Therefrom*, tr. R. C. Blitz, Cambridge, MA: MIT Press.

Hill, D. and Weingard, J. (1986) *Saturday Night*, New York: Beech.

Jevons, W. S. (1879) *The Theory of Political Economy*, 2nd edn, London: Macmillan.

Levins, R. and Lewontin, R. (1985) *The Dialectical Biologist*, Cambridge, MA: Harvard University Press.

MacIver, R. M. (1962) *The Challenge of the Passing Years*, New York: Simon and Schuster.

Manoilescu, M. (1931) *The Theory of Protection and International Trade*, London: P. S. King.

Marx, K. (1971) *Grundrisse*, ed. and tr. D. McLellan, New York: Harper and Row.

Putnam, H. (1975) *Mathematics, Matter, and Method*, Cambridge: Cambridge University Press.

Robbins, L. (1948) *An Essay on the Nature and Significance of Economic Science*, 2nd edn, London: Macmillan.

Samuelson, P. (1976) 'Spending up time with age in recognition of life as fleeting', in A. M. Tang, F. M. Westfield and J. S. Worley (eds) *Evolution, Welfare, and Time in Economics*, Lexington, MA: Lexington Books.

Schumpeter, J. A. (1934) *The Theory of Economic Development*, Cambridge, MA: Harvard University Press.

—— (1954) *History of Economic Analysis*, ed. Elizabeth M. Schumpeter, New York: Oxford University Press.

Shackle, G. L. S. (1972) *Epistemics and Economics*, Cambridge: Cambridge University Press.

Sharp, C. (1981) *The Economics of Time*, New York: John Wiley.

Solow, R. (1957) 'Technical change and the aggregate production function', *Review of Economics and Statistics* 39, August: 312–20.

—— (1974) 'The economics of resources and the resources of economics' (1973 Richard T. Ely Lecture), *American Economic Review Papers and Proceedings* 64, May: 1–14.

Sombart, W. (1930) *Die drei Nationalökonomien*, Munich and Leipzig: Duncker und Humblot.

Tani, P. (1986) *Analisi Microeconomica della Produzione*, Rome: Nuova Italia Scientifica.

Webber, R. (1982) 'Of time and manager', *The Wharton Magazine* 6, Spring: 21–7.

Wicksteed, P. (1894) *An Essay on the Coordination of the Laws of Distribution*, London: Macmillan.

Winston, G. (1982) *The Timing of Economic Activities*, New York: Cambridge University Press.

Zeckhauser, R. (1973) 'Time as the ultimate source of utility', *Quarterly Journal of Economics* 87 (4): 668–73.

PUBLISHED WRITINGS –
JOHN RICHARD HICKS

1928: 'Wage-fixing in the building industry', *Economica* 8, June: 159–67.

1930a: 'The early history of industrial conciliation in England', *Economica* 10, March: 25–39.

1930b: 'Edgeworth, Marshall and the "indeterminateness" of wages', *Economic Journal* 40, June: 215–31; reprinted in 1983a, pp. 72–84.

1931a: 'A reply' to M. Dobb, 'A note concerning Mr J. R. Hicks on "The indeterminateness of wages", *Economic Journal* 41, March: 145–6.

1931b: Review of W. W. M. Amulree, *Industrial Arbitration*, in *Economica* 11, February: 105–6.

1931c: 'The theory of uncertainty and profit', *Economica* 11, May: 170–89; reprinted in 1982a, pp. 11–27.

1931d: Review of W. H. Hutt, *The Theory of Collective Bargaining*, in *Economica* 11, May: 244–7.

1931e: Review of M. T. Rankin, *Arbitration Principles and the Industrial Court (An Analysis of Decisions 1919–1929)*, in *Economica* 11, November: 480–2.

1931f: 'Quotas and import boards' and (with W. Beveridge) 'The possibility of imperial preference', in W. Beveridge, *Tariffs: The Case Examined*, by a committee of economists under the chairmanship of Sir William Beveridge, London: Longmans, Green, pp. 210–29.

1932a: 'Marginal productivity and the principle of variation', followed by 'A reply' to Henry Schultz, *Economica* 12, February: 79–88; August: 297–300.

1932b: *The Theory of Wages*, London: Macmillan (Italian edn, 1934).

1932c: Review of D. M. Goodfellow, *A Modern Economic History of South Africa*, in *Economic Journal* 42, March: 109–11.

1932d: Review of D. H. Robertson, *Economic Fragments*, in *Economica* 12, May: 255–6.

1932e: Review of C. Bresciani-Turroni, *La Vicende del Marco Tedesco*, in *Economica* 12, August: 370–2.

1932f: Review of F. Simiand, *Le Salaire, l'évolution et la monnaie, Essai de théorie experimentale du salaire*, in *Economic Journal* 42, September: 451–74.

1932g: Review of L. Mises and A. Spiethoff (eds), *Probleme der Wertlehre*, in *Economic Journal* 42, September: 477–8.

1933a: Review of F. W. Taussig, *Wages and Capital*, in *Economica* 13, February: 101–4.

1933b: 'Gleichgewicht und Konjunktur', *Zeitschrift für Nationalökonomie* 4, June: 441–55; translated as 'Equilibrium and the trade cycle', *Economic Inquiry* 18, 1980, October: 523–34; reprinted in 1982a, pp. 28–41.

1933c: 'A note on Mr Kahn's paper' (on elasticity of substitution), *Review of Economic Studies* 1, October: 78–80.

1933d: Review of A. E. Monroe, *Value and Income*, in *Zeitschrift für Nationalökonomie* 4: 663–5.

1933e: Review of C. v Reichenau, *Die Kapitalfunktion des Kredits*, in *Zeitschrift für Nationalökonomie* 4: 668–9.

1934a: 'A reconsideration of the Theory of Value', part I; part II by R. G. D. Allen; *Economica*, New Series, 1, February: 52–76; May: 196–219; reprinted in 1981, pp. 5–29, 30–55; and in D. R. Helm, *The Economics of John Hicks*, Oxford: Basil Blackwell, 1984, pp. 25–48.

1934b: Review of K.S. Isles, *Wages Policy and the Price Level*, in *Economic Journal* 44, September: 473–5.

1934c: 'A note on the elasticity of supply', *Review of Economic Studies* 2, October: 31–7; reprinted in 1983a, pp. 237–45.

1934d: 'Leon Walras', *Econometrica* 2, October: 338–48; reprinted in 1983a, pp. 86–95.

1934e: Review of M. Fanno, *The Pure Theory of the Money Market*, and of G. Myrdal, *Monetary Equilibrium*, in F. A. Hayek (ed.) *Beiträge zur Geldtheorie*, in *Economica*, New Series, 1, November: 479–83; reprinted in 1982, pp. 42–5.

1934f: Review of P. H. Wicksteed, *Common Sense of Political Economy* (reprint), in *Economica*, New Series, 1, August: 351–4.

1935a: 'Annual survey of economic theory: the theory of monopoly' *Econometrica* 3, January: 1–20; reprinted in 1983a, pp. 132–52.

1935b: 'A suggestion for simplifying the theory of money', *Economica*, New Series, 2, February: 1–19; reprinted in 1967, pp. 61–82; in 1982a, pp. 46–63; in D. R. Helm *The Economics of John Hicks*, Oxford: Basil Blackwell, 1984, pp. 168–85; and in R. M. Starr (ed.) *General Equilibrium Models of Monetary Economics: Studies in the Static Foundations of Monetary Theory*, San Diego and London: Academic Press, 1989, pp. 8–23.

1935c: Review of C. E. Ross, *Dynamic Economics*, in *Economic Journal*, June: 336–7.

1935d: Review of H. von Stackelberg, *Marktform und Gleichgewicht*, in *Economic Journal*, June: 334–6.

1935e: Review of S. M. de Bernardi (ed.), *De l'utilité et de sa mesure par Jules Dupuit:écrits choisis et republiés* (Turin reprint), in *Economica*, New Series, 2, August: 341–2; reprinted in 1983a, pp. 329–30.

1935f: 'Wages and interest: the dynamic problem', *Economic Journal* 45, September: 456–68; reprinted in 1963b, pp. 268–85; and in 1982a, pp. 67–79.

1936a: Review of A. C. Pigou, *The Economics of Stationary States*, in *Economic Journal* 46 March: 98–102.

1936b: 'Mr Keynes's theory of employment', *Economic Journal* 46, June: 238–53; reprinted in 1982a, pp. 84–99.

1936c: 'Distribution and economic progress: a revised version', *Review of Economic Studies* 4, October: 1–12; reprinted in 1963b, pp. 286–303.

1936d: 'Economic theory and the social sciences', contribution to a symposium on the Social Sciences, *Institute of Sociology*.

1937a: 'Mr Keynes and the "classics"', *Econometrica* 5, April: 147–59; reprinted in 1967, pp. 126–42; in 1982a, pp. 101–15; and in D. R. Helm, *The Economics of John Hicks*, Oxford: Basil Blackwell, 1984, pp. 186–99.

1937b: *La Théorie mathématique de la valeur en régime de libre concurrence*, trans. G. Lutfalla, Paris: Hermann.

1939a: *Value and Capital*, Oxford: Clarendon Press (other edns: Spanish (Mexican),

1945; Japanese, 1950; French, 1956; Hindi, 1971; Polish, 1975; Urdu, 1975; Hungarian, 1978).

1939b: (with Ursula Hicks) 'Public finance in the national income', *Review of Economic Studies* 6, February: 147–55.

1939c: Review of R. G. D. Allen, *Mathematical Analysis for Economists*, in *Economica* 6, February: 92–4.

1939d: Review of A. G. Pool, *Wage Policy in Relation to Industrial Fluctuation*, in *Economica* 6, May: 233–5.

1939e: 'Mr Hawtrey on bank rate and the long-term rate of interest', followed by 'A reply' to Hawtrey, *Manchester School of Economic and Social Studies* 10: 21–39, 152–5; 'Mr Hawtrey . . .', reprinted in 1982a, pp. 116–26.

1939f: 'The foundations of welfare economics', *Economic Journal* 49, December: 696–712; reprinted in 1981, pp. 59–77; and in D. R. Helm, *The Economics of John Hicks*, Oxford: Basil Blackwell, 1984, pp. 126–43.

1940a: 'The valuation of social income', *Economica* 7, May: 105–24; reprinted in 1981.

1940b: 'A comment' on O. Lange's 'Complementarity and interrelations of shifts in demand', *Review of Economic Studies* 8: 64–5; reprinted in J. C. Wood and R. N. Woods, *Sir John Hicks: Critical Assessments*, 4 vols, London: Routledge, 1989, vol. I, pp. 42–4.

1940c: Review of H. Thornton, *An Enquiry into the Nature and Effects of the Paper Credit of Great Britain* [1802] edited with an introduction by F. A. Hayek, in *Economic History Review* 10: 182.

1941a: (with Ursula Hicks and L. Rostas) *Taxation of War Wealth*, Oxford: Clarendon Press (2nd edn, 1942).

1941b: 'The rehabilitation of consumers' surplus', *Review of Economic Studies* 8, February: 108–16; reprinted in 1981, pp. 101–13.

1941c: 'Saving and the rate of interest in war-time', *Manchester School of Economic and Social Studies* 12, April: 21–7.

1941d: 'Education in economics', *Manchester Statistical Society*.

1942a: *The Social Framework: An Introduction to Economics*, Oxford: Clarendon Press (other edns: Swedish, 1945; Spanish (Mexican), 1950; Greek (pirated), 1955; Portuguese, 1956; German, 1962; Sinhalese/Tamil, 1964).

1942b: 'The monetary theory of D. H. Robertson', *Economica*, New Series, 9, February: 53–7; extracts reprinted in 1982a, cf. pp. 127–31.

1942c: 'Maintaining capital intact: a further suggestion', *Economica*, New Series 9, May: 174–9.

1942d: 'Consumers' surplus and index numbers', *Review of Economic Studies* 9, Summer: 126–37; cf. 1981, pp. 114–32.

1942e: Review of Davis, *The Theory of Econometrics*, in *Economic Journal*, December: 350–2.

1942f: 'The budget White Paper of 1942', *Journal of the Institute of Bankers*.

1943a: (with Ursula Hicks) *Standards of Local Expenditure*, Cambridge: Cambridge University Press, National Institute of Economic and Social Research Occasional Papers.

1943b: 'History of economic doctrine', review of C. Rist, *History of Monetary and Credit Theory*, in *Economic History Review* 13: 111–15; reprinted in 1982a, pp. 132–9.

1943c: (with Ursula Hicks) 'The Beveridge plan and local government finance', *Review of Economic Studies* 11: 1–19.

1943d: 'The four consumer's surpluses', *Review of Economic Studies* 11, November: 31–41; cf. 1981, pp. 114–32.

1944a: 'The interrelations of shifts in demand: comment', a discussion with D. H. Robertson and O. Lange, *Review of Economic Studies* 12 (1): 72–5; reprinted in J. C. Wood and R. N. Woods, *Sir John Hicks: Critical Assessments*, 4 vols, London: Routledge, vol. I, pp. 97–101.

1944b: (with Ursula Hicks and C. E. V. Leser) *Valuation for Rating*, Cambridge: Cambridge University Press, National Institute of Economic and Social Research Occasional Papers.

1945a: (with Ursula Hicks) *The Incidence of Local Rates in Great Britain*, Cambridge: Cambridge University Press, National Institute of Economic and Social Research Occasional Papers.

1945b: 'Recent contributions to general equilibrium economics', *Economica*, New Series, 12, November: 235–42.

1945c: 'La théorie de Keynes après neuf ans', *Revue d'économie politique* 55: 1–11.

1945d: Review of A. C. Pigou, *Lapses from Full Employment*, in *Economic Journal*, December: 398–401; reprinted in 1982a, pp. 140–3.

1945e. *The Social Framework of the American Economy* (adaptation by A. G. Hart), New York: Oxford University Press.

1946a: 'The generalized theory of consumer's surplus', *Review of Economic Studies* 13: 68–74; cf. 1981, pp. 114–32.

1946b: *Value and Capital*, 2nd edn, Oxford: Clarendon Press.

1947a: 'World recovery after war: a theoretical analysis', *Economic Journal* 57, June: 151–64; reprinted in 1959a, pp. 3–19; and 1982a, pp. 148–61.

1947b: '"Full employment" in a period of reconstruction', *Nationalokonomisk Tidsskrift* 85: 165ff.; reprinted in 1982a, pp. 162–72.

1947c: 'The empty economy', *Lloyds Bank Review* 5, July: 1–13.

1948a: 'The valuation of the social income: a comment on Professor Kuznets' Reflections', *Economica*, New Series, 15, August: 163–72; extracts reprinted in 1981, pp. 98–9.

1948b: Review of F. Sewell Bray, *Precision and Design in Accountancy*, in *Economic Journal*, 58, December: 562–4.

1948c: 'L'économie de bien-être et la théorie des surplus du consommateur' and 'Quelques applications de la théorie des surplus du consommateur', *Economie Appliquée* 1, January–March: 432–46, 447–57.

1948d: *The Problem of Budgetary Reform*, Oxford: Oxford University Press (Spanish edn, 1957).

1949a: 'Devaluation and world trade', *Three Banks Review* 4, December: 3–23; reprinted in 1959a, pp. 20–39.

1949b: 'Les courbes d'indifférence collective', *Revue d'économie politique* 59: 578–84.

1949c: 'Mr Harrod's dynamic theory', *Economica*, New Series, 16, May: 106–21; reprinted in 1982a, pp. 174–92.

1950a: *A Contribution to the Theory of the Trade Cycle*, Oxford: Clarendon Press (other edns: Italian, 1951; Spanish, 1954; Japanese, 1954).

1950b: Articles on 'Value', 'Demand', 'Interest', 'Wages' and 'Rent', *Chamber's Encyclopedia*.

1950c: Part II of *Report of Commission on Revenue Allocation*, Nigeria, pp. 45–56; reprinted in 1959a, pp. 216–36.

1951a: 'A critical note on the definition of related goods: a comment on Mr. Ichimura's definition', *Review of Economic Studies* 18: 184–7.

1951b: 'Free trade and modern ecomonics', *Manchester Statistical Society*, March; reprinted in 1959a, pp. 40–65.

1951c: Review of C. Menger, *Principles of Economics*, trans. J. Dingwall and B.

Hoselitz, in *Economic Journal*, December: 852–3; reprinted in 1983a, pp. 333–4.

1952a: *The Social Framework*, 2nd edn, Oxford: Clarendon Press.

1952b: Review of T. Scitovsky, *Welfare and Competition*, in *American Economic Review*, September: 609–14; reprinted in 1982a, pp. 155–62.

1952c: 'Contribution to a symposium on monetary policy and the crisis: comments', *Bulletin of the Oxford University Institute of Statistics* 14, April–May: 157–9; August: 268–72.

1953a: Inaugural lecture: 'Long-run dollar problem', *Oxford Economic Papers*, New Series, 5, June: 117–35; extract reprinted in 1959a, pp. 66–84; revised version, 1983a, pp. 207–16.

1953b: 'A note on a point in *Value and Capital*' (a reply to Morishima), *Review of Economic Studies* 21: 218–21; reprinted in J. C. Wood and R. N. Woods, *Sir John Hicks: Critical Assessments*, London: Routledge, 1989, vol. 1, pp. 164–8.

1954a: 'The process of imperfect competition', *Oxford Economics Papers*, New Series, 6, February: 41–54; reprinted in 1983a, pp. 163–78.

1954b: 'Robbins on Robertson on utility', *Economica*, New Series, 21, May: 154–7.

1954c: Review of Myrdal, *The Political Element in the Development of Economic History*, trans. P. Streeten, *Economic Journal* 64, December: 793–6; reprinted in 1983a, pp. 343–6.

1955a: (with Ursula Hicks) *Report on Finance and Taxation in Jamaica*, Kingston, Jamaica, obtainable from Government Printer.

1955b: 'Economic foundations of wage policy', *Economic Journal* 65, September: 389–404; reprinted in 1959a, pp. 85–104; and in 1982a, pp. 194–209, 210–13.

1955c: *The Social Framework of the American Economy*, 2nd edn, adapted by A. G. Hart and J. W. Ford, New York: Oxford University Press.

1956a: *A Revision of Demand Theory*, Oxford: Clarendon Press (other edns: Spanish (Mexican), 1958; Japanese, 1958).

1956b: 'The instability of wages', *Three Banks Review* 31, September: 3–19; reprinted in 1959a.

1956c: 'Methods of dynamic analysis', in *Twenty-five Economic Essays in Honour of Erik Lindahl*, Stockholm: Ekonomisk Tidskrift; reprinted with addendum in 1982a, pp. 219–35; and in D. R. Helm, *The Economics of John Hicks*, Oxford: Basil Blackwell, 1984, pp. 200–15.

1957a: 'A rehabilitation of "classical" economics?' review of D. Patinkin, *Money, Interest and Prices: an Integration of Monetary and Value Theory*, in *Economic Journal* 67, June: 278–89; reprinted in 1967, pp. 143–54 as 'The "classics" again'.

1957b: 'National economic development in the international setting' and 'Development under population pressure', in *Bulletin of the Central Bank of Ceylon*; reprinted in 1959a, pp. 161–95 (revised version) and pp. 196–215.

1958a: 'The measurement of real income', *Oxford Economic Papers*, New Series, 10, June: 125–62; reprinted in 1981, pp. 142–88; and in D. R. Helm, *The Economics of John Hicks*, Oxford: Basil Blackwell, 1984, pp. 57–95.

1958b: 'Future of the rate of interest', *Manchester Statistical Society*, March; revised version, 1967, pp. 83–102.

1958c: 'A world inflation', *The Irish Banks Review*, September; reprinted in 1959a, pp. 121–51.

1959a: *Essays in World Economics* Oxford: Clarendon Press (including 'A Manifesto [on welfarism]', reprinted in 1981, pp. 135–41; 'Unimproved value rating (the case of East Africa)'; 'A further note on import bias', extract reprinted in 1983a, pp. 217–23; 'The factor-price equalization theorem' (other edns: Japanese, 1965; Spanish, 1967).

1959b: 'A "Value and Capital" growth model', *Review of Economic Studies* 26, June: 159–73.

1959c: Review of H. Leibenstein, *Economic Backwardness and Economic Growth*, in *Economic Journal*, June: 344–7.

1960a: *The Social Framework*, 3rd edn, Oxford: Clarendon Press.

1960b: 'Linear theory', *Economic Journal* 70, December: 671–709; reprinted in 1966 in *Surveys of Economic Theory*, vol. III, American Economic Association, London: Macmillan; and in 1983a, pp. 246–91.

1960c: 'Thoughts on the theory of capital: the Corfu Conference', *Oxford Economic Papers*, New Series, 12, June: 123–32.

1961a: 'Prices and the turnpike: the story of a mare's nest', *Review of Economic Studies* 28, February: 77–88; reprinted 1983a, pp. 292–307.

1961b: 'The nature and basis of economic growth', in J. R. Hicks *et al.* (eds), *Federalism and Economic Growth in Underdeveloped Countries*, London: Allen & Unwin, pp. 70–80.

1961c: 'The measurement of capital in relation to the measurement of other economic aggregates', in F.A. Lutz and D. C Hague (eds) *The Theory of Capital*, proceedings of a conference held by the International Economic Association on Corfu in 1958, London: Macmillan, pp. 18–31; reprinted in 1981, pp. 189–203.

1961d: 'Pareto revealed', review of V. Pareto, *Pareto's Letters to Pantaleoni*, *Economica*, New Series, 28, August: 318–22; reprinted in 1983a, pp. 338–42.

1961e: 'Marshall's third rule: a further comment', *Oxford Economic Papers*, New Series, 13, October: 262–5; extract reprinted in 1963b, pp. 376–8.

1962a: 'Liquidity', *Economic Journal* 72, December: 787–802; reprinted in 1982a, pp. 238–47.

1962b: 'Economic theory and the evaluation of consumers' wants', *Journal of Business* 35, July: 256–63.

1962c: Review of J. E. Meade, *A Neo-Classical Theory of Economic Growth*, in *Economic Journal* 286 (72): 371–4.

1962d: Review of A. K. Sen, *Choice of Techniques: an Aspect of the Theory of Planned Economic Development*, in *Economic Journal* 72, June: 379–81.

1963a: 'International trade: the long view', Cairo: Central Bank of Egypt.

1963b: *The Theory of Wages*, 2nd edn (with reprint and commentary), London: Macmillan (Spanish edn, 1973).

1963c: (with Ursula Hicks) 'The reform of budget accounts', *Bulletin of the Oxford University Institute of Statistics* 25, May: 119–26.

1963d: Review of M. Friedman, *Capitalism and Freedom*, in *Economica* 30, August: 319–20.

1963e: Review of F. Modigliani and K. J. Cohen, *The Role of Anticipations and Plans in Economic Behaviour and Their Use in Economic Analysis and Forecasting*, in *Economic Journal* 73, March: 99–101.

1965a: *Capital and Growth*, Oxford: Clarendon Press (other edns: Spanish, 1967; Italian, 1971; Polish, 1982).

1965b: Review of T. Scitovsky, *Papers on Welfare and Growth*, in *American Economic Review* 55, September: 882–3.

1965c: Review of R. G. Lipsey, *An Introduction to Positive Economics*, in *Economica* 32, May: 229–31; reprinted in 1983a, pp. 347–8.

1966a: 'Dennis Holme Robertson. 1890–1963: a memoir', in D. H. Robertson, *Essays in Money and Interest*, London: Collins, pp. 9–22.

1966b: 'After the boom', London, Institute of Economic Affairs Occasional Papers II.

1966c: 'Growth and anti-growth', *Oxford Economic Papers*, New Series, 18, November: 257–69.

1966d: Review of J. E. Meade, *The Stationary Economy*, in *Economic Journal* 76, June: 370–1.

1966e: 'Essays on balanced economic growth', *The Oriental Economist*, Tokyo.

1967: *Critical Essays in Monetary Theory*, Oxford: Clarendon Press (other edns: Spanish, 1971; Italian, 1971; Japanese, 1972).

1968: 'Saving, investment and taxation: an international comparison', *Three Banks Review* 78, June: 3–21.

1969a: *A Theory of Economic History*, Oxford: Oxford University Press (other edns: Swedish, 1970: Japanese, 1971; Portuguese (Brazilian), 1971; French, 1973; Norwegian, 1974; Spanish, 1974).

1969b: 'Automatists, Hawtreyans, and Keynesians', *Journal of Money, Credit and Banking*, 1 (3): 307–17; revised version 1977a, pp. 118–33.

1969c: 'Direct and indirect additivity', *Econometrica* 37, April: 353–4; reprinted in 1983a, pp. 308–11.

1969d: 'Maintaining capital intact: a further suggestion', in R. H. Parker and G. C. Harcourt (eds) *Readings in the Concept and Measurement of Income*, pp. 132–8.

1969e: 'The rehabilitation of consumer's surplus', in K. J. Arrow and T. Scitovsky (eds) *Readings in Welfare Economics*, pp. 325–35.

1969f: 'Value and volume of capital', *Indian Economic Journal* 17, October–December: 161–71.

1969g: 'The measurement of capital – in practice', *Bulletin of the International Statistical Institute* 43; reprinted in 1981, pp. 204–17.

1969h: Review of B. P. Pesek and T. R. Saving, *Money, Wealth and Economic Theory*, in *Economic Journal* 79, March: 129–31.

1970a: 'Expected inflation', *Three Banks Review* 87: pp. 3–34; extract reprinted in 1977a, pp. 108–17.

1970b: Review of M. Friedman, *The Optimum Quantity of Money*, in *Economic Journal* 80, December: 669–72; revised version, 1982, pp. 276–81.

1970c: 'Inflazione e interesse', *Bancaria* 26 (6): 675–82.

1970d: 'Capitalism and industrialism', *Tahqiqat Eqtesadi* (*Quarterly Journal of Economic Research*), Teheran, 7 (18), Spring: 1–13.

1970e: 'Elasticity of substitution again: substitutes and complements', *Oxford Economic Papers*, New Series, 22, November: 289–96; revised version, 1983a, pp. 312–26, 'Elasticity of substitution reconsidered'.

1970f: 'A neo-Austrian growth theory', *Economic Journal* 80, June: 257–81.

1971a: *The Social Framework*, 4th edn, Oxford: Clarendon Press (other edns: Japanese, 1972; Portuguese (Brazilian), 1972).

1971b: 'A reply to Professor Beach', 'Hicks on Ricardo on machinery', *Economic Journal* 81, December: 922–5; reprinted in J. C. Wood and R. N. Woods, *Sir John Hicks: Critical Assessments*, London: Routledge, 1989, vol. II, pp. 170–3.

1972a: 'Ricardo's theory of distribution', in M. Preston and B. Corry (eds) *Essays in Honour of Lord Robbins*, London: Weidenfeld & Nicolson, pp. 160–7; reprinted in 1983a, pp. 32–8.

1972b: 'Die österreichische Kapitaltheorie und ihre Wiedergeburt in der modernen Wirtschaftswissenschaft', *Zeitschrift für Nationalökonomie* 32: 91–101; English version, 1973a.

1973a: 'The Austrian theory of capital and its rebirth in modern economics', in J. R. Hicks and W. Weber (eds) *Carl Menger and the Austrian School of Economics*, Oxford: Clarendon Press, pp. 190–206; reprinted in 1983a, pp. 96–112.

1973b: 'The mainspring of economic growth', *Swedish Journal of Economics* 75,

December: 336–48; reprinted in 1977a, pp. 1–19; and in *American Economic Review* 71, 1981: 23–9.

1973c: 'Recollections and documents', *Economica* 40, February: 2–11; reprinted in 1977a, pp. 134–48.

1973d: *Capital and Time. A Neo-Austrian Theory*, Oxford: Clarendon Press (other edns: Italian 1973; Japanese, 1973; French, 1975; Spanish (Mexican), 1976).

1973e: (with H.C. Recktenwald) 'Walras's economic system', in H. C. Recktenwald (ed.) *Political Economy: A Historical Perspective*, London: Collier–Macmillan, pp. 261–6.

1973f: 'On the measurement of capital', *The Economic Science*, Nagoya University, Japan.

1973g: (with Ursula Hicks) 'British fiscal policy', in H. Giersch (ed.) *Fiscal Policy and Demand Management*, Tübingen: Mohr.

1974a: 'Capital controversies: ancient and modern', *American Economic Review* 64, May: 307–16; reprinted in 1977a, pp. 49–65.

1974b: *The Crisis in Keynesian Economics*, Oxford: Basil Blackwell (other edns: Italian, 1974; Spanish, 1976; Japanese, 1977; Hungarian, 1978).

1974c: 'Preferences and welfare', in A. Mitra (ed.) *Economic Theory and Planning: Essays in Honour of A. K. Das Gupta*, Calcutta: Oxford University Press, pp. 3–16.

1974d: 'Real and monetary factors in economic fluctuations', *Scottish Journal of Political Economy* 21 (3): 205–14; extract reprinted in 1977a, pp. 171–81; and in M. Monti (ed.) *The 'New Inflation' and Monetary Policy*, London: Macmillan, 1976.

1974e: 'Future and industrialism', *International Affairs*, April: 211–28; reprinted in 1977a, pp. 20–44.

1974f: (with N. Nosse) *The Social Framework of the Japanese Economy*, Oxford: Oxford University Press.

1975a: 'The permissive economy', in '"Crisis" 75 …?', London, Institute of Economic Affairs Occasional Papers 43.

1975b: 'Pareto and the economic optimum', Rome: Academia nazionale dei lincei.

1975c: 'The scope and status of welfare economics', *Oxford Economic Papers* 27 (3): 307–26; reprinted in 1981, pp. 218–39.

1975d: Annual survey of economic theory; 'The Theory of Monopoly', in E. Mansfield (ed.) *Macroeconomics: Selected Readings*, pp. 188–205.

1975e: 'The quest for monetary stability', *South African Journal of Economics* 43, December: 405–20.

1975f: 'Revival of political economy: the old and the new', reply to Harcourt, *Economic Record* 51, September: 365–7.

1975g: 'What is wrong with monetarism?', *Lloyds Bank Review* 118: 1–13.

1976a: Review of J. R. Whittaker (ed.), *The Early Economic Writings of Alfred Marshall (1867–1890)*, in *Economic Journal* 86, January: 367–9; reprinted in 1983a, pp. 335–7.

1976b: 'Forward trading as a means of overcoming disequilibrium', in B. A. Goss and B. S. Yamey (eds) *The Economics of Futures Trading: Readings*, New York: Wiley, pp. 63–7.

1976c: 'The little that is right with monetarism', *Lloyds Bank Review* 121: 16–18.

1976d: 'Must stimulating demand stimulate inflation?', *Economic Record* 52, December: 409–22; reprinted in 1982a, pp. 301–17.

1976e: '"Revolutions" in Economics', in S.J. Latsis (ed.) *Method and Appraisal in Economics*, Cambridge: Cambridge University Press, pp. 207–18; reprinted 1983a, pp. 3–16; and in D. R. Helm, *The Economics of John Hicks*, Oxford: Basil Blackwell, 1984, pp. 244–56.

1976f: 'Some questions of time in economics', in A. M. Tang, F. M. Westfield and J. S. Worley (eds) *Evolution, Welfare and Time in Economics: Essays in Honour of Nicholas Georgescu-Roegen*, Lexington, MA: Heath, Lexington Books, pp. 135–51; reprinted in 1982a, pp. 282–300; and in D. R. Helm, *The Economics of John Hicks*, Oxford: Basil Blackwell, 1984, pp. 263–80.

1977a: *Economic Perspectives: Further Essays on Money and Growth*, Oxford: Clarendon Press (other edns: Portuguese (Brazilian), 1978; Italian, 1980).

1977b: (with S. Hollander) 'Mr Ricardo and the moderns', *Quarterly Journal of Economics* 91, August: 351–69; reprinted in 1983a, pp. 41–59.

1978a: 'Capital, expectations and the market process', review note on L. M. Lachmann, *South African Journal of Economics* 46, December: 400–2.

1978b: 'La funzioni della moneta internazionale', *Bancaria* 34 (7): 661–7.

1978c: Review of R. D. Collison Black (ed.), *Papers and Correspondence of W.S. Jevons*, vols III–V, *Economic Journal*, June: 347–8; extract reprinted in 1983a, pp. 331–2.

1979a: 'The Ricardian system: a comment', *Oxford Economic Papers* 31, March: 133–4.

1979b: 'The formation of an economist', *Banca Nazionale del Lavaro Quarterly Review* 130, September: 195–204; reprinted in 1983a, pp. 355–64; and in D. R. Helm, *The Economics of John Hicks*, Oxford: Basil Blackwell, 1984, pp. 281–90.

1979c: 'Is interest the price of a factor of production?', in M. J. Rizzo (ed.) *Time, Uncertainty and Disequilibrium*, Lexington, MA: Lexington Books, pp. 51–63; reprinted in 1983a, pp. 114–28.

1979d: Review of E. R. Weintraub, *Microfoundations: The Compatibility of Microeconomics and Macroeconomics*, in *Journal of Economic Literature* 17, December: 1451–4; reprinted in 1983a, pp. 349–52.

1979e: 'The concept of income in relation to taxation and business management', *Greek Economic Review* 1, December: 1–14; reprinted in 1983, pp. 189–203.

1979f: 'On Coddington's interpretation: a reply', *Journal of Economic Literature* 17: 989–95; reprinted in J. C. Wood and R. N. Woods, *Sir John Hicks: Critical Assessments*, London: Routledge, 1989, vol. III, pp. 209–16.

1979g: *Causality in Economics*, Oxford: Basil Blackwell, and New York: Basic Books (other edns: Italian, 1981; Spanish (Argentinean), 1982).

1980a: 'IS–LM: an explanation', *Journal of Post Keynesian Economics* 3 (2), Winter: 139–54; reprinted in 1982a, pp. 318–31; and in D. R. Helm, *The Economics of John Hicks*, Oxford: Basil Blackwell, 1984, pp. 216–29; also published in J. P. Fitoussi (ed.) (1983) *Modern Macroeconomics Theory: An Overview*, Oxford: Basil Blackwell, pp. 49–63; and in G. K. Shaw (ed.) (1988) *The Keynesian heritage*, vol. 1, Schools of Thought in Economics series, no. 1, Aldershot: Edward Elgar, pp. 22–37.

1980b: 'Equilibrium and the trade cycle', translation of 'Gleichgewicht und Konjunktur', first published in German as 1933b, *Economic Inquiry* 18, October: 523–34; reprinted in 1982a, pp. 28–41.

1980c: Review of J. R. Presley, *Robertsonian Economics*, in *Canadian Journal of Economics* 13, August: 517–20.

1981: *Wealth and Welfare, Collected Essays on Economic Theory*, vol. I, Oxford: Basil Blackwell (including 'Valuation of the social income III: the cost approach', pp. 96–121); reprinted in D. R. Helm, *The Economics of John Hicks*, Oxford: Basil Blackwell, 1984, pp. 96–121.

1982a: *Money, Interest and Wages, Collected Essays on Economic Theory*, vol. II,

Oxford: Basil Blackwell (including 'The foundation of monetary theory, part IV, the credit economy', reprinted in D. R. Helm, *The Economics of John Hicks*, Oxford: Basil Blackwell, 1984, pp. 230–9).

1982b: 'Limited liability: the pros and cons', in T. Orhnial (ed.) *Limited Liability and the Corporation*, London: Croom Helm; reprinted in 1983a, pp. 178–88.

1982c: Forward to Andrew Shonfield, *The Use of Public Power*, Oxford: Oxford University Press.

1982d: 'Planning in the world depression', *Man and Development*, India.

1983a: *Classics and Moderns, Collected Essays on Economic Theory*, vol. III, Oxford: Basil Blackwell.

1983b: 'Culture as capital, supply and demand', Rome: Academia nazionale dei lincei.

1983c: 'A sceptical follower' (The Keynes Centenary), *The Economist*, 18 June, pp. 21–4.

1984a: 'The "new causality": an explanation', *Oxford Economic Papers* 36: 12–15.

1984b: 'Is economics a science?', *Interdisciplinary Science Review* 9 (3): 213–19; also published in M. Baranzini and R. Scazzieri (eds) (1986) *Foundations of Economics*, Oxford: Basil Blackwell, pp. 91–101.

1984c: (with S. K. Ghosh and M. Mukherjee), *The Social Framework of the Indian Economy. An Introduction to Economics*, India and New York: Oxford University Press.

1984d: 'Francis Ysidro Edgeworth', in A. E. Murphy (ed.) *Economists and the Irish Economy from the Eighteenth Century to the Present Day*, Dublin: Irish Academic Press, pp. 157–74.

1984e: 'Lineamenti storici dei metodi di controllo della moneta' (Methods of monetary control), *Bancaria* 40 (11): 1069–75.

1985a: *Methods of Dynamic Economics*, new edition of the first part of *Capital and Growth*, Oxford: Clarendon Press.

1985b: 'Sraffa and Ricardo: a critical view', in G. A. Caravale (ed.) *The Legacy of Ricardo*, Oxford: Basil Blackwell, pp. 305–19.

1985c: 'Keynes and the World Economy', in F. Vicarelli (ed.) *Keynes's Relevance Today*, London: Macmillan, pp. 21–7.

1986a: 'Towards a more General Theory' and 'Managing without money?', Symposium on Monetary Theory, Chung-Hua Series of Lectures by Invited Eminent Economists, 11, Taipei, Taiwan: The Institute of Economics, Academia Sinica, January, pp. 3–17, 19–29; the first paper reprinted in *Economia Politica* 3, 1986: 7–19; and in M. Kohn and S. C. Tsiang (eds) (1988) *Finance Constraints, Expectations and Macroeconomics*, Oxford: Oxford University Press, pp. 6–14.

1986b: 'Loanable funds and liquidity preference', *Greek Economic Review* 8, December: 125–31; reprinted as 'LF and LP' in S. C. Tsiang, *Finance Constraints and the Theory of Money*, selected Papers edited by M. Kohn, San Diego and London: Academic Press, 1989, pp. 351–58.

1986c: *A Revision of Demand Theory*, Oxford: Oxford University Press.

1986d: 'Rational behavior – observation or assumption?', in I. M. Kirzner (ed.) *Subjectivism, Intelligibility and Economic Understanding*, essays in honor of Ludwig M. Lachmann on his eightieth birthday, New York: New York University Press, pp. 102–10.

1986e: 'The abdication of money', *Hongkong Economic Papers* 17: 1–10.

1988: 'A conversation with Sir John Hicks about *Value and Capital*', *Eastern Economic Journal* 14: 1–6.

1989a: *A Market Theory of Money*, Oxford: Clarendon Press.

1989b: 'The assumption of constant returns to scale', *Cambridge Journal of Economics* 13, March: 9–17.

1989c: 'An accountant among economists: conversations with Sir John Hicks', *Journal of Economic Perspectives* 3, Fall: 167–80.

1990a: 'Ricardo and Sraffa', in K. Bharadwaj and B. Schefold (eds) *Essays on Piero Sraffa. Critical Perspectives on the Revival of Classical Theory*, London: Unwin Hyman, pp. 99–102.

1990b: 'The unification of macro-economics', *Economic Journal* 100, June: 528–38.

1990c: 'A Self-Survey', in A. Courakis and C. Goodhart (eds) 'The monetary economics of John Hicks', *Greek Economic Review* 12, Supplement: 1–7.

1991a: 'Postscript', in L. W. McKenzie and S. Zamagni (eds) *Value and Capital Fifty Years Later*, London: Macmillan, pp. 471–6.

1991b: 'The Swedish influence on *Value and Capital*', in L. Jonung (ed.) *The Stockholm School of Economics revisited*, Cambridge: Cambridge University Press, pp. 369–76.

Helm, D. R. (ed.) (1984) *The Economics of John Hicks*, Oxford: Basil Blackwell.

Wood, J. C. and Woods, R. N. (eds) (1989) *Sir John Hicks: Critical Assessments*, 4 vols, London: Routledge.

NAME INDEX

SUBJECT INDEX